Philip II, Alexander the Great

and the

Macedonian Heritage

Edited by

W. Lindsay Adams
The University of Utah

and

Eugene N. Borza
The Pennsylvania State University

UNIVERSITY
PRESS OF
AMERICA

Copyright © 1982 by

University Press of America, Inc.

P.O. Box 19101, Washington, D.C. 20036

All rights reserved

Printed in the United States of America

ISBN (Perfect): 0-8191-2448-6
ISBN   (Cloth): 0-8191-2447-8

Library of Congress Catalog Card Number: 81-43664

DF
233
P477
1982

In Memoriam

HARRY JAMES DELL
1933-1981

*. . . semper aut discere aut docere
aut scribere dulce habui.*
— Bede

CONTENTS

PREFACE vii
CONTRIBUTORS ix
ABBREVIATIONS xi

The essays in this volume are arranged in chronological order of their topics.

EUGENE N. BORZA
    The Natural Resources of Early Macedonia   1-20

M. B. HATZOPOULOS
    The Oleveni Inscription and the Dates of Philip II's Reign   21-42

J. R. ELLIS
    Philip and the Peace of Philokrates   43-59

CHARLES D. HAMILTON
    Philip II and Archidamus   61-83

E. A. FREDRICKSMEYER
    On the Final Aims of Philip II   85-98

E. BADIAN
    Eurydice   99-110

N. G. L. HAMMOND
    The Evidence for the Identity of the Royal Tombs at Vergina   111-127

PETER GREEN
    The Royal Tombs at Vergina: A Historical Analysis   129-151

ROBERT WYMAN HARTLE
    The Search for Alexander's Portrait   153-176

LLOYD L. GUNDERSON
    Quintus Curtius Rufus: On His Historical Methods   177-196

STANLEY M. BURSTEIN
    Arsinoe II Philadelphos: A Revisionist View   197-212

FRANK W. WALBANK
    Sea-power and the Antigonids   213-236

W. LINDSAY ADAMS
    Perseus and the Third Macedonian War   237-256

ERICH S. GRUEN
    Macedonia and the Settlement of 167 B.C.   257-267

JOHN PAUL ADAMS
    Polybius, Pliny and the Via Egnatia   269-302

PREFACE

This collection of Macedonian essays has its origin in a symposium held at the Art Institute of Chicago on 5-6 June 1981. The symposium, "Alexander the Great . . . Before and After," was sponsored by the Art Institute and Ares Publishers, Inc., and was designed to complement the Art Institute's installation of the touring exhibition of Macedonian antiquities, "The Search for Alexander." The sponsors contacted Harry J. Dell, Professor of Ancient History in the Univerity of Virginia, a well-known scholar of ancient Macedonia, and asked him to organize the program.

After inviting a number of scholars and arranging for their topics, Dell became seriously ill with cancer. When it became apparent that he would not be able to continue his work, the final preparations were taken over by Al. N. Oikonomides and Eugene N. Borza, the latter replacing Dell as chairman of the symposium. Harry Dell died on 11 May 1981, and it was agreed by the participants that the symposium, held less than a month later as originally scheduled, would be dedicated to his memory.

There was a strong feeling among the symposiasts that their papers should be kept together and published as a tribute both to Dell and to the successful symposium which he had organized but not lived to enjoy. Ten of the symposiasts — J. P. Adams, W. L. Adams, Borza, Burstein, Ellis, Fredricksmeyer, Green, Gunderson, Hammond and Hartle — revised their papers for publication. Badian, Gruen, Hamilton, Hatzopoulos and Walbank accepted invitations to join in the commemorative volume. The collection of fifteen essays has thus emerged as a tribute to a friend and colleague, and as a testament to the vigor of contemporary studies of ancient Macedonia.

What evolved in this volume was a cooperative effort among a company of scholars, a fact that the editors recognize with pleasure and gratitude. The special advice and assistance rendered on occasion by John Adams, Peter Green, Lloyd Gunderson and Nicholas Hammond are particularly acknowledged. The editors have depended heavily on one another for encouragement.

The publication was made possible by a gift from a donor who prefers to remain anonymous, but whose generosity will earn the thanks of all those interested in ancient Macedonia. Publication was assisted by a grant from the College of the Liberal Arts of The Pennsylvania State University, through the office of Thomas F. Magner, Associate Dean for Research. The Departments of History of The University of Utah and The Pennsylvania State University supported the enterprise by underwriting some of the telephone, postage and photocopy expenses incurred by the frequent communications between editors and contributors. Lee Thomassen's sharp eye and knowledge of *Makedonika* made him a valuable editorial assistant. Patti Hartranft, Production Manager of Collegian Inc., designed the book and supervised the type-setting and technical preparation of camera-ready copy. The editors are grateful that the editorial board of University Press of America agreed to produce the book.

The single remaining acknowledgement is expressed in the dedication.

W. LINDSAY ADAMS
EUGENE N. BORZA

February 1982

CONTRIBUTORS

John Paul Adams. Assistant Professor of Classics, The Pennsylvania State University.

W. Lindsay Adams. Associate Professor of Ancient History, The University of Utah.

E. Badian. Professor of History, Harvard University.

Eugene N. Borza. Professor of Ancient History, The Pennsylvania State University.

Stanley M. Burstein. Professor of Ancient History, California State University, Los Angeles.

J. R. Ellis. Reader in Classical Studies, Monash University.

E. A. Fredricksmeyer. Professor of Classics, University of Colorado.

Peter Green. Professor of Classics, The University of Texas at Austin.

Erich S. Gruen. Professor of Ancient History, University of California, Berkeley.

Lloyd L. Gunderson. Professor of Classics, St. Olaf College.

Charles D. Hamilton. Professor of Ancient History, San Diego State University.

N. G. L. Hammond. Emeritus Professor of Greek, University of Bristol.

Robert W. Hartle. Professor of Romance Languages, Queens College and the Graduate School, City University of New York.

M. B. Hatzopoulos. Fellow of The National Hellenic Research Foundation, Research Centre for Greek and Roman Antiquity.

Frank W. Walbank. Emeritus Professor of Ancient History and Classical Archaeology, University of Liverpool.

ABBREVIATIONS

AA	Archäologischer Anzeiger
AAA	Athens Annals of Archaeology
AJA	American Journal of Archaeology
AJAH	American Journal of Ancient History
AJP	American Journal of Philology
AM	Archaia Makedonia
AncW	The Ancient World
ANRW	Aufstieg und Niedergang der römischen Welt
ASNP	Scuola normale superiore di Pisa, Classe di lettere e filosophia, Annali.
ArchEph	Archaiologikē Ephemeris
ASAtene	Annuario della R. Scuola archeologia di Atene
AthMitt	Mitteilungen des deutschen Archäologischen Instituts, Athenische Abteilung
BCH	Bulletin de Correspondence Hellénique
Berve, *Alex*	H. Berve, *Das Alexanderreich aus prosopographischer Grundlage* I-II (Munich, 1926)
BIAB	Bulletin de l'Institut archéologique bulgare
BIFAO	Bulletin de l'Institut français d'archéologie orientale
BSA	Annual of the British School at Athens
Bull. epig.	Bulletin épigraphique
CAH	Cambridge Ancient History
CJ	The Classical Journal
CQ	Classical Quarterly
CP	Classical Philology
CRAI	Comptes rendus de l'Académie des inscriptions et belles-lettres
CSCA	California Studies in Classical Antiquity
CW	The Classical World
Deltion	Archaiologikon Deltion
EphDac	Ephemeris Dacoromana
FGrH	F. Jacoby, *Die Fragmente der griechischen Historiker*
G & R	Greece & Rome
GGA	Göttingische gelehrte Anzeigen
GGM	C. Mueller, *Geographici Graeci Minores*

GRBS	Greek, Roman and Byzantine Studies
Hist Mace I	N. G. L. Hammond, *A History of Macedonia. Historical Geography and Prehistory* (Oxford 1972)
Hist Mace II	N. G. L. Hammond and G. T. Griffith, *A History of Macedonia. 550-336 B.C.* (Oxford 1978)
HSCP	Harvard Studies in Classical Philology
IG	Inscriptiones Graecae
JARCE	Journal of the American Research Center in Egypt
JdI	Jahrbuch des k. deutschen archäologischen Instituts
JFA	Journal of Field Archaeology
JHS	Journal of Hellenic Studies
JNES	Journal of Near Eastern Studies
JRAI	Journal of the Royal Anthropological Institute
JS	Journal des savants
MemAcInscr	Mémoires présentés par divers savants à l'Académie des inscriptions et belles-lettres
OGIS	Orientis Graeci Inscriptiones Selectae
PM	*Philip of Macedon*, ed. M. B. Hatzopoulos and L. D. Loukopoulos (Athens 1980)
PMI	J. R. Ellis, *Philip II and Macedonian Imperialism* (London 1976)
PPS	Proceedings of the Prehistoric Society
Praktika	Praktika tēs en Athēnais Archaiologikēs Hetairias
RE	Pauly-Wissowa, *Real-Encyclopädie der klassischen Altertumswissenschaft*
REG	Revue des études grecques
RendIstLomb	R. Istituto Lombardo di scienze e lettere, Rendiconti
RGV	M. Andronikos, *The Royal Graves at Vergina* (Athens 1978); reprint of "Vergina: the Royal Graves in the Great Tumulus," *AAA* 10 (1977) 1-72
RhM	Rheinisches Museum für Philologie
RivFC	Rivista di filologia e d'istruzione classica
RivStorAnt	Rivista Storica dell'antichità
"RT"	M. Andronikos, "Regal Treasures from a Macedonian Tomb," *National Geographic* 154 (1978) 54-77
"RTP"	M. Andronikos, "The Royal Tomb of Philip II: an unlooted Macedonian Grave at Vergina," *Archaeology* 31.4 (Sept.-Oct. 1978) 33-41

SB	*Sammelbuch griech. Urkunden aus Aegypten*
Search	*The Search for Alexander. An Exhibition* (Boston 1980), catalogue of the exhibition.
SEG	*Supplementum Epigraphicum Graecum*
SGDI	*Sammlung der griech. Dialekt-Inschriften*
SicGym	*Siculorum Gymnasium*
SIG	Dittenberger, *Sylloge Inscriptionum Graecarum*
SIMA	*Studies in Mediterranean Archaeology*
TAPA	*Transactions of the American Philological Association*
Tod, *GHI*	M. Tod, *A Selection of Greek Historical Inscriptions* II (Oxford 1948)
ŽA	*Živa Antika*
ZAes	*Zeitschrift für ägyptische Sprache und Altertumskunde*
ZPE	*Zeitschrift für Papyrologie und Epigraphik*

Philip II, Alexander the Great

and the

Macedonian Heritage

The Natural Resources of Early Macedonia

EUGENE N. BORZA

Abstract

Macedonia produced the finest ship-timber in the Mediterranean world, according to the testimony of ancient writers. The recent excavations of Macedonian artifacts wrought from precious metals is visible evidence of the gold and silver resources of the region. Access to both the forest and mineral resources of Macedonia was considered important by the Greek cities, and the fortunes of some fifth and fourth-century B.C. Macedonian kings is a reflection of their struggle to maintain their independence from foreigners interested in the resources of their lands.

Abundant rainfall, excellent high-grazing land and alluvial plains made Macedonia relatively prosperous, at least by Greek standards. Yet, the region suffered from endemic malaria, and great swamps in the main alluvial plains restricted settled agriculture. The coastline of central Macedonia in antiquity intruded quite far into the Emathian plain, giving the heartland an irregular and inconvenient shape. It is likely that cereal grains and vegetables were grown, and the wooded slopes of nearby mountains held abundant wildlife. No oil was produced, as the Macedonian climate was too severe for the olive. Wine was imported, and probably was also made locally.

Part of the analysis of this material derives from archaeological and literary sources, and part emerges from analogs with modern Macedonia, as the ecology of the region in modern times is similar to that of antiquity.

One of the most enduring impressions of those who visit the exhibition of Macedonian antiquities now touring this country is of the astonishing array of items fabricated from precious metals. The gold and silver artifacts are a major lure, as every museum-keeper can testify. But we are reminded that beneath the romance and propaganda associated with the marketing of Alexander the Great to a modern audience lie a people and a land — a land abundant in natural resources. What follows is intended to convey some sense of that land and to address in particular three topics: timber, precious metals and cultivation.

I.

"The best timber which comes into Greece for the carpenter's use is Macedonian. . ." Theophrastus (*Hist. Plant.* 5.2.1) thus sums up one of Macedonia's most valuable natural resources, her great deciduous and evergreen forests. Nearly one-third of all forested land in Greece today is in Macedonia, and there may be an increase in that figure if government forestry efforts of recent years are successful. Much of the Macedonian countryside above about 200 m. is forested, although largely without the dense appearance of European and American wooded areas. Greek forests normally produce less underbrush and thus are more open. Theophrastus (*Hist. Plant.* 3.3.1) lists no fewer than 34 varieties of mountain and plains trees; the precision of his account of Macedonian plant life is due both to his own experience there and to his extensive use of Macedonian sources.[1]

The forests in populated places in mainland Greece were reduced quite early on, so that by the Classical period the Greeks were forced to turn elsewhere for wood.[2] Macedonia had forests aplenty, partly because of her suitable mountain slopes and arable riverside land, and partly because Macedonian forests, even when exploited, were done so by a small population and were able to regenerate themselves through abundant rainfall. Timber was needed in Greece for both ships and domestic uses. Only a few places in the eastern Mediterranean produced ship timber, and of these Macedonia was not only the closest to Greece but also produced the most desirable woods.[3] These included oak, with which Macedonia had been heavily covered since *ca.* 7000 B.C. — used for keels —, and fir, pine and beech, used for

---

[1] E.g., *Hist. Plant.* 3.3.4; 3.3.8; 3.4.1; 3.8.7; 3.9.2.

[2] A. C. Johnson, "Ancient Forests and Navies," *TAPA* 58 (1927) 199, whose conclusions are supported by the data cited in J. R. A. Grieg and J. Turner, "Some Pollen Diagrams from Greece, and their Archaeological Significance," *Journ. Archaeo. Science* 1 (1974) 177-94. Grieg and Turner's pollen analysis shows that in the Lake Kopais region of Boiotia the forests had been decimated since at least the Bronze Age.

[3] Theoph. *Hist. Plant.* 4.5.5.

The Natural Resources of Early Macedonia

masts, yardarms and hull sheathing.[4] There can be little doubt that the export of these timber resources to a wood-starved Greek world was one of Macedonia's most important commercial enterprises.[5]

Among the major forested areas were the mountains above the Strymon and the plain of Philippi,[6] the Pierian mountains[7] and Mt. Vermion, the latter known even today for its variety of wooded land and wildlife.[8] There were also extensive forests in northwestern Macedonia (today timber harvesting is a major industry in the Pisoderion pass above Florina), but these were probably too distant from the Aegean to have shared much in the region's economic life. The forests were then, as now, mainly in the mountainous areas of the countryside. The lower slopes and drier ground at plain's edge may have also supported groves, but the great Emathian and Strymonian plains were probably unforested then as today.[9]

Bintliff[10] has argued that the plain of Emathia was heavily forested in Neolithic times, this based on analyses of pollen cores taken near Yiannitsa. But Yiannitsa is on the edge of Mt. Paiko's terrace-land, and to extrapolate from its vegetation the flora of the plain makes no more sense than to use Vergina, or sites on the lower slopes of Mt.

---

[4] *Ibid.*, 5.1.7; 5.7.1-4; also Johnson (supra n. 2) 200-201; Grieg and Turner (supra n. 2) 191; and M. Cary, *The Geographic Background of Greek and Roman History* (Oxford 1949) 27.

[5] For some details see H. Michell, *The Economics of Ancient Greece* (Cambridge 1940) 282, with notes; also Johnson (supra n. 2) 199-206, and a useful summary in E. C. Semple, *The Geography of the Mediterranean Region. Its Relation to Ancient History* (London 1932) 276-77.

[6] Grieg and Turner's pollen diagrams (supra n. 2) show especially heavy concentrations of oak and pine.

[7] Especially pine; see Semple (supra n. 5) 282 (after Leake), and N. G. L. Hammond, *Hist Mace* I 125.

[8] *Hist Mace* I 10. There is a restaurant in Athens which has occasionally served boar advertised as being from "Macedonian Mt. Vermion." The meat is delicious.

[9] *Contra* Hammond, *Hist Mace* I 14. That lignite beds in Macedonian plains are evidence of early forestation (as Hammond says) is certain, but lignite (an immature form of coal) is Tertiary in origin, and thus has little bearing on the periods under consideration here. Moreover, Hammond's argument that Neolithic settlements were sited on lake, river and marsh edges (true) "presumably because the plains themselves were forested" neglects the fact that some primitive peoples in both Europe and America were able to live quite well in forested areas. I would suggest that these early inhabitants of Macedonia lived where they did because the plains were too swampy for dwelling. Hammond himself recognized that the Neolithic site at Nea Nikomedeia lay at marsh-edge.

[10] John Bintliff, "The Plain of Macedon and the Neolithic site of Nea Nikomedeia," *PPS* 42 (1976) 241-62, esp. 261.

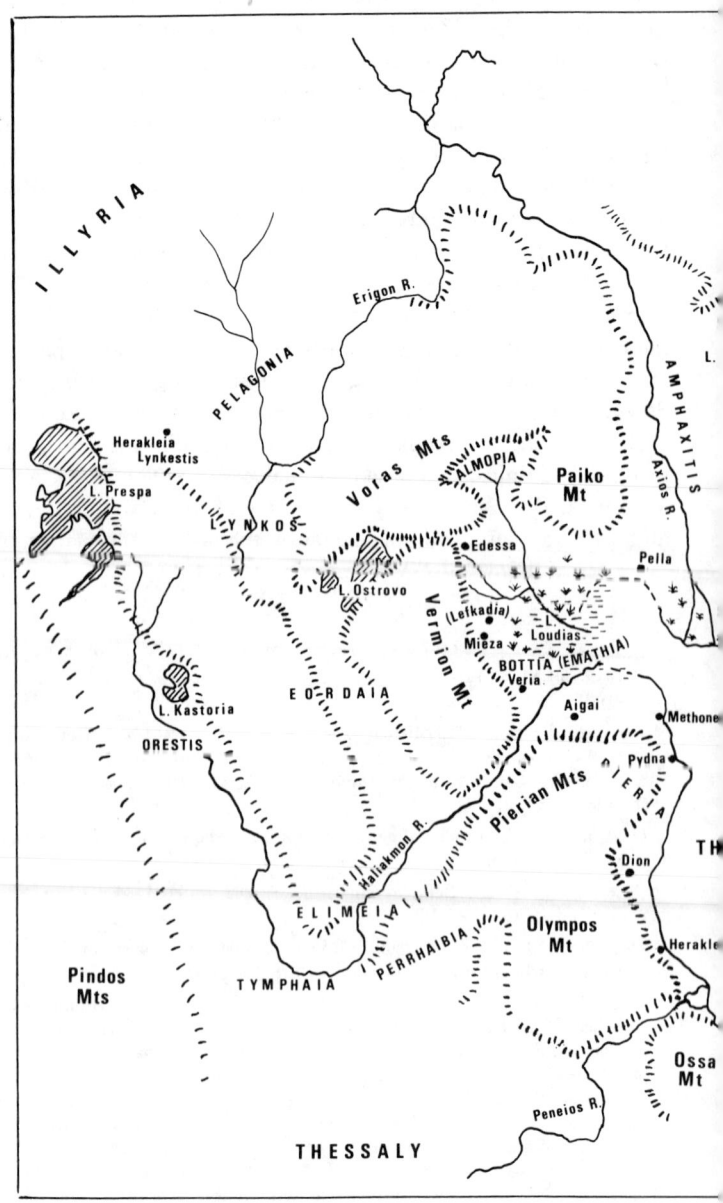

Macedonia, showing some Classical and Hellenistic sites. Map by E. N. Bo

The Natural Resources of Early Macedonia

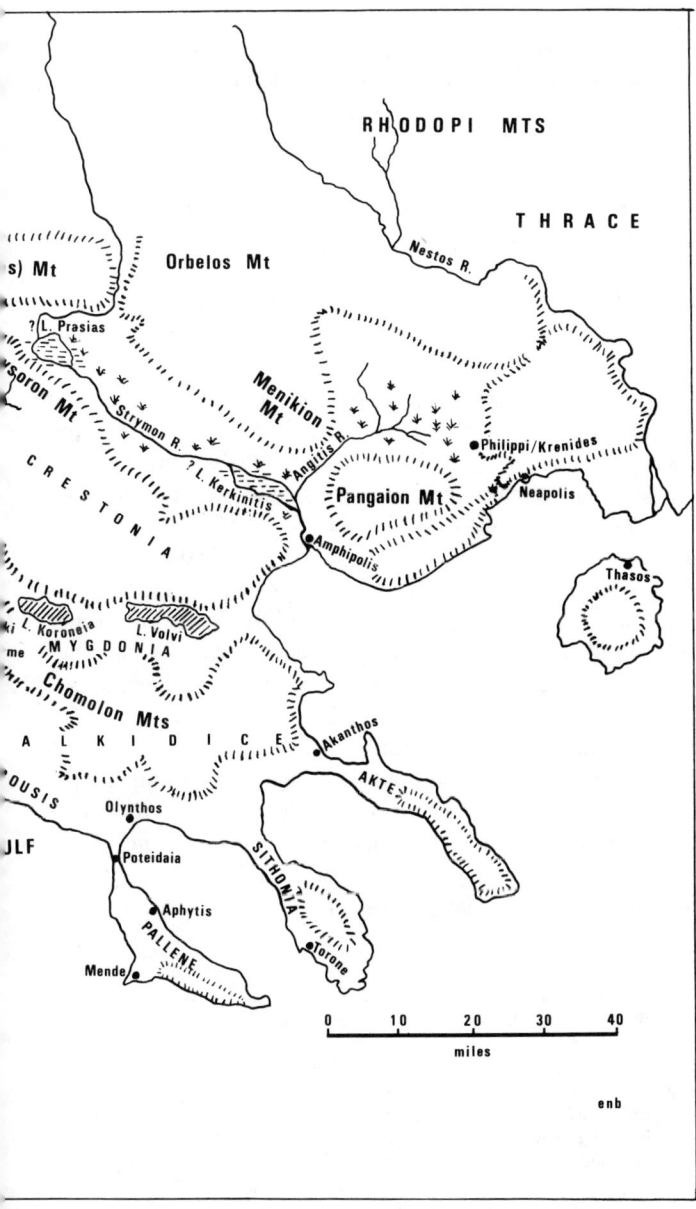

Vermion for a similar purpose. If by "plain" is meant the land below the piedmont, evidence must be used from these lowland areas. That Bintliff offers the remains of wild pig from the Neolithic site at Nea Nikomedeia proves nothing about plains woodland, as the slopes of Mt. Vermion, famous for its boar even today, lie only a few miles to the west.[11]

What remains is Bintliff's view that the "plain" was well wooded until quite recently, and that the present open landscape is due to deforestation in the period between the mid-nineteenth century and *ca.* 1939. His main nineteenth-century source is E. M. Cousinéry, *Voyage dans la Macédoine* (Paris 1831), who claims to have seen plenty of woods stretching from Veria to the sea along the Haliacmon[12] and throughout Bottiaia and the western plain. One wonders if Cousinéry had observed the same Macedonian plain seen by other nineteenth-century visitors to the region. No traveller's account seen by me mentions woodland on the plain. Col. Leake (1806) described a vast marsh and generally uncultivated area up to the Vermion slopes. Holland (1812) saw forests only in the plain of Katerini; his descriptions of the Emathian region mention marshes, rivers, mountains, but no woodland. In 1861 Heuzey observed an "open" plain. In the same year Tozer saw only tamarisk bushes north of the swamp. In 1863 Mackenzie and Irby described the plain as "for the most part desert," and contrasted the "weary level of the treeless plain" with the fertility of the glens below Edessa. In 1874 Baker saw a plain "almost treeless," by contrast to the Vermion piedmont. In brief, there were no forests in the modern period (the rich piedmont excluded), as far as we can tell. To visitors, both ancient and modern, the central part of the Emathian plain was flat, open space, including a narrow, fertile, coastal strip, vast marshes and a nuclear lake. Bintliff's statement (p. 261) that "there is not a trace in former days

---

[11] Supra n. 8.

[12] Perhaps this is a reference to the Pierian piedmont. If so, it may be confirmed in part by Heuzey; see Léon Heuzey and H. Daumet, *Mission Archéologique de Macédoine* (Paris 1876) 117.

References to the information which follows: William Martin Leake, *Travels in Northern Greece* III (London 1835) 260 ff.; Henry Holland, *Travels in the Ionian Isles, Albania, Thessaly, Macedonia, &c, during the years 1812 and 1813* (London 1815) 305 ff. and 329; H. F. Tozer, *Researches in the Highlands of Turkey, including visits to Mounts Ida, Athos, Olympus and Pelion* I (London 1869) 154; G. M. M. Mackenzie and A. P. Irby, *Travels in the Slavonic Provinces of Turkey-in-Europe* (London 1867) *passim*; and James Baker, *Turkey in Europe* (London 1877) 344-45. Holland (p. 328) describes timber (though not from the central plain) as a major export from Thessalonike in 1812.

of the present day open plain environment" must be set against the overwhelming evidence of nineteenth-century observers. Indeed the "present day open plain environment" would appear to be close to its natural state in late prehistoric and historical times. The forests of ancient Macedonia were then where they are today, on mountain slopes and in higher elevations.

It is curious that a people who possessed the finest ship-building materials in the Greek world themselves never developed a seafaring tradition during the Classical period. (Although the kingdom of Macedon developed formidable naval forces during the Hellenistic period, when her extensive foreign interests demanded such a commitment; see F. W. Walbank, "Sea-power and the Antigonids," elsewhere in this volume.) One suspects that this has to do with a lack of ports (save for Pella, briefly) in the Macedonian heartland as well as with other internal matters. Certainly it is one more factor establishing a distinction between the Macedonians and the maritime Greeks who lived nearby and in the south.

One final point about timber. That the forest products of Macedonia were prized by Greeks is a matter of the historical record, especially in the fifth century B.C. That Macedonia provided timber to Athens is certain; we have inscriptions to prove it.[13] And we are aware of the keen interest displayed by Athenians and Peloponnesians in this region, which in Athens' case began in the sixth century B.C., and did not cease with the Peloponnesian War.[14] Macedonian kings, and in particular Perdiccas II, fought desperately to maintain

---

[13] E.g., *IG* I² 71 (treaty of Athens with Perdiccas II) and *IG* I² 105 (Athenian honors to Archelaus; now see Meiggs and Lewis, *GHI* no. 90, with bibliography cited); also note 14 infra.

No thorough study of the timber trade yet exists, although we anticipate the publication of such a work soon by Russell Meiggs. Some useful information has been summarized by Homer A. Thompson in a paper presented at the University Museum of the University of Pennsylvania symposium: "The Mediterranean Market: aspects of trade in classical times," 13 October 1979. See pp. 12-14 of the circulated typescript of the paper: "Commerce in Building Materials in Ancient Athens." On the uses of timber in ship-building see L. Casson, *Ships and Seamanship in the Ancient World* (Princeton 1971), and J. S. Morison and R. T. Williams, *Greek Oared Ships, 900-322 B.C.* (Cambridge 1968).

[14] In the later fifth century no one could challenge Athens' naval supremacy while she had access to northern timber. With, however, the loss of Amphipolis, Brasidas' disruptive campaign in the north, and the Peloponnesians' growing ability to secure their own timber resources from Persia and Thessaly, Athens' position became precarious. She was forced into treaty arrangements with Macedon (supra n. 13) to insure the timber supply, and was thus enabled to continue the struggle. If Brasidas' scheme to interdict completely the flow of Macedonian timber and divert

control over a kingdom directly threatened from without, and endangered from within by internal factions supported from afar. In my view, one of the central themes in this continuing instability was timber, as Athens strove by every means to maintain access to her most important supply of ship timber, while Sparta attempted to interdict that access. Macedonian monarchs were precariously balanced midst the shoals of later-fifth-century Greek turbulence, and the Macedonians switched sides several times during the Peloponnesian War. One suspects that at least some of the misunderstanding of the age of Philip II was a reflection of Athenian memory of what must have appeared to have been Macedonian perfidy and whimsy in the fifth century. A fresh look at the history of fifth-century Greece might well add a new dimension to the standard bi-polar interpretation, as we see a third force — Macedon, and her timber — as a factor in the continuing struggle between Peloponnesians and Athenians.

II.

Macedonia was as renowned in the Greek world for her gold and silver resources as for her timber.[15] It was not so much that large quantities of gold and silver were produced as that Macedonia provided precious metal to the Greek world when other sources were unavailable. Western and central Macedonia west of the Axios river, while possessing some mineral resources, do not appear to have been worked in antiquity. A gold mine at Kozani, for example, seems not to have been in operation in ancient times, and there is reason to doubt Strabo's statement (14.680) that Mt. Vermion was a gold-producing center.[16] It is only when one crosses the Axios that he enters the region of mineral wealth. Many of the rivers of trans-Axios Macedonia produce gold-bearing sands, most of the Rhodopi

it to Spartan use had succeeded, the war might have ended nearly two decades earlier (Michell 281, supra n. 5).

For more on these complex issues (with sources cited) see Michell 281-82 (supra n. 5) *ATL* III 308-25, Meiggs and Lewis *GHI* no. 91 (with additional bibliography), G. E. M. de Ste. Croix, *Origins of the Peloponnesian War* (Ithaca, N.Y. 1972) 80-81, J. W. Cole, "Perdiccas and Athens," *Phoenix* 28 (1974) 55-71, and, for the whole period, Hammond, *Hist Mace* II, *passim*.

[15] In general see O. Davies, *Roman Mines in Europe* (Oxford 1935) 226-37, "Ancient Mines in Southern Macedonia," *JRAI* 62 (1932) 145-62, and "Notes on Mining," App. I in W. A. Heurtley, *Prehistoric Macedonia* (Cambridge 1939). Hammond, *Hist Mace* I 12-14, gives a convenient summary of the many mineral resources of Macedonia, and a brief description of gold and silver resources appears in *Hist Mace* II 69-73.

[16] Davies, *JRAI* (supra n. 15) 147.

streams being slightly auriferous. These same streams also were a source of magnetite iron-bearing sands, but it is unknown whether these were worked in ancient times.[17] Gold slags dating from the early Bronze Age exist in the Axios-Gallikos basin and in the corridor of lakes Volvi and Koroneia; in the former region these date from the late Bronze and early Iron ages. The gold native to the Axios-Gallikos was heated to make the grains coagulate; slag, the archaeologist's clue, was the residue. Little else seems to have been mined. The tin route from Britain to the Mediterranean lay outside Macedonia, and the residents of the area do not appear to have had access to it. In brief, the Macedonian mineral output seems to have been small during the Bronze Age. Only a bit of prehistoric iron was worked, and there is no evidence of silver before the Iron Age. The early inhabitants of the region seem to have been pasturers and farmers, not metal workers, possessing little need for and interest in the mineral resources of their land.[18]

It was in the sixth century B.C. that Macedonia became, in Davies' words, "an Eldorado" to the Greeks. Under Thasian and Athenian influence, and encouraged by Macedonian eastward expansion and the rising general demand for precious metals, mining became an important activity in trans-Axios Macedonia in the later sixth and early fifth centuries B.C. There appear to have been three main areas of mineral exploitation. The first of these was the basin of the upper Gallikos (ancient Echedoros) river, always more productive than the neighboring Axios to the west as a center for both the working and smelting of gold.[19] This may be the site of Aristotle's "Paeonian placers,"[20] where it was said that the rain washed the soil away, leaving gold. Moreover, if one accepts the view that Lake Prasias was located in the northern part of the Strymon plain, one might also place close to the headwaters of the Gallikos the silver

---

[17] *Ibid.* 228-29.

[18] Davies-Heurtley (supra n. 14) 254. In their use of gold the early inhabitants of Macedonia lagged behind not only their Aegean contemporaries, but also their northern Balkan counterparts. The oldest major find of gold in the world (as of 1978) is at Varna, near the Black Sea coast of northeastern Bulgaria. Dated to *ca.* 4600-4200 B.C., the cemetery-finds at Varna establish southeastern Europe as an early center of metal working innovation; at present it appears that Macedonia was not affected by this development. See Colin Refrew, "Varna and the social context of early metallurgy," *Antiquity* 52 (1978) 199-203.

[19] Davies, *JRAI* (supra n. 15) 151-52.

[20] *Mir. Ausc.* 833b.45; Davies, *Roman Mines* (supra n. 15) 232.

mine mentioned by Herodotus (5.17) as being so rich as to produce a talent a day for Alexander I.[21]

The second area comprises the adjacent regions of Philippi and Mt. Pangaion. The Thasians established an outpost at Krenides in the sixth century which was eventually lost to local tribes, then refounded by the Thasians shortly before being taken over by Philip II in 356 B.C. and renamed Philippi. Philip was the first Macedonian monarch to produce extensive gold coinage, and his source of metal was undoubtedly the Philippi-Pangaion region.[22] Several mining areas in or about the Philippi plain are known, the primary method of gold retrieval having been through placer extraction, that is, by the use of running water in sandy or gravelly deposits. The Mt. Pangaion area was the most renowned producer of precious metal in Macedonia. It was well known by the Greeks at least as early as the late sixth century B.C.,[23] and there is evidence suggesting that the area may have been worked as early as the seventh century.[24] It is not certain whether it was gold or silver that was first produced at Pangaion. It would appear to have been silver, both because the Laurion mines in Attica were not yet fully exploited, and because the local tribal coinage is of silver, abundant, and of good quality.[25] Gold may not have been extracted from the local pyrites until the fifth or even fourth century. This would explain Diodorus' comment (16.8.6-7) that the Pangaion mines were insignificant until the time of Philip II, who improved them and increased their output. "Insignificant" can refer only to gold production, for surely the region had been producing significant quantities of silver for some time. Thus Philip was the first to exploit fully the gold-bearing potential of the mines, and, by doing so, he became wealthy and,

---

[21] Davies, *Roman Mines* (supra n. 15) 235, locates this mine near the present Mt. Dysoron just east of the head of the Gallikos. If, however, "Mt. Dysoron" in antiquity referred instead to the whole range of hills forming the western boundary of the Strymon plain, and if the ancient Lake Prasias was in the lower Strymon plain, Alexander I's famous high-yield mine might have been in the Pangaion region.

[22] Davies, *JRAI* (supra n. 15) 155.

[23] Arist. *Ath Pol* 15.2; Hdt. 5.23.

[24] Davies, *JRAI* (supra n. 15) 157-58, who also includes a description of Pangaion itself. Davies regards the account of S. Casson, *Macedonia, Thrace and Illyria* (Oxford 1926) 63 ff. as being of little value on the question of the location and character of the Pangaion mines.

[25] Discussion of the tribal coinages of eastern Macedonia can be found in Hammond, *Hist Mace* II 74-91 and in Martin Price, *Coins of the Macedonians* (London 1974) 1-10.

according to Arrian (Anab. 7.9.3), issued gold coins,[26] organized mercenaries and bribed Greeks. One of the most astonishing aspects of M. Andronikos' royal tomb discoveries at Vergina was the large quantity of well wrought gold among the finds. This gold production continued sporadically until the Romans closed the mines in 167 B.C.

The third among the major mining areas was in the mountainous territory extending from the Volvi-Koroneia lake corridor to the southern slope of the central Chalkidian ranges. Perhaps no other region of Macedonia contains the remains of so much ancient mining activity. These Chalkidic mines were probably not worked before the middle of the fourth century.[27] Whether they were opened in the mid-fourth century and helped Olynthos challenge Philip, or were opened by Philip himself is not certain. What is clear, however, is that once begun, this area became one of the most heavily mined in Macedonia, as numerous slag heaps, shafts and galleries in the region testify.[28] The Chalkidic mines were among those closed by Rome (Livy 45.29) in 167 B.C., and the region was virtually deserted by Strabo's time. Only in the Turkish period did some gold-working reappear, and today mining is again a major occupation among the inhabitants, mainly for iron, magnesite, chrome, manganese and small amounts of gold, silver, lead and copper.

By modern standards mineral extraction techniques were primitive in ancient Macedonia.[29] Itinerant Balkan gold-washers, known in Roman times, may have existed earlier, and in deep mines machinery was simple. Extensive human labor, whether slave or free, was cheap. Thus numerous small mines could be worked profitably under conditions considered impossible today. In antiquity the mines of eastern Macedonia produced enough gold and silver to support

---

[26] The fullest treatment of Philip's coins is now George Le Rider, *Le Monnayage d' argent et d'or de Philippe II frappé en Macédoine de 359 à 294* (Paris 1977), some points of which are summarized in Le Rider, "The Coinage of Philip and the Pangaion Mines," *PM* 48-57.

[27] In the Acanthian speech at Sparta of 383 B.C. (Xen. *Hell.* 5.2.16-17) virtually every resource of the Chalkidike and Olynthos is mentioned, including wealth in ships and timber, revenues from commerce, large populations and abundant food. Mineral wealth is absent from the list, suggesting that the mines were not yet being exploited. The wealth of Pangaion, however, is noted.

[28] Davies, *Roman Mines* (supra n. 15) 233-34. Leake III (supra n. 12) 159-61 describes the residue of silver mining of more recent origin witnessed by him in the eastern Chalkidike in 1806.

[29] Davies (supra n. 14) 7, 231 and *passim* for full discussion.

excellent local coinages, make the region attractive to foreigners, help support the ambitions of Macedonian kings from Alexander I to Perseus, and enable Macedonia to enjoy the reputation of being one of the most important precious-metal sources in the ancient Mediterranean world.

III.

The evidence for agriculture in ancient Macedonia includes literary sources, archaeological remains (including botanical analyses) and analogues with modern Macedonia. The model for the analogue requires that natural ecological factors such as climate or sea level (which can affect alluvial plains and coastline configurations), be similar if one hopes to use empirical data from the modern era to reconstruct the ancient environment. I have argued in detail elsewhere[30] that the climate of modern Greece is like that of antiquity. Moreover, recent studies of the sea level have shown that the level of the Mediterranean has not varied more than about 30 cm. (about one foot) over the last 3000 years. The apparent changes as evidenced by the existence of submerged sites are generally the result of land subsidence caused by local seismic or tectonic disturbances, common in this geologically active part of the world.[31] Thus we appear to be dealing with a set of ecological factors that provide some evidence for the past.

As an agricultural area, Macedonia is, by comparison with much of Greece, blessed by nature. The region possesses large alluvial plains, abundant rainfall throughout the year, and cultivable terrace lands on the lower slopes of mountains. Moreover, Macedonia's major rivers flow yearround, permitting both natural and artificial irrigation for crop and pasture land. The large mountain ranges also provide well watered summer pasture on their upper slopes and basins, a phenomenon that has sustained herdsmen for centuries.

Thus any consideration of agricultural conditions in the historical period must take into account a virtually unchanged sea level and climate, and we must be prepared to show by analogy with the modern experience the uses to which the land was put. The main agricultural areas lay along river banks where the ground was not water-logged, in higher plains such as Pelagonia, Almopia and the

---

[30] "Some Observations on Malaria and the Ecology of Central Macedonia in Antiquity," *AJAH* 4 (1979) 111.

[31] *Contra* Hammond, *Hist Mace* I 145; for my arguments on the sea level (with technical literature cited) see "Observations on Malaria" (supra n. 29) 110-11.

upper half of the Philippi plain, along the terrace lands of the Emathian and Strymonian plains, in narrow coastal plains like those of Pieria and Crousia, and in hills which held both water and soil, such as those of Mt. Paiko and the central Chalkidice. The land was used to grow cereal grains and vegetables, and to raise domestic animals.

The transhumance of sheep — the system of alternating pasturage between the lowlands in winter and the mountains in summer — was widely practiced.[32] The higher basins and meadows of Macedonian mountains are ideally suited for summer pasturage, as are many such places in Greek and Balkan highlands. The manure produced by the animals in winter was a major source of fertilizer available to ancient farmers. If left to rot in manure piles and compost heaps for a year, the manure eventually came to enrich his soil.[33] And in much of Macedonia — where wood is available — it was not necessary to use dung cakes for fuel, a practice which of necessity has contributed to the enduring cycle of soil impoverishment throughout much of the Middle East.

Agriculture and transhumance can co-exist if there is no severe competition for the land. Farmers resist any encroachment upon their cropland by large flocks. In the case where the village is organized to a high degree, and land is available, uncultivated common ground may be given over to herds for winter grazing so as not to disturb crops. If, however, the competition for the same ground becomes intense, sheep and goat herding normally decline.[34] Eventually one no longer finds the mix of farmer and herdsman in the lower towns. As the practice of agriculture expands, herdsmen move to higher ground. In western Macedonia especially there are dozens of villages lying at elevations higher than the normal farming ones that serve mainly as winter residences and forage depots, and which are abandoned by herding families each summer when the flocks graze in upland meadows. In central and eastern Macedonia, on the fringes of the Thessalian plain, in Epiros, Boiotia, the Argolid and the Corinthia, the author has seen the temporary winter quarters of

---

[32] A point correctly emphasized by Hammond, *Hist Mace* I 7-8 and 15, and in *Migrations and Invasions in Greece and Adjacent Areas* (Park Ridge, N.J. 1976) *passim*; also see Cary (supra n. 4) 18-19.

[33] Semple (supra n. 5) 406-17.

[34] In modern Macedonia this has happened during the past half century, as the legal ownership and intensive use of land for non-pasturing purposes has become prevalent.

herdsmen and their flocks, but always in areas not given over to agriculture. When the division between farmer and herdsman is complete, both suffer somewhat to survive. The herdsman is denied lusher lowland winter grazing, and the farmer is without his most useful form of fertilizer. In modern times the farmer can compensate with chemical fertilizers; but there is no alternative for the herdsman except eventually to abandon his transhumant existence or to join others to raise animals on an industrial scale.[35]

Much of the mountainland of Macedonia between the upper timbered slopes and the lower cultivated areas is covered with maquis, the wild scrub common in Mediterranean lands. What is lacking in Macedonia that is ubiquitous in level places and on gentle slopes in Greece is the olive tree. The olive is not a feature of the Macedonian landscape. This sturdy tree, which seems to thrive where all else fails, is in fact extremely sensitive to cold, and needs well drained soil. It prefers lime soil, but is not particular. It will not flourish above about 600 m., although this varies from region to region depending upon latitude and proximity to the sea.[36] A few olives will grow, for example, on the lower slopes of Mt. Vermion, where they catch sea breezes from the Thermaic gulf and thereby avoid the frosts of the Emathian plain below. The Pierian coastal plain and perhaps (only by modern analogy) the terraces above the plain of Philippi supported olives in quantity in antiquity.[37] One must reach the Mediterranean climes of the Chalkidice before seeing the great groves we normally associate with the Greek countryside.[38] It was Pliny (*NH* 15.1.1), quoting Theophrastus, who remarked that the olive will grow only within forty miles of the sea. Except for the

---

[35] I have not here considered the truly nomadic herding families, a fascinating feature of Balkan life for centuries, but one which may not have directly affected Macedonian life in the historical periods of antiquity.

[36] Great Britain, Admiralty, Naval Staff, *Greece* II (London 1944) 66-68, and W. B. Turrill, *The Plant Life of the Balkan Peninsula. A Phytogeographical Study* (Oxford 1929) 242.

[37] Although the pollen analysis of the Philippi plain shows no evidence of olives from the Classical period; see Grieg and Turner (supra n. 2) passim.

[38] There is a striking example of the results of climate change as one crosses the major transverse Chalkidian mountain barrier, the Cholomon ridge, from the northern, "Macedonian," half of the Chalkidike to its southern (Mediterranean) slope. Within a few hundred meters of the crest on the southern slope the first olive groves appear. This may be seen along the road from Palaiokastro, through Polygyros, down to the Kassandrian gulf. The transition is also visible, though less suddenly and dramatically, along the coastal road from Thessalonike to the Potidaia isthmus.

few places noted, the Macedonian homeland was virtually without Athena's gift.[39]

Not so Dionysus'. The vine is sturdier than the olive tree, suffering winter frosts without damage, needing only well drained soil, spring rain and periods of prolonged sunshine just before vintage time. Most of Macedonia fulfills these conditions, save only the higher elevations and the lowland swamps. The slopes of Mt. Vermion around Naoussa produce arguably the best red wines of modern Greece. Leake spoke well of famous wines in western Macedonia,[40] but it is not known whether either place produced vines in antiquity. We should be surprised if they did not, although the only evidence we have for outstanding ancient wines in northern Greece is for the wines of Thasos and the Chalkidice.[41]

---

[39] *Contra* Hammond, *Hist Mace* I 181 and 205, who claims that in Classical times olives grew in abundance in the central plain and hillsides and in Crestonia. He offers as evidence a fragment of Theopompus (F237 = Athen. 3.77D) which states that Philip II was fortunate in that olives bore in the spring [!] in Crestonia. This view is unacceptable. First, it conflicts with Hammond's own (correct) statement (p. 5) that the climate of Macedonia is unsuitable for the olive. Second, the Theompompus fragment makes no reference to the region of the central plain, an area of extensive swampland inhospitable to the olive; the trees need well drained soil. Moreover, even if we assume (as did Hammond) that Philip had drained the plain (and that the weather was warmer then so as not to produce the frosts which prevent olive production today), it would have taken decades for the newly reclaimed area to produce olives in quantity, by which time Philip was long in his tomb.

Finally, the Theopompus fragment itself is a botanical nightmare: the spring harvest of "figs, vines and olives." Vines are not harvested in the spring; grapes require the warmth and dryness of late summer and early autumn to mature. The Macedonian vintage occurs during the early autumn. E.g., the author has witnessed the vintage in the northwestern Chalkidian village of Agia Trias, just across the bay from Thessalonike, and only 30 miles southeast of the area described by Theopompus; the vintage in that year (1977) was in late September.

Olives are harvested in October-December, depending upon local conditions. Pliny (*NH* 15.13-14) refers to some Italian olives being harvested in February and March, but not in spring in Greece, as Theopompus puts it. Indeed, even the possibility of a second sprouting is excluded. Nowhere in his discussion of twice-bearing and late-bearing trees does Theophrastus (*de Caus. Plant.* 1.13.4-14.2), who presumably knows about such things, mention the olive. The second bearing of some plants may occur at the end of a long, warm autumn, but not in the case of fruits such as grapes and olives, which take a long time to mature. The point of this odd passage of Theompompus is that Philip was fortunate in all things, citing as examples an exaggerated version of olive, fig and grape harvests. Its purpose is rhetorical. Indeed it could be argued that the passage was intended to show how fortunate Philip was to have found such fruits elsewhere (exaggeration aside), indicating that he was not thus blessed at home.

[40] At Siatista along the Elimean-Orestian frontier; see *Travels in Northern Greece* I 306-307.

[41] "The Symposium at Alexander's Court," *AM* 3 (forthcoming).

One would give much for some information about the ancient Macedonian wine trade, especially since the consumption of wine — much of it *akratos*, or unmixed — was such a central activity in the Macedonian court, as both literature and the Vergina artifacts testify. We have one clue, however. In response to my inquiries, Prof. Ph. Petsas kindly informed me that several hundred amphora stamps had been preserved from the excavations at Pella. These have not been published, and they have not been available for examination. But quite by chance, I was able, at very short notice and without preparation, to examine the photo archives of the stamps. I can report that at least in the periods represented in the excavations thus far, Pella was importing wine from, among other places, Mende, Torone and Thasos. And we would not be wrong to assume that local wines were produced in abundance as well.

What do we know of the shape of the central (Emathian) plain? First, it is clear from the work of Hammond and Bintliff and others that an inlet of the Thermaic gulf stretched quite far inland in the fourth century B.C. Second, it has been argued that Philip II was responsible for a land reclamation project in the Emathian plain.[42] No direct evidence for this scheme exists, although Theophrastus (*de Caus. Plant.* 5.14.6) mentions that Philip drained and reclaimed the land around Philippi. This area, the lower part of the plain which begins above Drama and runs down to the Kavalla ridge separating it from the sea, is hardly analogous to the central plain. The Philippi plain is an ill-drained alluvial basin, fed by numerous small streams falling from the mountains which lie to the northeast. The plain's natural drainage narrows to a single stream where the Angitis river pierces the Pangaion-Menikion mountain barrier to flow into the lower Strymon plain. The drainage of the Philippi plain was accomplished with relative ease in modern times by the erection of a pumping station at the Angitis canyon bottleneck.[43] If Philip were responsible for draining the Philippi plain shortly after he took it in 356 B.C. he may have solved the drainage problem in some similarly simple fashion, given the primitive hydraulic skills of his day. The Emathian plain, however, presents a much different situation. It is huge and complex, fed by major rivers, and resists any single easy method for flood control and reclamation, as modern experience has shown. It took a major effort by Greek and American hydraulic

---

[42] Hammond, *Hist Mace* I 149 and 160.

[43] Admiralty Handbook *Greece* II (supra n. 35) 140 and pl. 57.

engineers to reclaim the area in the 1920's and 1930's. One doubts that ancient Macedonian technology and the royal purse were up to this formidable task. That the region around Philippi was reclaimed is arguable; if true, one might even suggest that Philippi was drained because the central plain was marshy, and Philip was pressed for cultivable land. Whatever the case may have been, Philippi's drainage cannot serve as an analogue for the great central plain.

If the sea level were several feet lower in antiquity it might be argued that drainage was naturally more efficient than it is today, and thus the Emathian plain was less swampy. But the sea level in historical times has remained virtually unchanged, and the silting process by which Lake Loudias was formed indicates that the plain was ill-drained in antiquity. It is thus best to suggest that the area was undrained, as it remained until the recent program of reclamation.

The marshy areas in the Emathian and Strymonian plains, plus the numerous mountain streams that drain into them, have made Macedonia highly malarious for much of its history until quite recently. This scourge decimated hundreds of thousands of Balkan and Anatolian refugees who settled the region in 1912-1924 and the French, British and German armies who fought along the Macedonian front in 1916-1918.[44] Malaria continued to be endemic in Greece until the 1950's, and as late as 1936 was the fourth leading cause of death after senility. The northern marshlands of Thrace and Macedonia were among the most heavily infected regions, as the conditions are conducive to the proliferation of two species (marshbreeding and stream-breeding) of *Anopheles* mosquitos which carry the deadly plasmodium parasite.

Malaria was known by the writers of the Hippocratic corpus in the fifth century B.C. Indeed their description of the malaria fever stages is so precise that until recently the pathological nomenclature describing symptoms was based on phrases from the Hippocratic handbook. Recent attempts to suggest that Greece was malaria-free in Classical times have not been convincing.[45] If we accept the notion

---

[44] The horrors — and humor — experienced by the British Salonika Force continued to be recalled for at least the following three decades in The Official Journal of the Salonika Re-union Association, entitled (appropriately enough) *The Mosquito*. I am indebted to Prof. Ph. M. Petsas for sending me a photo-copy of the cover of an issue of *The Mosquito*, no. 75 (September 1946).

[45] Details in Borza, "Observations on Malaria" (supra n. 29). I take this opportunity to add two pieces of evidence suggesting the possibility of malaria in the Emathian plain in antiquity. Both were brought to my attention by Dr. M. B. Hatzopoulos, to whom I am grateful. In Athen. 8.348e and 8.352a there are references to what may

that malaria was endemic in Greece at least by the fifth century B.C. (perhaps introduced fully into the area by Xerxes' armies), and we know that the Macedonian environment was as conducive to the disease then as now, we have little reason to doubt that it was a factor in Macedonian history. The effect on the population was to maintain a high mortality rate among the young and the weak. Long-term residents develop some forms of resistance, although these may have been mitigated somewhat in Macedonia because of the unusually long mosquito season caused by the residence of two Anopheline species which breed at different times of the year. The human population has little opportunity to recover from Anopheline attack and develop natural defenses; it was no wonder that Macedonia was regarded in modern times as the most malarious region in the world outside the tropics.

Malaria does not depopulate a region, but it contributes to generally poor health and reduces the inhabitants' work efficiency. One assumes that the highlanders of western Macedonia, and those who lived in the uplands of central Macedonia, were generally malaria-free. One also suspects that those whose livelihood depended on farming the fertile lowlands in malarious regions kept to the highest, driest ground available, living and working on the terrace lands bordering the deadly marshes. All the known prehistoric and historical sites of the Emathian plain — Aegae, Veria, Nea Nikomedeia, Lefkadia, Edessa and Pella — are located on higher ground bordering the central marshland. Not enough site studies exist for eastern Macedonia, nor has its ancient ecology been yet well enough defined to generalize about the patterns of land-use and settlement there.

The ecological character of the central Macedonian homeland is becoming clear. Emathia was a vast marshland and sea inlet bordered by fertile terrace land. Farmers tilled the slopes, and may even have reclaimed small patches at the marsh's edge. The mountain meadows above were exploited by pasturers. Timber was widely available. Wine was undoubtedly produced locally in abundance, although better wines were imported from Thasos and the Chalkidice from at least the fourth century. Oil was imported; whether from the Chalkidice or from the south is not known.

The expansion of the Macedonian kingdom out of this irregular

---

be taken as splenomegaly and jaundice (both are common symptoms of malaria) in the early to mid-fourth century B.C.

The Natural Resources of Early Macedonia

crescent-shaped territory can be seen both as a response to the perceived need for security and as a desire for resources not available in Pieria and Emathia. Clearly the acquisition of the passes and routes into western Macedonia and Thessaly can be regarded as a security measure, the interest in these areas marking the policy of Macedonian kings from the sixth century B.C. The attraction of eastern Macedonia certainly lies in the precious metal resources of the mountain regions bordering the plains of the Strymon and Philippi. This is clear from the time of Alexander I on. One suspects that in the fourth century the grazing and forage land of the Strymon plain and of the northwestern Chalkidice may have whetted Philip II's appetite for a stable base for horse production and maintenance, not to mention his desire for strategic and mining purposes to reclaim the kingdom of his illustrious fifth-century predecessors.

Macedonia was by Greek standards a prosperous region, although its central part was awkwardly arranged around the Emathian core. The inconvenience of this irregular, crescent-shaped territory, including its lack of direct access to eastern Macedonia, was undoubtedly a contributing factor in the movement of the capital from Aegae to Pella about the turn of the fifth and fourth centuries. Pella, located near the junction of the main east-west and north-south Balkan land routes, was strategically more advantageous and also provided a better outlet to the sea. In time the population increased, foreign and local demand for Macedonian metals and timber grew, the need for cultivable land both for crops and forage was evident, and the desire for security produced an expansion of Macedonian interests in several directions.[46]

Much remains to be considered. I have not dealt with internal economic arrangements such as the ownership of land, the distribution of wealth generated by what we assume are royal resources, such as forests and mines, and the means by which, say, Athens paid for her timber, or the Macedonians for their oil. The evidence on these matters is slim and the subject not much studied.[47] But we do come

---

[46] For which *ibid.*, 106-109.

[47] Much of the best evidence concerns the Hellenistic period. See, for example, the paper of Erich S. Gruen, "Macedonia and the Settlement of 167 B.C." (elsewhere in this volume), which discusses the reorganization of royal resources made by Rome at the end of the Third Macedonian War. The Romans recognized that gold, silver and timber were important sources of revenue and (one might add) wealth for the potential resurgence of Macedonian nationhood.

away with a vivid impression of a relatively rich land whose abundance was exploited to the extent that a primitive technology and frequent political instability permitted. This abundance was probably responsible in part for supporting a nation whose kings and people were among the most dynamic in the ancient Mediterranean world, and who provoked respect — if not fear — from Asians, Greek and Romans alike.

The Pennsylvania State University

The Oleveni Inscription and the Dates of Philip II's Reign

M. B. HATZOPOULOS

Abstract

This study attempts a reevaluation of the evidence concerning the dates of Philip's accession and of his murder. Since Beloch the generally accepted view places these events in summer 359 and in summer 336, respectively. The recently republished fourth-century Oleveni inscription, which records a campaign of a king Philip against the Dardanians, is incompatible with these dates. After a reexamination of the literary sources in connexion with recent archaeological finds, the writer comes to the conclusion that Philip succeeded his brother Perdikkas between *ca.* July and October 360, and was murdered *ca.* October 336.*

Eleven years ago Fanoula Papazoglou gave a new edition of an inscribed stele (see Fig. 1) built in as the left-hand door-post in the chapel of St. Anne, one kilometre to the west of Oleveni, a small

---

*I wish to thank Dr. J. R. Ellis for reading this paper and making valuable suggestions on both form and substance. I am also grateful to Professor Fanoula Papazoglou, who has offered me constant help and advice. Neither, of course, is in any way responsible for the opinions expressed here. My thanks are equally due to Professor D. Pandermalis, who kindly showed me and sent me a photograph of the unpublished inscription of Dion, and to Professor M. Andronikos, who with his usual generosity gave me some of his time in order to explain to me the secrets of the royal tombs of Vergina.

The following abbreviations will be used:

Beloch, *Geschichte*   K. J. Beloch, *Griechische Geschichte* III, 1-2 (Berlin and Leipzig 1922-23).

village six kilometres to the south of the Makedonian town of Monastir (Bitola), the ancient Herakleia Lynkou:[1]

[. . . 3 lines . . .]
4 [. . . . T A . . A N . .]
[. .]στενα[. . . . . .]
[. .]φοι ταῦτα [εἰ]ς τοὺς
[. . . ΣΑΧΡΑ . Ν] ἀν[α-
8 [γρά]ψαντες εἰς σ[τή-
[λην] ἀνά[θ]ετε ἐν τῶι
ἐπιφαν[ε]στάτωι τ[ό]πωι
ἔτους ͵Ϛί Πανήμου [. .
12 [. .]κατλεστῶν [οἱ πα-
[ρ]αταξάμενοι ἐπὶ
τοῦ βασιλέως Φιλίπ-
που πρὸς Δαρδανε[ῖς
16 [. Α . . . . ή]σαντες

Bosworth, *Commentary*	A. B. Bosworth, *A Historical Commentary on Arrian's History of Alexander* I (Oxford 1980).
Gutschmid	A. Gutschmid, *Kleine Schriften* (Leipzig 1889-94).
Meyer, *Forschungen*	E. Meyer, *Forschungen zur alten Geschichte* I-II (Halle 1899).
Papazoglou, *Historia*	Fanoula Papazoglou, "Les origines et la destinée de l'Etat illyrien," *Historia* 14 (1965) 143-79.
Papazoglu, *Tribes*	Fanula Papazoglu, *The Central Balkan Tribes in Pre-Roman Times* (Amsterdam 1978).
Papazoglou, *ŽA*	Fanoula Papazoglou, "Inscription hellénistique de Lyncestide," *Živa Antika* 20 (1970) 99-113.
Prestianni Giallombardo, *RivStorAnt*	Anna Maria Prestianni Giallombardo, "Diritto metrimoniale, ereditario e dinastico nella Macedonia di Filippo II," *RivStorAnt* 6-7 (1976-77) 81-110.
Prestianni Giallombardo, *SicGym*	Anna Maria Prestianni Giallombardo, "ΦΙΛΙΠΠΙΚΑ I. sul "culto" di Fillippo II di Macedonia," *SicGym* 28 (1975) 1-57.
Prestianni Giallombardo, *Helikon*	Anna Maria Prestianni Giallombardo, "Aspetti giuridici e problemi cronologici della reggenza di Filippo II di Macedonia," *Helikon* 10-11 (1973-74) 191-209.
Schaefer	A. Schaefer, *Demosthenes und seine Zeit*, I-III.2 (Leipzig 1856-58), I-III² (Leipzig 1885-87).
Sordi, *Diodorus*	Marta Sordi, *Diodori Siculi Bibliothecae Liber XVI*, Biblioteca di studi superiori 56 (Florence 1969) 123.

NOTES

[1] Papazoglou, *ŽA* 99-113; cf. Papazoglu, *Tribes* 154-55; 555-56; 653 n.11 and 14. A relatively different edition of this text had been presented by N. Vulić, "Antički spomenici naše zemlje," *Spomenik Srpske Akademije nauka* 98 (1948) 21, no. 53. The two versions are conveniently reproduced in Papazoglu, *Tribes* 556.

Dates of Philip II's Reign

The most important parts of the inscription, the reading of which is fortunately beyond doubt,[2] are the 11th line, with the date, a day of the month of Panemos of the 16th year of a king, and lines 12-16, which allude to a battle under a king named Philip against the Dardanians. What we have here is undoubtedly a dedication in commemoration of distinguished service[3] preceded by an official document referring to it.[4] The obvious question is naturally that of the date of the document and of the identity of "King Philip." Professor Papazoglou's well argued and prudent conclusion was that palaeographic and historical considerations were in favour of Philip II and not Philip V (who is the only other possible candidate), but that she could not commit herself definitely. The more I studied the palaeographical arguments the more they seemed to me overwhelming,[5] and were it not for a chronological difficulty, to which I shall

---

[2] Since the first editor, Vulić, did not explicitly state that he had studied the monument himself, and Professor Papazoglou had been able to work only from a copy which I. Mikulčić of Skopje had the kindness to send her, I attempted to examine the inscription myself. Unfortunately, for reasons beyond my control it was not possible for me to reach Oleveni. Professor Papazoglou kindly visited the site in my behalf. In a letter she was able to confirm the exactness of Mikulčić's copy and in particular to ascertain that the reading of the date was beyond doubt.

Through the continuing interest and kindness of Professor Papazoglou, I have, since submitting the first draft of this paper, received a photograph of the inscription itself, printed from a negative just discovered in the National Museum of Belgrade. The photograph (infra Fig.1), without affecting the general understanding of the text, permits new readings at several points. I intend to present a new edition of the inscription in the near future.

[3] Whatever the exact reading and meaning of the last word, there can be no doubt that the stele celebrated a victory to which the dedicants had significantly contributed.

[4] For another example of recognition of military service by a Macedonian king; cf. *IG* X 2,1,1.

[5] Cf. Fanoula Papazoglou, "Un témoignage inaperçu sur Monounios l'Illyrien," *ŽA* 21 (1971) 183-84. I reexamined all the dated Macedonian documents of the royal period. We now have a royal letter which can be securely dated in the 16th year of Philip V (Cf. D. Pandermalis, "Λατρεῖες καί ἱερά τοῦ Δίου Πιερίας" *AM* II (1977) 340-41. A mere comparison between the letter forms of the two documents — those of the unpublished Dion inscription were known to me through Daux's description (*BCH* 95 [1971] 275) and now thanks to Professor Pandermalis' kind permission I was able to examine the stone and to obtain a photograph (infra Fig. 2) of it — is sufficient to convince of the utter improbability of their being contemporary. Nor is it possible to draw an argument from the peripheral position of Oleveni, in order to explain the striking differences in the forms of the letters. Alkomena (Bučin) in Derriopos is even more peripheral, but the lettering of the royal document recently discovered there (F. Papazoglou, "Nouveau fragment d'acte de la chancellerie macédonienne," *Klio* 52 [1970] 305-15; cf. G. Daux, "En

Fig. 1. The Oleveni Inscription. Courtesy of F. Papazoglou.

Dates of Philip II's Reign

Fig. 2. Royal Letter of Philip V, dated to the 16th year of his reign, from Dion in Pieria. Courtesy of D. Pandermalis.

return presently, I would have unreservedly accepted the context suggested in the article. What had impressed Professor Papazaglou as no mere coincidence was the fact that the great Illyrian war, during which Philip II crushed the Dardanians, is usually dated (following Diodoros) in the campaign season of 344,[6] which belongs to the Macedonian year that is also usually considered as the 16th regnal year of Philip II. On the other hand we know of no Dardanian campaign of Philip V in summer 206 which corresponds to the campaign season of the 16th year of his reign.[7]

The geographical setting of the events referred to is controversial and can be exhaustively discussed only within the wider context of the Illyro-Macedonian relations in the fourth century. I can only present here some conclusions fully argued elsewhere:[8]

1) Diodoros,[9] perhaps after Ephoros,[10] is formal: Philip waged this war against the Illyrians, the hereditary enemies of his house; he invaded Illyria, devastated the countryside, took many towns and returned to Macedonia laden with booty. These hereditary enemies can be no others than the Illyrians bordering the Macedonian kingdom on the Northwest, who already under Grabos[11] and before

---

marge des "Mélanges Klaffenbach," *BCH* 95 [1971] 274-75) is indistinguishable from that of contemporary documents found in the heartland of the Macedonian kingdom.

[6] Papazoglou, *ŽA* 106, and *Historia* 156.

[7] For the date of Philip's accession, see Chr. Habicht, "Epigraphische Zeugnisse zur Geschichte Thessaliens unter der makedonischen Herrschaft," *AM* 1 (1970) 274-75, with previous bibliography, to which should be added Chr. Makaronas, "'Ἐπιστολή τοῦ βασιλέως Φιλίππου τοῦ Ε΄," *Arch Eph* (1934-35) 117-27.

[8] I am at present engaged in a reexamination of the evidence in a study of fourth-century Macedonian historiography. Older bibliography can be found in Papazoglou, *Historia* 156-58, and in N. G. L. Hammond, "The Kingdoms in Illyria, ca. 400-167 B.C.," *BSA* 61 (1966) 244-45. For some more recent views cf. Ellis, *PMI* 134-36 and 274-75, and Griffith, *Hist Macc* II 469-74 and 684-85.

[9] Diod. 16.69.7.

[10] According to N. G. L. Hammond, "The Sources of Diodorus XVI: Part One," *CQ* 31 (1937) 90-91, (cf. *eiusdem*, "The Sources of Diodorus XVI: Part Two," *CQ* 32 [1938] 148-51), this notice as well as the following one (Diod. 16.69.8) about Philip's activities in Thessaly, come from a "text-book" mentioning the most important events of the period. On the other hand, Marta Sordi, who for the Greek affairs in the 16th book of Diodoros, admits only one subsidiary source besides Ephoros-Demophilos, assigns this paragraph on Illyria implicitly (cf. Sordi, *Diodorus*, XXVII and XXX) — as she does explicitly for the immediately following paragraph on Philip's intervention in Thessaly (Sordi, *Diodorus* XVIII, XXVIII and 124) — to Ephoros.

[11] Cf. Diod. 16.22.3.

him under Bardylis had fought against Philip himself, both his brothers and his father.

2) The most plausible interpretation of Diodoros is that this time Philip did not, as in the past, limit himself to compelling the Illyrians to join forces with him[12] but actually annexed some towns and territory which belonged to them. It is therefore likely that the extension of the Macedonian frontiers in the Pelagonian plain and the southernmost foothills of Mt. Skardos (Šar Planina) date from this campaign.

3) Pompeius Trogus[13] knew of a victorious war of Philip against "Illyrian Kings" to be dated at the same period. His epitomator's[14] more detailed expression, *Dardanos ceterosque finitimos fraude captos expugnat*, leaves little doubt as to the meaning of this plural and the identity of these kings described collectively as Illyrians:[15] Philip did not fight only against his Illyrian hereditary enemies but also against the Dardanians, who make then their first entrance in Greek history.

4) A special feature of this war, which may have extended, all taken together, over one campaign season, was the population transplants for the securing of a defensible frontier.[16] A case in point is the conquest of Sarnous, which must be situated on or near the Illyrian, Dardanian and Macedonian frontier, in the vicinity of modern Debrešte, and which commanded the entrance to the Pelagonian plain. It is in this area of the strategic *fauces Pelagoniae* or *fauces ad Pelagoniam* or *angustiae quae ad Pelagoniam sunt*[17] that must have taken place the momentous encounter which is the most probable

---

[12] Cf. Diod. 16.22.3.

[13] Pomp. Trog. *Prol.* 8: *Ut Illyrici reges ab eo victi sunt.*

[14] Just. *Epit.* 8.6.3.

[15] The most plausible explanation is that Pompeius Trogus (or more probably his source), like most ancient authors, considered — rightly or wrongly (cf. Papazoglou, *Tribes* 211-18) — the Dardanians as part of the greater Illyrian family and included them in the "Illyrians." (For a different view, see Papazoglou, *Historia* 159).

[16] Cf. J. R. Ellis, "Population Transplants under Philip II," *Makedonika* 9 (1969) 16, and *PMI* 136 and 274-75; Hammond, *Hist Mace* II 661; H. J. Dell, "The Western Frontier of the Macedonian Monarchy," *AM* 1 (1970) 121-22, and "Philip and Macedonia's Northern Neighbors," *PM* 94. A. W. Pickard-Cambridge, *Demosthenes and the Last Days of Greek Freedom* (New York and London 1914) 303, dates these population transplants to 345; Ellis, *Makedonika* 14, rightly suggests that they must have extended over a much longer period.

[17] Livy 31.34.6, 33.3, 28.5, with Papazoglu, *Tribes* 157, n. 90. For a different opinion, see Hammond, *Hist Mace* I 60.

candidate for the historical event referred to in the Oleveni inscription.

With the scarce notices that survive we cannot hope for a full reconstruction of the famous campaign that culminated in the pitched battle against Pleuratos which nearly cost Philip's life. Here is what can be retrieved from some miserable fragments and incidental allusions in ancient authorities. At the beginning of the campaigning season the Macedonian king, having heard that the Illyrians and the Dardanians were planning to invade Macedonia, entered Illyria first at the head of his Royal Bodyguards.[18] He hastened to the στενά τῆς Πελαγονίας[19] to deal with the Dardanians, who were coming down the Treska valley into the Pelagonian plain, before they joined forces with the Illyrians.[20] King Philip won the day but, instead of contenting himself with the repulsion of the danger that threatened Macedonia, he engaged in a reckless pursuit of king Pleuratos, during which the enemy rallied and the Macedonians suffered near disaster. Philip himself sustained a severe wound to the collar bone and was nearly killed, 150 bodyguards were wounded and one of them, Hippostratos, probably the nephew of Attalos and brother of Kleopatra, Philip's future wife,[21] was killed, presumably while trying to save the life of his king.[22] It would seem that the near disaster suffered by the Macedonian forces caused bitter controversy concerning the responsibility of the king himself, of the Bodyguards[23] corps

---

[18] See Griffith, *Hist Mace* II 709. (For a different suggestion, cf. N. G. L. Hammond, "A Cavalry Unit in the Army of Antigonus Monophthalmus: Asthippoi," *CQ* 28 [1978] 130 and n. 8). The two campaigns considered by Griffith as possible candidates are in fact one and the same (*vide infra*). Whether he had with him a detachment of Thessalians, as conjectured Marta Sordi (*La lega tessala fino ad Alessandro Magno* [Rome 1958] 282, n. 6, and *Diodorus* 123) from a Thessalian dedication to Athena Itonia (*AnthPal* 9.743), cannot be ascertained.

[19] Cf. Hammond, *Hist Mace* I 60, n. 1.

[20] For a similar overall strategic view but in a very different geographic and ethnic setting, cf. Griffith, *Hist Mace* II 471-72. Nothing can be made out of Theopompos *FGrH* 115 F 182, Οἰδάντιον· πόλις Ἰλλυριῶν.

[21] Satyros, *FHG* 3.161 F 5 (=Athen. 13.557 D).

[22] Marsyas of Pella, *FGrH* 135/6 F 17; cf. W. Heckel, "Marsyas of Pella, Historian of Macedon," *Hermes* 108 (1980) 456, and Dem. 18.67 with *schol. ad loc.*; Sen. *Controv.* 10.5.6.

[23] The *hetairoi* of Marsyas, the *pedzetairoi* of Theopompos (or Anaximenes), the *sōmatophylakes* of Diodoros (cf. the *phylakes* of Isokrates). For the use of the term *sōmatophylakes* to describe the *agēma* of the Footguards (the *hypaspistai* of Alexander's reign), see now Bosworth, *Commentary*, 72 and 323; for the term *pedzetairoi* used in

as a whole and of some of the Bodyguards in particular. The first two points can be gained from veiled but insistent allusions of Isocrates.[24] The third one, which in my opinion explains the otherwise incomprehensible relationship between the king, his future wife (and her family) and his assassin-to-be, underlies Diodoros' romanticised story of the second "Pausanias," who died in battle during an Illyrian war against a king named Pleurias, while trying to save the life of king Philip, and whose death was avenged by his friend Attalos.[25]

Whatever the exact identity of the dedicants the correspondences between the situation inferred from our epigraphic document and what we know about Philip's campaign against the Dardanians is striking. Even the tantalising letters forming the word ΣΤΕΝΑ in the fifth line of the inscription can but bring to mind τὰ στενὰ Πελαγονίας, the *fauces Pelagoniae*, where our bitterly fought battle must have taken place.

In these circumstances my acceptance of Professor Papazoglou's suggestion would have been unreserved, were it not for my conviction that the Illyrian campaign referred to cannot have taken place in 344 but only one year earlier, in the campaign season of 345. This was first seen in the last century by K. G. Böhnecke and A. Schaefer,[26] who pointed out that since the reorganisation of Thessaly by Philip was already an accomplished fact by Autumn 344, there was no time for both a Thessalian intervention and an Illyrian war (followed by a long convalescence) earlier in the same campaign season and that Diodorus was in fact bringing retrospectively up to date Philip's activities since the end of the Third Sacred War.[27] G.

Philip's reign to describe this same corps, see Griffith, *Hist Mace* II 705-13. There is no cogent reason, *pace* N. G. L. Hammond, "A Note on Pursuit in Arrian," *CQ* 28 (1978) 138, to believe that at the moment of Pleuratos' rally Philip was engaged in a cavalry pursuit; cf. Diod. 16.93.4-7 and Philip's great battle against Bardylis (Diod. 16.4.3-7), where he fought at the head of the *agēma*; cf. G. T. Griffith, "Philip as a General and the Macedonian Army," *PM* 62.

[24] Isok. *Ep.* 2 (the responsibilities of the king): 3, 9, 11, 12; (criticism of the Bodyguards): 5, 6. Isokrates is obviously establishing a disparaging comparison between the Macedonian *pedzetairoi* and the Spartan *hippeis*.

[25] Diod. 16.93. 4-7, with P. Foucart, "Etudes sur Didymos," *MémAcInscr* 38,1 (1909) 118-21.

[26] K. G. Böhnecke, *Forschungen auf dem Gebiete der Attischen Redner und der Geschichte ihren Zeit* (Berlin 1843) 428-29, 435 and 735; Schaefer II² 345, n. 3; cf. II¹ 324, n. 2.

[27] For Böhnecke's and Schaefer's wide following, but also for the persistence of different opinions, see, e.g., F. R. Wüst, *Philipp II von Makedonien und Griechenland*

Cawkwell,[28] starting from a very different premise, the dating of the Persian appeal and of Python's embassy to Athens, also concluded that Isocrates' *Second Letter to Philip* (and consequently the campaign against the barbarians he refers to) must be moved back to 345.[29]

Rather than return to an untenable date or dismiss as just another caprice of History the striking correspondence between Philip's Dardanian war of the literary tradition and Philip's Dardanian war of the Oleveni inscription one should perhaps better reconsider the chronology of Philip's reign or, to put it more specifically, whether Panemos of the 16th year of Philip's reign should be actually dated to 344 or rather to the previous year.

After the pioneer work of a number of German scholars Beloch's[30] thorough examination of the Macedonian king lists seem to have definitively settled the main chronological questions, or at least those concerning the beginning and the end of the reign of Philip II. For more than half a century his conclusions have remained virtually unchallenged. It is characteristic in this respect that the relatively numerous works on the subject which have been published in the last five years, either do not discuss the matter as such or even explicitly state that the question in fact does not arise. The only notable exception, thanks to Ellis' highly stimulating article on Amyntas Perdikka,[31] Philip's controversial nephew, is the recent debate on Philip's regency, which has incidentally touched the length of his reign and accordingly the dates of his accession and of his death.[32]

(Munich 1938) 54-56, and, more recently, P. Cloché, *Un fondateur d'empire, Philippe II, roi de Macédoine* (Saint-Etienne 1955) 180-81, and *Histoire de la Macédoine* (Paris 1960) 205-206; Sordi (supra n. 18) 282, n. 6, and *Diodorus* 123; Papazoglou, *Historia* 156-57; Hammond, *BSA* (supra n. 8) 245; and Papazoglou, *ŽA* 106.

[28] G. L. Cawkwell, "Demosthenes' Policy after the Peace of Philocrates, I," *CQ* 13 (1963) 126-27, and *Philip* 114-15; Cawkwell's views have met with acceptance by most recent studies. See, e.g., Ellis, *PMI* 136 and 275, n.34; Dell (supra n. 16) *PM* 95; and Griffith, *Hist Mace* II 469-74.

[29] The argument from the location of Pleuratos' kingdom is not valid for the reasons already mentioned.

[30] Beloch, *Geschichte* 2, 49-80.

[31] J. R. Ellis, "Amyntas Perdikka, Philip II and Alexander the Great," *JHS* 91 (1971) 15-24; also his "The Security of the Macedonian Throne under Philip II," *AM* 1 (1970) 68-75.

[32] Besides Ellis' two studies cited supra n. 31, see also his articles "The Stepbrothers of Philip II," *Historia* 22 (1973) 351-53, and "The Unification of Macedonia," *PM* 38; D. Kanatsoulis, "Πότε ὁ Φίλιππος β' ἔλαβε τὸν τίτλον τοῦ βασιλέως," *Makedonika* 9 (1969) 237-42; Hammond, *Hist Mace* II, 651, n. 1; and Griffith, *Hist*

Dates of Philip II's Reign

Although the reasons that lie behind Beloch's[33] choices are not always easy to guess, his conclusions are clear and can be readily summarised: 1) Between the different traditions that assign to Philip between 23 and 27 years he considers Diodoros' figure of 24 years as the only correct one and dismisses the rest as "einander widersprechenden Angaben." 2) He also accepts Diodoros' dating of the beginning of Philip's reign on the Attic-Olympic year 360/59, but places the actual time of Perdikkas' death and Philip's accession in Summer 359, rejecting all ancient evidence on the dealings between the new Macedonian ruler and the Odrysian king Kotys, who was murdered several months before that date. 3) He rejects or at least modifies the unanimous ancient tradition, which implies that Alexander's accession and consequently Philip's death took place in October 336, at the *earliest*, and moves it back some two months before. Beloch's conclusions call for certain remarks:

The ancient tradition concerning the length of Philip's reign is both richer and — in some cases at least — less simple to dismiss without further discussion whenever it does not agree with one's chronological system. Richer, for there is another group of evidence not mentioned by Beloch, which assigns to Philip only 21 or 20 years;[34] less simple to dismiss, because, although the figures of 27 (viz. 26) years of the "bad lists" have been convincingly explained away by Schwartz[35] as a scribal error, Justin's 25 years are confirmed by Orosius (3.12.1; 14.10), whose direct and independent access to

---

Mace II 702-704; R. M. Errington, "Macedonian 'Royal Style' and its Historical Significance," *JHS* 94 (1974) 25-28; Prestianni Giallombardo, *Helikon* 191-209, and *SicGym* 39-47.

[33] Beloch, *Geschichte* 2, 59-61.

[34] Ioannes Antiochenus, *FHG* 4, 555, F40; Pseudo-Symeon, a passage from the unpublished part of his *Chronography* included in the doctoral dissertation of A. Markopoulos, Ἡ χρονογραφία τοῦ ψευδο-Συμεὼν καὶ οἱ πηγές της (Ioaninna 1978) 93-94; Kedrenos I, pp. 264-65, ed. B. G. Niebuhr (Bonn 1838); Joel, *Chronographia Compendiaria*, p. 7, ed. B. G. Niebuhr (Bonn 1837). I wish to thank my colleague, A. Markopoulos, who kindly informed me about the references to Philip II and Alexander the Great in the work of Pseudo-Symeon.

[35] E. Schwartz, "Die Königslisten des Eratosthenes und Kastor," *Abhandlungen des Göttingischen Gesellschaft der Wissenschaften*, Phil.-hist. Kl. 40 (1894) 79-93; cf. A. Momigliano, *Filippo il Macedone* (Florence 1934) 41, n. 1. The same applies to the 23 years of Synkellos p. 495 (cf. p. 501), which was probably also a scribal error (cf. Schwartz, 75) for Eusebios' 27 (viz. 26) due to a mechanical repetition of $\overline{KT}$, as Philip was the 23rd Macedonian King (495: Μακεδόνων κγ' ἐβασίλευσε Φίλιππος ἔτη κγ').

Pompeius Trogus has now been successfully vindicated,[36] whereas the emendation of Satyros' text is both arbitrary and palaeographically indefensible. Moreover there is another element which Beloch should have taken into consideration before dismissing as "einander widersprechenden" some of the figures that did not fit into his system: Philip's age at his death in relation to his age at his accession to power.

According to Pausanias (8.7.6) Philip died at the age of 46, while in Justin's account (*Epit.* 9.8.1) he dies at 47. Beloch[37] considers the two pieces of evidence as equally trustworthy and concludes that Philip was born either in 382 (336 + 46) or in 383 (336 + 47), which in turn has led to the even more extravagant conclusion that Philip came to power at the age of 23 or even 24.[38] In fact the figures of Philip's age at his death are not to be separated from the figures of the length of his reign, on which they are based. The mechanism of such ancient computations was magisterially analysed in the case of Alexander by E. Meyer,[39] who showed that Aristoboulos'[40] statement that Alexander lived 32 years and eight months (instead of 32 years and 11 months)[41] does not represent a different tradition about the date of Alexander's birth but only the result of the mechanical method of computation followed by Aristoboulos, which was based on the combination of two different data: the age of Alexander at his accession to the throne, which is conventionally given as 20 years,[42] and the length of his reign, for which he adopts the round figure of 12 years and 8 months.[43] The great German historian concluded that "die Analyse des aristobulischen Datums mag als Musterspiel für all ähnlichen Angaben dienen."[44] Beloch[45] accepted Meyer's conclu-

---

[36] L. Piccirilli, "Una notizia di Trogo in Giustino e in Orosio," *ASNP* ser. III, no. 1 (1971) 301-306.

[37] Beloch, *Geschichte* 2, 66.

[38] Schaefer II², 16; G. L. Cawkwell, *Philip of Macedon* (London and Boston 1978) 27; Griffith *Hist Mace* II 208.

[39] Meyer, *Forschungen* II, 445-48.

[40] Arr. *Anab.* 7.28.1; cf. *FGrH* 139 F 61.

[41] Cf. G. F. Unger, "Diodors Quellen im XI. Buch," *Philologus* 41 (1882) 82-83.

[42] Sources in Beloch, *Geschichte* 2, 68.

[43] Sources in Beloch, *Geschichte* 2, 59.

[44] Meyer, *Forschungen* II, 448.

[45] Beloch, *Geschichte* 2, 59-60, and others after him; cf. Bosworth, *Commentary* 46, who curiously ignores Meyer's analysis and arguments.

sions but failed to apply them to Philip's case. Actually, the *Souda* (*s.v.* Κάρανος which gives the conventional age of Philip at his accession as 22 years, offers additional confirmation of Justin's and Orosius' figure and leaves little doubt that the two different figures of Philip's age at his death do not reflect *two different traditions about the date of his birth* but result from the combination of this conventional age with *two different traditions about the length of his reign* (24 or 25 years respectively). The same *Souda* entry may also help us explain Satyros' figure of 22 years, which is avowedly the most difficult to understand. The information preserved by this Hellenistic biographer is in several cases unique[46] and is generally considered as trustworthy.[47] Accordingly the first reaction is to attribute the aberrant figure to a scribal error.[48] Both Hammond and Griffith[49] rightly reject these manipulations for reasons that they do not state, but which must obviously be first of all palaeographic. In fact, while one could, if need be, admit that $\overline{\text{KΔ}}$ might be copied as $\overline{\text{KB}}$ there is no obvious way in which a hypothetical -εἴκοσι καὶ τέταρσιν could have been copied as εἴκοσι καὶ δύο, the actual reading of the manuscript. The other explanation that comes to mind is that Satyros is referring to Philip's actual years of reign, i.e., 24 minus a two-year period of guardianship.[50] This solution, attractive as it is, cannot be retained, if for no other reason, because in that case nearly half of Philip's marriages introduced by the statement: "In the twenty-two years of his reign" would have taken place *before* the beginning of the period to which they are supposedly ascribed. In fact the clue to the right solution is probably provided by an oversight in one of Griffith's notes,[51] where it is stated that the *Souda* (*s.v.* Κάρανος too assigns to Philip a 22-year reign. Griffith must have been misled by the undeniable similarities between the two texts. Since another characteristic detail common to the *Souda* entry and to Satyros' biography of Philip rules out the

---

[46] E.g., the complete list of Philip's wives, the name of Kleopatra's brother, the name of Philip's and Kleopatra's child.

[47] Cf. P. Foucart (supra n. 25) 118-20; Beloch, *Geschichte* 2, 72; Griffith, *Hist Mace* II 681, n. 1; Prestianni Giallombardo, *RivStorAnt* 81-83 and 108; W. Heckel, "Philip II, Kleopatra and Karanos," *RivFC* 107 (1979) 386-87.

[48] Böhnecke (supra n. 26) 608, n. 4, followed by Beloch, *Geschichte* 2, 60 and others.

[49] *Hist Mace* I 651, n. 1, and II 209, n. 2.

[50] Gutschmid, 35; Unger (supra n. 41) 80, n. 4, and, more recently, Hammond, *Hist Mace* II 651, n. 1; cf. Hammond's *A History of Greece to 322 B.C.*² (Oxford 1967) 536-38, and Griffith, *Hist Mace* II 702.

[51] *Hist Mace* II 702, n. 3.

possibility of a mere coincidence[52] and renders highly probable the derivation of the latter from the former or of both from a common original, and since the internal cohesion of the *Souda* entry excludes an error on the part of its author,[53] the error must be sought in the Satyros fragment. But rather than accuse Satyros of misunderstanding his source, it is simpler to attribute the error to Athenaios, who has obviously rewritten and heavily abridged Satyros' original text in order to insert it in his work.[54] If such is the case, Satyros is another piece of evidence about Philip's age at his accession and has nothing to do with a hypothetical "verdrängung" of Amyntas IV.[55] If some trace of the distinctions between Philip's rule as a guardian and his rule as a king is to be sought in the ancient tradition, it probably lies

---

[52] Satyros; *FHG* 3,161 F3 apud Eust. ad Il. p. 990, 34: . . . ὁπηνίκα Φίλιππος τὸν ὀφθαλμὸν ἐξεκόπη ὀϊστῷ βληθεὶς ἐν πολέμῳ ὑπὸ 'Αστέρος . . . *Souda, s.v.* Κάρανος: Μεθωναίοις δὲ τοῖς ἐπὶ Θρᾴκης πολεμῶν τὸν ὀφθαλμὸν ἐπηρώθη, 'Αστέρος τινὸς ὄνομα βαλόντος αὐτὸν βέλει. .

[53] One could theoretically consider the possibility that the author of the *Souda*'s entry introduced the word γεγονώς after ἔτη either inadvertently, under the influence of the current expression τόσα ἔτη γεγονώς, or because he happened to know from some other source that Philip had actually acceeded at 22 years. Such an error is in fact excluded because the presence of γεγονώς, the punctual value of ἄρξας, and consequently the meaning of the phrase, are guaranteed by the whole context which opposes the relatively uneventful reign of the elder brothers to the demoniac activity of Philip once he acceeded to power.

[54] The cause of the error can only be conjectured, but a possible reason for this confusion may be the fact that the original text mentioned in the same (or rather in several contiguous sentences) the age of the king at his accession, the length of his reign, the age at which he died, his different marriages and the names of his children (cf. Just. *Epit.* 9.8.1). The incomprehensible reading of the manuscript: ἐν ἔτεσι γοῦν εἴκοσι καὶ δύο οἷς ἐβασίλευσεν has been emended in order to make sense to: ἐν ἔτεσι γοῦν εἴκοσι καὶ δυσίν οἷς ἐβασίλευεν by Schweighäuser and Kaibel respectively. The first emendation could be defended palaeographically, if one supposed an original reading $\overline{KB}$, which was transcribed in full words by a copyist at a time when the feeling of the dative had receded. But it would still leave intact the problem of the meaning which is much more serious. The replacement of the aorist (ἐβασίλευσεν) by the imperfect (ἐβασίλευεν) proposed by Kaibel attenuates but does not resolve the paradox of a phrase, which however manipulated can only be translated: "In the twenty-two years of his reign . . . he married Audata of Illyria, and had by her a daughter, Cynna; he also married Phila. . ." (Gulick's translation in the Loeb edition) and is particularly inappropriate to introduce his seven marriages. If, on the other hand, Satyros' original contained information similar to that of the *Souda* one could understand much better the awkwardness of Athenaios' expression and his errors such as εἴκοσι καὶ δύο (from ἔτη εἴκοσι καὶ δύο γεγονώς) and the use of the aorist which constitute in fact the last surviving evidence of the original meaning of a sentence that Athenaios has not managed to obliterate completely.

[55] Gutschmid, 35.

Dates of Philip II's Reign

in the figures of the Byzantine chronographers, who seem to subtract a four-year period of anarchy after his death.[56] If such is the case, only the two figures of 24 and 25 ought to be taken into consideration. The slightness of the discrepancy between them points unmistakably not to two different starting points but to two different chronological systems.[57] Now we know that the system of Diodoros' chronographic source is based on the Attic-Olympic year,[58] which must also have been the basis of the Athenian Diyllos, the common source of both Diodoros' last chapters of Book 16 and Pausanias' synopsis of Macedonian history (8.7.5-8).[59] Pompeius Trogus' source's alternative chronological system can be no other than that of Macedonian regnal years, which is only to be expected from someone familiar with the Macedonian court and writing the history of a Macedonian king, like Theopompos.[60] Although he does not explicitly say so, it is obvious that Beloch can ascribe 24 years to a reign that according to him lasted from Summer 359[61] to Summer 336 only because he implicitly[62] follows one of the rules laid down in the pioneer work of E. Meyer: that the first new calendar year after the accession counts

---

[56] [25 − 4 = 21] + 4 = 25, or [24 − 4 = 20] + 4 = 24; for the references see n. 33 supra. Gutschmid's hypothesis (p. 48) that this is done in order to make space for a 17-year reign of Alexander does not carry conviction, for in this case there would have been no vacuum to fill with a four-year period of anarchy. Moreover, since Kedrenos (I 271) assigns to Alexander a 12-year reign, he would have needed five, not four, extra years, if he had wanted to obtain a total of 17 years. As we shall see, however, a four-year guardianship is precisely what the historical context seems to require (cf. Prestianni Giallombardo, *Helikon* 204-208, with older bibliography).

[57] This was Gutschmid's (in my opinion unwarranted) suggestion (pp. 34-35), that the 25-year figure goes back to Philip's appointment to a "Theilfürstenthum" shortly before Perdikkas' death.

[58] E. Schwartz, *s.v.* "Diodorus," *RE* 5 (1903) 665-66; Meyer, *Forschungen* 446-47; C. B. Welles, Introduction to the eighth volume of the Loeb *Diodorus* (Cambridge, Mass. 1963) 1; Sordi, *Diodorus* VII-VIII.

[59] For Diyllos as Diodoros' source for book XVI, see Hammond, *CQ* 89-91; Sordi, *Diodorus* XXX-XXXIII. I accept this thesis and believe that Pausanias 8.7.5-8 derives from the same source.

[60] The dependence of books 7, 8 and 9 of Justin's (viz. Pompeius Trogus') *Philippika* on the *Philippika* of Theopompos is the inescapable conclusion of any detailed study of fourth-century Macedonian historiography. For some recent appreciations, Marta Sordi, "Il soggiorno di Filippo a Tebe nella propaganda storiografica," *Storia e propaganda*, ed. Marta Sordi, Contributi dell' Istituto di storia antica 3 (Milan 1975) 58; Hammond, *Hist Mace* II 9, 12, 661; Griffith, *Hist Mace* II 208 and 285.

[61] Beloch, *Geschichte* 2, 61; 2, 60.

[62] Cf. Beloch, *Geschichte* 2, 61.

as the *second* regnal year of a ruler.⁶³ Indeed, according to Diodoros' Attic-Olympic chronological system it suffices that Philip came to power at any time before mid-summer 359, in order that the year 360/59 be reckoned as his first regnal year. But if the evidence from Pompeius Trogus' computation according to the Macedonian chronological system is not to be ignored, then the twenty-five years that it assigns to Philip can only mean that he came to power before the first of Dios (*ca.* October) 360. In other words the combination of the two data based on the two alternative chronological systems point to the period between July and October 360 as the time of the great Macedonian defeat by the Illyrians, which brought about Perdikkas' death and Philip's accession to power. Beloch's reasons for excluding this possibility are not clear and even less cogent. The premises of his reasoning that the only right figure of Philip's reign is 24 years and that they are to be counted according to the Macedonian chronological system⁶⁴ are either arbitrary or erroneous. As we have seen, the 25-year figure is equally well attested and there is no doubt that Diodoros and his source followed not the Macedonian but the Attic-Olympic chronological system, whose New Year falls in mid-summer. His other allegedly decisive argument⁶⁵ that according to a scholion on Aischines (2.31), in the Attic year of Kallimedes (360/59) the Athenian forces on the Macedonian coast were under the orders of Timotheos, whereas according to Diodoros (16.3.5) immediately after Philip's accession⁶⁶ they were commanded by Mantias, does not carry more weight. Indeed the reference to Diodorus is misleading, since the Sicilian historian clearly dates the activity of Mantias too by the same archon year of Kallimedes (360/59). As there is no other cogent reason to manipulate the one or the other piece of ancient evidence, the obvious conclusion is that, as it had already happened in the immediately previous years,⁶⁷ there was more than one

---

⁶³ Meyer, *Forschungen* 440-53; cf. Schwartz (supra n. 35) 82; K. J. Beloch, *Griechische Geschichte* IV,2 (Berlin and Leipzig 1927) 48; Bischoff, *s.v.* "Kalender," *RE* 10 (1919) 1586-87; Makaronas (supra n. 7) 124-25; F. W. Walbank, *Philip V of Macedon* (Cambridge 1940) 297.

⁶⁴ Cf. supra n. 62.

⁶⁵ Cf. Beloch, *Geschichte* 2, 61.

⁶⁶ Beloch, *Geschichte* 2, 61.

⁶⁷ S.Dušanić, "Plato's Academy and Timotheus' Policy, 365-359 B.C.," *Chiron* 10 (1980) 112, n. 5.

Athenian strategos *peri Makedonian*.⁶⁸ Moreover the dating proposed here makes it unnecessary to reject the ancient evidence⁶⁹ which connects Philip already in power with the Odrysian king Kotys, assassinated in the later half of 360.⁷⁰ In fact all favours and nothing opposes our dating of Philip's accession between July and October 360.⁷¹

Although Beloch rightly makes use of Meyer's principle of "Antedatierung," in his attempt — however erroneous — to fix the beginning of Philip's reign, he discards it completely when it comes to determining the date of his death. For a corollary of the same rule that requires that any number of months, however few, between the accession and the following New Year count as the first year of a ruler is that any number of months, however many, between New Year and the death of a ruler are left out of his reign and are reckoned as part of the first year of his successor, or as Meyer⁷² put it epigrammatically: "sein Tod fällt in das erste Jahr seines Nachfolgers." Therefore, since, according to the unanimous ancient tradition,⁷³ Alexander's first regnal year begins in the first of Dios 336/35 (*ca.* October 336), Philip's assassination must have taken place after — even if only a few days after — that date. Nevertheless Beloch

---

⁶⁸ Tod, *GHI* II, no. 143, p. 133, lines 15-16. In fact Beloch's argumentation runs in circles. In his list of the Athenian generals *epi Thrakēs* Beloch (*Geschichte* 2, 247) puts Mantias under the archon year of Eucharistos (359/8) with the note that Diodorus places him in 360/59. Thus Mantias' generalship, which had helped date Philip's accession, is in its turn dated by Philip's accession and so the circle is complete. The fact that Beloch here apparently does not exclude the possibility of Mantias' joint generalship with Timotheos in 360/59 probably means that he had abandoned the reasons implied in his earlier work *Die attische Politik seit Perikles* (Leipzig 1884) 319, for positively dating Mantias generalship to 359/58. Actually the unique reference for this revision of the ancient evidence was to a page of (the first edition) of Schaefer's work's on Demosthenes (III 2, 214), where the great German scholar moved back Mantias' generalship from 360/59 to 359/58 on the grounds that in 360/59 Mantias was only a treasurer. The inscription (*IG* II-III² 1622, lines 435-39) on which this assumption was based has long since been dated to 377/76 (cf. I. Kirchner, *Prosopographia Attica* II [Berlin 1903] 48-49 and now J. K. Davies, *Athenian Propertied Families* [Oxford 1971] 364-68, no. 9667).

⁶⁹ Hegesandros, *FHG* 4, 413-14, F 4 apud Athen. 6.248E; Theopompos *FGrH* 115, F 31.

⁷⁰ Beloch, *Geschichte* 2, 87.

⁷¹ This is the way Pletho understood the relevant ancient authorities more than half a milennium ago. See Gemistos Plethon *Hellen.* 1.13, ed. H.G. Reichard (Leipzig 1770); cf. Clinton, 282, n.p.

⁷² Meyer, *Forschungen* 443.

⁷³ Sources in Beloch, *Geschichte* 2, 59.

rejects Meyer's[74] inescapable conclusion and prefers to put the fatal celebration at Aigai in August on subjective grounds. While there is no reason to manipulate ancient evidence in order not to leave Philip "inactive,"[75] it is true that the fatal celebrations at Aigai must have taken place very soon after our "terminus post quem" of the 1st of Dios, in order to leave time for Alexander's southern campaign and his arrival at the borders of Attica in late November.[76]

Is it possible to be more precise? I think that the main narrative of Philip's assassination offers a clue. Indeed an attentive reading of Diodorus' account (16.91.2-95.1) reveals that the celebrations at Aigai did not at all originate with the wedding, but rather that the wedding was made to coincide with a religious festival which had its independent existence. The key phrase is:[77] "Straightaway he set in motion plans for gorgeous sacrifices to the gods joined (συνετέλει) with the wedding of his daughter Cleopatra," where συνετέλει evidently retains its etymological meaning of "celebrate jointly." A near repetition of the same expression is to be found in the beginning of the next chapter (16.92.1): "So great numbers of people flocked together from all directions to the festival, and the games and the marriage were celebrated in Aegae in Macedonia." This is in complete accord with all the other expressions used by Diodoros[78] to

---

[74] Beloch, *Geschichte* 2, 59-60; Meyer, *Forschungen* 447; cf. J. G. Droysen, *Geschichte des Hellenismus* (Gotha 1877) 98 and 354.

[75] Beloch's argument is probably not valid, as E. Borza, "Philip II and the Greeks," *CP* 73 (1978) 243, n. 15, has recently pointed out.

[76] Cf. Böhnecke (supra n. 26) 616-18. This was perfectly possible as Alexander's advance was so rapid that it took everybody by surprise; Cf. Bosworth, *Commentary* 51, with references and P. Goukowsky's notes in his edition of *Diodore de Sicile, Bibliothèque historique, livre XVII* (Paris 1976) 168. Alexander's hurry to proceed southwards would explain the extreme haste with which Philip's tomb was constructed and to which M. Andronikos, "The Royal Graves in the Great Tumulus," *AAA* 10 (1977) 56, and "The Royal Tombs at Aigai (Vergina)," *PM* 212-18, has repeatedly drawn attention. Cf. now his article "The Royal Tomb at Vergina and the Problem of the Dead," *AAA* 13 (1980) 168-78. N. G. L. Hammond, *Alexander the Great. King, Commander and Statesman* (Park Ridge, N.J. 1980) 42, has Alexander waiting in Macedonia until "autumn." This annoying discrepancy with Justin *Ep.* 11.2.5, to which Hammond drew attention himself in the paper which he read at the Chicago symposium, need no longer be one. [See Hammond's paper elsewhere in this volume. — *Ed.*]

[77] Diod. 16.91.4; trans. C. B. Welles in the Loeb. Cf. Doxapatres ad *Aphth.* pp. 475-76 (ed. Walz). This impression is not invalidated by Just. *Epit.* 9.6.2; Oros. 3.14.7; and Stob. *Anth.* 98.70, who simply choose to stress one side of the festivities.

[78] Diod. 16.91.3, 91.5-6, 92.5, 94.2.

describe the event. F. Täger[79] had already thought that we were dealing with a genuine religious festival, which he interpreted as Dionysiac. Prestianni Giallombardo[80] rightly points out that Dionysos was not included in the *twelve Olympian* gods who were honoured at the festival.[81] Actually, G. Kleiner[82] and K. Lange had already pointed out the "Dian" aspect of Philip's real or alleged — but on some sort of actual basis — incipient divinisation.

Yet, it is the striking parallel of another text of Diodoros[83] which offers, in my opinion, the clue to the solution. The festival described in this second passage is the Olympia, which was celebrated in the month of Dios every year.[84] It is commonly assumed that not only this passage of Diodoros but also all the other ancient references exclusively concern the festival at Dion. Actually things are not as simple. Besides Diodoros only Dion Chrysostomos and Ulpian[85] mention Dion as the place of celebration of the festivities they describe (the Olympia of 337 and 348 respectively) and in the latter instance it is probably a mere inference of the author, since he is simply paraphrasing Diodoros' description of the festival of 335. Otherwise there is simply no evidence as to where the Olympia referred to by Demosthenes himself, the scholiast of Thucydides, the fragment of Apollodoros or Philostratos[86] were celebrated. The only justification for situating them at Dion is the more or less tacit

---

[79] *Charisma. Studien zur Geschichte des antiken Herrscherkultes* I (Stuttgart 1957) 174-78.

[80] Prestianni Giallombardo, *SicGym* 31, n. 95, with rich bibliography.

[81] Diod. 16.92.5; cf. 16.95.1.

[82] G.Kleiner, "Alexanders Reichsmünzen," *AbhBerl* 1947, 5, 39, nn. 12-14. K. Lange, "Zur Frage des Bildnisgehaltes bei Köpfen auf Münzen Philipps II. und Alexanders III., des Grossen von Makedonien," *Wissenschaftliche Abhandlungen des deutschen Numismatikertages in Göttingen 1951* (Göttingen 1959) 30.

[83] A comparison of Diod. 16.91-92 with 17.16 reveals a number of parallel phrases.

[84] Cf. P. Girard, "La trilogie chez Euripide," *REG* 17 (1904) 159; W. Baege, *De Macedonum sacris* (Halle 1913) 10-13; F. Geyer, *s.v.* "Makedonia," *RE* 14 (1929) 697-771, and *Makedonien zur Thronbesteigung Philips II* (Munich and Berlin 1930) 100-101; J. N. Kalléris, *Les anciens Macédoniens* I (Athens 1954) 249-53; D. Kanatsoulis, "Τό κοινὸν τῶν Μακεδόνων," *Makedonika* 3 (1956) 98; A. B. Bosworth, "Errors in Arrian," *CQ* 26 (1970) 119-21 and *Commentary* 97, with references, to which may be added the epigraphic evidence: D. M. Robinson, "Inscriptions from Macedonia 1938," *TAPA* 49 (1938) 64-65 (cf. J. and L. Robert, *Bullépigr* [1939], 169).

[85] Diod. 17.16.3-4; Dion Chrys. *Orat.* 2.2; Schol. Dem. 19.192 (401).

[86] Dem. 19.192; Schol. Thuc. 1. 126; Apollodorus, *FHG* 1.434, F 35 = Schol. Apolloni I, 599; Philostratos, *Apoll.* 1, 34. Philostratos, in fact, thought that the Olympia of 348 referred to by Demosthenes had been celebrated at Olynthos!

assumption that this was the only city of Macedonia where such a festival took place. There is however a very explicit piece of ancient evidence (Arr. *Anab.* 1.11.1) stating that after the destruction of Thebes "Alexander returned to Macedonia, where he offered the traditional sacrifice (established by Archelaus) to Olympian Zeus and celebrated the Olympian games at Aegae: others add that he held games in honour of the Muses." It is true that Baege, followed by Geyer, Kalléris and Bosworth[87] consider it as an "error in Arrian." In fact nothing is less sure. "If that source (i.e. Arrian's source) was, as is generally thought, Ptolemy, the error is incomprehensible," admits Bosworth,[88] and goes on to explain it as a misunderstanding by Arrian of the source's account of the history of the festival: a New Year ceremonial sacrifice to Zeus in the old capital, Aigai, which was later transferred to Dion and associated with the newly established festival of the Muses, the Olympia. This is probably an unnecessary complication. As Hammond[89] recently pointed out, "What was attributed to Archelaus was only the dramatic festival at Dium and the sacrifice to Zeus of Olympus and the Muses at this festival . . . The Aegae festival was different and presumably older." Arrian's statement is indeed unambiguous. On the faith of his principal source (probably Ptolemy) he attributes to Alexander two different actions: 1) the sacrifice to Olympian Zeus established by Archelaos (at Dion), and 2) the Olympian games at Aigai. Then he adds that according to others (the Kleitarchean tradition) Alexander also held games in honour of the Muses (at Dion). Rather than believe that Arrian and even less his source (Ptolemy), who had a first hand knowledge of Macedonia, mixed up Aigai with Dion, it is more economical to suppose that Diodoros or even his source Kleitarchos, who seems never to have set his foot in Macedonia, failed to distinguish between two festivals more or less synonymous and consecrated (at least partly) to the same deity, and then attributed to the better known one the totality of the information concerning both. In fact there must be no doubt that all the Macedonian communities held more or less lavish celebrations in honour of Zeus in the month of Dios, which was

---

[87] Baege (supra n. 84) 7-8; Geyer (supra n. 84) *RE* 716, and *Makedonien* 100; Kalleris (supra n. 84) I 251, n. 2; and Bosworth (supra n. 84) *CQ* 119-21, and *Commentary* 97.

[88] Bosworth (supra n. 84) *CQ* 120.

[89] Hammond, *Hist Mace* II 150; cf. now Hammond, *Alexander* (supra n. 76) 309-10.

consecrated to him.[90] It must not have been difficult to insure that the two (not merely local but state) celebrations at Aigai and at Dion did not coincide, and that the king accompanied by his court and his guests might move in time from one place to another in order to attend both.[91]

This concelebration of a royal wedding with the great autumn festival that marked the beginning of the New Macedonian Year is not without precedent. Apparently such was the case of Philip's marriage with Olympias,[92] and most probably of his marriage with Philinna,[93] which are among the few earlier Macedonian weddings that can be dated with some precision. In fact we are dealing with an ancestral custom that from time immemorial until our day requires that weddings in Macedonia take place at the great October festival, first of Zeus Olympios and later of Saint Demetrios (26 October),[94] which, together with the Xandika and later Saint George's festival (23 April), constituted officially in pagan times and unofficially in the rural communities until recently the major landmarks of the year.[95]

---

[90] There is epigraphic evidence from the Hellenistic period suggesting that there were sacrifices and festivals common to all Macedonian communities; Makaronas (supra n. 7) 118 and 123, and Fanoula Papazoglou, "Nouveau fragment d'acte de chancellerie macédonienne," *Klio* 52 (1970) 310 and 314.

[91] Two connected festivals in honour of the same god and taking place in the same month are not unusual (cf. Synoikia and Panathenaia in honour of Athena in Hekatombaion or Dipolieia and Diisoteria in Skirophorion in Athens). It is possible that the celebration of the Olympia at Aigai as well explains their later celebration in nearby Beroia, which after the decline of the old capital (See, however, Ph. Petsas' review of D. Kanatsoulis' history of Macedonia in *Makedonika* 17 [1977] 450) seems to have inherited its cults and its functions as the ceremonial capital of Macedonia.

[92] Prestianni Giallombardo, *RivStorAnt* 96, n. 46; cf. Beloch, *Geschichte* 2, 68 and now P. Green's paper elsewhere in this volume.

[93] Cf. Beloch, *Geschichte* 2, 69; Ellis, *PMI* 61 and 212; Prestianni Giallombardo, *RivStorAnt* 91; Griffith, *Hist Mace* II 225, with chronological table, p. 722.

[94] G. F. Abbot, *Macedonian Folklore* (Cambridge 1903) 155; "The marrying season among the Macedonian peasants is the end of October, about the time of the Feast of St. Demetrius (Oct. 26th o.s.). At that time of year the labours of the field are over, the vintage just concluded, and the villages are in possession of the two essentials for merry-making: leisure and wine." Cf. M. Delacoulonche, "Mémoire sur le berceau de la puissance macédonienne des bords de l'Haliacmon et ceux de l'Axius," *Archives des Missions Scientifiques et Littéraires* 8 (1859) 87-88: It is perhaps not a mere coincidence that the festival of St. Demetrios lasted nine days, exactly like the Olympia to which it had succeeded; cf. T. L. F. Tafel, *De Thessalonica eiusque agro, dissertatio geographica* (Berlin 1839) 227.

[95] Stella Georgoudi, "Quelques problèmes de la transhumance dans la Grèce ancienne," *REG* 87 (1974) 169, n. 54.

To sum up. According to the chronology proposed here, Philip came to power at the age of 22 in late Summer 360 and was assassinated during the celebration of the Olympia in October 336. As his first regnal year he reckoned the year that began *ca.* October 361 and ended *ca.* October 336, and his 25th (and last) the one that began *ca.* October 337 and ended *ca.* October 336. Accordingly the great war against the Illyrians and the Dardanians dated to the 16th year of his reign took place in the campaign season of 345. The Oleveni inscription in itself throws no new light on the question of Philip's regency. It is obvious that Philip in any case, once he had become a king — much earlier than the date of our inscription — would have started counting his regnal years from the date of his accession to power.[96] The most likely hypothesis remains the one exposed for the first time by A. Aymard and was later developed by A. M. Prestianni Giallombardo.[97] Amyntas Perdikka was never a king in Philip's life-time.[98] After Perdikkas' death no king was proclaimed; Philip became and remained ἐπίτροπος until late 357 or early 356, a date which corresponds to the situation described by Justin (*Epit.* 7.5.10: *graviora bella*, the coalition between the Illyrian, Paionian and Thracian kings, later joined by Athens)[99] and the four-year period of "anarchy" of the chronographic tradition.

The National Hellenic Research Foundation,
Research Centre for Greek and Roman Antiquity

---

[96] Cf. Antigonos Doson in *IG* X,2,1,2.

[97] A. Aymard, "Tutelle et usurpation dans les monarchies hellénistiques," *Aegyptus* 32 (1952) 85-96; Prestianni Giallombardo, *Helikon* (*passim*), and *SicGym*, 39-45.

[98] Anna Maria Prestianni Giallombardo did not see that this still remains the most important argument in favour of Ellis' main thesis, which she so vehemently attacks.

[99] Diod. 16.22.3; Tod, *GHI* II, no. 157, pp. 167-70.

Philip and the Peace of Philokrates

J. R. ELLIS

Abstract

The formation of the Peace of Philokrates coincided closely with Philip's settlement of the Third Sacred War, and its terms were designed to elicit a certain stance on Athens' part in that settlement. The conventional view, deriving less from Demosthenes' (as well as Aischines') data than from the slant he gives them, is that the destruction of Phokis and the consequent promotion of Theban interests were his aims. But the evidence, direct and inferential, points rather to the opposite view, that what Athens expected from the settlement of the war — the salvation of Phokis and the advancement of Athens, both to Thebes' disadvantage and cost — was also what Philip desired and planned. That this result did not occur was due in part to Philip's own miscalculation but also to skillful opposition within Athens by those who preferred to see Theban power preserved for the moment when it might be combined with that of Athens against Macedonian encroachment.

The year 346 B.C., when the so-called Peace of Philokrates ended ten years of war between Athens and Philip II of Macedon, is one of the most abundantly documented of ancient times. Unfortunately most of the evidence is from the trial of Aischines in 343, in which Demosthenes' prosecution-speech and Aischines' defence are both representative only of Athenian viewpoints, both designed to persuade the *dikastai* rather than to clarify the events of 346, and both written for delivery in changed circumstances in which honesty about those events was arguably no longer the best or most expedient policy. The interests and intentions of Philip in offering the peace and dictating its terms are not documented at all and, if they are to be understood, must be inferred not only on general Macedonian grounds but from these same forensic sources.

In *Philip II and Macedonian Imperialism*[1] I based my treatment of the affairs surrounding the Peace of Philokrates and the settlement of the Third Sacred War on the view that Philip's first aim was to reduce the power of Thebes and to favour Athens — despite the facts that Thebes was one of his Amphiktyonic allies[2] and that Athens had been at war with him, "the war for Amphipolis," as it came to be called in Athens,[3] for a decade.

In some of its essentials this interpretation was not mine. I concurred in general with the argument advanced first by Rohrmoser, in 1874, and later by Beloch, by Wüst and recently by Markle.[4] So far there has not been any published attack on the detail of my own particular interpretation. But two authors[5] have challenged Markle's revival of this thesis,[6] and my purpose in this paper is to defend my own interpretation, which differs from Markle's in some respects but is no less questioned by their criticisms. I begin by setting out the evidence and assumptions of my own reconstruction. The basic premises are either contained in or follow directly from the speeches *peri tēs parapresbeias* of Demosthenes and Aischines:

i) In 346, when Philip was preparing to enter Central Greece on the request of the major Amphiktyonic states engaged in their long and debilitating war with Phokis, two things were clear where Athens and Thebes were concerned. Thebes was among Philip's Amphik-

---

[1] *PMI*, esp. Chapter IV, pp. 90-124. The following abbreviations are used in the notes below.
PMac — G. C. Cawkwell, *Philip of Macedon* (London 1978).
"PPhil" — G. C. Cawkwell, "The Peace of Philocrates again," *CQ* 28 (1978) 93-104.
Peace — M. M. Markle III, *The Peace of Philocrates* (diss., Princeton 1970).
"PStrat" — M. M. Markle III, "Philip's strategy in 346," *CQ* 24 (1974) 253-68.

[2] An alliance between Philip and the Thebans was in force by the time of the king's first, halfhearted intervention in Central Greece (in 347): Diod. 16.58.3. Pausanias believed that it was first formed in 354 or 353 (10.2.5) and other circumstances favour such a view: Ellis, *PMI* 258 n.67 and Griffith, *Hist Mace* II 345.

[3] Isok. 5.2; Ais. 2.70.

[4] J. Rohrmoser, "Kritische Betrachtunger über die philokrateischen Frieden," *Zeitschr. österr. Gymn.* 25 (1874) 789-815; Beloch, *Griech. Gesch.* iii, 1 502 ff., esp. 506; F. R. Wüst, *Philipp II von Makedonien und Griechenland in den Jahren von 346 bis 338* (Munich 1938) 1 ff.; Markle (supra n. 1), *Peace* and "PStrat".

[5] Cawkwell (supra n. 1), "PPhil" and *PMac* (supra n. 1) 108 ff.; Griffith, *Hist Mace* II 345.

[6] The attack was made on Markle's article, not on the much more detailed treatment of the question in his dissertation.

tyonic allies, and Athens had been his enemy since 357/6.[7] It was therefore natural to assume that his entry into the war would favour Thebes (among others) and disadvantage Athens. As Demosthenes says,[8] he had already sworn oaths to the Thebans and had agreed to help them subjugate Boiotia, their control over which had weakened during the exhausting years of the Sacred War. Such was the *natural* expectation.

ii) What had occurred at Thermopylai on 23 Skirophorion 346 (the date of the *homologia Philippou kai Phōkēōn*) and the days following, with the Peace of Philokrates by then in effect, did disadvantage (or at least disappoint and anger) the Athenians and did favour Thebes.[9] What happened, that is to say, should have been expected.

iii) Yet Demosthenes and Aischines agree[10] that the Athenians expected the settlement, on the contrary, to favour Athens and to disadvantage Thebes. They expected their Phokian allies to be saved. They expected Thebes to be stripped of her control of Boiotia. They expected, among other gains, that Oropos and Euboia would be returned to Athenian control.[11] It follows, I infer, that someone had persuaded the Athenians to anticipate an outcome quite opposed to natural expectation.

iv) As (again) both Demosthenes and Aischines agree, Philip himself made no public promises, verbally or in writing.[12] (Logic complements the evidence: if Philip really planned to betray an existing ally he would hardly advertise his intention in advance.) The only possibility — because for the Athenians to have believed in such an apparently unnatural scenario it must have been conveyed to them by or via a source they trusted — is that this intelligence was promulgated by Athens' own envoys, those (or some of them) who travelled to Pella on the first and second embassies, to learn Philip's wishes and then to get his signature to the treaty. This is, of course, the charge Demosthenes brings in particular against Aischines and more promiscuously against all other envoys but himself.[13] In essence then I accept the truth of Demosthenes' accusation. Philip must in

---

[7] Supra notes 2 and 3.
[8] Dem. 19.318.
[9] Dem. 19.42-47, 321; Ais. 2.136.
[10] *Ibidd.*
[11] Dem. 5.10, 6.29 f., 19.20 ff.; Ais. 2.119 f.
[12] Dem. 19.316 ff., 321; Ais. 2.119.
[13] Dem. 19.188-98, 230 f.

private conversation have asked the envoys to pass on to the Athenian *demos* the news that he planned (in brief) to damage Thebes, to favour Athens and to save Phokis. They must have done so and successfully. But why did they believe him? Was he telling the truth? (It was not, after all, what he might have been expected to do or, in the event, what he did.) And, if it was the truth, why then did he change his policy when it came to the actual settlement?

These are questions to be answered. One must ascertain Philip's own interests regarding Athens and Thebes and how such informally transmitted plans both for the settlement of the war and for his peace and alliance with Athens might have been intended to further them. In maintaining the belief that Athenian expectations *were* justified one would need to be able to show too why Philip did not, or could not, achieve the settlement he and most Athenians hoped for.

v) There is one further premise. After the settlement of the Sacred War, except for Demosthenes no envoy condemned Philip or his peace; no other envoy even condemned Philokrates, who had proposed the main enabling *psephismata*. The second of those observations is stated explicitly by Demosthenes;[14] the first, I think, may be assumed because, if Demosthenes had been able to add another's condemnation to his own during the trial of Aischines, there can be little doubt that he would have done so. Demosthenes himself, of course, not only condemned the peace, but also Philip, Philokrates, Aischines and everyone else on the second embassy; that at least provided an example for others. But no one else joined in.

To return to the questions posed: the first four premises led me to the unavoidable conclusion that Athenian expectations of the settlement and the peace must have come via her own envoys out of their more-or-less private conversations with the Macedonian king. But how are we to explain his evident success and their apparent gullibility (especially since at that time he was publicly denying what they must have been saying)?[15]

The first possibility is that the envoys were bribed by Philip — all, that is, but Demosthenes. But these were prominent men, some at

---

[14] Dem. 19.116-118. In the circumstances, the trial *in absentia* of Philokrates, the other envoys' refusal to dissociate themselves from their erstwhile colleague (whose flight had, however undeservedly, by now labelled him guilty in the public mind) is striking. One would rather expect them to condemn him unbelieving than to stand firm in the face of a populace happy to hunt scapegoats.

[15] Dem. 19.320 f.

least of whom had served their city well in the past.[16] They must all have been experienced enough in public affairs to know the fate awaiting those found guilty of accepting bribes. For whichever reason, they could not all have been bought. Yet, so far as we can tell, they all acted uniformly. Bribery as an explanation is implausible.

Conceivably the envoys might have felt that Athens must be protected by peace with Philip when the Macedonian army was admitted by its friends into Central Greece. That being so they might have concluded that, although Philip was probably lying, only such distortions could persuade the Athenians to accept the peace that security dictated. This too is unacceptable. The envoys in that case would also be well aware that the actual settlement would within days expose both the lie and their connivance in it. They would then have the bracing task of pleading that it had been in fact from the very best of motives that they had fed the *demos* an untruth, a lie that the enemy himself had denied in word and refuted in action. Further, had they made their false assurances only for the greater good of peace and security they would presumably (as Demosthenes did) have felt free to make this public the moment their end was achieved (as indeed on this view it was) when the Macedonian forces had returned to the north leaving Athens untouched. But they did not. (Demosthenes did; and this may be the explanation in his case. But it will not do for the others.)

Plausibly, but only just, they were tricked by Philip, persuaded that his aims were not what they really were and, when events disclosed their mistake, shrank from underlining their foolishness by public confession. This too I reject. It is not credible that none of the others made any attempt to defend or justify himself by condemning the arch-dissembler. Demosthenes had; and so could others. Did they fear, even afterwards, to jeopardize the treaty by impeaching its architect? Not likely. Once his troops had withdrawn Athens was relatively safe. Philip could be openly excoriated without destroying his peace. Many felt no qualms, including Demosthenes. But the other envoys said nothing.

I see only one other possibility. The envoys were convinced by the king that his genuine interests made the enfeeblement of Thebes and the favour of Athens expedient to him. (From which it should follow

---

[16] For Ktesiphon (and Phrynon): Ais. 2.12 f.; Iatrokles, Philokrates and Aristodemos: Ais. 2.15-19; Nausikles: Diod. 16.37.3, 38.2; Aischines: Ais. 2.79, Dem. 19.10 f.; nothing is known beforehand of Kimon, Derkylos or the allied representative Aglaokreon.

that this programme could be rationally explained and justified to men who would naturally be skeptical.) Then, although Philip proved unable to carry the plans to fruition, the envoys must have continued to believe that his interests coincided with Athens', and that, if enough good will could be fostered, there remained a possibility that he could and would achieve his end in some other way. For that reason they did not condemn him for deception; they did not denounce his peace; they did not castigate Philokrates, even though by 343 — when they declined Demosthenes' formal challenge — all three had become very unpopular in Athens. This, it seems to me, is the only credible explanation.

I argued in *Philip II and Macedonian Imperialism* that Philip had no interest in ruling Greece. The peninsula was far from wealthy; it was fragmented and difficult to control, many of its *poleis* imbued with a propensity for independence that would give trouble to the most masterful of overlords; its heavy-armed militias were dangerous to him. Even could he subjugate the states of the peninsula at the cost certainly of a great many Macedonian lives, there would be too little gain for the conqueror. He preferred, I suggested, to direct his power towards the east where the rewards were greater and, perhaps, the costs lower.[17] But, whatever his long-term hopes, he had to be sure that the strongest military forces of southern and central Greece could not damage Macedonia. Athens alone, despite her powerful navy, was no serious threat. In ten years of war she had done him virtually no harm, perhaps none at all. Thebes alone, with her powerful infantry drawn from the hoplite class of Boiotia, was not much more dangerous, since Philip securely controlled Thessaly and the passes leading from Thessaly to Macedonia. The real danger lay in a combination of the Athenian navy and Thebes' army. Philip had to be sure that he did nothing to drive the two into alliance against him. The best means of preventing that was to divide them, preferably by weakening the more dangerous (at least by removing Theban control over Boiotia and if possible by maintaining Phokis as an impediment to her recovery), and to win the allegiance of Athens, militarily no serious problem to him in opposition but an inestimable complement to his own strength in coalition. [18] Then, too, when he turned

---

[17] *PMI* 8 ff., 91 f., 101 f., etc., and especially 209 f., 227 ff.

[18] It is instructive to note the bombastic nonsense to which Demosthenes (6.6-9) must resort when attempting to explain why Philip should *wish* to favour Thebes at Athens' expense. I am grateful for Peter Green's observation that if it should come

eastwards the Athenian navy could offer him important assistance; and afterwards her trading network might once again extend to the eastern Aegean and the ports of Asia Minor as freely as it had done a century before.

My reading of Philip's aims in the Peace of Philokrates and the settlement of the Sacred War as they emerge by inference from the Attic orators is therefore in close agreement with my analysis of his shorter- and longer-term interests regarding peninsular Greece and perhaps the east.

In 346, then, Philip intended to turn against his Theban ally. Athens, on the other hand, he hoped to make his colleague, whose own interests would supplement rather than compete with those of Macedonia — in much the same way as Sparta (and later Thebes) had been the Persian king's "partner" in the Peace of Antalkidas and subsequent *koinai eirēnai*, the one as "guarantor"of the settlement, more remote but overwhelmingly powerful if provoked, the other as its local "executor."

But if this was all so, then Philip must keep such an aim from the Thebans until it was too late for them to hinder the strategy and until he was certain of Athens' firm support. Thus he could make no public pronouncements, no written promises, except in the most general terms. ("I would write more explicitly of the benefits I shall confer on you," as Demosthenes quotes from one of his letters, "if I were certain that the alliance too would be made.")[19] Instead he would have to communicate his intentions by means of Athens' envoys. Then, if Thebes should grow alarmed, he could deny what others were saying in Athens. He was successful up to this point: the Athenians got the message and believed it; and, although the Thebans were suspicious enough to call out all their troops, they took no action against him.[20] Yet he did not do what he intended. Why?

Before answering that we should consider why alliance was vital to Philip — not just peace but "peace and alliance," as he em-

---

to all-out war Athens would be the most difficult of enemies to defeat, for the reasons which Perikles enumerated (Thuc. 2.13). It was better for Philip for that reason too to have her on — rather than offside.

[19] Dem. 19.40 ("the alliance too," i.e., as well as peace, as Griffith, *Hist Mace* II 339 points out); taken out of context three years later these words will easily carry the burden of deviousness Demosthenes wishes. Also [Dem] 7.33.

[20] Ais. 2.137

phasized.[21] Not because of any regard for Athens' hoplites. They could not themselves be decisive at Thermopylai. After the signing by Philip of the treaty the Athenian assembly (on 16 Skirophorion, again on Philokrates' motion) confirmed the peace and alliance, extended them to Philip's descendants and added a rider promising that, if the Phokians did not surrender Apollo's temple to the Amphiktyons, Athens would give assistance to Philip against "those who prevented it."[22] Not *epi tous Phōkeas*, or some such, but *epi tous diakōluontas*, apparently an ambiguous device to allow Athenian troops to be brought into play against Thebes; because it was the Thebans, when it became clear that the settlement would not destroy their Phokian enemies, who would oppose the whole arrangement (and indeed, when their suspicions were aroused, called out their full levy to do so).[23] A few days later, on 18 or 19 Skirophorion, a written message (or perhaps more than one) arrived from the king asking his new ally to send troops. Through Demosthenes' opposition, all other envoys but Aischines being absent on the third embassy, Athens refused.[24]

Philip's reason for wanting these soldiers is straightforward. The Macedonian army with its Thessalian and other allies was at the Pass of Thermopylai. Ahead of it were the Phokians, occupying the three strategic fortresses, Nikaia, Alponos and Thronion; but Philip was in contact and negotiating with their tyrant Phalaikos.[25] Somewhere beyond were the Thebans, presumably awaiting Philip's orders to advance on the Phokian positions.[26]

As the Athenians expected, Philip wanted to turn the tables on Thebes. To do so without a bitter and bloody struggle he would first have to come to some arrangement with Phalaikos and then he would have to convince the Thebans that they had no hope of winning. On the former, it seems, he was already working. Essential to the latter were the Athenian hoplites. First, and less importantly, they would (presumably) be behind the Theban position; caught between the

---

[21] Dem. 19.40; see note 19. Also, for example, 19.41, 48; Ais. 2.17, 110, [Dem.] 12.22.

[22] Dem. 19.47-49.

[23] Ais. 2.137.

[24] Ais. 2.136 ff. I do not accept the slant given these events by Dem. 19.122-127.

[25] Dem. 19.34, 58; 18.32; Ais. 2.130; Diod. 16.59.2. The varied use of prepositions leaves it unclear whether Philip camped on the far side of the pass, inside it or on the near side but short of the Phokian-held fortresses. See also *PMI* 106 with 266 n.67.

[26] The reconstruction is slightly imaginative but there are not many possible variants and something of the sort is implied at Ais. 2.138-141 and Dem. 6.14.

forces of Philip and Athens the Thebans would be more likely to surrender without battle. But secondly, and more importantly, when the Thebans realized what was happening their best chance of salvation would lie in immediately seeking alliance with Athens. They would then have an ally at their backs and the Athenian navy to turn Philip's position and to carry the war to his territory; Philip, for his part, would be faced with the most dangerous of Greek alliances. Athens, though now his ally, had been formally at peace with him for only a few days after a decade of hatred. He could not yet be sure whether he could trust her. He needed her troops as a warranty, both (after the point of no return) to Thebes and (before it) to himself, of her commitment to his cause, to demonstrate to both that Thebes would get no help from her neighbour. Without such proof it was all too likely that the Thebans *in extremis* would declare war on him, retreat to a defensible position and send envoys to Athens. The whole settlement was likely to slip away. He needed the Athenian hoplites not to fight but to convince the Thebans that they must not.

So when Athens refused his formal request he was obliged to do instead as his Amphiktyonic envoys were expecting,[27] to do what he had told Athens' envoys he did not want to do. The reason why his plans, in which the Athenians believed, did not come to fruition was quite simply that Athens at the last moment would not send her troops.[28]

Now Aischines makes all this clear, especially in chapters 136-138 of his speech *Peri tēs parapresbeias*. No modern student has built it out of his imagination. The only argument is over whether Aischines really knew what Philip wanted and whether he is telling the truth about it. I maintain that he did and was. At his trial in 343 it was in his interest to explain this to the jurors; it was in Demosthenes' interest to hide it.

Such an explanation makes sense of the behaviour of Aischines between early 346 and 343 (and later). Previously opposed to Philip and known for that opposition, he changed his mind on the first

---

[27] It seems however that at least the Thessalians, or some of them, may for several weeks have had an inkling of what was afoot: Ais. 2.136.

[28] One reason for the refusal is provided at Ais. 2.137; see also below *PMI* 119 and 270 n. 138, where I follow Markle, *PPhil* (supra n. 1) 239 ff. in accepting that it was at this time (on which schol. Ais. 1.169) that Timarchos and Demosthenes initiated their prosecution of Aischines for *parapresbeia* as a means of discrediting the only other envoy remaining in the city. For the background to the decision: Dem. 19.122.

embassy to Pella.[29] Less realistically than Demosthenes he had earlier wished to stake Athens' security on a defensive Hellenic treaty aimed at keeping Philip beyond Thermopylai.[30] This was unpractical for two reasons: one, that many Greek states had no particular reason to fear the king's entry and certainly no sympathy for Athens in her "war for Amphipolis"; two, that Philip's forces, backed by many Amphiktyons, were simply too strong to be resisted by any but the desperate or the foolhardy. Athens was the only state at sufficient risk to have an interest in war — and only then if enough others would stand with her. No one would, so she had to talk peace.

In Pella Aischines must have heard what Philip *said* he wished. This was not what the Athenians had expected. Most of the envoys, including Aischines and Philokrates, were delighted.[31] Not so Demosthenes. But except for him there is henceforward no identifiable opponent of Philip's plans among the ambassadors.[32] Aischines became an enthusiastic proponent of Philip's peace.

Four months later at Thermopylai the settlement was effected, but not in the way Athens desired or (now) anticipated. And yet Aischines, a man who (on the standard view) had been cruelly hoodwinked by Philip's lies, or had been caught out in his own, continued in the coming months and years to press for a positive

---

[29] Dem. 19.10-16. Aischines (2.12-20) challenges none of this, though the two versions exhibit the colouring that suits their respective authors. But Demosthenes accuses Aischines of changing course between the two assemblies of 18 and 19 Elaphebolion, whereas, I have proposed, the *volte-face* occurred in Pella but was camouflaged for good political reasons until the 19th: *PMI* 112 and 268 n. 98.

[30] *PMI* 100 ff. with 265 notes 50-51. Cawkwell, "Aeschines and the Peace of Philokrates," *REG* 73 (1960) 416 ff., and "PPhil" (supra n. 1) 93-98, has in Markle's view and mine conflated the decree of Euboulos with another, milder decree seeking Hellenic support and dated early in 346. Markle has dealt with the two decrees in detail: *PPhil* (supra n. 1) App. 1, and "PStrat" (supra n. 1) 257; now see also Griffith, *Hist Mace* II 330 n. 1.

[31] So much seems implied in Ais. 2.38-43 (and note the first words of 44 and the record of testimony at 46).

[32] Ais. 2.43 with 49-54 (referring to the later stages and aftermath of the first embassy) implies that Demosthenes at this early stage, though he took no overt action until after the second embassy, may have been trying to pave the way for a later challenge on his fellow-envoys' credit. (On my interpretation he had just, like the others, learnt Philip's plans and opposed them. But, accepting that Athens must have peace, and on Philip's terms, he expedited the formation of the treaty while hoping and planning to sabotage the consequences it was to have.) Since opinion in Athens in Elaphebolion was strongly in favour of a *koinē eirēnē*, as the allied *synhedrion* proposed, no envoy, except presumably Philokrates, seems to have declared himself openly in favour of Philip's peace and alliance until the king's emissaries had ruled out the former on the morning of 19 Elaphebolion; see note 29 above.

attitude towards the peace and for its extension on better terms for Athens. He did not swerve from that course however unpopular the treaty became, when Philip's credit in Athens was low and when the politically expedient thing was to dissociate himself utterly from the king and all his arrangements. The same was true of the other envoys. Yet, one might almost say, Philokrates in effect signed his death-warrant (though, when the time came, he fled before it could be executed) rather than repudiate the peace. For his part Aischines went on fighting (in his defence speech of 343) for Philip's credibility when his life too was at stake.[33] To resort to the charge of bribery is too easy.[34] This was a man who not only understood and believed what Philip said he wished to do and committed himself to it publicly, but did not afterwards hold him responsible when it was not realized.

It is no objection that there was no love lost between Athens and Thebes, at this time or most others. A state's perception of the threats to its security may change rapidly, and old alignments and ideologies adapt readily enough to new circumstances. Many rival states have suddenly discovered each other's virtues when a greater common threat appeared. One might adduce examples from any period (the United States of America and the People's Republic of China during the 1970s, for one) but the most apposite occurred in 339: then, when Athens and Thebes both found their interests at risk, these two very states stood together in opposition to Philip at Chaironeia, the enmities and rhetoric of past years not forgotten but temporarily irrelevant. But prerequisite to any such eventuality would be that Thebes emerge undamaged and Athens disgruntled from the settlement of 346. It was that which the king sought to avoid.

Griffith concedes the "short-term" advantage to Philip in weakening Thebes and so increasing his ability to control Central Greece. But he objects that it would have meant alienating Thebes while Athens' loyalty could not yet be counted on. Yet it could equally well be maintained that to alienate Athens while Thebes could not be

---

[33] Even at the trial of Timarchos in winter 346/5, only a few months after the disappointment of late Skirophorion 346, Aischines could speak warmly of Philip (1.166 ff.).

[34] Griffith (*Hist Mace* II 337 n. 4) seems certain that Philokrates was bribed but is unsure over Phrynon and Aischines. I do not deny that envoys or politicians (or prelates or professors) have their price, but I should need better evidence that they have been bought than the charges of their opponents or a change in their public policy. Philokrates' resort to flight to avoid trial in a fiercely anti-Macedonian atmosphere in which, regardless of desert, his condemnation was nearly certain is no proof of his guilt.

counted on was hardly more satisfactory, and that was more or less what the eventual settlement did achieve. My own position is that the realisation of his plan to enfeeble Thebes while saving the Phokian people would be the best possible means of winning Athenian favour, to say nothing of the other benefits he could then offer his new ally.[35]

Cawkwell holds that Philip had to maintain Greek respect by punishing Phokis, for the Phokians "were universally condemned for their sacrilege."[36] Two points may be made. In the first place, the Greek states did not "universally" (or even "generally") condemn Phokis. The evidence of one extreme contemporary opinion[37] and the judgements of three late and notorious moralists[38] count for little against the hard fact that those prepared to stand and be counted in support of the Phokian cause (or anti-Theban enough to forget other causes) included not only Athens but Sparta, Korinth, Epidauros, Megara, Sikyon, Phleious and probably Argos, not to mention Delphi itself and Lokris who (though these last probably had little option) with the others listed had sent *naopoioi* to participate in the affairs of the "rebel" Amphiktyony under Phokian patronage in the early years after 356.[39]

Strategically this was no negligible group. These friends of Phokis, as it seems they must be regarded, would if so minded be easily capable of keeping any Peloponnesian allies of Thebes south of the Isthmus where they could do little harm. Morally their views must be

---

[35] For hints over the destruction of Theban power, the restoration of Oropos and Euboia to Athens and even the cutting of a canal through the neck of the Chersonesos at Macedonian expense see supra n. 11. There are also signs that at least rumours were heard, perhaps as early as this, about a Macedonian plan for an eastern campaign ([Dem.] 7.35, Diod. 16.60.4 f., Isok. 5.16 f., 73 ff. with *Ep.* 3.3) and Athens' part in it ([Dem.] 7.35).

[36] Cawkwell, *PMac* (supra n. 1) 110; cf. at "PPhil" (supra n. 1) 102 the more moderate "generally condemned."

[37] Ais. 2.142 refers to the harsh demand of the Oitaians, close neighbours of Phokis who had no doubt suffered in this war and perhaps before.

[38] Diod. 16.61-64; Justin 8.2; Paus. 10.2.4 ff.

[39] *Fouilles de Delphes* iii, 5 (Paris 1932) No. 19 lines 33-36, 41-44, 63-65, etc. Diod. 16.29.1 names Athens and Sparta "and some other Peloponnesians." Argos, it seems, was sympathetic to the Phokian cause, as the attendance of its *naopoioi* at the meeting of autumn 356, after the laying of the Theban charge against Phokis implies; but it may have backed off once war actually broke out. See N. G. L. Hammond, "Diodorus' narrative of the Sacred War," *JHS* 57 (1937) 63 for the chronology of these lists, and now C. Roux, *L'amphictionie Delphes et le temple d'Appollon au. IVe s.* (Paris 1979) 233.

held to carry a good deal of weight.[40] Militarily they comprise some of the peninsula's more significant forces. And all of these Amphiktyons, it must be presumed, would have been happy about the suppression of Thebes and the salvation of Phokis. The truth is that many must have been able to see the Sacred War as a Theban ploy designed to cut back a neighbour's power,[41] and such states were not likely to be much more disturbed by subsequent Phokian sacrilege than were the Athenians — and little trace of pious horror survives in their orators.[42]

Moreover, the question of the sacrilege, even for those who took it seriously, could be easily rationalised. It was simple to draw a line between the common people of Phokis and the tyrants, with their hired mercenaries, who could be held exclusively responsible for the pollution.[43] Provided "those responsible" were punished there was no need on religious grounds to torment the Phokian majority.

It is possible, however, that one state whose opinion mattered to Philip might have been less than ecstatic over such a settlement. Cawkwell and Griffith both emphasize that Philip's closest allies, the Thessalians, would want more, for "they were animated by the most bitter hatred of the Phokians."[44] There is certainly some evidence that such feelings were present, mutual and of long standing,[45] and in recent years, moreover, the two had been on opposite sides of the Sacred War. But, even if the average Thessalian flushed purple at the mention of Phokis, he was none the less open to persuasion, presumably, that the diminution of Theban power was at least as

---

[40] It is interesting in this regard to note that sixteen years before, when the Arkadian leaders commandeered Olympian treasures for similar reasons, there was eventually (but not immediately) a reaction that forced them to desist. But the fact that they had done so seems, once they had stopped, to have upset no one: Xen. *Hell.* 7.4.33 ff. I am grateful to P. D. Londey for drawing my attention to this parallel.

[41] As Diod. 16.28.4 comments, over the beginnings of the war there was "a great deal of confusion and disagreement throughout Greece."

[42] The exception is at Ais. 2.131, 133, but Aischines is here defending himself against Demosthenes' charge that he had personally been responsible for the Phokian surrender and punishment (130; cf. Dem. 19.51 ff.) and must do so by arguing that the responsibility was their own, partly (but far from predominantly) because of the sacrilege. Even so he confines any condemnation to the tyrants themselves.

[43] Supra n. 42. In fact, of course, such a distinction *was* drawn and no doubt it served to avoid an all-out Phokian stand on Phalaikos' orders. Unfortunately, though, as things turned out it was the wrong people who were punished.

[44] Cawkwell (supra n. 1), "PPhil" 102 and *PMac* 110; similarly Griffith, *Hist Mace* II 345 n. 1.

[45] Hdt. 7.176, 8.27-30; Ais. 2.140.

beneficial to his own country as the rape of the Phokians — at least if both could not be had together. And Demosthenes, for one, seems convinced that a primary ambition among the Thessalians at this time was the recovery of their old Amphiktyonic privileges,[46] the prospect of which Philip could confidently hold out to them as the consequence of a reduction of Theban influence. Of all Philip's allies the men of Thessaly were those with the greatest fund of *existing* good will on which the king could draw; of all parties involved they were the most likely to start with enough sympathy for their archon, Philip himself, to give genial attention to his reasons. By all means he had to keep this ally happy. But the destruction of Phokis — *if* this was a Thessalian ambition at Thermopylai — was not the only means of ensuring that. And Philip was peculiarly well placed (and would soon, if all went well, be even better placed) to offer others.[47]

Cawkwell refers to the "absurdity" of thinking that with the Macedonians and Thessalians under his command Philip needed Athens' unimpressive hoplite force.[48] In military terms he is no doubt correct. But, as I have already argued, it was the Athenian commitment, much more than her actual troops, that interested him.[49] He clearly felt that he needed, whatever the proclaimed rationale behind his intervention, to settle this war without a bloodbath.[50] (Sufficient reason, though there were probably others, was that with sympathy abroad for both sides a bloodletting would certainly alienate some and might disgust everyone.) Thus the relative leniency of the punishment, further ameliorated in later years. Thus too, I think, Macedonian soldiers accompanied their Theban counterparts when the Phokians were being resettled in

---

[46] Dem. 5.23, 8.65.

[47] This is not to underestimate the finesse Philip would have needed to effect this settlement. Aischines may have believed that it was in part Thessalian pressure that brought about what *did* happen; such may be the implication of 2.140 f. But properly speaking he is here referring to the confused situation *following* Athens' refusal to send the hoplites (*tōn Ath. hoplitōn ou parontōn*), when the preferred form of settlement is on the point of being abandoned. At that time, with Phalaikos and his mercenaries already gone, the Thessalians evidently feared that they were to get nothing for their pains and joined Thebes in pressing Philip to act.

[48] Cawkwell (supra n. 1), "PPhil" 103 and *PMac* 110; similarly Griffith, *Hist Mace* II 347.

[49] Here and above on this subject I defend my own position, which differs somewhat from that of Markle, "PStrat" (supra n. 1) 256 f.

[50] As is recognized by Griffith, *Hist Mace* II 343 and 450 f., and Cawkwell, *PMac* (supra n. 1) 110 f.

Philip and the Peace of Philokrates

villages — not, as Demosthenes implied,[51] to terrorise the victims but to prevent the Thebans from doing so, or worse.[52] But far more destructive than a last-ditch Phokian resistance (which Philip could and did avoid by diplomacy and compromise) would have been a desperate defence by the full Theban levy, an attempt the Thebans, if they were to be the losers, might well deem worth making while the possibility of getting Athenian help remained. The Athenian hoplites would not, probably, need to strike a blow; but they needed to be there, under Philip's orders and behind the Theban position.

This all the envoys understood, however circumspect they had to be in explaining it to the Athenian *demos*. When, after the assembly of 16 Skirophorion[53] a third embassy was detailed to carry formal word of Philokrates' final *psephisma* to Philip, who was known to be at Thermopylai,[54] Demosthenes on this occasion refused nomination. An indefinite profession of intent — all that the decree formally contained where military aid was concerned — was not at all the same thing as having the troops themselves. And Demosthenes' aim, with peace now achieved and Athens therefore as safe as possible from Macedonian invasion, was to make sure that they did not go. He had no wish to see Thebes lost to Athens (if the time should come) as an effective ally. His reminder that Philip still held Athenians hostage (for all that they had been promised free release soon afterwards) and his warning that the king might add the soldiers to them, combined with his attack (with Timarchos) on Aischines, was sufficient, so far as we know, to procure the rejection of Philip's request on *ca.* 20 Skirophorion.[55] So the preferred settlement lapsed and Philip fell back on the less desirable alternative, known now as the Peace of Philokrates.[56]

I readily concede that theories about unrealised intentions generally make better fiction than history. But there are reasons in this case

---

[51] Dem. 19.81.

[52] See in general *PMI* 122-24, Cawkwell, *PMac* (supra n. 1) 107 f., and Griffith, *Hist Mace* II 450-56.

[53] Supra notes 22 and 23.

[54] Supra notes 25 and 26.

[55] Supra n. 28.

[56] The two alternative strategies are referred to by Markle as "Plan A" and "Plan B". I have suggested that the treaty with Athens would be more appropriately known as "the Peace of Demosthenes," since Philokrates' *psephismata* (like Demosthenes' before he changed tack) had actually been designed to effect Philip's preferred strategy, rather than the alternative (*PMI* 125-27).

for being less damning. Firstly, this is not a fantasy conjured out of the air. Some people, including many Athenians, thought at the time that Philip's intention was to effect what did not occur. The main question, details aside, is whether they were right, and I have argued that they were. Secondly, this theory, I believe, makes the most consistent sense of the large body of tendentious and often contradictory extant evidence relating to the events of 346 and following years. In my book I interpreted those events in the light of this theory and found it effective in either removing or rationalising the difficulties (a task which has not, except in small part, been repeated here). Thirdly, this hypothesis makes very good sense not only of the consistency of men like Aischines (and, on his side of the fence, Demosthenes) in the three or four years after the peace but also of Philip's attempts over that period (before he abandoned the struggle as hopeless in late 343)[57] to remake the treaty in a form more acceptable to his no-better-than-nominal ally. I have held that Athens' hoplites were critical to a particular set of circumstances in 346. This is why he insisted upon peace and alliance; his request for the troops came under the terms of his alliance with Athens, not of any Amphiktyonic requirements or sanctions.[58] But (on this view), once the settlement at Themopylai, however it worked out, was over and done with, that requirement was no longer relevant and the treaty's terms might as well be renegotiated if Philip was serious about his relationship with the Athenians, to whom they were unpalatable. And we next find him, in 344, offering the Common Peace he had denied earlier.[59]

Lastly, a hypothesis that has Philip intending in 346 to weaken Thebes, to preserve Phokis against her recovery, to strengthen

---

[57] *PMI* 353-56.

[58] The enabling decree was the same one that ratified the treaty and extended it to Philip's descendants (Dem. 19.47-49).

[59] I do not follow Cawkwell's point (*PMac* [supra n. 1] 111) that the "only one answer" to the question why Philip wanted *alliance* was that he needed Athens' navy for his plan to attack Persia. I agree that he did want her navy. But if, by the time of Python's embassy of 344, he was prepared to accept a common peace in place of alliance ([Dem.] 7.18 ff., 30 f.) and if the terms under which he (or, as it turned out, Alexander) did get use of the navy were those of the treaty of Korinth, itself a common peace, then I do not understand how one can suppose that alliance, and not common peace, was the only possible activating mechanism or that Philip thought it was. (Conversely, if the alliance he obtained could not, in the event, shift a squad of hoplites up the road to Thermopylai, what could he have thought were its chances of propelling the Athenian navy to Miletos?)

Athens' general standing in Central Greece and above all to win her allegiance has the supreme virtue that it seems to coincide precisely with what Philip much more certainly tried to execute when, after Chaironeia, he was in a very much stronger position to arrange matters according to his inclination.[60] Unfortunately by that time the failures of earlier years, and especially of the treaty of 346, had rendered a happy rapprochement with Athens quite impossible.[61]

Monash University

---

[60] On which see, for example, Cawkwell, *PMac* (supra n. 1) 167 f. and Griffith, *Hist Mace* II 609-11.

[61] I am grateful to P. D. Londey for his suggestions and critical comments on a draft of this paper.

Philip II and Archidamus

CHARLES D. HAMILTON

Abstract

The reign of Archidamus (*ca.* 359-338) is a rather neglected topic in modern scholarship, although there are several points of contact with Philip II in his rise to ascendancy in Macedon. The present study argues that Archidamus' policy was a failure for Sparta, while at the same time offering to Philip a key to the control of the Peloponnesus. After Epaminondas' liberation of Messene, Archidamus remained inflexible in his determination to reduce Megalopolis and to reconquer Messene. During the Third Sacred War, Philip recognized this as the central fact of Peloponnesian politics, and he was able to exploit conditions there to his advantage after the Peace of Philocrates and the settlement of the Phocian war. Sparta's continuing threats and hostility to Argos, Megalopolis, and Messene provided Philip with an easy means of securing allies in southern Greece. The result of Sparta's intransigent isolation was Philip's invasion of the Peloponnesus late in 338 and his settlement of border disputes to the advantage of his allies. Thus, with Sparta humbled and isolated, Philip could well afford to acquiesce in her proud but futile refusal to join the League of Corinth.

There are numerous puzzling aspects of the relationship between Archidamus and Philip II. For example, why did the Spartans not take more vigorous action against the Macedonians in the Sacred War? Why did they apparently not resist Macedonian intervention in the Peloponnesus after the Peace of Philocrates? Why did they remain aloof from the Greek coalition which Demosthenes helped organize to face Philip at Chaeroneia? Why did Philip invade the Peloponnesus after that battle and strip away border territories from

Sparta to hand them over to her enemies? Any why, finally, did Philip allow Sparta, alone of all the Greeks, to remain outside the League of Corinth? It is the purpose of this paper to examine the later career of Archidamus in relation to Philip II.[1]

Archidamus had become king only a few years before the outbreak of the Sacred War, but he had been active for at least a decade prior to his accession. By then, not only had he acquired a military reputation through participation in four or five campaigns,[2] but his political attitudes had matured as well. Like his father, Agesilaus, he appears to have shared feelings of hatred and resentment toward Thebes for her military and diplomatic triumphs over Sparta. He also stood firmly opposed to the realities of newly independent Messenia and the recent foundation of Megalopolis as capital of Arcadia.[3] Throughout his career Archidamus was to remain firmly attached to these cardinal points of foreign policy: reduction of Megalopolis and Messene; reassertion of Spartan control of the Peloponnesus; and opposition to Thebes.

In 356 Isocrates composed the unfinished *Letter to Archidamus*.[4] In it the author urges the king to undertake feats of military enterprise which would confer great benefits on all of Greece. Isocrates was referring to his most cherished project, the panhellenic crusade, and he would write a similar appeal ten years later to Philip.[5] But nothing came of Isocrates' idea at this time, perhaps because word of the outbreak of the Sacred War, and of Archidamus' part in it, had reached the orator and dashed his hopes.[6] The letter is testimony

---

[1] There is no full-length study of Archidamus' reign. Useful though short studies will be found in B. Niese, *s.v.* "Archidamos (4)," *RE* 1 (1894) 467-69; P. Poralla, *Prosopographie der Lakedaimonier* (Breslau 1913) 33-34; P. Cloché, "Sur le rôle des rois de Sparte," *Les Études Classiques* 17 (1949) 362-66; for chronological matters, Ed. Meyer, *Forschungen zur alten Geschichte* II (Halle 1899) 504-507 should be read with caution.

[2] He escorted the survivors of Leuctra back to Sparta and served several times in the 360's in the Peloponnesus; Xen. *Hell*. 6.4.18-19, 7.1.28-32, 7.4.20-25 and 7.5.12-13; *Ages*. 33, 34.6. Diod. 15.54-55 has him, mistakenly, fighting at Leuctra.

[3] Isoc. 6 (*Archidamus*) *passim*; cf. Xen. *Hell*. 7.4.8-10; Diod. 15.76.3, and F. Blass, *Die attische Beredsamkeit* II² (Leipzig 1892) 299.

[4] Section 16 affords the date; Isocrates says he was 80 then.

[5] See Isoc. 5 (*To Philip*) and S. Perlman, "Isocrates' 'Philippus' — a Reinterpretation," *Historia* 6 (1957) 306-317 for discussion.

[6] The dates of the opening years of the Third Sacred War are a much discussed and probably insoluble problem. I follow here the arguments of N. G. L. Hammond, "Diodorus' Narrative of the Third Sacred War," *JHS* 57 (1937) 44-78 = *Studies in Greek History* (Oxford 1973) 486-533, which seem to me persuasive and cogent.

however that Archidamus had acquired a sufficient reputation to be considered as a potential leader of a panhellenic expedition to Asia, and that the fortunes of Sparta had not yet sunken so low as to remove the state from consideration as one of the leaders of Greece.

An invitation more to Archidamus' liking reached him when Philomelus of Phocis sought his aid. The Thebans, after the war in Leuctra, had sought and received judgment against the Spartans for their unlawful seizure of the Cadmeia in 382. The Spartans had failed to pay the fine assessed, and on this occasion the Thebans succeeded in having the Amphictyons vote to condemn them anew.[7] Philomelus traveled to Sparta and approached Archidamus in private, arguing that the Lacedaemonians had an equal interest in the attempt to annul the decrees, and disclosing his plan to seize the temple. Archidamus approved of the proposal, but said that he would not openly assist Philomelus at this point. Instead, he promised to cooperate in private by supplying money and mercenaries, and in fact he gave the Phocian fifteen talents.[8]

Philomelus proceeded to seize Delphi. He then attempted to justify his acts by personal propaganda, annulling the Amphictyons' decrees against both Phocis and Sparta, and tearing down the *stelae* on which they were inscribed. Only after a successful battle with the Locrians, and the reception of a favorable oracle from the priestess — obtained by coercion — did Philomelus send out envoys to numerous states in an official attempt to gather support and neutralize opposition. The Phocian envoys succeeded in persuading Athens, Sparta and some other Peloponnesian states to aid them.[9]

Archidamus no doubt lobbied strenuously with his countrymen in support of the Phocian request, for he was later held chiefly responsible for the war and the sacrileges committed by the Phocians in using the sacred treasures for military purposes in the course of the war.[10] Pausanias puts the Spartan decision down to hatred for Thebes, pure and simple, and clearly anti-Theban feeling counted

---

[7] Diod. 16.23.3-4, 29.2-4.

[8] Diod. 16.24.1-3. It is important to recognize the role here of Archidamus in a private capacity, in distinction to that of the Spartan state officially at 16.29.2. Although Hammond (supra n. 6) does not adduce this fact, it adds weight to his arguments against the "doublet" theories of Cloché, Beloch and others.

[9] Diod. 16.24.4-5, 25.1-3, 27.1-5, which I interpret, following Hammond (supra n. 6) 488-99, as reflecting two separate stages in the war, rather than a "doublet" version of the same events.

[10] Diod. 16.63.1.

for much.¹¹ The Spartans could not forgive the Thebans for their activities in the Peloponnesus in the 360's, but furthermore, the Thebans' recent act in persuading the Amphictyons to condemn them, along with the Phocians, still rankled. By accepting the Phocian alliance the Spartans thereby gave approval to Philomelus' actions, including the figurative rejection, as well as the literal destruction of the Theban-inspired Amphictyonic decrees. Thus, Sparta had the opportunity to check Thebes on the level of diplomacy and propaganda. But, on quite another level, there were potential advantages of a more practical sort to Sparta from this policy. If Thebes were to find her hands tied, militarily, in Central Greece, and be unable to intervene in the Peloponnesus (as she had done at least as recently as 361),¹² the Spartans would have an opportunity such as they had not enjoyed since Leuctra to attempt to revise the situation in the Peloponnesus. Within two years, in fact, they launched a military and diplomatic effort to precisely this end. For Sparta, therefore, the Phocian alliance offered several advantages and few apparent risks: through it they could register an effective protest against Thebes' manipulation of the Amphictyonic Council and also hope to engage Thebes in war in Central Greece which would give them a freer hand in the south. What was not foreseen was the involvement of Philip in the war, and with that the entire complexion of things changed.

Initially Sparta played a relatively unimportant part in the military activities of the Sacred War proper. She was inactive for several years, apparently awaiting a propitious opportunity. At the end of 354, a request for aid reached Thebes from Artabazus, a rebellious satrap of the Persian King. The Thebans assented to this request and sent their general Pammenes with a force of 5,000 men to Asia Minor.¹³ His departure took place most probably in early spring 353, and Onomarchus lost little time in exploiting his absence by leading a reformed mercenary army into Boeotia.¹⁴

Sparta, which had taken no part in the fighting thus far, and whose aid to Phocis seems to have been limited to moral support and allowing recruiting agents to operate within her territory, seized this opportunity to act. She marched against her old rival, Argos, and a

---

[11] Paus. 3.10.1-3.

[12] Diod. 15.94.1.

[13] Diod. 16.34.1-2.

[14] Diod. 16.32.2-4, 33.1-4. For the chronology, see Hammond (supra n. 6) 502-510.

battle was fought in which the Spartans were victorious, capturing Orneae on the Argive frontier.[15] This auspicious event marked the beginning of a brief period of renewed Spartan activity to reassert her predominance in the Peloponnesus. But while the victory over Argos was heartening, the Spartans knew very well that they faced several strong enemies close at hand. Since the 360's their territory had been ringed round by Argos, Megalopolis, and Messene, and they had been isolated by their refusal to recognize Messene in 362. In order to reduce the Messenians to subjection again, Sparta would need to find allies, and to proceed step by step. Thus, she turned to diplomacy first and we know about her proposals from Demosthenes' speech *For the Megalopolitans*.

In autumn 353, or the winter following, Archidamus proposed a general settlement of territorial disputes, based on ancient claims. It was proposed that Athens regain possession of Oropus, recently seized by Thebes; that Thespiae, Plataea, and Orchomenus regain their independence from Theban control; that Elis recover parts of Triphylia and Phlius the district of Tricanarum; and that certain of the Arcadians get back the land which had belonged to them.[16] The Megalopolitans, fearing that the implementation of these proposals would mean the dispersal of their population and loss of independence, sent envoys to Athens to seek alliance; the Spartans countered with envoys of their own; and Demosthenes delivered a speech on behalf of the Megalopolitans in which he took it as axiomatic that the real objective of the Spartans was the conquest of Messene, which would follow upon the neutralization of Megalopolis.[17] As Demosthenes correctly saw, Archidamus' objective was to augment Sparta's position, not to resolve old problems on the basis of justice.[18] His fear, however, that Sparta would use her power, if she succeeded in her designs, against Athens, was baseless. He failed to convince the

---

[15] Diod. 16.34.3. Again, I follow Hammond (supra n. 6) 519-21 in dissociating this incident from the campaign of 351 (cf. 16.39.1-7).

[16] Dem. 16.11, 4, and 16. While there is little direct evidence that Archidamus was the author of these proposals, the indirect evidence of his past policies and his influential position at the time leads to this suggestion. See the introduction to the speech in the Loeb edition by J. H. Vince, *Demosthenes* I (London and Cambridge, Mass. 1954) 437, where Archidamus' authorship is asserted without argument or reference to source. See Xen. *Hell*. 7.4.1, 11, 13-35.

[17] On the background, derived from the speech itself, see Blass (supra n. 3) III.1, 288 and Vince (supra n. 16) 437-38. Dem. 16.8-10.

[18] Dem. 16.16-18.

Athenians of this, and Athens, under the guidance of Eubulus, chose to accept neither the Megalopolitan nor the Spartan proposal for alliance.[19] Was Athens' decision to remain neutral a check to Archidamus' diplomacy? Granting that Archidamus' principal concern was to secure allies to aid him in an attack upon Megalopolis, the outcome could still be viewed as a partial victory. Athens refused to help Sparta, but neither did she lend her aid to Megalopolis, so that Archidamus was free to march against that city without worrying about Athens, as he did soon after.[20] As for the other points of his proposal, it seems clear that Archidamus gained a certain measure of very useful good will, even if no territorial changes took place at this time. Onomarchus had invaded Boeotia in 353 and seized Orchomenus, and the proposal to restore that city to independence would have won his approval as a measure to weaken Thebes.[21] Furthermore, by espousing the claims of Elis and Phlius to border territories long in dispute,[22] he secured the favor of the governments there, which in any case had had ties of long standing to Sparta. Phlius' dispute was with Argos, and Elis' with the Arcadians, so that Archidamus had adroitly manipulated the situation to his own advantage. When he turned from diplomacy to warfare, Argos and Megalopolis would need to watch their flanks lest Phlius and Elis intervene while they were occupied with meeting Archidamus' advance. Finally, by suggesting internal changes in Arcadia which would have weakened Megalopolis seriously, Archidamus was again championing the cause of disaffected elements there which had been forced against their will to remain under the control of Megalopolis.[23] This issue would lead to open war soon enough, but in 352 Sparta's attention was drawn elsewhere.

The Phocian star had risen again in the meanwhile. Under Onomarchus another army had been recruited, Thessaly temporarily bribed into inaction, and Boeotia invaded.[24] It was at this point that Philip II first became involved in the war, in alliance with the Thessalians against Lycophron of Pherae. He was defeated in two battles by Onomarchus, and forced to withdraw. Returning in spring

---

[19] Vince (supra n. 16) 438.
[20] Diod. 16.39.1ff; Paus. 4.28.2.
[21] Diod. 16.33.3-4.
[22] Cf. Xen. *Hell*. 7.4.11 for Phlius and 7.4.13-35 for Elis.
[23] Diod. 15.94.1-3.
[24] Diod. 16.32.3-4, 33.2-4.

of 352, Philip met Onomarchus again in Thessaly, where he inflicted a severe defeat upon him at the Battle of the Crocus Field.[25] After this, he marched to Thermopylae to exploit his victory, but a combined force of Athenians, Achaeans and Spartans checked his progress. Philip did not tarry long before turning northwards towards Thrace. His intervention in the conflict in Central Greece was of short duration, and he would be involved elsewhere for the next several years, but he would return to play the decisive role in the settlement of the Sacred War.

The prospect of Macedonian troops south of Thermopylae had greatly alarmed the Athenians and produced the first actual commitment of Spartan forces in the Sacred War.[26] The quite unexpected reversal of Phocis' fortunes and the defeat and death of Onomarchus forestalled any plans Archidamus might have made for a Peloponnesian campaign in 352. Instead, Sparta sent a thousand men to assist Phayllus, the new Phocian commander, and the rest of the year was taken up with campaigning in Locris and Boeotia. At the end of the campaigning season the Spartans presumably returned home, and in the following year they requested and received a reciprocal force of Phocians in their war in the Peloponnesus.[27]

In spring of 351 Archidamus resumed the enterprise which he had initiated through his diplomacy in 353 and had suspended during the Macedonian threat to Central Greece; he invaded and overran the country of Megalopolis.[28] Diodorus says merely that the two states were at variance, but it is clear that Archidamus' invasion is consistent with his previous policy. The Megalopolitans were not equal to Archidamus' forces, so they called upon their allies, and the Argives, Sicyonians, and Messenians came out in full force to their aid; in addition, the Thebans sent 4,000 foot and 500 horse. The Spartans, in their turn, were reinforced by 3,000 Phocians and 150 horse under Lycophron. They had thus, Diodorus says, "mustered an army capable of fighting."[29] No other Spartan allies are mentioned, but it is likely that both Elis and Phlius aided Sparta, and Diodorus failed to note this. His report states that the extra-Peloponnesian allies of Megalopolis outnumbered those of Sparta by

[25] Diod. 16.35.1-6.
[26] Diod. 16.37.2-3; Dem. 19.84; Justin 8.2.8.
[27] Diod. 16.39.3.
[28] Diod. 16.39.1.
[29] Diod. 16.39.3.

almost 1500, and while the Spartan forces exceeded those of Megalopolis alone, the combined armies of Argos, Sicyon, and Messene must have far outnumbered the Spartans at this period. It is hard to see how the Spartan coalition could be described as "capable of fighting" and could in fact win several encounters in the ensuing warfare, if they were substantially outnumbered. I suggest, therefore, that the earlier efforts of Archidamus in diplomacy may have borne fruit, and that Elis and Phlius may have contributed to Archidamus' army at the outset of the campaign, in hopes of aggrandizement along their own frontiers. However that may be, the fighting itself was on the whole indecisive. In the earlier stages of what appears to have been a full season of campaigning, the Spartans initially had the advantage, capturing Orneae again, checking the Argives and Thebans in an indecisive battle, and storming Helissus in Arcadia. The tide turned, and the Thebans then scored victories in three encounters. Finally, the Spartans won an important battle which brought the fighting to an end. Shortly thereafter they concluded an armistice with Megalopolis, and the Thebans returned home.[30]

The failure of the campaign of 351 must have been a bitter disappointment for Archidamus. He had calculated that the Sacred War would distract the rest of Greece, and Thebes in particular, sufficiently to allow him to regain at least some measure of Sparta's ancient control of the Peloponnesus. His expectations were dashed and, if anything, the effort suggested that he had overextended Sparta's resources. There is no evidence of further attempts by Sparta to reassert her predominance by military means during Archidamus' reign, and we must wonder whether the failure of Archidamus' diplomacy and military leadership may not have diminished his prestige and influence within Sparta. In any case, he does not reappear in the sources until 346, when he took 1000 soldiers to Phocis in a vain attempt to secure the fortifications of Thermopylae against Philip.[31] But the consequences of 351 were even more serious for Sparta. Her supporters in the few states still favorably disposed toward her found themselves facing increasing opposition, and strife and confusion began to spread.[32] Isocrates paints a dismal picture, which must be substantially true, even if exaggerated, in which the

---

[30] Diod. 16.39.4-7 gives the military activities; cf. Paus. 4.28.2.

[31] Diod. 16.59.1; Aeschin. 2.133.

[32] Dem. 18.18. Perhaps the revolution in Elis took place at this time; see K. J. Beloch, *Griechische Geschichte* III², 1 (Leipzig 1922) 541 for discussion, and infra n. 78.

Spartans found themselves isolated and distrusted by the Peloponnesians, harried constantly by the Messenians, and obliged to be on their guard almost daily, in defence of themselves or their borders. But their worst fear, he says, is that the Thebans may settle the Phocian question and return to inflict still greater misfortunes upon them.[33] Isocrates' analysis, although overly generalized and inaccurate in some details,[34] nonetheless suggests a decline in Sparta's fortunes between 351 and the date of the speech, 346. This situation did not go unnoticed elsewhere.

When Philip decided to intervene in the Sacred War at the invitation of the Thessalians, he must have begun to give thought to matters in central and southern Greece, and perhaps already to consider what his position would be should his intervention prove successful. After being checked at Thermopylae, he marched to the north on other enterprises, but he was not inattentive to the course of events in the south. According to Demosthenes, Philip observed conditions in the Peloponnesus in the latter part of the Sacred War, which were evident enough in any event, and decided to exploit the situation to his own advantage.[35] Philip's policy was based on the mistakes of others, he says, and it was skillfully developed to his own ends. Archidamus' diplomatic and military efforts from 353 to 351 had made several things clear, and the astute Philip was quick to draw the correct conclusions from these events. The useful lessons which he learned were several. First of all, Sparta was militarily unprepared for any major undertakings outside the Peloponnesus; her only campaign, consisting of a mere thousand soldiers sent to Thermopylae, in contrast to the Achaeans' 2000 and the Athenians' 5000, demonstrated this. On the other hand, her troops were not to be dismissed lightly, for they had fought well under Archidamus. Next, three states stood in virtually permanent opposition and hostility to Sparta: Argos, Megalopolis, and Messene. Third, internal rivalries divided many of the Peloponnesian states into factions and thus provided opportunities for intervention. And finally, Sparta's central concerns in foreign policy were the reconquest of Messenia and, to that end, the weakening of both Argos and Megalopolis. To Philip, the options must have seemed very clear: to

---

[33] Isoc. 5.49-50.
[34] Isoc. 5.51. It was incorrect to say that they were distrusted by *all* the Peloponnesians, and an exaggeration to allege that *most* of the Greeks hated them.
[35] Dem. 18.19.

thwart Sparta, ally with her Peloponnesian foes; to court her, offer her aid against those same foes. Philip was technically at war with Sparta already (as the result of the Amphyctionic declaration of war), and there is no indication that he nurtured any sense of gratitude to her for the help rendered to his father Amyntas in the Olynthian campaign of 382-379.[36] By establishing good relations with Sparta's Peloponnesian enemies he could secure the support of numerous allies and neutralize Sparta, thus controlling the situation in the Peloponnesus without direct military intervention. The opportunity was too good to pass up. Furthermore, if Philip had already begun to think about leading a Greek force into Asia Minor against the Persian King,[37] he might have reasoned that Sparta was best kept isolated and incapable of participating in such an enterprise. Sparta, alone of the Greek states, had a reputation of championing the panhellenic cause, however well or ill deserved, as Isocrates' *Letter to Archidamus* indicates.[38] Philip will not have wanted a rival for leadership of an undertaking of this sort. Consequently, he began to formulate his Peloponnesian policy. Its genesis lay in the events of the late 350's.

The last five years of the Sacred War, from 351 to 346, witnessed increasing desecration of the Delphic shrine at the hands of Phalaecus, Phayllus' successor and the last commander of the Phocian forces. The Delphic treasures had not proved to be inexhaustible, and the Phocians and their enemies were worn out and eager for an end to hostilities by late 347.[39] Factional strife broke out in Phocis, and Phalaecus had been temporarily deposed from command of the mercenary troops. Philip meanwhile, after having attended to affairs closer to Macedon, in the Thraceward area and the Chalcidic peninsula, was ready once again to turn his attention southwards. The Athenians, who had attempted to check his advances without success on several occasions, were ready to treat for peace and sent envoys for that purpose to Pella. The stage was set for the Peace of Philocrates and the settlement of the Third Sacred War. It is not possible here, nor is it even desirable, to attempt to disentangle the web of charge and countercharge woven several years

---

[36] Cf. Xen. *Hell.* 5.2.11ff; Diod. 15.19.

[37] I find the analysis of J. R. Ellis, *PMI* 92, very persuasive on this topic.

[38] See the discussion of Cloché (supra n. 1) 363-64 and, on the use and abuse of panhellenic propaganda in general, S. Perlman, "Panhellenism, the Polis and Imperialism," *Historia* 25 (1976) 1-30.

[39] Diod. 16.59.1ff.

after these events by the rival Athenian orators, Demosthenes and Aeschines. We shall endeavor, however, to follow the thread of diplomacy between Sparta and Philip during this period.

When precisely Philip began to implement his policy of winning over adherents among the Peloponnesian states hostile to Sparta is impossible to say. Demosthenes implies that Philip started to "bribe traitors" in various Peloponnesian cities and to promote disorder there toward the latter part of the Sacred War, although the first clear piece of evidence of such activity appears to belong to 348.[40] At that time Aeschines denounced Philip for stirring up trouble in Arcadia, and produced Ischandrus, an Arcadian aristocrat, to testify. The result was an Athenian embassy headed by Aeschines which unsuccessfully attempted to draw envoys from various states to Athens to deliberate on a common Greek war against Philip. Isocrates, writing in 346 in *To Philip*, represents Philip's enemies as charging that he was claiming that he intended to assist the Messenians if he could resolve the Phocian question, although his real object was the subjugation of the Peloponnesus; furthermore, the Argives, Messenians and Megalopolitans, as well as others, were said to be prepared to join forces with Philip to destroy the Spartans.[41] If the allegations which Isocrates reports are grounded in fact, even if perhaps exaggerated, they show that Philip was well advanced in laying the groundwork of his Peloponnesian policy. In 348, when Aeschines decried his intervention in Arcadia, he may have only begun to win over supporters in the Peloponnesus, but by the late winter of 347-46 Philip had made considerable headway in Argos and Messene as well.

The Spartans will have known about Philip's intrigues in Arcadia, but they did not answer the appeal of Aeschines' embassy.[42] We can only speculate about the reasons for their inactivity. Perhaps they minimized the danger from Philip's intrigues, or they were skeptical of the possibilities of success in forming such an anti-Macedonian coalition. What finally brought them face to face with Philip again was the development of the Phocian War. After the deposition of Phalaecus early in 347, his three successors in command achieved some military victories. The Thebans, in turn, appealed to Philip,

---

[40] Dem. 18.19; 19.10-11, cf. 303ff; Aeschin. 2.79. On the date, see Ellis, *PMI* 100-101.

[41] Isoc. 5.74-75; cf. Dem. 5.18.

[42] Aeschin. 2.79.

who sent a small force of Macedonians under Parmenio. As a result, the Phocian government appealed for aid to Athens and Sparta late in 347, specifically asking for troops to occupy three fortified places which held the approaches to Thermopylae. Both Athens and Sparta assented.[43] When he discovered resistance stiffening, Philip shifted course. Philip had made only a limited commitment of troops in answer to the Theban request, and the course of subsequent negotiations to end the Sacred War, as well as its final settlement, shows that Philip was reluctant to act in such a way as to augment Thebes' power significantly. The prospect of a major conflict with Phocis, Athens and Sparta, which might endanger his gains elsewhere and which would be costly to him, was not particularly attractive. Consequently he undertook to effect changes in the Phocian situation and to establish peace with Athens, the strongest of his opponents.[44] Both his efforts were successful. Phalaecus was returned to power in Phocis, and when the Athenian general Proxenus reached Phocis and inquired about arrangements to occupy Alponus, Thronium and Nicaea, the Greek approaches to Thermopylae, he was coldly rebuffed. When Archidamus himself, in command of a thousand hoplites from Sparta, arrived some time later for the same purpose, he too was refused entry with the remark that the Phocians feared the danger from Sparta more than that from home.[45] While these events were taking place, in winter 347-46, Philip informed the Athenians of his wish to have peace and alliance with them. The Demos voted to dispatch an embassy to secure terms, and the envoys returned at the end of March with Philip's proposals: peace and alliance for Philip and his allies on one hand, for Athens and hers on the other; both sides to retain their possessions as of the time of ratification; and the exclusion of Phocis and several others from the peace. After considerable discussion and debate, and not without misgivings, especially over the exclusion of Phocis, the Demos accepted Philip's proposal, on the motion of Philocrates.[46] Philip himself had already gone off on a campaign to Thrace for the duration of spring, 346, but the news of his diplomatic achievement doubtless reached him there.

During his sojourn in Thrace, there was a rush of activity in the

---

[43] Aeschin. 2.132; Diod. 16.59.1.
[44] See Ellis, *PMI* 100-102, for the background and analysis.
[45] Aeschin. 2.133-34; Diod. 16.59.1.
[46] See Ellis, *PMI* 107-113, for detailed discussion of this topic.

Greek states to salvage what they could from the situation through diplomacy. Sparta in particular felt herself isolated once again. Phalaecus had rejected her offer of military aid, thus effectively eliminating any possibility of successful resistance to the Macedonian entry into Central Greece. His act must have seemed puzzling at the time, but Philip's agreement to allow him and his mercenaries to retire from Phocis in the summer, without bearing any responsibility for their sacrilegious behavior, may provide the explanation. It seems likely that a secret pact had been arranged between the two early in 346, according to which Phalaecus, recognizing that his resources were exhausted and the war lost, agreed to hold the fortifications until Philip was ready to occupy Thermopylae, in order to save his own skin.[47] The Athenian alliance precluded any hope of cooperation from that quarter. The Spartans surely felt that it was now only a matter of time before Philip returned from Thrace, marched south, and settled the Sacred War to his advantage and that of his allies, Thessaly and Thebes. The resurgence of Theban influence in Central Greece and the possibility of renewed intervention in the Peloponnesus was especially alarming to Sparta, as Isocrates remarked in *To Philip*.[48] Diplomacy seemed to offer Sparta her only means of avoiding a difficult and dangerous situation. She sent envoys to Pella, therefore, in the spring. While Philip tarried in Thrace, his capital buzzed with throngs of anxious and impatient envoys, for in addition to Sparta, Athens, Thebes, Thessaly, Phocis, and probably Argos, Messene and Megalopolis had also sent embassies.[49]

No detailed account exists of the negotiations which took place upon Philip's return to Pella in June. We must rely on the divergent and hardly impartial, if not outright false, assertions made by Aeschines and Demosthenes after the fact. Each of these men, in any event, sought to justify his part in the negotiations and concentrated on the Athenian objectives of their embassy.[50] There is no direct factual report of the conversations between the Spartans and Philip, but Demosthenes suggests that Philip promised to grant what they wanted, and Aeschines implies that the Spartan envoys were so

---

[47] For this suggestion see Ellis, *PMI* 106 and 119-20, and G. L. Cawkwell, *Philip of Macedon* (London 1978) 109.

[48] Isoc. 5.49-50.

[49] Aeschin. 2.104, 136-37; Dem. 9.11; and see Isoc. 5.74 which suggests the presence of the Peloponnesian states.

[50] See Ellis, *PMI* 113-15, and Cawkwell (supra n. 47) 92-95.

encouraged by Philip that they clashed openly with the Theban representatives.[51] Assuming that these reports reflect accurately the Spartans' perception that they had obtained from Philip what they sought, we must ask what the possible points of discussion between them might have been. The Spartans might have wished to treat with Philip on three issues: 1) Philip's attitude toward Sparta for her role in the outbreak of the Sacred War, and the attendant question of imposing sanctions on her for her part in the war; 2) her concern about the fate of Phocis and the possibility of the extension of Theban power; and 3) the question of the Peloponnesian states, and Macedonian intervention there against her interests. There is some direct evidence that the second point above was a common concern of the Spartans and Athenians,[52] but we can support the first and third points only by appeals to the logic of the situation and by inference from the actual settlement of the Sacred War. Before attempting to gauge the success of Sparta's diplomatic effort, however, we must first try to discern what Sparta could have offered to Philip as a *quid pro quo*.

Philip's object seems to have been to settle the Sacred War without much bloodshed, and with as much general assent as he could muster among the Greek states. He was probably already thinking ahead to the Asia Minor expedition, and for that he would require settled conditions in Greece.[53] He held the decisive power at this point, but his position was curious. He had entered the Sacred War as the ally of Thessaly and Thebes, and he had represented himself as the champion of Delphic Apollo, so that religious propaganda was important to him.[54] He could not very well hope to maintain the fiction of fighting to save the shrine from its sacrilegious despoilers if he did not punish *some* of the offenders. Yet he did not want to see Phocis destroyed root and branch — the penalty for temple robbery was to hurl the offenders from the cliffs, and the Otaeans savagely demanded the penalty be meted out to the adult males at the Amphictyonic meeting later that summer[55] — for practical as well as humanitarian reasons. Philip's treatment of Olynthus demonstrates

---

[51] Dem. 19.76-77; Aeschin. 2.136-37.
[52] Aeschin. 2.115ff; Dem. 19.19-21.
[53] So Ellis, *PMI* 91-92.
[54] Justin 8.2.1-2; cf. Polyb. 9.33.6.
[55] Aeschin. 2.142; cf. Diod. 16.61-64.

that he was quite capable of such cruelty when he deemed it necessary. In order to resist pressures from Thebes and Thessaly to crush Phocis, Philip would find the support of other states useful. The Peace of Philocrates, which Philip would finally ratify a few days after leaving Pella for Thermopylae at Pherae, made Athens his ally.[56] The only other major state involved in the Sacred War, save Phocis itself, with which Philip had as yet to reach an accord, was Sparta. He wanted two things from her. The first was her assent and participation in the settlement of the war. Some Phocians had to be punished, that was inevitable; but if only the guilty suffered, as Aeschines had argued, and the Spartans agreed to the proceedings, they could be assured that Philip would restrain his allies from calling for punishment for Sparta. Secondly, a peaceful Peloponnesus, which meant Sparta's renunciation of hostile ambitions towards Megalopolis and Messene and acceptance of the status quo, was essential to Philip.[57] Such terms were not likely to be acceptable to Archidamus, of course, as his career to this point suggests. But he appears to have been in Phocis at the time of the negotiations in Pella, and we have suggested that he suffered a loss of prestige after 351 at home in Sparta. Let us suppose that the Spartan envoys at Pella agreed to participate in Philip's settlement of the war, in order to restrain potential Theban gains in Central Greece and again in the Peloponnesus, and also agreed to accept the Peloponnesian status quo, to forestall further Macedonian or Theban meddling there. Opposition to such a compromise was to be expected in Sparta, but that could be met when it was raised, at a later date. The most pressing immediate issue was the Phocian question and the containment of Theban ambition in Central Greece. It is quite possible that the Spartan envoys regarded these terms as a fair bargain. For their part, then, they agreed to a role in Philip's settlement of the Phocian war, and to acceptance of the Peloponnesian status quo, at least for the moment (which in any case they were powerless to alter at this point). In exchange, Philip gave assurances that Phocis would not be destroyed to Thebes' advantage; that Sparta would not be punished for her role in the war; and a promise to end Macedonian meddling in the Peloponnesian question. Such a scenario may help to explain the subsequent sequence of events.

---

[56] Aeschin. 2.137; cf. Ellis, *PMI* 116.

[57] Isoc. 5.73-74 and cf. Ellis, *PMI* 150, for Philip's later insistence on this point.

When the various envoys left Pella they were expecting Philip to save Phocis and to humble Thebes. The Thebans even mobilized in alarm.[58] At Pherae, Philip finally gave his oath to the Athenians, who returned home. Philip then marched to Thermopylae and requested his new allies, the Athenians, to send a force to him. In the brief interval, the Phocian government had once again sent to Athens for help against Philip.[59] This development only makes sense if they had lost confidence in their commander, Phalaecus, and had begun to suspect him of seeking to save himself at any price. The Athenians refused Philip's request, now mistrusting his intentions.[60] The Spartans, according to Demosthenes,[61] detected a trap when Philip had reached Thermopylae, and they too withdrew. This reference can only be to the force which Archidamus was commanding in Phocis, and the decision to withdraw, that is, to take no part in Philip's settlement, will have been the policy of the commander in the field, Archidamus. It is impossible to know whether Archidamus made this decision because he had been apprised of the results of the negotiations at Pella and refused to agree to the status quo in the Peloponnesus, which amounted to the recognition of the right of Messene to exist, or because he suspected, with the Phocian government, that Philip might allow Phalaecus to escape unpunished.[62] Philip was disappointed, both at the Athenian refusal to send troops and at the Spartan withdrawal. Pressed by the Thessalians to take action, he soon announced the "Convention between Philip and the Phocians," which allowed Phalaecus to withdraw with his mercenaries, and then he accepted the surrender of the Phocian cities. Finally, he asked the Amphictyonic Council to convene to decide the fate of Phocis.[63]

At the meeting of the Amphictyonic Council in mid-summer 346 the fate of Phocis was decided. Demosthenes branded it as disastrous, but in fact the Phocians suffered far less than they might.[64] The cities

---

[58] Aeschin. 2.137.
[59] Dem. 19.58-59.
[60] Aeschin. 2.137.
[61] Dem. 19.76-77.
[62] My reconstruction differs from Ellis' interpretation of events on this point; see *PMI* 117, n. 134.
[63] Dem. 19.61ff; Diod. 16.59.3; cf. Ellis, *PMI* 120, n. 146.
[64] Dem. 19.64ff and 81.

were torn down and the population resettled in small villages, but there was neither execution nor enslavement. The sacred monies were to be paid back at a stiff rate, sixty talents per year. Those responsible for the temple-robbery were placed under a curse, but this seems not to have weighed very heavily on Phalaecus and his mercenaries. For the future, Phocis was to be defenceless, but at least the land and its inhabitants had been spared. The two votes which Phocis had held in the Amphictyony were given to Philip, and he presided over the Pythian Games.[65] Phocis' allies in the war escaped retribution. Neither Athens nor Sparta was ejected from the Amphictyony, as Delphic inscriptions verify; Pausanias' report that Sparta was expelled, although erroneous, may reflect a proposal to that effect which was made but effectively defeated.[66] Throughout the deliberations, one suspects that Philip worked actively to moderate the more extreme demands which his allies, the Thebans and Thessalians in particular, may be expected to have made. He seems to have wanted, still, to bring over both the Athenians and Spartans to his camp, despite their failure to cooperate shortly before. There is no record that the previous fines levied on Sparta for her seizure of the Cadmeia, and still unpaid, were demanded now; nor is there any hint of censure for Archidamus for his role in supporting Philomelus, although many obviously held him chiefly responsible for the war.[67] Philip probably worked to achieve this, in the hope that the Spartans, and Archidamus himself, would be gratified and would agree to compromise by modifying their Peloponnesian policy. The Spartans boycotted the proceedings and they remained steadfast in their refusal to recognize Messene.

The settlement of the Third Sacred War marked a turning point in Greek history, for thenceforth Philip had a forum and a formal role in Greek matters. It also marked a turning point in Spartan-Macedonian relations. The apparent intransigence of Archidamus convinced Philip that Sparta could not be won over by reason and compromise. Thus, in the aftermath of the Sacred War, Philip reconsidered his Peloponnesian policy. Spartan diplomacy at Pella can, at best, be viewed as a limited success. In the long run, it was a failure and Archidamus must bear much of the blame for this failure.

---

[65] Diod. 16.60; Justin 8.5; Aeschin. 2.142ff.
[66] *SIG* 241B 1.76f, cf. 1.117 and C 1.143; Paus. 10.8.2.
[67] Diod. 16.63.1; Paus. 3.10.3.

Over the next several years, Philip undertook a vigorous campaign to win over Argos, Messene, Megalopolis, and other states in the Peloponnesus. Unfortunately, most of what we know of his activities derives from the hostile speeches of Demosthenes. The orator viewed Philip's policy as one of corruption and bribery, intended only to serve his own ends, which are represented as the conquest of Greece. Demosthenes provides a catalogue of names of those in various states who succumbed to Philip's overtures, and who were thus guilty of "treason."[68] Although there is little evidence for Sparta's response to Philip's advances, we have at least the point of view of the Peloponnesian states involved, in Polybius' defence of their relationship to Philip.[69] Polybius refutes Demosthenes' charges of treason, arguing that the Athenian's was not the only possible outlook on the matter.[70] He defends leaders in Thessaly and Boeotia, as well as those in Argos, Messene, and Arcadia against Demosthenes' charges, but he argues that the Messenians and Arcadians in particular were justified because by their alliance to Philip they brought about liberty in the Peloponnesus, and the restoration of territory taken from their states by Sparta.[71] Polybius is writing in reference to the settlement which Philip effected in the Peloponnesus after Chaeroneia, but the motives which he attributes to the Messenians and Arcadians are valid throughout our period. Thus, Philip seems to have represented himself as, and to have been accepted as, the champion of the independence of these states. This fact is important to note as we attempt to trace the growth of his power in the area, and the Spartan response.

At some point in late summer or autumn 346 an Athenian embassy was dispatched to Sparta, although its object is not recorded. In response to this embassy, the Argives, Messenians, Megalopolitans and other Peloponnesians remonstrated with Athens, thinking that the Athenians were promoting Spartan policy.[72] Demosthenes says no more than this about the incident, but if the Peloponnesian states suspected Athens of intriguing with Sparta against them at this time, they will have been more than receptive to the overtures which Philip

---

[68] Dem. 19.260-62; 18.64 and 295 contain the names of the states involved and the individuals in them who were corrupted.

[69] Polyb. 14.18.1-15.

[70] Polyb. 14.18.11-12.

[71] Polyb. 14.18.5-7; cf. 9.33.6.

[72] Dem. 5.18.

Philip II and Archidamus

made not long afterwards. It is possible, although not at all certain, that the Spartans had begun hostilities with the Messenians again at the conclusion of the Sacred War, and the request for Athenian aid which Pausanias says the Messenians made to Athens may belong to this context.[73] In any case, Philip did not delay to approach the enemies of Sparta in the Peloponnesus, and he soon struck an alliance with Messene and started to furnish mercenaries and supplies to that state and Argos, presumably for the warfare with Sparta.[74] He also ordered the Spartans to renounce their claims to Messenia.[75] These developments can only be dated by reference to the time of the speech in which Demosthenes alludes to them, which is after mid-summer 344. They had probably occupied much of the previous year and a half, and Demosthenes proposed an Athenian embassy to the Peloponnesus to counteract the growing pro-Macedonian sentiment there.[76] Philip countered with diplomacy of his own, sending Pytho of Byzantium to Athens to attempt to patch up the peace by offering to renegotiate his treaty with Athens. The effort failed, but at least things did not come to an open breach yet.[77] Once again, although they were central to any Peloponnesian settlement, we have no information on the reaction of the Spartans to these developments. We must conclude that they remained opposed to any accommodation with the Messenians and that they resented the interference of Macedon. They seem to have eschewed diplomacy in favor of more direct, military means. The single detailed example we know of occurred in 343.

In that year, strife broke out in Elis.[78] Two factions were struggling for power, one of them pro-Spartan and the other presumably inclined toward Macedon. While the Spartans were preparing to go to the aid of their partisans, the Messenians anticipated them and gained entry to the city by a ruse. The pro-Spartan faction was driven into exile. The loss of Elis, one of Sparta's few remaining Peloponnesian allies, to the Messenian-Macedonian cause, seems to have been

---

[73] Paus. 4.28.2. Alternatively, their request may belong at the time of Demosthenes' speech *For the Megalopolitans*; cf. V. Ehrenberg, s.v. "Sparta," *RE* 3A.2 (1929) 1415.

[74] Dem. 6.15, cf. 9; Paus. 4.28.2.

[75] Dem. 6.13.

[76] Dem. 6.19ff; 18.79. See Ellis, *PMI* 143.

[77] Dem. 18.136; 7.18ff; and Ellis, *PMI* 143-44.

[78] Paus. 4.28.4-7; Dem. 19.260, 294.

the catalyst which brought Archidamus to our notice for the last time. He had been on the verge of setting out on an expedition to south Italy, in response to a summons from the Tarentines, who were fighting with their Lucanian neighbors. In the midst of his preparations, another opportunity presented itself in a call for assistance from the city of Lyctus, in Crete. That city had been taken by Phalaecus and his mercenaries who were then in the employ of Cnossus. Archidamus went to Crete first, took and restored Lyctus to its rightful inhabitants, and then sailed off to Italy.[79] He spent an indeterminate amount of time campaigning there before meeting his death in battle, presumably on the very same day as Chaeroneia, in 338.[80] Two questions need to be asked in this connection: when, and why, did Archidamus sail to Italy? Diodorus puts these events under 346/5, relating them to the fortunes of Phalaecus and his men, but this is too early, and results from his habit of beginning his narrative under one year and continuing it to its logical conclusion, regardless of duration. He further relates that, after Archidamus' departure from Crete, the mercenaries were hired by Elean exiles. They returned to the Peloponnesus and were defeated and captured by the Eleans and their Arcadian allies in an abortive attempt to recapture Elis.[81] This incident is likely to have occurred not long after the original disturbance which led to the exile of the pro-Spartan faction and, therefore, probably in 342.[82] The sources are not very helpful in explaining the reason for Archidamus' expeditions. Diodorus mentions the kinship between Tarentum, Sparta's ancient colony, and that city, offering this as the reason for the sending of an army and a fleet under Archidamus.[83] Theopompus suggests that life in Sparta had become too confining, and that Archidamus was eager to go abroad.[84] The truth is much more likely to lie in Sparta's ever more urgent need for money. Like his father before him, Archidamus made the decision to undertake the expedition to Italy, and then to Crete, in order to earn sufficient funds to enable his state to accomplish otherwise unattainable goals. He was not merely an

---

[79] Diod. 16.62.4.

[80] Diod. 16.88.3, cf. 63.1.

[81] Diod. 16.63.3-5.

[82] See Beloch (supra n. 32) 541 for discussion of the date; and cf. 594-95.

[83] Diod. 16.62.4.

[84] Theopomp. *FGrH* 115 F232.

adventurer. When Elis went over to Philip, assisted by Philip's allies, the Messenians,[85] Archidamus and the Spartans must have been greatly frustrated at their inability to strike back effectively. Archidamus did not turn his back on Sparta or the Peloponnesus in 342, but rather he judged the need pressing, and the moment opportune, for his departure.[86] That he would never return, of course, he could not have known.

During Archidamus' absence, the increasing tension and hostility in Greece came to a head. Sparta, however, elected not to fight with the coalition Demosthenes had formed at Chaeroneia. The principal reason for Sparta's obdurate neutrality may have been Archidamus' absence. His son Agis held the regency, but he had not yet built enough influence to win the ephors over to such a serious step as open warfare with Macedon.[87] The government was probably reluctant to make any crucial decisions in foreign policy before Archidamus returned. Sparta's participation at Chaeroneia is unlikely to have made a decisive difference to the outcome of the battle in any event, but she was to be punished for her neutrality, by a seeming miscarriage of justice.

Within a short time of his settlements with Thebes, Athens, and the other states which had opposed him, Philip came to the Peloponnesus. From Corinth or, more probably, from Argos, Philip issued a series of demands to Sparta. What precisely they were is not known, but judging from his subsequent actions, they will have consisted of a series of demands for the adjustment of border disputes between Sparta and her Peloponnesian neighbors, Argos, Tegea, Megalopolis, and Messene.[88] Agis, king since the news of his father's death, seems to have met with Philip, but he refused to make any

---

[85] Paus. 4.28.5-6.

[86] Demosthenes and Callias were partially successful in 342 in bringing over a number of states into alliance against Philip, and these included Messene, Megalopolis, and Argos. Archidamus may thus have judged the time ripe to attempt to renew his efforts through the recruitment of a mercenary army, which would require the funds he hoped to earn in south Italy. For the diplomacy, see Dem. 9.72; Aeschin. 3.95ff; *IG* II² 225; schol. Aeschin. 3.83 and Dem. 18.64.

[87] See E. Badian, "Agis III," *Hermes* 95 (1967) 171-72.

[88] For recent discussion of this topic, see Ellis, *PMI* 203-204, and Cawkwell (supra n. 47) 168-69. The evidence is late and rather muddled in precise details: Plut. *Mor.* 216A, 218E, 233E, 235A; Stob. *Flor.* 7.59; Front. *Strat.* 4.5.12; Val. Max. 6.4.E4; Cic. *Tusc. Disp.* 5.14.42. C. Roebuck, "The Settlements of Philip II in 338 B.C.," *CP* 43 (1948) 73-92 provides a detailed discussion at 210-15 which is of great value, particularly in assessing the merit of the sources.

territorial concessions.[89] As a result, Philip marched to Laconia with his Peloponnesian allies, including Elis as well as the states named above, and ravaged Sparta's territory. Sparta itself was not taken, although Philip could undoubtedly have done so, and crushed the state forever.[90] In the aftermath of his invasion, Philip then proceeded to settle the claims of his allies by stripping from Sparta disputed districts along her borders with Argos (Thyreatis), Tegea, (Scyritis) Megalopolis (Belemina), and Messene (Denthalis).[91] He may have sanctioned the redistricting by a special court appointed "from all the Greeks" and, if so, this may have been a function of the new League of Corinth.[92] Whatever the pretended legal basis, however, the new territorial adjustments seem to have been remarkably long-lived, enduring down into Roman times.[93] The Spartans, we may suppose, were neither happy with the settlement, nor present among "all the Greeks" who ratified it, since they alone of the Greeks refused to accept Philip's invitation to join the League of Corinth.[94] Thus they stood alone, in utter isolation, at the beginning of Agis' reign. Philip ignored them.

Philip's treatment of Sparta after Chaeroneia needs explanation, for it is puzzling at first glance. At a time when he was attempting to win over the Greeks to the settlement which he would propose in the League of Corinth, he apparently launched an unprovoked attack upon a neutral state which had scrupulously avoided confronting him militarily in the Athenian-Theban coalition. Furthermore, he seemingly rewarded those of his allies who had not joined with him at Chaeroneia, in supporting their territorial claims at Sparta's expense. Upon closer investigation, however, Philip's policy demonstrates his appreciation of the complexities of Greek interstate relations. In particular, if his real objective was to settle affairs in Greece not in order to rule it but to permit himself a safe point of departure for Asia,[95] then his settlement of the Peloponnesian question makes a great deal of sense. He had known for almost a

---

[89] Plut. *Mor.* 216B.
[90] Plut. Mor. 219F, 235B; Paus. 3.24.6, 5.4.9; Polyb. 9.28.6f.
[91] Paus. 2.38.5, cf. 2.20.1 and 7.11.1f; 8.35.4; Polyb. 9.28; Tac. *Ann.* 4.43.3.
[92] See the discussions in Ellis, *PMI* 204, and Cawkwell (supra n. 47) 169.
[93] Tac. *Ann.* 4.43.3.
[94] Plut. *Mor.* 240A; Justin 9.5.3.
[95] The suggestion of Ellis, *PMI* 92 and 205, which I accept.

decade that Sparta steadfastly refused to recognize Messene's independence and was opposed to Megalopolis' predominance in Arcadia. She had shown that she would never assent to these realities. Therefore, if concord within the Peloponnesus was impossible, Sparta's recalcitrant belligerence must be properly focused. By granting the disputed territories to her Peloponnesian enemies, Philip sought to achieve two objectives. First, he expected to gain the goodwill of those who benefited by the settlement. Secondly, he hoped to direct future Spartan aggression against these states, rather than against Macedon. There was nothing to be gained by destroying Sparta utterly, and much to be risked by such an act. Many Greeks admired the Spartan way of life and the Spartan achievement, even if they might not agree with specific Spartan policies. To have crushed Sparta militarily, enslaved the population, and destroyed her temples in a brutal display of superior force would have been counterproductive.[96] On the other hand, we need not necessarily see in this merely a Machiavellian maneuver to create a "bogeyman" to keep Philip's Peloponnesian allies in check.[97] An obdurate Sparta, stolidly refusing to join the new League of Corinth, gave some substance to Philip's claim that it was to be a voluntary organization.[98] Philip was attentive to propaganda, and he saw in his settlement of the Spartan-Peloponnesian question a means of making a good deal of political capital. The key to his policy had been furnished by Archidamus, as early as 351. The rebellion of Agis which culminated in the Battle of Megalopolis, eight years later, proved that Philip had miscalculated, but not seriously.[99] The assessment of Alexander, upon hearing the news of the battle, suggests that Sparta's importance had ended with the reign of Archidamus.[100]

San Diego State University

---

[96] One might compare the situation at the end of the Peloponnesian War, when Sparta made political capital of refusing to destroy Athens even though her allies pressed for this. See C. D. Hamilton, *Sparta's Bitter Victories* (Ithaca 1979) 47-48, 50-54 for discussion.

[97] For this suggestion, see Cawkwell (supra n. 47) 169.

[98] See Ellis *PMI* 298, n. 125.

[99] On Agis' rebellion against Macedonian control, see Badian (supra n. 87).

[100] Plut. *Ages.* 15.4: "It would seem, gentlemen, that while we have been conquering Darius here, over there in Arcardia there has been a battle of mice."

On the Final Aims of Philip II

E. A. FREDRICKSMEYER

Abstract

According to the traditional and prevailing view, the final aims of Philip II, in contrast to those of his son Alexander, were reasonable, cautious, and limited. There is some evidence to indicate, however, that they were in fact much more ambitious. This paper examines the evidence and concludes that there is a good possibility, which must not be discounted, that on the eve of his invasion of Asia Philip hoped to conquer and supersede the Great King, to establish in all parts of his greater empire, as far as possible, an absolute monarchy, and to secure, finally, his own deification. It is likely that deification was not merely an end in itself for Philip, for the sake of the glory of it, but that he hoped to establish a theocratic basis for his absolute monarchy, and to institutionalize this new kingship for his successors. If this is correct, Alexander in his policies and ambitions followed Philip's *paradeigma* more closely than has been hitherto acknowledged. It may well have been the apprehensions on the part of some Macedonian nobles over Philip's final ambitions which led to his assassination in the summer of 336 B.C.

Introduction. Philip was assassinated in July 336 B.C. on the eve of his invasion of the Persian Empire. Officially, as an assignment of the League of Corinth, the war was to be a crusade against the Persians for the injuries inflicted by them on the Greek gods and temples in their invasion of 480-79 B.C.[1] Beyond this, Philip harbored ambitions of his own. What were they?

In their assessment of Philip's final aims, historians have been

---

[1] Diod. 16.89.2; Polyb. 3.6.13. Cf. Arr. 2.14.4; 3.18.12; Polyb. 5.10.8.

influenced, consciously or unconsciously, by the contrast between Philip and his more dramatic son, Alexander. Alexander is seen as the youthful conquerer of titanic ambitions who won for himself new worlds and changed the course of history. Philip, however, is seen as prudent and cautious, and middle-aged, who pursued a purely national Macedonian policy, and whose final aims against Persia were limited to the annexation of Asia Minor or at most the conquest of the eastern Mediterranean seaboard, to secure his domain in Europe. This perception is given weight by the *auctoritas* of the leading historians in the field, and at present it remains virtually unchallenged. It may well be correct.[2] But it rests entirely on speculation and inference. There exists not a single piece of evidence which directly attributes these goals to Philip. On the other hand, there is some specific evidence to the effect that Philip's aims by the end of his life were considerably more ambitious. The case for this conclusion has occasionally been argued before, at least in part, but without securing acceptance.[3] It deserves further examination. *Audiatur et altera pars.*

The Background. First, let us consider whether in Philip's time, say around 338 B.C., a war of conquest against the Persian Empire was thought to have a realistic chance of success. The Empire was a heterogeneous entity comprised of many peoples, races, and traditions held together precariously by the dynasty of the Achaemenid kings, who laid claim to absolute dominion by grace of their supreme

---

[2] F. Schachermeyr is representative. He concedes that Philip's aims may have extended to Syria and Egypt. But: "Von grundsätzlicher Bedeutung [ist es] dass Philip über den somit umschriebenen Mittelmeerraum niemals hinausgegriffen hätte, dass ihm also der Radikalismus ferne lag, etwa das gesamte Perserreich zu gewinnen." *Alexander der Grosse* (Vienna 1973) 62. Cf. J. Kaerst, *Geschichte des Hellenismus* I³ (Leipzig and Berlin 1927) 272 ff.; Ed. Meyer, *Kleine Schriften* (Halle 1910) 245 f., 291, 293 f., 297; G. Radet, *Alexandre le Grand* (Paris 1931) 81; U. Wilcken, *Alexander the Great* (New York 1967; with notes and bibliography by E. Borza) 30; G. Wirth, "Dareios und Alexander," *Chiron* 1 (1971) 143 f.; Ellis, *PMI* 227 ff., 308 n. 72; Griffith, *Hist Mace* II 633 and 691. F. Geyer, *RE* 19 (1938) 2299, grants that he might have gone as far as the Euphrates.

[3] Most important, F. Hampl, *Die griechischen Staatsverträge des 4. Jahrhunderts* (Leipzig 1938) 89 ff. See also H. U. Instinsky, *Alexander der Grosse am Hellespont* (Bad Godesberg 1949) 39 f.; H. Berve, *Griechische Geschichte* II (Freiburg 1963) 244. Cf. V. Chapot, "Philippe II de Macedoine," in *Hommes d'etat* I, ed. A. B. Duff and F. Galy (Paris 1936) 102; P. Cloché, *Un fondateur d'empire. Philippe II roi de Macédoine* (Saint Etienne 1955) 278. However, note also the view of A. Momigliano, *Filippo il Macedone* (Florence 1934) 166: "Fino a che punto Filippo mirasse di portare la sua conquista dell' Asia nessuno naturalmente sa, e il primo a non saperlo era forse Filippo stesso."

On the Final Aims of Philip II

deity Ahuramazda, that is, by right of conquest. In the fourth century, the Empire was weakened by a series of rebellions and secessionist movements by subject peoples and ambitious satraps. A potential invader out to conquer the Great King could expect, to a considerable extent, mere token resistance or active cooperation, especially in the Western parts of the Empire. And the Persians were known to be militarily inferior to the Greeks. For decades now the Persian kings had succeeded in maintaining or restoring the territorial integrity of the Empire only with the help of Greek mercenaries, who provided the only effective infantry the Persians could muster. The Persians' strength lay in their cavalry, but at Chaeronea Philip proved the superiority not only of the Macedonian infantry over the Greek hoplites but also, by implication, of the Macedonian cavalry over their Persian counterparts.[4]

Moreover, there were on record several attempts, either planned or attempted, to conquer the Great King and seize his kingdom. In 401 B.C. the younger Cyrus with the help of Greek mercenaries invaded the interior of the Empire with the design of challenging the Great King for the throne of Asia. Cyrus was killed in the battle at Cunaxa near Babylon, but in this battle and in their subsequent retreat to the Black Sea the Greeks demonstrated their superiority over the Orientals.[5] Isocrates expressed the opinion (5.92) that if it had not been for Cyrus, the Greeks "would have overthrown the power of the King." In 396 B.C. the Spartan king Agesilaus undertook an offensive against the Persians in Asia Minor, and Isocrates claimed (4.144) that "he conquered almost all the territory this side of the Halys river." It was believed that Agesilaus' intention was to march into the interior in order to overthrow the Great King and destroy his Empire.[6] But difficulties in Greece forced him to abandon his plan and return home. Not long afterwards, Jason of Pherae conceived similar ambitions which were, however, brought to naught by his assassination in 370 B.C. It was thought that Jason hoped to make himself master of the Balkan peninsula, and then to invade and destroy the Persian Empire.[7] Xenophon quotes him as saying (*Hell.* 6.12):

---

[4] For a judicious assessment of the *Machtverhältnisse* at this time, see P. A. Brunt, Loeb *Arrian* I, LXIII-LXVIII, with refs.

[5] See, conveniently, H. Bengston, *Griechische Geschichte*[4] (Munich 1969) 262 ff., with refs.

[6] Xen. *Hell.* 4.4.41; *Ages.* 1.36; cf. 7.7; Plut. *Ages.* 15.

[7] Xen. *Hell.* 6.1.8-12; Isoc. 5.119.

E. A. Fredricksmeyer

It is even easier to reduce [the Great King] to subjection than to reduce Greece. For I know that everybody there, save one person, has trained himself to servitude rather than prowess, and I know what manner of force it was — both that which went up with Cyrus and that which went up with Agesilaus — that brought the King to extremities.[8]

In 346 B.C. Isocrates addressed an open letter to Philip in which he appealed to Jason in urging Philip to unite the Greeks and lead them in a war against the Persians (5.120):

Now since Jason by use of words alone advanced himself so far, what opinion must we expect the world will have of you if you actually do this thing; *above all, if you undertake to conquer,* [*helein*] *the whole empire of the King* or, at any rate, to wrest from it — to use a current phrase — "Asia from Cilicia to Sinope."

After detailing some of the advantages to be obtained for the Greeks from a conquest of Asia Minor (5.120-23), Isocrates continues (5.123): "If however you do not succeed in these objects [i.e., seizing the whole Empire or Asia Minor], this much you will at any rate easily accomplish, — the liberation of the cities which are on the coast of Asia."

On the eve of Philip's invasion, by mid-summer of 336 B.C., this last-stated minimum goal had already been largely achieved, in Philip's sense, by his advance force under Parmenio and Attalus. He would not have launched, with the greatest possible fanfare, the main invasion of Asia only to put the finishing touches to these operations conducted by his subordinates. As for the other two objectives, Isocrates presents the first one, the conquest of the Persian Empire, as the most desirable. But he quickly proceeds to a discussion of the second one, the seizure of Asia Minor, not, as has been thought, because he considered the conquest of the Empire unrealistic, but because he considered the seizure of Asia Minor more profitable for the Greeks. Isocrates thought consistently in terms of Greek, specifically Athenian, interests, and understandably so.[9] At the same

---

[8] This and the following translations from the Greek are from the Loeb editions, with minor changes.

[9] U. Wilcken, *Philip II. von Makedonien und die panhellenische Idee* (Sitzungsberichte der Preussischen Akademie der Wissenschaften. Berlin 1929) 296 f. See also S. Perlman, "Isocrates' 'Philippus' — a Reinterpretation," *Historia* 6 (1957) 317, and G. Dobesch, *Der panhellenische Gedanke im 4. Jr. v. Chr. und der "Philippos" des Isokrates* (Österreichisches Archäologisches Institut. Vienna 1968) 144 ff.

time, he hoped to be taken seriously as a counselor of practical policy. We may be reasonably sure that Isocrates considered the conquest of the Persian Empire as feasible, or at least that he expected Philip and a large part of the audience to consider it feasible.[10]

Two years later, in 344 B.C., Isocrates wrote again to Philip. After rebuking him for taking unnecessary risks in battles with barbarians (Illyrians), he says (*Ep.* 2.11):

> As to the barbarians with whom you are now waging war, it will suffice you to gain the mastery over them only so far as to secure the safety of your own territory, *but the king who is now called Great you will attempt to overthrow [kataluein].*[11]

In 338 B.C., after Philip's victory at Chaeronea, Isocrates once again called on Philip to lead the Greeks against the barbarians and to compel them, except for those who would fight on his side, to be subject to the Greeks. And he adds (*Ep.* 3.5): "And to accomplish this from your present status is much easier for you than it was for you to advance to the power and renown you now possess from the kingship which you had in the beginning."[12]

In the fall of 338 B.C. Philip formalized his domination of Greece achieved at Chaeronea by the establishment of the League of Corinth and then placed before it the proposal of a panhellenic crusade against Persia. Those of the Greeks who would have opposed the plan were in no position to do so, and Philip was elected for the purpose *strategos autokrator,* generalissimo with full powers (Diod. 16.89.2-3).

---

[10] See also Isoc. 5.124-26, 132, 139, 141. Cf. M. Markle, "Support of Athenian Intellectuals for Philip: A Study of Isocrates' *Philippus* and Speusippus' *Letter to Philip,*" *JHS* 96 (1976) 86: "Isocrates understood that, if he was to win the favor of Philip by his pamphlet, he must not be taken for a dreamy intellectual who, though unaware of the means for carrying out his proposal, presumed to advise the world's most successful military leader." Already around 380 B.C., in the *Panegyricus,* Isocrates said (4.166): "Whenever we [i.e., the Greeks] transport thither [to Asia] a force stronger than his [the Great King's], which we can easily do if we so will, we shall enjoy in security the resources of all Asia. Moreover, it is much more glorious to fight against the King for his empire than to contend against each other for the hegemony." And in the same speech (4.131) he noted, as well, that it lay in the power of the Lacedaemonians, in cooperation with the Athenians, "to reduce *all* barbarians to a state of subjection to the whole of Hellas." See also 4.154, 186, and G. A. Lehmann, "Die Hellenika von Oxyrhynchos und Isokrates' 'Philippos'," *Historia* 21 (1972) 393. Some allowance, of course, must be made for rhetorical exaggeration in Isocrates.

[11] For the date of the letter, see Markle (supra n.10) 88 n. 15.

[12] On the authenticity of the letter, see Markle (supra n. 10) 89 n. 21.

E. A. Fredricksmeyer

The historian Polybius clearly perceives, however, that Philip's motive was not a desire to punish the Persians for the greater glory of the Greeks, but personal opportunism and the desire for conquest and glory. After stating that Philip was encouraged by the successes of the Ten Thousand and of Agesilaus, Polybius says (3.6.12-13) that Philip

> perceived and reckoned on the cowardice and indolence of the Persians compared with the military efficiency of himself and his Macedonians, and further fixing his eyes on the splendor of the great prizes which the war promised, he lost no time, once he had secured the good will of the Greeks, but seizing on the pretext that it was his urgent duty to take vengeance on the Persians for the injurious treatment of the Greeks, he bestirred himself and decided to go to war, beginning to make every preparation for the purpose.[13]

The Conquest of the Persian Empire. In the spring of 336 B.C. Philip, according to Diodorus (16.91.2-3), "wanting to enter upon the war with the gods' approval, asked the Pythia *whether he would conquer [kratēsei] the king of the Persians.* She gave him this response: 'The bull stands wreathed. The end is near. The one who will smite him stands ready.' Since the response was ambiguous, Philip accepted it in a sense favorable to himself, namely *that the Persian would be slaughtered like a sacrificial victim.*"[14] After noting that in the end the oracle foretold Philip's own death, Diodorus says (16.91.4):

> In any case, he thought that the gods supported him and he was

---

[13] Cf. J. G. Droysen, *Geschichte des Hellenismus* I (Berlin 1877) 50: "[Dareios] mochte ahnen, wie sein ungeheures Reich, in sich zerrüttet und abgestorben, nur eines äusseren Anstosses bedürfe, um zusammensubrechen."

[14] Diodorus' sources in the latter part of book 16 remain very much in doubt. See esp. Griffith *Hist Macc* II 459; C. B. Welles, *Diodorus of Sicily* VIII (LCL) 4 f.; N. G. L. Hammond, "The Sources of Diodorus Siculus XVI," *CQ* 31 (1937) 79 ff.; M. Sordi, *Diodori Siculi Bibliothecae Liber XVI* (Florence 1969) XII ff. The information must be taken on its merits. Most historians regard it as historical.
The oracle is cited in identical form by Paus. 8.7.6. H. D. Parke and D. E. W. Wormell consider it authentic: *The Delphic Oracle* (Oxford 1956) I 238; II, no. 266. J. Fontenrose considers it spurious: *The Delphic Oracle* (Berkeley 1978) 67. But it is to be noted that Fontenrose's whole approach in this book seems excessively sceptical and rationalistic. However, if the oracle as quoted is not authentic, but the remainder of Diororus' account is substantially accurate, we should suppose that Philip doctored it for his own end.

On the Final Aims of Philip II

very happy *that Asia would be made captive [aichmalōtou] under the hands of the Macedonians.*[15]

Diodorus continues (16.91.4-92.3) that Philip thereupon made plans for a great festival and splended sacrifices to the gods. When the occasion arrived, at a state banquet the famous actor Neoptolemus recited several poems which had been commissioned by Philip on the subject of the impending war. In one of them he addressed the great wealth of the Persian king, suggesting that "it could some day be overturned by fortune," and predicting the death of the Great King. After remarking that the remainder of the poem went on in the same vein, Diodorus continues (16.92.4):

> Philip was enchanted with the message and was completely *occupied with the thought of the overthrow [katastrophēn] of the Persian king, for he remembered the Pythian oracle which bore the same meaning as the words quoted by the tragic actor.*

We have seen that Philip took the oracle to mean *that Asia would be made subject (aichmalōtou) to the Macedonians.* Thus the statement that Philip expected the *overthrow (katastrophēn)* of the Persian king appears to mean not that he expected to win some battles and seize some territory but that he expected to take his kingdom from him.

Two years later, Alexander crossed the Hellespont to start the war which Philip had planned. Diodorus, apparently on the authority of Clitarchus, says (17.17.2) that he

> hurled his spear from the ship and fixed it on the ground and then leapt ashore himself the first of the Macedonians, signifying *that he received Asia from the gods as his spear-won [doriktēton] property.*[16]

Two years after this, at Marathus, in northern Syria, Alexander wrote a letter to Darius in which, according to Arrian (2.14.7-9), he called himself *Lord of all Asia* and *King of Asia*, and claimed that *he held the country by gift of the gods.*[17] Although Alexander was painstakingly

---

[15] "Asia" at this time usually was synonymous with the Persian Empire. See, e.g., P. A. Brunt, "The Aims of Alexander," *G&R* 12 (1965) 208. Sometimes, however, as used by Greek writers, it connotes only "Asia Minor." But in light of Diodorus' statement a little further on (16.92.4) that Philip expected the "overthrow" (*katastrophēn*) of the Persian King, it more probably here means "the Persian Empire."

[16] Cf. Just. 11.5.10. See W. Schmitthenner, "Über eine Formveränderung der Monarchie seit Alexander dem Grossen," *Saeculum* 19 (1968) 31 ff.; E. Badian, "Alexander the Great, 1948-67," *CW* 65 (1971) 83.

[17] On the letter, no doubt authentic, see esp. Schachermeyr (supra n. 2) 222 ff., and

scrupulous in his dealings with the gods, he apparently did not seek an oracle before the start of the invasion.[18] Why not? And how could he nevertheless both at the Hellespont and again now claim Asia as gift of the gods? At the Hellespont, Alexander claimed to receive Asia from the gods as *doriktētos*, while Philip had interpreted his oracle for the war as signifying that Asia would be *aichmalōtos* under Macedonia. The two words mean virtually the same thing. The conclusion is justified that just as Alexander inherited from Philip the project of the war and its official slogan, so he also applied to himself the oracle which Philip had received for the war, and Philip's interpretation of it, to wit, that he would conquer the Persian Empire.[19]

Absolute Monarchy. How would Philip rule over his vast new domain? It was reasonably apparent that it could not be administered easily, if at all, as an appendage of Macedonia. The most feasible, possibly the only, arrangement would be the one which also Alexander aspired to from the beginning, that is, to become the new king of Asia.[20] There is evidence that this is indeed what Philip had in mind. We learn from a fragment of Philodemus (*Rh.* II, 61 ed. S. Sudhaus) that Aristotle

> tried to warn Philip against the [Achaemenid] kingship and the Persian succession (ἐ[κ] βασιλείας παρεκάλει [Φ]ίλιππο[ν] τότ[ε] καὶ τῆς Περσικῆς διαδ[ο]χῆς).

This information not only corroborates the belief that Philip aimed to conquer the Persian Empire, but it also indicates that he meant to supersede the Great King, for otherwise there would have been no point for Aristotle to advise against it.

Why would Aristotle advise against it? The Persian kingship, as virtually all rule in the Orient, meant absolute rule. The Orientals knew no other, and any limited rule, even if considered desirable on

---

A. B. Bosworth, *A Historical Commentary on Arrian's History of Alexander* I (Oxford 1980) 232.

[18] See Parke-Wormell (supra n. 14) I, 240 and 242; II, 110; J. R. Hamilton, *Plutarch. Alexander. A Commentary* (Oxford 1969) 34 f.

[19] Cf. Instinsky (supra n. 3) 29 ff., Hampl (supra n. 3) 92 ff.; P. A. Brunt (supra n. 15). The oracle was reinforced for Alexander at Gordium and perhaps also at Siwah. See E. A. Fredricksmeyer, "Alexander, Midas, and the Oracle at Gordium," *CP* 56 (1961) 160 ff.

[20] With respect to Alexander, see, e.g., H. Berve, "Die Verschmelzungspolitik Alexanders des Grossen," *Klio* 31 (1938) 145, and J. B. Bury, *A History of Greece* (London 1900) 747.

some theoretical ground, was not practically feasible. The whole Persian Imperial system, from the court ritual to the dynastic religion and art, served above all the enhancement and glorification of the power and majesty of the Great King.[21] Even though Philip probably did not intend to adopt in detail the Persian Imperial system, it was yet clear that his Asiatic kingship would necessarily mean an absolute monarchy over the Asiatics. And it was predictable that this situation would also affect Philip's relationship with the Macedonians and Greeks in Asia, and eventually also his role as king of Macedonia and as Hegemon of the League. No doubt it was the fear that Philip's Achaemenid succession would have a harmful effect on Greece, in particular that his preponderant power as king of (or over) Asia would eventually reduce the Greeks to the status of mere subjects, that moved Isocrates in his address to Philip to propose only *en passant* the seizure of the whole Empire, and that likewise moved Aristotle, like Isocrates a fervent Hellenist, to advise Philip against the Persian kingship. Similarly Aristotle later urged Alexander, perhaps after the latter's proclamation as King of Asia in Oct. 331 B.C. (Plut. *Alex.* 34.1), to treat "the barbarians as a despot [*despotikōs*] but the Greeks as a leader [*hēgemonikōs*]" (Plut. *Mor.* 329 B).[22] And in 327 B.C. Aristotle's nephew, Callisthenes, forfeited his life by opposing Alexander's design to apply his Oriental kingship to the Greeks.[23]

The desire for power was Philip's driving motivation from the beginning of his career, as the record shows, both in his expansionist foreign policy and in his self-aggrandizement at home. Beyond this, it has been shown recently, with some probability, that in the development of his court system and the organization of his kingship, Philip followed to a considerable extent Persian models. In particular the institutions of the court aristocracy recruited in part from foreigners, the Royal Pages, the Hypaspists, the initiation of a harem for political ends, all seem to have been patterned more or less closely on their Persian counterparts.[24] Evidently Philip here followed a carefully designed program. It has been said that in the development

---

[21] See H. H. von der Osten, *Die Welt der Perser* (Stuttgart 1956) 59 ff.; R. Frye, "The Institutions," in *Beiträge zur Achämenidengeschichte*, ed. G. Walser, Historia Einzelschrift 18 (Wiesbaden 1972) 83 ff.

[22] E. Badian, "Alexander the Great and the Unity of Mankind," *Historia* 7 (1958) 440-44, dates the advice nearer to Alexander's accession in 336 B.C.

[23] See esp. Schachermeyr (supra n. 2) 370 ff.

[24] D. Kienast, *Philip II. von Makedonien und das Reich der Achämeniden* (Munich 1973). For the Persian models, see Frye (supra n. 21).

of his own supra-national kingdom there was no other model at hand.[25] True. But just as the very soul of the Persian system was the principle of the absolute sovereignty of the Great King, so Philip in imitating this system no doubt also hoped to increase, as much as possible, his own power over the Macedonians. It seems reasonable to conclude that Philip's aim may well have been, after the conquest of the Persian king, to establish an absolute monarchy, as far as possible, in all parts of his empire.

Deification. Beyond this, there is evidence that Philip aspired to the supreme honors. *A priori*, his divine descent from Zeus and Heracles, in addition to his royal rank, placed him in a position of superiority over most mortals.[26] And it appears that, beginning with 359 B.C., several Greek cities accorded Philip divine or near-divine honors as benefactor or savior.[27] Moreover, after Chaeronea Philip commissioned the construction at Olympia of a temple that was to house, apparently, a dynastic cult for himself and his family (Paus. 5.20.9-10; cf. 5.17.4).[28] The edifice was completed around the time of Philip's assassination.

On the morning of the assassination, Philip staged a parade into the theatre crowded with people from everywhere. His own entry was preceded in solemn procession by the statues of the Twelve Gods. And accompanying them was Philip's own statue. Diodorus says (16.92.5):

> Along with lavish display of every sort, Philip included in the procession statues of the Twelve Gods wrought with great artistry and adorned with a dazzling show of wealth to strike awe in the beholder, and along with these was conducted a thirteenth statue, suitable for a god, that of Philip himself, so that the king exhibited himself enthroned among the Twelve Gods.

As Philip himself reached the entrance, the assassin struck. Diodorus relates the deed and then comments (16.95.1):

> Such was the end of Philip, who had made himself the greatest of the kings in Europe in his time and because of the greatness of his

---

[25] Kienast (supra n. 24) 33.

[26] Hdt. 8.137; Thuc. 2.99; Isoc. 5.105, 127.

[27] See Fredricksmeyer, "Divine Honors for Philip II," *TAPA* 109 (1979) 39-61; C. Habicht, *Gottmenschentum und griechische Städte*² (Munich 1970) 12-16 and 245.

[28] See Fredricksmeyer (supra n. 27) 52-56. For a different interpretation, see Griffith *Hist Mace* II 691 ff.

kingdom had made himself a throned companion of the Twelve Gods.

This information may be taken to mean that through the exhibition of his statue in the procession Philip indicated to the audience that he deserved divine honors, that he deserved them on par, and perhaps in conjunction, with the Twelve Gods, and that he deserved them by virtue of his power as king.[29] Apparently there were those in the audience who were willing to grant these honors on the spot. According to a report preserved by the Macedonian compiler and polymath Ioannes Stobaeus (4.34.70 p. 846 ed. Wachsmuth-Hense) the tragic actor Neoptolemus, the same who on the preceding day had recited the portentous poetry, was an eye-witness and later commented that he had seen Philip "taking part in the procession and *being invoked (epiklēthenta) as the thirteenth god.*" There is no reason to doubt the historicity of this information. It provides corroboration for the report of Diodorus.

We may be quite certain that at the end of the procession, in the theatre, sacrifices were planned to the Twelve Gods, and the presence of Philip's statue with theirs in the procession on an equal level must have caused many in the audience to expect that Philip too was to receive a sacrifice. Yet it is difficult to believe that this was really Philip's plan. On this occasion, on the eve of the panhellenic war against Persia, it was important for Philip to court popular good will. His deification, or self-deification, now would surely have provoked as much resentment as approval. It is reasonable to postulate, therefore, that Philip's intention was, after first raising the expectation of his deification, then conspicuously to refrain from it, to demur. Thus he would impress the people with his restraint yet also serve notice, or at any rate suggest, that he deserved the honors and that they might be granted at some time in the future.

At what time? Most modern historians appear to think that the occasion for the procession was the wedding celebration of Philip's daughter and Alexander of Epirus.[30] This is not quite correct. The wedding celebration seems to have been concluded on the previous day. At any rate, certainly the main occasion for this day's activities was the celebration of the imminent invasion of Asia and of the

---

[29] Fredricksmeyer (supra n. 27) 56-58. Contra Griffith *Hist Macc* II 682 f. and 695.

[30] A Schäfer, *Demosthenes und seine Zeit* III (Leipzig 1887) 67, and Ellis *PMI* 223 have it right.

oracle's prediction for it (Diod. 16.91.4).[31] If then at the very celebration of the projected conquest of Persia Philip served notice that he deserved divine honors, but abstained from them at this time, despite the eagerness of some of his partisans, the suggestion was clear that he hoped to obtain them at the time when he would have achieved his goal. Philip commissioned his temple at Olympia on the eve of his proposal to invade Persia, and it was completed, as has been noted, around the time of his assassination. But here too it is difficult to believe that Philip intended to initiate a cult at this time. There certainly is no evidence for it. It is probable therefore that both at Olympia and at Aegae Philip intended the same effect, to serve notice that he expected divine honors after his conquest of the Persian king.

In this light, a statement which Isocrates made in his last address to Philip assumes added significance (*Ep.* 3.5):

> Be assured that a glory unsurpassable and worthy of the deeds you have done in the past will be yours when you shall compel the barbarians — all but those who have fought on your side — to be serfs to the Greeks, and when you shall force the king who is now called Great to do whatever you command. *For then will naught be left for you except to become a god [theon genesthai].*

If Philip had already previously received divine honors in several places, including Athens, it is highly probable that Isocrates meant the statement literally, and that he expected others, and Philip himself, to take it literally. We may have here, then, Isocrates recommending *expressis verbis* what Philip himself at Olympia and Aegae only suggested, namely, deification after the conquest of the Great King.

For what purpose? The cult at Olympia, if instituted, would be a dynastic cult. The suggestion at Aegae was that Philip deserved a cult as king, by virtue of his great power. If, as noted, Philip had already received cults in several individual locales, including Athens, Isocrates' statement that after conquering the Great King Philip "become a god," without limiting qualification, amounted to the suggestion that he receive a universal cult, as ruler of his empire.[32]

---

[31] I assume therefore that the invasion was to start very soon afterwards, that is, in the late summer or fall of 336 B.C. Philip probably intended to use the bases secured by Parmenio as winter quarters and from there start his main push down the coast and inland in the spring of 335 B.C.

[32] Isocrates did not think of Greece as a potential part of Philip's empire. He

On the Final Aims of Philip II

This might have been its own end, for the glory of it. But perhaps Philip, forever the pragmatist and politician, wanted more. As for his association with the Twelve at Aegae, it is noteworthy that their cult consituted, or was part of, the state cult at Athens and probably most, or all, other Greek cities, as well as in Macedonia.[33] At Athens, the oaths taken by these gods were officially binding on the city.[34] The same may have held true of other cities. It is quite possible therefore that by association with the cult of the Twelve, perhaps as *Theos Triskaidekatos*, Philip hoped to be acknowledged as an official deity in the Greek communities and even in Macedonia, and thus to acquire there a supralegal and constitutional status.[35] In 324 B.C. Alexander requested divine honors from the Greek cities,[36] and it is reported in the case of Athens that a cult was proposed for him as *Theos Triskaidekatos* (Ael. *VH* 5.12). The same might have happened elsewhere. Those who made the proposal no doubt knew what Alexander wanted. And Alexander had been present at Philip's procession with the Twelve at Aegae. It is therefore quite likely that Philip on that day at Aegae provided the model for Alexander's design twelve years later.

As for Persia, the Great King did not receive divine honors, but he was nevertheless considered to be of divine descent, to be possessed of a divine quality, and to hold an intermediate position between god and man.[37] In view of this fact, and of Herodotus' statement (1.135) that there was "no nation which so readily adopts foreign ways as the Persians," it would not seem difficult for Philip to introduce his deification in Asia. In 327 B.C. Alexander attempted to introduce

---

considered a monarchical system indispensible for all others, but contrary to the spirit of the Greeks (5.107,154). Cf. Perlman (supra n. 9) 310 ff.; K. Bringmann, *Studien zu den politischen Ideen des Isokrates, Hypomnemata* 14, Göttingen 1965) 99 ff. But there were those who welcomed the possibility of Philip's monarchy over Greece. See K. von Fritz, "Die politische Tendenz in Theopomps Geschichtsschreibung," *A&A* 4 (1954) 56 f. Cf. also Markle (supra n. 10) 87 ff.

[33] O. Weinreich, in Roscher's *Ausführliches Lexikon der griechischen und lateinischen Mythologie* IV (1924-27) 764 ff.; U. von Wilamowitz-Moellendorff, *Der Glaube der Hellenen* II (Berlin 1932) 351 n. 1; Berve, *Alex* I 87; K. Atkinson, "Demosthenes, Alexander, and Asebeia," *Athenaeum* 51 (1973) 313 ff.

[34] Atkinson (supra n. 33) 331 f.

[35] *Ibid.* 330.

[36] E. A. Fredricksmeyer, "Three Notes on Alexander's Deification," *AJAH* 4 (1979) 1 ff.

[37] G. Widengren, "The Sacral Kingship of Iran," *Numen*, Supplement 4 (Leiden 1959) 242-57. Cf. R. Frye, *The Heritage of Persia* (London 1962) 95 f.; *id., Persia* (New York 1969) 23.

among *all* his subjects, Greeks and Macedonians as well as Asiatics, the Persian *proskynesis*, obeisance.[38] To the Persians, *proskynesis* to the Great King did not mean worship but it nevertheless acknowledged his status as semi-divine.[39] To the Greeks and Macedonians, *proskynesis* meant worship.[40] It has been argued, perhaps correctly, that Alexander on this occasion attempted to introduce his cult as god of his empire.[41] If this is correct, and if this was also Alexander's final aim in 324 B.C., we may see here again the influence of Philip.

Conclusion. The possibility should not be discounted that in 336 B.C. Philip hoped, *deis volentibus*, to conquer and supersede the Great King, to establish in all parts of his greater empire, as far as possible, an absolute monarchy, and to secure, finally, his deification as ruler, to the end of providing a theoretical support for absolute monarchy. As things turned out, it was Alexander who conquered the Persian Empire, and he did so in less than ten years. In 336 B.C. Philip may have expected, with longevity apparently running in the family, to live another twenty or even thirty years. If we remember that Cyrus the Great undertook the conquest of his, the Persian, empire from a power-base quite inferior to Philip's at this time, a fact which Philip no doubt appreciated, and that Antigonus Monophthalmus not many years later set out, at age 63, to make himself master of Alexander's empire, it is not difficult to believe that at age 46 Philip harbored comparable ambitions. It may have been the apprehensions on the part of some Macedonian nobles over Philip's final aims that led to his assassination on that fateful day at Aegae in 336 B.C.[42]

University of Colorado

---

[38] Arr. 4.10.5 ff.; Curt. 8.5.5. ff.; Plut. *Alex.* 54.3 ff.

[39] Widengren (supra n. 37)

[40] E. Badian (supra n. 16) 43; W. W. Tarn, *Alexander the Great* II (Cambridge 1950) 360.

[41] Meyer (supra n. 2) 314 ff.; Tarn (supra n. 40) 359 ff. Cf. L. Edmunds, "The Religiosity of Alexander," *GRBS* 12 (1971) 386 f.

[42] I wish to thank my colleagues for valuable criticisms and observations on an earlier version of this paper read at the Alexander Symposium at the Art Institute of Chicago on June 5, 1981, and Professor Erich Gruen, as well as the editors, for carefully reading the manuscript, as a result of which the paper has been further improved. Any remaining faults are entirely my own responsibility. Finally, I wish to take this opportunity to express my appreciation to my brother-in-law, John English, M.D., for the pleasure of many stimulating conversations over the years on Philip and Alexander.

Eurydice

E. BADIAN

Abstract
There is no justification for the view, recently advanced, that "Eurydice" became a throne name for Argead queens. Arrian's use of the name for Philip II's last wife Cleopatra must, as Tarn suggested, be a mere error.

It is well known to specialists in the history of Alexander the Great that Philip II's last wife Cleopatra (as we know her from the rest of the tradition) is, on one and only one occasion (Arr. 3.6.5), referred to *obiter* as Eurydice. The point as such is of so little *prima facie* interest that most scholars working on Philip II or Alexander, though aware of it, have not bothered to discuss it.[1] Some older scholars followed Berve in accepting (without argument) R. Schneider's suggestion that the lady changed her original name of Eurydice to Cleopatra on marrying Philip. This lacks even the technical merit of reconciling the sources and, but for Berve's authority, would surely have been deservedly forgotten. Tarn, again without argument, suggested that it was simply an error: one of numerous instances in authors of all periods (and examples among modern scholars could easily be added) of the purely accidental and (at times) psychologically explicable confusion of one well-known name with another, which should simply be recognized for what it is and ignored.[2]

Recently a more interesting suggestion has emerged, perhaps independently in several places, but most carefully argued and

---

[1] E.g., Ellis, *PMI*; Griffith in *Hist Mace* II.

[2] W. W. Tarn, *Alexander the Great* (Cambridge 1948) II 262 n. 1 — noted by Heckel (cit. next note) 156 n. 6.

supported by a specialist in Alexander prosopography, W. Heckel.[3] Heckel took up a suggestion by Grace Macurdy[4] that "the name Eurydice . . . had a tendency to become dynastic like the name Cleopatra in Egypt." The confusion between dynastic names (like Arsaces or Ptolemy) and throne names that this shows is not worth discussing here: the two phenomena certainly merge into each other, and both are due to the desire to impress the image of continuity and (in some sense) legitimacy upon the minds of the subjects. Macurdy, oddly enough, does not seem to have applied her idea to Philip II's wife; but Heckel's attempt to do so imparts a certain interest to the whole question, and it certainly calls for careful examination.

The first and (I think) only securely attested instance of throne names in Macedon is found in the cases of Alexander the Great's immediate successors: Arrhidaeus, who assumed the name of Philip (III), and his wife Adea, who assumed the name Eurydice.[5] The psychological reasons behind these changes are obvious enough. The "election" of Alexander's mentally impaired brother to succeed him had been fiercely contested at Babylon, and he was badly in need of an image of legitimacy. Now, the name "Arrhidaeus" was indeed a good Argead name, found more than once before.[6] But no Arrhidaeus had ever sat on the Argead throne. Arrhidaeus owed his election to the fact that he was a son of Philip II, and the whole debate, as reported by our main source (Curtius in Book 10), shows that the opposition of the army was not to the rule of a possible future son of Alexander the Great, but to the very present proposal of putting Perdiccas in a position where he might, especially if no son were born to Alexander, assume the diadem himself. Moreover, his mother, of course, had not been a Macedonian, but the Thessalian

---

[3] W. Heckel, "Cleopatra or Eurydice?" *Phoenix* 32 (1978) 155-58. See also A. B. Bosworth, *A Historical Commentary on Arrian's History of Alexander* (Oxford 1980) 282 f., written without knowledge of Heckel. Bosworth takes the idea to an extreme that Heckel would clearly not contemplate: " . . . it seems that Eurydice was the established name for a Macedonian queen."

[4] G. Macurdy, *Hellenistic Queens* (Baltimore 1932) 25.

[5] Respectively Arr. *Succ.* (*FGrH* 156) F1.1; Diod. 18.2.4; and Arr. *ibid.* F9.23. I must, incidentally, put in a plea, as against (e.g.) Heckel and Bosworth, that Arrian's *Successors* should be cited from Jacoby's collection of the fragments, where the facts as to the tradition can at least be readily seen. Citation as though from a surviving work only obscures them (cf. infra n. 18).

[6] See O. Hoffmann, *Die Makedonen* (Göttingen 1906) 34 ff.

Philinna;[7] so the claim to royal blood, which had secured him election, needed all the emphasis it could get.

As for his wife Adea, she was, just like him, of royal Argead blood on her father's side, but of rather inferior descent on her mother's. Her father was Amyntas son of Perdiccas, whom Philip II had superseded as king, but allowed to live and, towards the end of his own life, married to Cynnane, Philip's own daughter by an Illyrian wife. This would make their offspring three quarters Argead, and well placed in any future struggle for the succession.[8] The offspring turned out to be female and was allowed to live, when Amyntas himself was eliminated by Alexander at some time before the beginning of his Asian campaign. Her name was almost certainly not Macedonian or Greek — perhaps Illyrian, like her mother's; and even if Greek, as has been authoritatively claimed, by no means fit for a queen. She too needed a new name: and what better than that of Philip II's mother, the most recent non-controversial Macedonian queen no longer alive? Whether the choice of name was also intended to convey the new queen's intention to play an active part in policy and politics, as Philip's mother had done, we cannot even guess.[9]

A further suggestion is perhaps worth making: the return to the well-established names of Philip II and his mother might also have the desirable effect of invoking the time before Alexander's eastern campaigns with all their consequences — most of which, by now, the Macedonian soldiers disliked. A suggestion of a return to old Macedonian ways would surely be welcome.

No far-fetched explanation, no precedent, need be invoked, it is clear, to explain the throne names adopted by Philip III and his wife. If a precedent were needed, to suggest the idea in the first place (however obvious the need for its application), we must at least consider the Persian precedents that would by now be familiar. As far as we can see, no Great King, since the ill-omened Xerxes, had borne

---

[7] See Berve, *Alex* II, no. 781 *init*.

[8] See Berve, *Alex* II, nos. 23, 61, 456. On the possible (but not demonstrable) political importance of this marriage, see further below. Whether Philip was originally regent for Amyntas is irrelevant.

[9] For ᾿Αδέα (as in the *codices*) rewritten ῾Αδέα see Hoffmann (supra n. 6) 216: he thus identifies it with the Attic ῾Ηδέα = ῾Ηδεία and can claim it as good Greek. I am not easily convinced that a Macedonian princess would be given a name we can most closely render as "Honey." On Philip II's mother and her part in politics, see (whatever it may be worth in detail) Justin 7.4.7-5, *fin*. Adea-Eurydice certainly lost no time in making her active interest in politics clear.

any name other than (to use the familiar Greek forms) Artaxerxes or Darius. Indeed, Diodorus reports a Persian law, supposedly passed after the death of Artaxerxes II, that imposed the name of Artaxerxes on all his successors (15.93.1). If there ever was such a "law," it was certainly not totally observed. But it is worth noting that, when Bessus proclaimed himself King after killing Darius III, he indeed called himself Artaxerxes (Arr. 3.25.3), and it has recently been suggested that Arses, about whose royal style we have no certain information, may have done likewise.[10] Moreover, it is clear from Babylonian documents that various Persian kings did adopt a royal name which was not their original name.[11] Although we know of no such precedent for queens,[12] that of kings might have sufficed for Philip, and his then for Eurydice.

The only attested changes of name on accession to the Argead throne — those of Philip III and Eurydice — can therefore be seen to be sufficiently motivated by the special conditions in which they took place, and the idea of such a change, if explanation be needed, can be explained without any Argead precedent whatsoever.

This argument, of course, does not aim at *disproving* the existence of such Argead precedents; merely to show that they are not to be hypothesized on the basis of the only attested pair — whether as required precedents or as themselves somehow supported by these later parallels. This at least clears the ground for an examination of the name changes that have been suggested for the earlier history of the dynasty, and above all of the alleged use of "Eurydice" as a throne name.

It is perhaps worth pointing out that in the case of Argead *kings*, in whom our sources are inevitably more interested and on whom we, on the whole, have ample information, so such allegations have been

[10] See my note in K. H. Kinzl (ed.), *Greece and the Ancient Mediterranean in History and Prehistory* (Berlin and New York 1977) 40 ff. On "Xerxes II" (who ruled, if at all, only a few months and about whose intentions with regard to his name we know nothing) see W. Hinz, *s.v.* "Xerxes" (2), *RE* 9A (1967) 2101.

[11] See A. Sachs, "Achaemenid Royal Names in Babylonian Astronomical Texts," *AJAH* 2 (1977) 129 ff. Note Artaxerxes I (131), Darius II (*ibid.*), Artaxerxes II (133-39), Artaxerxes III (139-43), Darius III (143). The names we find in the Babylonian records are all represented in the Greek, though the reasons for the equivalents chosen are not always explicable.

[12] I cannot accept F. Schachermeyr's suggestion (*Alexander in Babylon* [Vienna 1970] 22) that Barsine, Alexander's royal wife, renamed herself Stateira. No instance to parallel such a change is known, while instances of errors over names in Arrian are indeed known and well attested (see Heckel [supra n. 3] 155 f.).

made. Macedonian kings are generally agreed to have been content with their own names, down to and including Alexander the Great. For queens, of course, the evidence is often thin and unreliable, especially if their sons did not in the end succeed to the throne. No one, apart from Satyrus, was much interested in the various ladies whom Philip II is said to have married *kata polemon*.[13] In fact, Olympias seems to be the first Macedonian queen who did arouse more general interest.

But let us start with Philip II's mother Eurydice. She is called by late (but probably good) sources an Illyrian, even though her mother was the daughter of Arrhabaeus of Lyncestis, who claimed Corinthian Bacchiad descent. Her father was probably, as ingenious combination and emendation established very plausibly in the nineteenth century, an Illyrian chieftain named Hirras.[14] How did she come by her Greek name? Certainly, no other name is mentioned by any source (and we have an almost contemporary one, Aeschines 2.26). There is nothing surprising if the daughter of a lady descended from the Bacchiads was given a good Greek mythological name. It was Otto Hoffmann who first suggested (*obiter* and as a possibility, while recognizing that the hypothesis was not necessary) that she may have had an Illyrian name, which she exchanged ("eingetauscht") for the Greek one when she became queen of Macedon; and he duly compared, as a parallel, the only attested case of this kind, that of Adea-Eurydice.[15] Heckel repeats this (not referring to Hoffmann). Now, it is technically accurate that "we do not know if she held the name already or if she took it at the time of her marriage" — we

---

[13] See the well-known fragment of Satyrus *ap.* Athenaeus 13.557b-c.

[14] For the combination see Hoffmann (supra n. 6) 160-63. He was not (it seems) aware of Plut. *Mor.* 14B f., which seems decisive for the form "Hirras." For a different view see Hammond, *Hist Macc* II 14 ff., discussing the form of the name (16), with a partial report of the textual transmission in the sources and the remedies suggested. He exhorts the reader not to be "misled" by the sources that call Eurydice (i.e., by implication her father) an Illyrian. After correctly quoting Strabo (14), he dreams up a "regency" by Sirras (his form of the name) for a "minor" Arrhabaeus and proceeds to imply (15) that Strabo intended to describe both Eurydice and her father as Bacchiads. (He does not explain why, in that case, Strabo carefully and specifically applied the term only to Eurydice's grandfather Arrhabaeus — as the quotation he prints makes clear.) Since this would not be so if Sirras were an Illyrian, he concludes that Eurydice's father was a member of the royal house of Lyncestis and both he and Eurydice were full Bacchiads. As the argument is part circle, part fiction, there is no *prima facie* case to discuss. But he suggests no change of name.

[15] Hoffmann (supra n. 6), 162 (-3) n. 68. Bosworth (supra n. 3) rightly ignores the suggestion.

know very little indeed about her. But proper method surely demands that there should be some positive reason why a change of name might be suggested; and Hoffmann's parallel, as we saw earlier, is not relevant even in support. What should be noted is that Gygaea, Amyntas' earlier wife, retained her name; at least, no one has yet suggested the contrary.[16] Of course, it was (if indeed it was her name) a good Argead name, but we know nothing about her except for the names of her sons: they make it certain that she was at one time regarded as a Macedonian queen. In any case, if we are to believe that Philip's mother Eurydice had to change her name, we have not so far disengaged any support for that notion. As an alternative to Heckel's statement, quoted above, we might suggest that "we have *no reason to think* that she adopted the name only at the time of her marriage."

Support, of a kind, comes with the next Illyrian wife of a Macedonian king: Audata, Philip II's first wife on Satyrus' list. Berve[17] asserts, as a matter of fact and without argument, that she "nach ihrer . . . Verbindung mit Philipp den Namen Eurydike annahm." In fact, her Illyrian name is attested only once, by Satyrus *ap.* Athenaeus. So is her Greek name Eurydice — and, as it happens, again by Arrian. But in this instance, unlike that of Cleopatra with which we started, we do not have Arrian's text. We have the name in Photius' summary of Arrian's *Successors*.[18] "Eurydice" is here named, not (as in Satyrus — though he also mentions her daughter, as he mentions the children of the other wives where he knew them) for her own sake, but purely as the mother of Cynnane (whose precise name, fortunately, we need not worry about). Arrian (or Photius) gives us no further information about her, though he adds something on every other character with whom she is associated.[19] Since these

---

[16] The actual name, very corrupt, has been disengaged from Justin 7.4.6. The common emendation, which seems secured by the name of Alexander I's sister, should not (I think) be questioned. In any case, however, the lady was not called Eurydice.

[17] Berve, *Alex* II, p. 229.

[18] *FGrH* 156 F9.22. This fragment contains Photius' summaries of books 6-9. S. 22 must have stood in one of the earlier of these books, perhaps 7. (It is the tenth modern section out of 26.) This, incidentally, shows how misleading references such as Heckel's (who, using a different text, refers to "*Succ.* 1.22") really are: cf. supra n. 5.

[19] ἡ δὲ Κυνάνη Φίλιππον μὲν εἶχε πατέρα, ὃν καὶ Ἀλέξανδρος, ἐκ δὲ μητρὸς Εὐριδίκης ἦν, γυνὴ δὲ Ἀμύντου, ὃν ἔφθη Ἀλέξανδρος κτεῖναι, ὁπότε εἰς τὴν Ἀσίαν διέβαινεν. (Another sentence explains that Amyntas was Philip's nephew.)

confess that we can make nothing of the collection of names, of which Olympias is not even the last: since no contemporary source, and no Alexander history either, tells us that she used any other name, it is difficult to believe that she was called Stratonice after being called Olympias; and if Myrtale was, as Justin says, the name she bore when *parvula*, it is difficult to see when she would have been called Polyxena, which (according to Plutarch) came earlier. It is best to be highly sceptical as to whether Olympias' name was changed at any time, or if it was, as to what it had been before or when precisely it was changed; and it would certainly be unwise to believe that she changed it again in her old age. But whatever the facts about this, she certainly is nowhere said to have been called Eurydice.

Heckel appears to accept Macurdy's suggestion that "Olympias, who was originally called Myrtale [this follows Justin, without revealing the context], took the former name only after Philip's Olympic victory of 356"! He goes on to conclude that "Philip was inclined to experiment with names for their propagandist value": adding the names of his daughters, Thessalonike and Europe, to the change of name postulated for Olympias, he concludes that in 337 Philip "revived the name Eurydike for the young Kleopatra." Now, quite apart from the confusion over Olympias, this is making confusion worse confounded. For the names of the daughters are not alleged to have been changed, merely given to them at birth; and the use of propagandist names for one's children went back a long way in Greece and did not wait for Philip II to invent it: we remember that three of Themistocles' daughters were called Nicomache, Asia and Italia, and that Cimon called a son Lacedaemonius. All this has nothing to do with changing names or with the adoption of throne names. In fact, Heckel has only one answer to the uncomfortable fact that Olympias was not called Eurydice: "The answer must lie in the fact that Eurydike was only gradually developing into a dynastic name and its use had not yet become a fixed practice."

This might be acceptable, despite all methodological doubts, if there were later a time when the "practice" was complete. Now, we know that Alexander, for one, did not give the name Eurydice to either of the barbarian queens he married. Nor does the name ever appear (with one exception we shall soon come to) among the wives of the non-Argead Successors, who so often tried to endow themselves

---

called Myrtale, took the former name only after Philip's Olympic victory of 356." There is no mention of Plutarch's evidence on her names.

with some shadow of legitimacy in their claims to the Macedonian throne. And we have already seen that the change of name by Adea is to be explained in different and simpler ways. The "gradual development," posited as conveniently explaining why Olympias never adopted that name when she is credited with no fewer than four, in fact never came to any fruition. The development as such is a myth.

So much for negative disproof. More positive disproof may be added. The name "Eurydice" was given by Antipater and later by Lysimachus to a daughter.[25] Antipater's daughter married Ptolemy I in 321 or soon after. She was presumably born some time after 340 (no previous husband is known). Hence at that time, whatever precisely it was, it was possible to give the name without any implications of a claim to the throne, a claim that would in fact arouse royal suspicion. (We remember that in Persia it was *not* possible for a noble child to be called Darius or Artaxerxes.) Lysimachus' daughter, presumably by Nicaea, must have been born between the time of that marriage (not long after the death of Perdiccas) and *ca.* 310; for by 293 we find her married already to Antipater, son of Cassander, and fleeing with him to her father's court when they were expelled by Demetrius Poliorcetes.[26] So, not long after Adea had so conspicuously changed her name, in the only such change by a Macedonian queen actually attested (as distinct from modern conjectures, more or less plausible), the name "Eurydice" was not associated with a claim to the Macedonian throne; though it is, of course, theoretically possible to argue — and I expect someone will do so, sooner or later — that Lysimachus' daughter too was not originally called Eurydice, but adopted that name when she married Antipater, thus bringing the "gradual development" to completion. Henceforth, in any case, no more is heard of that name on the Macedonian throne.

It only remains to consider Heckel's argument that the name "Eurydice" for Cleopatra in Arrian should be accepted, because "we have every reason to believe that Arrian copied precisely what Ptolemy wrote" (p. 156). Whether or not Ptolemy somewhere gave the facts about his exile and that of Alexander's other friends, there is certainly no reason to think that this was given, as Arrian gives it, precisely at this point, in the form of an inaccurate flashback. Nor is

---

[25] See Willrich, *s.v.* "Eurydike" (16 and 18), *RE* 6 (1909) 1326-27.

[26] See "Eurydike" (18), *ibid.*, 1327.

there any reason to think that Arrian was directly consulting Ptolemy at this point: it is at least as easy to believe that he added the flashback, in this vague form, because he needed some background for Harpalus and found that he had so far failed to give any. It is unlikely that Ptolemy had done the same.

Heckel gives a reason for positing the use of Ptolemy here (p. 155 n. 1): "Ptolemy's must certainly be the (deliberately?) misleading suggestion that he became *somatophylax* very soon after his return from exile (3.6.6)." This comment is rather disconcerting, since Heckel actually refers to another article of his,[27] where he gets the main point right: "*Arrian's comment* that Ptolemy was rewarded for his loyalty to Alexander . . . by being appointed *somatophylax* (Arr. 3.6.6) *anticipates the events of Arr. 3.26 f.*" (My italics, except for the Greek term.) He in fact filled the vacancy caused by the events that may be called the Philotas affair.

What Heckel quite rightly recognized in *Historia*, but forgot in *Phoenix*, is that the comment is Arrian's, and that it refers — and is *meant* to refer — to the later appointment. The comment is not Ptolemy's, and it is not misleading, whether deliberately or not. Arrian gives a list of the positions the friends of Alexander in due course attained, and he can be shown to have had no intention of claiming that those appointments were "very soon" after the men had returned from exile. Nearchus' appointment to the satrapy of Lycia belongs, as Arrian knew as well as we do, to 334; and that of Laomedon to take charge of the barbarian captives "because he knew two languages" (whatever precisely Arrian means) cannot predate the Asian expedition: there is no implication that Laomedon knew Thracian or Illyrian: he presumably, as Brunt has suggested, knew either Persian or Aramaic. Arrian picks out, in the case of each of these men, the first major appointment he knows of. In Ptolemy's case, this was precisely his appointment as *somatophylax*, before which surprisingly little is known about him.[28]

There is, in fact, no reason to think that those loyal boyhood friends who had suffered exile on his behalf were, as a body, treated by Alexander with particular distinction. We may suspect some disappointment, in some cases. They certainly did not receive unusually early promotion. Laomedon never did receive a major

---

[27] "The *Somatophylakes* of Alexander the Great: Some thoughts," *Historia* 27 (1978) 225.

[28] On this, see Berve, *Alex* II, p. 330.

post, and Arrian was presumably hard put to it to find anything to report. Although his position as what we might call Chief of Intelligence was undoubtedly an important one in our eyes, it involved no fighting or command and cannot have ranked very high in Macedonian eyes. We never, in fact, hear of his doing any fighting. After Alexander's death, he rose to a satrapy, the key satrapy of Syria: it may be suspected that there were men at Babylon who did not want it to be in the hands of a strong and able leader. In any case, there too he seems to have done no fighting and was easily dislodged.[29] We know that Alexander was very aware of loyalty and of disloyalty. But it is clear that he took no chances where military command was concerned. Harpalus (for the reason Arrian gives) and Laomedon (for reasons we can see for ourselves) never got there at all. Ptolemy, presumably, took a long time to prove his qualities — and even then did not prove himself, to Alexander's satisfaction, a candidate for senior military command.

The story of the false Eurydice, like every problem concerning Alexander the Great, turns out to have some bearing, after all, on the nature of our sources, on the customs of the Macedonian monarchy, and on the character of Alexander himself. That the answer to the immediate problem — a simple error in Arrian — must be what Tarn saw long ago should now be beyond reasonable question. But the specialists who ignored this minor puzzle were perhaps unwise to do so.[30]

Harvard University

---

[29] See *RE* 12 (1925), *s.v.* "Laomedon" 6 = 7 (two long articles on the same person by different authors [Stähelin and Bux], both printed without comment by the editors).

[30] I should like to thank my colleagues in the Ancient History Seminar at the Freie Universität Berlin and in the Philology and Ancient History Seminars at the University of Göttingen for allowing me the use of their libraries and typewriters during my visits to those cities for other academic purposes: this kindness alone made it possible for me to complete this little work of *pietas* towards a friend. I should also like to thank Professor W. Lindsay Adams for a useful suggestion on my argument.

The Evidence for the Identity of the Royal Tombs at Vergina

N. G. L. HAMMOND

Abstract

New evidence has been released by Professor M. Andronikos in the three years since I wrote my article " 'Philip's Tomb' in Historical Context" (n. 1, infra), and I have had the advantage of being shown round the excavations by Professor Andronikos in the summer of 1978. I express my gratitude to him for his generosity and constant helpfulness. Various points of construction have emerged. The Great Mound is entirely man-made. Under the Mound and above the three built tombs there is a tumulus of red soil, of which the purpose is not obvious. In the soil of this tumulus two skeletons and two funerary headstones have been found, but no explanation of their presence there has been advanced. The discovery of a third tomb, unplundered, has added one startling piece of evidence, and it has provided an analogy for the larger unplundered tomb. We can now compare the details of the construction of the three tombs and speculate on the development of this kind of burial. We know now that the great fresco portrayed a Royal Hunt, and that of the huntsmen one mounted man alone is of mature age and the other nine are youthful. The analysis of the cremated remains in both chambers of the large tomb and those in the third tomb have been completed and are of great interest.

Thus the gradual disclosure of evidence from late November 1977 until now has made the excavation into a moving target for the enquiring scholar. It seems appropriate at this time to take stock of our interpretation.

Three years have passed since I wrote an article in which I set the historical framework and supported some of Andronikos' conclusions

N. G. L. Hammond

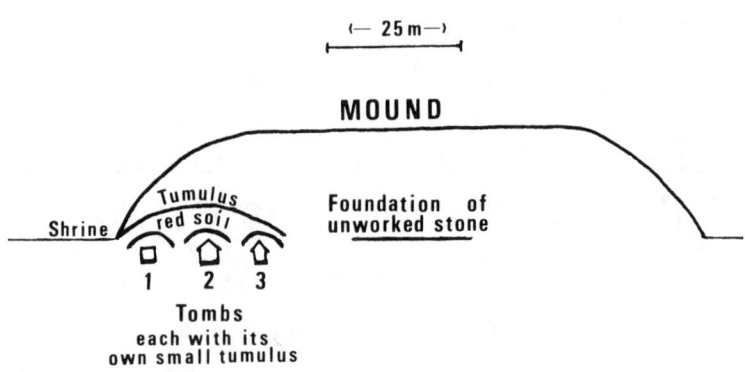

Fig. 1. Sketch plan of a section of the Great Mound (N. G. L. Hammond).

about the largest tomb at Vergina.[1] Meanwhile Andronikos has released more information, and I had the privilege of being shown the site by him in summer 1978 and of hearing him lecture at the British Academy in 1979. So it is appropriate now to review the situation, with the proviso that almost everything is subject to the final publication by Andronikos of his discoveries.

The Great Mound (Fig. 1) is now known to be artificial, made systematically with successive layers of waterproof clay, packed earth and compacted rock. The lowest layer of rock was 3 m thick and had to be removed by a mechanical digger; so it is not surprising that earlier excavators, digging downwards from the top, got no further than the top layers and that Andronikos' team, digging in the same way, took several months to reach the bottom. Why build so huge a Mound, of 110 m in diameter and 15 m high? There are in Macedonia two mounds at Kourinos[2] and one at Amphipolis;[3] the

---

[1] "Philip's Tomb' in historical context," *GRBS* 19 (1978) 331-50.

[2] I visited these in July 1978. One, excavated by Daumet (see L. Heuzey and H. Daumet, *Mission archéologique de Macédoine*, [Paris 1876], 242 f.), contained a built-tomb with a long built *dromos*. The other had just been illegally attacked by a bulldozer, which had revealed one plinth of poros stone probably from a built-tomb. I reported this to the local authority. Ancient Pydna was near Kourinos (see *Hist Mace* I 127 f.).

[3] The mound at Amphipolis, *ho hypermegethēs tymvos*, was apparently 140 m in diameter and more than 20 m high; it was built in the Hellenistic period over an area which already contained burials of different periods, beginning in the Early

The Evidence for the Identity of the Royal Tombs at Vergina

former are half the size and later in date, and each covers a built tomb. The nearest in date and in size are those built overseas by Alexander III: a memorial to Demaratus 39 m high "and great in circumference" (a cenotaph, made by the army, while the cremated remains were sent to Corinth),[4] and a huge mound over the tomb of Hephaestion.[5] The plan of Alexander III to build such a mound "like the greatest of the pyramids in Egypt" as a tomb for his father Philip (i.e. over the existing burial) was rejected together with the other plans by the army at Babylon.[6] But the idea of a giant Mound at Aegeae was sown, and we can hardly doubt that our Mound at Aegeae was the result.

Whom does the Mound commemorate? Andronikos expected to find the answer at the centre of Mound. There he disclosed an area of unworked stone, 20 m long but narrow, with 3 m high walls at each narrow end; and round about there were chips of the same stone and chips of marble, which indicated that the building had been of cut masonry and had contained marble statues. Analogies at Dodona and elsewhere suggest a stoa for the display of spoils and for the statues of commanders. Of Philip's conquests or of Alexander's? We shall answer that question later. Since the contents of the stoa and even its worked masonry were removed presumably for display elsewhere, it may be that the Mound was positioned to commemorate rather those buried under it, namely the greatest kings of the Macedonians, of whom one was certainly Philip. If so, it was just what Alexander had intended.

The secondary tumulus over a group of built-tombs is not known elsewhere. Its purpose may be inferred from the tumuli over groups of cist tombs at Vergina and elsewhere,[7] namely in each case to cover the burials of the leading members of a family over some generations. Under this secondary circular tumulus Andronikos has found below

---

Iron Age, but its purpose seems not to have emerged. Its size is in *Praktika* (1965) 49; the reports in following volumes of *Praktika* and concurrently in *Ergon* (1971) 62, (1972) 30, (1973) 42, (1974) 38, (1975) 52, (1977) 33, (1978) 17 and (1979) 13 leave one in something of a haze.

[4] Plut. *Alex.* 56.2.

[5] Plut. *Alex.* 72.5; for its colossal size see Diod. 17.115.2-5.

[6] Diod. 18.4.5-6; arguments for the genuineness of these plans in N. G. L. Hammond, *Alexander the Great: King, Commander and Statesman* (Park Ridge, N.J. 1980) 300 ff.

[7] For example, at Visoî in Pelagonia, at Pateli in Eordaea, and in Albania (see N. G. L. Hammond, *Migrations and Invasions in Greece and adjacent areas* (Park Ridge, N.J. 1976) *passim*.

the original ground level three built tombs and in the upper part of the tumulus two funerary headstones and two skeletons, presumably of persons who wished to be associated with the dead below. This tumulus was probably built after the construction of the largest tomb, i.e., Tomb 2, because that tomb is more or less at the central point.

Can we put a bracket of dates over the burials within the confines of the secondary tumulus? At this stage let us consider only the archaeologists' best criterion, pottery, and the dates given by Andronikos, for whose judgment anyone who has worked with his report of the Cemetery of Tumuli at Vergina will have the highest respect.[8] In Tomb 2 the pottery was unused and so interred probably close to the date of making. In the main chamber, the king's one, the pots and in particular a clay lamp were dated *ca.* 350-320, and in the antechamber alabastra, other pots and in particular a "Cypriote amphora" *ca.* 350-320. On the cornice of Tomb 2 sherds from the little pyre were dated to *ca.* 340. In Tomb 1 there were two pots and some sherds, which were dated to the middle period of the fourth century. For Tomb 3 Andronikos has given a date not later than 325, without saying whether it was on the strength of the pottery. Then on the burnt area, used for ritual purposes, by the shrine and near the edge of the secondary tumulus, the sherds were dated 350-325, the later date giving the last instance of ritual worship at this spot. The datings provided at six *separate* places are cumulatively compelling. Those from the unused pottery are very strong. Still a margin should be allowed: I propose for Tomb 2 (both burials) down to 315 as the extreme limit, but with 340 as the mean, especially in view of the date for the little pyre on the cornice; for Tomb 1, Tomb 3 and the ritual area allowances of 15 years. The total bracket will then be *ca.* 370 to *ca.* 310.

The shrine, found next to a tomb only here in Macedonia, must mean worship after death of the person buried in Tomb 1 and very probably of the person buried in Tomb 2's main chamber. The only Macedonian kings of the period *ca.* 370-310 whose worship is attested are Amyntas III, *ob.* 370, and Philip II, *ob.* 336; thus the presumption is strong that the former's remains lay in Tomb 1 and the latter's in the main chamber of Tomb 2. Worship ceased *ca.* 310, the year in which the last male descendant of Amyntas died.

Tomb 1 is a glorified cist-tomb, 3.50 x 2.09 x 3 m high, roofed with removable flat plinths of poros stone, and covered by its own

[8] M. Andronikos, *Vergina* I. *To Nekrotapheion tōn Tymvōn* [in Greek] (Athens 1969).

The Evidence for the Identity of the Royal Tombs at Vergina

tumulus. It is entirely unlike the "trench-burials" of varying sizes which were found in groups under large tumuli in the Cemetery of Tumuli at Vergina (Andronikos [supra n. 8] 151). We must look elsewhere for its origin. At Argos[9] in the Peloponnese, from which the Temenid dynasty had come to Macedonia in the seventh century, as we know from the decision of the Hellenodikai at Olympia and from the evidence of Herodotus and Thucydides,[10] there have recently been found tumuli originating in the Middle Helladic period but reused in the Protogeometric and Geometric periods for burials in cist-tombs; and at Argos there are also in the Geometric period examples of the "large built cist-tomb" (as it is called by E. Deilaki, supra n. 9) which contained armour, weapons and offerings. The first king in the seventh century may have introduced this type of burial, of which Tomb 1 at Vergina is merely an unusually large example.

Tomb 1 was constructed before the vault came into use at Aegeae. Now the earliest description of a vaulted tomb under ground level was given by Plato in *Laws* 947D, written some years before his death in 347: "a tomb underground, built of poros stone, vaulted and oblong, and . . . over it a circular tumulus of soil."[11] Plato proposed to provide such a tomb for the most prestigious citizen of his ideal state, and he derived the idea presumably not from the Greek city-states, where it was unknown, but from Macedonia, where his disciple, Euphraeus, lived for a time in the 360s at the court of Perdiccas 3. Tomb 1, then, may date from before the late 360s.

The king buried there might have been either Amyntas III or Alexander II; but as the latter reigned for less than two years, he can

---

[9] Andronikos (supra n. 8) 164, found no cist-tombs in the tumuli he excavated. See the reports by E. Deilaki in *Delt* 26 (1971), *Chron* 28 (1973) 95 and 99. Her book, *The Tumuli of Argos* (Athens 1980) deals only with prehistoric burials.

[10] We have no outside evidence on which to challenge the verdict of the Hellanodikai or the acceptance of the Temenid Macedonian family tree by Herodotus and Thucydides. Those who choose to reject the tradition act on theoretical grounds alone.

[11] θήκην δὲ ὑπὸ γῆς αὐτοῖς εἰργασμένην εἶναι ψαλίδα προμήκη . . . κύκλῳ χώσαντες. The Scholiast here used the other word for a vault ἀψίδα. He mentioned an underground sewer, and we may compare Sophocles fr. 367 στενὴν δ' ἔδυμεν ψαλίδα. The word ψαλίς, meaning "scissors" describes the V shape, as in the "scissor-tailed flycatcher." Insufficient weight has been given to this passage by R. A. Tomlinson, "Vaulting techniques of the Macedonian Tombs," *AM* II 473 ff. and T. D. Boyd, "The Arch and Vault in Greek Architecture," *AJA* 82 (1978) 83 ff., P. W. Lehmann, "The so-called Tomb of Philip II: a Different Interpretation," *AJA* 84 (1980) 527, and W. L. Adams, "The Royal Macedonian Tomb at Vergina," *AncW* 3 (1980) 67 ff.

be excluded from any possible worship. Thus we conclude that the king for whom Tomb 1 was built was Amyntas III. There may have been others buried there as well, since Andronikos mentioned finding "many bones" on the floor; analysis of the bones may provide more information. The tomb was rifled perhaps by the Gallic mercenaries of Pyrrhus in 274 (Plut. *Pyrrhus* 26.6 and Diod. 22.12; they threw out the bones), or else by the Romans in 168 B.C. after the defeat of Perseus. The violent destruction of the shrine was no doubt due to the Romans.

I turn next to Tomb 3. Round the neck of the silver funerary urn there lay a gold wreath of oak-leaves and acorns, the prerogative of some king, as in the main chamber of Tomb 2 and as on Hellenistic coins. Traces were found of a folded cloth, gold-decorated, like the cloth in the antechamber of Tomb 2; and there were gilded greaves as in Tomb 2, some fine gold jewelry, and 27 silver goblets (the main chamber of Tomb 2 had 20). All these indicate that the tomb is royal. We may recall that Arrhidaeus put on Alexander's royal garment at a crucial moment (Curt. 10.7.13). A spear-shaft was wrapped with gold foil, which indicates that it was a ceremonial piece. Strigils, curry combs and the chariot-race portrayed on the fresco inside the tomb reveal the interests of a young athletic horseman. The cremated remains in the silver urn have been analysed: they are those of a boy of 12 to 14 years (such analysis being particularly dependable for this young age). Since Alexander IV was born in 323 and died in 310, he is the person buried in Tomb 3. There is no possible alternative. The construction of the tomb resembled that of Tomb 2, being two-chambered, vaulted and without a pediment, the last feature showing that it is pre-Hellenistic,[12] and that it is close in date to Tomb 2.

Tomb 2 has one inscribed object: a tripod commemorating a victory in the games at Argos, dated by the lettering to *ca.* 450. Its presence in a royal tomb can mean only that it had been won by an ancestor of the dead man, an ancestor who had competed successfully at the place of the Temenid family's origin, perhaps Amyntas, son of Alexander I and grandfather of Amyntas III. Other objects show that Tomb 2 is that of a king: the heavy gold coffer, the gold wreath of oak-leaves and acorns, the gold-wrapped sceptre 2 m long, the

---

[12] I use the term vaguely to indicate that almost all, if not all, built-tombs with pediments are of third-century date. The circumstances of the boy Alexander's death were no doubt reported as natural at the time; the rumour that Cassander had him murdered circulated presumably after Cassander's death. Pausanias 9.7.2 attributed the boy's death to poisoning.

The Evidence for the Identity of the Royal Tombs at Vergina

ceremonial shield of gold, silver and ivory, the sets of fine greaves, and the diadem of gilded silver.

Much confusion has arisen over the diadem. The word *diadēma* merely means a headband. It was worn by ordinary men in many countries, but in Macedonia it was the mark of the king (Curt. 10.6.4; 10.8.20; Arr. 7.22.4 *to diadēma to basilikon*). The earliest representation (Fig. 2) is on the coinage of Alexander I, dating from *ca*. 477 onwards: a cloth diadem with two long ends hanging down, worn on top of his hat.[13] A similar cloth diadem with two long ends was worn by Alexander III on the top of his *kausia*, this diadem being lighter than the hat itself (Arr. 7.22.2). Such a cloth diadem with a single end (as would result, for instance, from a slip-knot) is shown on the Tarsus medallion of Philip II; and again with two long ends on the Philip II plate[14] and on a "Porus medallion" of Alexander III. The simpler diadem of cloth with no loose ends is shown on the head of a young man, probably Caranus, the mythical founder of the Temenid dynasty in Macedonia, on the coins of Archelaus (Fig. 3) and of some later kings;[15] and again on the marble head of Philip II (so identified by Gisela Richter).[16] The diadem in the main chamber of Tomb 2 is a version in precious metal of the simpler kind of diadem, adjustable either because it was worn sometimes on top of a *kausia* and sometimes bare-headed, or because it was worn by successive kings. This diadem could have been made for any Macedonian king from Alexander I onwards.

The armour in the main chamber is of interest for dating. An oxydised spearhead was struck to the wall some 5 m up; this must have belonged to a sarissa-shaft which has mouldered away. Since the

---

[13] The Macedonian kings, not unreasonably, wore two kinds of hat, both of felt, the floppy *petasus* and the stiffer *kausia* (Alexander III, for instance, in Athen. 12.537e-f). Alexander I probably wore the *kausia* for hunting. Demetrius had on his *kausia* a woven diadem with long ends hanging down his back (Athen. 12.535f).

[14] The Philip II plate is published in *PM* 179.

[15] See *Hist Macc* II 8-13 and 138, arguing that Caranus was first introduced into the genealogy of the Macedonian kings in the reign of Archelaus.

[16] G. M. A. Richter, *The Portraits of the Greeks* III (London 1965) 253 fig. 1708. The suggestion of Lehmann (supra n. 11) 529 n. 21, that Roman copyists added diadems of varying kinds to the Tarsus medallion and the marble head of Philip presupposes that copyists were as independent and academic as the suggester; its falseness is proved by the coins showing the marble head's type of diadem from Archelaus onwards, and now by the diadem with ends on the Philip II plate, which is an original.

Fig. 3. Young man, probably Caranus, wearing a cloth diadem without ends. Didrachm of Archelaus.

Fig. 2. Alexander I wearing on top of his hat a cloth diadem with long ends hanging down his back. Octadrachm.

The Evidence for the Identity of the Royal Tombs at Vergina

sarissa was invented by Philip II in 359,[17] we have a *terminus post quem* for Tomb 2. The cuirass with shoulder-pieces, gold lion-heads and leather kirtle, and the pommel of the sword are all as worn by Alexander in the Alexander-Mosaic, and the cuirass with shoulder-pieces is as on the Tarsus medallion of Philip II. The use of iron for the cuirass and for the helmet is paralleled by the use of iron, "polished to look like silver," for the helmet and the gorget of Alexander at the battle of Gaugamela (Plut. *Alex.* 32.5).[18] This armour is entirely appropriate to the time of Philip II's death (we may compare the reverence for Alexander's armour in Curt. 10.6.4).

The cremation of a corpse on a wood-pyre, even with a high wind, as in *Iliad* 23.215 ff., did not consume the teeth and the bones. Thus the remains of the man in the coffer of the main chamber of Tomb 2 have been analysed as those of a man between 35 and 50 years old, which enables us to exclude Amyntas III (*senex decessit*, Justin 7.4.8) and also both Alexander II and Perdiccas III, who died in their twenties. We are left with Philip II who died at the age of 46, and Philip III Arrhidaeus who was about 40 at the time of his death in 316.

On entering the main chamber Andronikos picked up a group of five miniature ivory heads, and he reported later the finding of others. Trunks and limbs in gold and ivory were also found. The earliest examples of such miniature figures until then were in a Macedonian built tomb of the third century to the number of some twenty.[19] The practice of providing gold-and-ivory likenesses of the dead man for his tomb was first mentioned in Diodorus 17.115.1, where the Friends of Alexander III competed in preparing such *eidola* of Hephaestion. So Alexander might well have arranged to place such an *eidolon* of Philip in his tomb. As the group of five heads was in the place of honour beside the coffer, the chances are considerable that one of the five heads is that of the dead man. One head can be dated to the time of its making: for Alexander III is portrayed as a very

---

[17] As argued in my forthcoming article in *Antichthon* (1981).

[18] Owning abundant deposits of iron, Philip was able to equip his infantry with new weapons (Diod. 16.3.1 f.) by employing local ironsmiths, who may well have developed an expertise in making some pieces of armour in iron.

[19] In "A New Monumental Chamber Tomb with Paintings of the Hellenistic Period near Lefkadia (West Macedonia)," *AAA* 6 (1973) 87-92 K. Rhomiopoulou mentioned twenty-one ivory heads, mostly male and obviously portraits, as her illustration of one showed, at Lefkadhia. For a dead king the heads would portray his Friends in particular.

young man, probably before his accession to the throne in 336, and the portrait is much less flattering than those made in his later years. Another head undoubtedly is of Philip II in middle age; for it shows the damaged eyebrow-bone and the blind right eye, both due to a wound in 354,[20] and it has many resemblances with other portraits of Philip, especially in the prominent horizontal eyebrow-bones.[21] The other three heads, one male with the same eyebrow-bones and two female, are probably those of Amyntas III and Eurydice (the parents of Philip) and Olympias; for we know that Philip arranged in the winter of 338/7 for the making of five lifesize gold-and-ivory statues of his parents, himself, Olympias and Alexander which were to be placed in his new building at Olympia, the Philippeum.[22] These heads enhance the likelihood that Tomb 2 is that of Philip II.

The painting on the large space (5.15 m x 1.16 m) below the cornice did honour to the man buried within. The subject is the climax of a hunt and shows attacks on a stag, two boars and a lion, the last being extant in Macedonia in the fourth century.[23] A mounted man, coming up from behind, is about to strike with his spear this lion, which is held at bay, facing two men and the dogs. The horseman is undoubtedly the king; for it was his prerogative to give the *coup de grâce* to the quarry (Curt. 7.6.7) and in particular to the royal beast, the lion (cf. Curt. 8.1.14), and in addition he was required by customary law to hunt always on horseback (Curt 8.1.18, keeping the reading of A: *scivere gentis suae morem*). Thus a didrachm of Amyntas III shows a rider, probably the king, about to attack a lion (Figs. 4 and 5). There are two other figures on horseback; it is to be presumed that they were members of the royal house, coming under the same law. These two and the seven huntsmen on foot are all young. While the two princes may be above the age of the royal pages (fourteen to eighteen), the seven on foot are certainly pages "attending the king in the hunt" (Curt. 5.1.42, *venantesque comitantur* [sc. regem]). The only mature man is the horseman who is about to kill the lion, i.e. the king. Of the two princes one has his back to the viewer, probably because he was to be played down at the time of the

---

[20] Especially *FGrH* 115 (Theopompus) F 52 and *FGrH* 135/136 (Marsyas) F 16.

[21] Clearly on the Philip plate and on the Tarsus medallion.

[22] Paus. 5.20.10.

[23] Xen. *Cyn.* 11.1.

The Evidence for the Identity of the Royal Tombs at Vergina

Fig. 4. Rider striking downwards with his spear, and

Fig. 5. lion teasing a spear. Didrachm of Amyntas III.

painting,[24] and the other, seen full face, has the central position in the picture and is wearing a laurel wreath. He is presumably the successor of the dead king and the commissioner of the picture. Such a combination of king and successor cannot apply to Perdiccas III and Philip II (or Amyntas IV) or to Arrhidaeus and Alexander IV, because the ages are wrong, and we are forced to conclude that the two are Philip II and Alexander III.[25]

Tomb 2 was built in two stages. The first stage was a single chamber, being to that extent like Tomb 1 but being different in having a vaulted top, a two-leaved door and larger dimensions, 10 x 55 x 6 m. This chamber was sealed off while the plastering of the inside walls was still incomplete and while the inner side of the door was unfinished. The explanation is surely that the dead king's successor was in such a hurry to complete the obsequies of his predecessor and presumably to go away from Aegeae that he left the interior of the chamber in an unfinished state. If the dead king is Philip and the successor is Alexander, he had every reason to rush south. Bypassing a Thessalian force at Tempe (cf. Justin 11.2.5), *citato gradu in Graeciam contendit*, "he hastened at full speed into Greece" (cf. Polyaenus *Strat.* 4.3.23).

The second stage was the construction of an ante-chamber, of which the interior was completed with a painted dado and a painted band of rosettes, and of a facade with attached columns, a two-leaved door, a flat cornice and below it the fresco which we have described. We see here an immediate forerunner of the standard Macedonian built-tomb, with two chambers, vaulted roof, two two-leaved doors, applied columns and outside fresco. But Tomb 2 differs in having, like Tomb 3, no pediment and in having a burial in the ante-chamber (other built-tombs with two burials have both in the back chamber). Tomb 2 is larger than any other built-tomb in Macedonia. If it was built on the instructions of Alexander for Philip, it is another example of Alexander's large-scale ideas.

The antechamber of Tomb 2 has the following objects which are appropriate to the burial of a queen: a gold coffer, a gold wreath of

---

[24] Such as Amyntas, son of Perdiccas, or one of the sons of Aëropus, if they were members of the royal house, as I have argued in "Some passages in Arrian concerning Alexander the Great," *CQ* 30 (1980) 457 f.

[25] The details of the fresco which I have cited have been mentioned by Andronikos in articles and in the lecture to the British Academy in London, now published as "The Finds from the Royal Tombs at Vergina," in the *Proc. of the Brit. Acad.* for 1979.

The Evidence for the Identity of the Royal Tombs at Vergina

myrtle as worn by queens on Hellenistic coins, a gilded pectoral with horsemen in relief, a gold-decorated purple cloth,[26] and a gold quiver-cover. The cloth enfolded the cremated remains, which on analysis proved to be of a woman 23 to 27 years old. This age excludes from consideration the wife of Arrhidaeus, Eurydice, who as the product of the short-lived marriage of Cynna to Amyntas, son of Perdiccas, was born in 335 or so and was killed in 316 around the age of 19.[27] Philip was well off for wives who were probably of the required age in 336. One, the Macedonian Cleopatra, married in 337, can be excluded because she and her brothers were put to death in connection with the death of Attalus, which occurred later than the funeral of Philip and probably in 335.[28] The others are a Getic princess, Meda, married in 341, and a Scythian princess whom Philip may have married in 340; for her father the Scythian king, Atheas, undertook to adopt Philip as his heir, and such adoption entailed marriage to the heiress (Just. 9.2.1). The Scythian type of quiver-cover, a pile of arrows and the horsemen on the pectoral are particularly appropriate to a Scythian queen; for the Scythians excelled in mounted archery. The timely death of this queen, whether Getic or Scythian, to match the death of the king may not have been due to accident. For suttee was practiced by some Thracian tribes (Hdt. 5.4), the Getae (Steph. Byz. *s.v.Getia*) and the Scythians (Hdt. 4.71.4).[29]

There were many offerings in the antechamber, and in view of the haste with which the main chamber was closed some of them may have been meant for the king's chamber. This has been taken to be so for an uneven "pair" of gold-engraved greaves which was in the ante-chamber, and the argument was advanced that since Philip was

---

[26] Such cloth was characteristic of royalty; cf. Athen. 12.535f and 538d, and Curt. 8.9.24, for instance.

[27] Philip married Audata in 358 at the earliest; their daughter, Cynna, could have been born at the earliest in 357, assuming that she was their first born, so that she was at most 20 by 337. She married Amyntas, son of Perdiccas; this was probably in 337, since she lost him "quickly" (*tacheōs:* Polyaenus 8.60) and he was put to death before summer 335, when her hand was offered to Langarus (Arr. 1.5.4). Eurydice, born to Amyntas and Cynna at the earliest in 336 or 335, was hardly more than 19 or 20 at the most in 316. I do not follow W. L. Adams' arguments (supra n. 11), 72 n. 60.

[28] See the order of events in Diod. 17.2.1 and 17.5.2; for the killing of Cleopatra see Hammond, *Alex. the Great* (supra n. 6) 39.

[29] Argued more fully in *GRBS* (supra n. 1) 335 f., at which time the analysis of the woman's remains was not known.

lame this pair was intended for his chamber. In fact, there were already three matching pairs of greaves in his chamber. In any case, the illustration of the uneven "pair" (No. 159 in *Search*) shows that the short greave was for the left leg, whereas Philip was wounded in the right leg, both in the shin in 345 and in the thigh in 339, the latter wound being said to have lamed him.[30] Perhaps "one of his and one of hers" were put there for the lady by mistake!

The king and the queen were cremated presumably on one and the same pyre. Other objects, affected by intense fire and cremated no doubt on the same pyre, were placed in a brick tray on top of the vault before its stucco had dried: namely a spear-head set upright as "the killer," two swords, horse trappings, pieces of ivory (? from pommels or harness), a few gold acorns and a bronze oenochoe. If the dead king was Philip, there is an immediate explanation for the tray and its contents, which have not been found with any other built-tomb. The spear-head is the weapon of a king's Bodyguard, and the assassin, Pausanias, was one: the two swords are those of the two men condemned for connivance and killed "by the tumulus" of Philip (Justin 11.2.1 *ad tumulum*);[31] the trappings are those of the horses brought by the assassin to the gates of the theatre (Diod. 16.94.3, twice; and Justin 9.7.9 *equos*); the gold acorns may have survived from a wreath placed on the corpse of the king; and the bronze oenochoe had held the wine with which the pyre's flames were doused, as in *Iliad* 24.791 (cf. 23.220), and it was then thrown into the embers.

Lastly, the small pyre on top of the cornice had sherds, dated *ca.* 340 by Andronikos, and bones of birds or small animals, so that it was of a purificatory nature. The explanation of this is at hand, if the dead man was Philip II. For the corpse of his assassin was hung for display and finally burnt "above the remains of Philip" (Justin 9.7.11).[32] The natural place for display was on top of the cornice. It had to be purified.

In conclusion it is important to cover all the details of the evidence as they emerge and not to pick on just one or two details. In my previous article I mentioned as conceivable candidates for the tombs

---

[30] Didymus *in Dem.* col. 12.63 f. τὴν δὲ κν[ήμη]ν τὴν δεξιάν, if so restored, and 13.3 f. τὸν δεξιὸν αὐτοῦ μηρόν (cf. Justin 9.3.2 *in femore*).

[31] Fuller discussion and documentation in *GRBS* 19 (supra n. 1) 342 f.

[32] Justin's source, ultimately I think Satyrus, kept the facts but pinned onto them a case against Olympias, which is totally unconvincing to me.

The Evidence for the Identity of the Royal Tombs at Vergina

at Vergina (only two tombs being known then) Arrhidaeus, Eurydice and Cynna, but I rejected them for various reasons.[33] Further evidence since then has strengthened my reasons. Let us consider the matter. We begin with Diyllus (*FGrH* 73 F I: paraphrased in Diod. 19.52.5). "Cassander, returning from Boeotia and burying the king and the queen at Aegeae and with them Cynna, the mother of Eurydice, and honouring them in other appropriate ways, held a contest in single combat, in which four of his soldiers took part." The natural inference from this statement is that Cassander buried all three in one tomb, which will not fit Tomb 2; and if we suppose that he buried only the king and the queen in one Tomb and the queen mother in another place altogether,[34] we have no explanation for the differences in time as shown by the stages of construction of Tomb 2, for the unfinished interior of the main chamber, or indeed for the separation in different chambers of the king and the queen, since of the two she was the dynamic and effective character. Next, the analysed remains in the queen's coffer are of a woman aged 23 to 27, whereas Eurydice died about the age of 19; so she cannot be the occupant of the antechamber of Tomb 2.

If we assume that only Arrhidaeus was buried in this tomb, i.e., in the main chamber, we still have no explanation for the hunting-scene. For no one would entrust the conduct of such a hunt to a man as "slow-witted and epileptic" as Arrhidaeus (*FGrH* 155 F 1, [2]), and the youth about to kill the lion, if he be the successor, cannot be the child Alexander IV. Nor is worship of Arrhidaeus conceivable, if the position of Tomb 2 implies worship; nor is an ivory head of Olympias likely to have been placed by Cassander beside the coffer of Arrhidaeus, when it was Olympias who had ordered the murder of Arrhidaeus and Eurydice. Finally, if Arrhidaeus lies in the main chamber, what reason can be advanced for the contents of the brick tray and for the small pyre on the cornice? The cap may fit at one point, the age of Arrhidaeus in relation to the remains in the coffer in the main chamber, but that is very far from enough.

The reconstruction which seems best to fit the evidence at present available is as follows. In 370 Alexander II built Tomb 1 to receive the remains of Amyntas III, the first member of his side of the descent

---

[33] In *GRBS* 19 (supra n. 1) 337 f.

[34] As proposed by Lehmann (supra n. 11) 530 n. 41, and Adams (supra n. 11) 71. See also A. M. Prestianni Giallombardo and B. Tripodi, "Le tombe regali di Vergina: quale Filippo?" *ASNP*, ser. III, 10, 3 (1980) 989 ff.

from Alexander I to become king;[35] for that reason Alexander II chose a site apart from the tombs of earlier kings. Adjacent to the tomb he built a shrine, perhaps called the Amyntaeum as at Pydna, and worship of Amyntas as a god was practiced there. We do not know as yet whether Amyntas was cremated; the report of "many bones" suggests perhaps that he was not cremated and that others were buried there later.

In 336, after the assassination of Philip II, Alexander III spent several weeks in organizing affairs in Macedonia and enquiring into the background of the assassination. Meanwhile some progress was made in the building of a tomb for Philip, which Alexander had planned to a size which no subsequent built-tomb in Macedonia achieved. The trial was held and the guilty were sentenced. Then "Alexander took all possible care of his father's funeral" (Diod. 17.2.1), placing in the tomb offerings which were superb both in quality and quantity.[36] The king's chamber was closed before its interior was fully finished, because Alexander had to hasten away and deal with conditions in the Greek states. His deputy supervised the completion of the ante-chamber, the placing of the queen's remains and the addition of many offerings. The assassin's spear and horses, and two "conspirators" were burnt upon the pyre, and the iron, bronze, ivory and gold pieces were laid in a brick tray above the vault. And on the cornice, where the assassin's corpse had hung and then been burnt, a small fire of purification was lit. Alexander chose to site this tomb close to Tomb 1, in order that the worship accorded to Philip as a god might be made at the shrine. Tombs 1 and 2, each having its own small tumulus which showed above ground level, were now covered with an extensive tumulus of red soil (as "in the Macedonian manner" near Bukhara; Plut. *Alex.* 72.5; Curt 7.9.21 and 11.2.1).

In 321, when the corpse of Alexander III was diverted to Egypt, the Macedonians probably placed trophies from Persia and statues of Alexander and his special commanders in a stoa constructed close to the tumulus of red soil. In 316, when Arrhidaeus, Eurydice and Cynna were killed, Cassander buried their remains in a tomb somewhere outside the periphery of the great Mound. In 310, when

---

[35] See stemma in *Hist Mace* II, facing p. 176.

[36] When Alexander III died, the objects placed on his throne were the diadem, the royal robe, the armour and the ring of the dead king. Such objects were placed in the tomb of Philip II. See Curt. 10.6.4.

the last male of the line, Alexander IV, died, he was buried in a tomb which was placed within the circumference of the tumulus of red soil. After 336 and before 310 the corpses of two men, not cremated, and two funerary headstones were placed in the upper soil of this tumulus; it had no doubt been their wish to be associated with the dynasty of Amyntas.

After 310 worship ceased at the burnt area by the shrine. Then or later (a point which the complete excavation may have decided) a great Mound, such as Alexander had planned to commemorate Philip, was erected perhaps to commemorate the dynasty which had ended, that of Amyntas's branch of the Temenid family.

St. Olaf College

Illustration credits:
All coin illustrations were reproduced from the author's chapter in *Ancient Greek Painting and Iconography*, Warren G. Moon, editor (Madison 1982), published by the University of Wisconsin Press, whose permission to use these materials is gratefully acknowledged.

The Royal Tombs of Vergina:
A Historical Analysis

PETER GREEN

Abstract
Any verdict on the identity of these tombs' occupants must remain provisional until Professor Andronikos' final report is made public, and even then certainty seems unlikely. External evaluation by physical anthropologists of the cremated bones, and by archaelogists of the pottery and other artifacts, e.g., the ivory heads, may reduce the margin of doubt, but cannot eliminate it altogetce, and apply firm conclusions from this to the Vergina finds. A general consensus has been reached on the identification of Vergina as Aegae, and the Great Tumulus as the royal Macedonian necropolis. There is also general agreement that the finds are to be dated within the second half of the 4th century B.C. Since we possess a full prosopography of the Argead royal house for this period, it should be possible to provide rational candidates for the occupancy of all three tombs. From a detailed analysis I conclude that, as our evidence at present stands, the only possible occupant of Tomb III is Alexander IV; that the likeliest candidate for Tomb I is Philip II's early wife Phila; and that Tomb II, on balance, probably housed Philip II and Cleopatra-Eurydice.

Of necessity, any verdict on the identities of the persons buried in the three tombs thus far (September 1981) excavated at Vergina must remain provisional. Indeed, without further substantial evidence it is doubtful whether an indisputable decision can be reached. At present we have no independent external evaluation of two crucial groups of source-material: the bones and the pottery. Professor Manolis Andronikos has made public only the conclusions reached by his own consultant Greek physical anthropologist concerning the first, and his own opinions as regards the second. That is his undoubted right prior to the final excavation report, but it makes the historian's task difficult. We are required to build hypotheses on largely unconfirmed evidence. We must take it on trust that the bones in Tomb II are of a man in his forties, those in the antechamber of a woman "between twenty-three and twenty-seven," those in Tomb III of "a boy twelve to fourteen years old," and, most intriguingly, those in Tomb I of a girl in her twenties, a baby, and a large-boned man.

In his original report Andronikos did not speculate on the age or sex of the bones, since the physical anthropologist's findings were not yet available. It was thus possible for Hammond to speculate that Tomb I, despite the evidence of its murals, contained Amyntas III, Philip II's father. Later Andronikos wrote, apropos Tomb II, that "two teeth, a molar and a wisdom tooth, have been judged by an anthropologist as belonging to a man of more than 32 years. (Philip was 46 at his death.)" In his next two articles he avoided the question altogether. It was only in *The Search for Alexander*, the museum catalogue published in 1980, that he offered more specific assertions: that the bones in Tomb II "belong to a man forty to fifty years old," that those in the antechamber were of a woman in her mid-twenties (23-27). It was left for Robin Lane Fox, using personal and unpublished information supplied by Andronikos, to acquaint scholars with the three mysterious occupants of Tomb I, glossed over in Andronikos's published work as "a large number of bones" and

Abbreviations

Adams	W. Lindsay Adams, "The royal Macedonian tomb at Vergina: an historical interpretation", *The Ancient World* 3 (1980) 67-72.
Calder	William Musgrave Calder III, "Diadem and barrel-vault: a note", *AJA* 85 (1981) 334-5.
Fredricksmeyer	E. A. Fredricksmeyer, "Again the so-called tomb of Philip II", *AJA* 85 (1981) 330-334.
Giallombardo-Tripodi	Anna Maria Prestianni Giallombardo and Bruno Tripodi, "Le tombe regali di Vergina: quale Filippo?", *Annali della Scuola Normale Superiore di Pisa,* class. lett. fil., 10 (1980) 989-1001.
Green, AM^2	Peter Green, *Alexander of Macedon 356-323 BC: a historical biography* (Harmondsworth 1974).
Hammond, PTHC	N. G. L. Hammond, " 'Philip's Tomb' in historical context", *GRBS* 19 (1978) 331-350.
LF-*AG*	Robin Lane Fox, *Alexander the Great* (London 1973).
LF-*SA*	Robin Lane Fox, *The Search for Alexander* (Boston 1980).
PWL	Phyllis Williams Lehmann, "The so-called tomb of Philip II: a different interpretation", *AJA* 84 (1980) 527-531.
"RTV"	M. Andronikos, "The Royal Tomb at Vergina and the Problem of the Dead," *AAA* 13 (1980) 168-78.

The Royal Tombs of Vergina: A Historical Analysis

"some bones scattered around in disorderly fashion."[1] Some of this testimony, then, has been deliberately down-played; some of it (e.g., that on the age of the bones in Tomb I) has been disputed; none of it has been exposed to the scrutiny of outside experts; all of it figures largely in any theory of identification hitherto introduced. These are warning signs that we disregard at our peril.

A similar state of affairs exists over the dating of the pottery. From the start Andronikos opted for the third quarter of the century, though he conceded that a lower date of 320 was possible.[2] With time he grew more specific: "vases made about 340-330 B.C.," "it would be possible to make out a case for dating all the finds to *ca.* 340"; "the pottery dates the tomb to around the middle of the fourth century B.C., perhaps to about 340 B.C.": "the sherds found above the facade dated the tomb to around 340 B.C."[3] Lindsay Adams is by no means the only scholar to feel that "one might justifiably pick a much later date". If 320, why not 316? How narrow a limit can be imposed on stylistic grounds? Is it really possible to date a few pieces of fourth-century pottery within twenty years either way of a median point? And is it not common for burial-goods in such a tomb as this slightly to predate the sepulchre itself?[4] Once again, in default of a final excavation report and external expert corroboration, the historian should be wary of resting too weighty a hypothesis on problematical evidence of this sort.

Dating by purely aesthetic criteria, especially where the material for comparison is so inadequate (indeed, in some cases virtually non-

---

[1] See *AAA* 10 (1977 [1979]) 1-39 (in Greek), 40-72 (in English), reprinted separately 1978 as a monograph, *The Royal Graves at Vergina* [*RGV*]. This, apart from newspaper interviews, constitutes Andronikos's original report. Hammond's speculations on Amyntas: PTHC 338. The evidence of the teeth: "*RT*" 75. The articles that avoid the problem are those in "RTP" and *PM*. Andronikos's latest word on the age of the bones is to be found at *Search* 37 and "RTV" 172 and his remarks about the bones in Tomb I at *PM* 205 and *Search* 27. Professor E. N. Borza, who has corresponded with Andronikos on this last point, quotes him as fully recognizing the serious historical implications of the find. Lane Fox on the bones in Tomb I: LF-*SA* 80, 92-93. I am grateful to Mr. Lane Fox for confirming to me, by letter, that his information came directly from Andronikos.

[2] *RGV* 48: cf. Hammond, PTHC 335, PWL 528 n. 3, "RTP" 35.

[3] "RT" 70, "RTP" 35, *PM* 229, *Search* 27.

[4] Adams, 68 n. 14, cf. PWL 528 nn. 3 and 4. The final point made here, one, I think, with which no serious archaeologist would disagree, I owe to Professor Borza, who with great generosity allowed me to read the draft typescript of his paper, "The Macedonian Royal Tombs at Vergina: Some Cautionary Notes," forthcoming in *Archaeological News*.

existent) offers even greater risks of mere subjectivism. (One recalls Proust's telling remark, put in Saint-Loup's mouth, that mere adherence to the latest aesthetic formula was no true test of real intelligence.) How can Andronikos claim that the ivory heads and the wall-paintings found "are, with no use of special pleading [sic] . . . definitely in the third quarter of the century"? These things are unique: what yardstick is he using? We are not told. Is it really possible to place the relief heads on the silver vessels within the decade 340-330? The dating of Tomb III is even odder. As reported by *The Times* shortly after its discovery, a pottery lamp enabled Andronikos to date this burial "in the second quarter of the fourth century, 375-350 B.C.," and to speculate that the occupant might be Amyntas III, Alexander II, Ptolemy of Alorus, or Perdiccas III. However, in the two preliminary accounts of Tomb III that he has published, this lamp is conspicuous by its absence. Instead, Andronikos now dates the tomb, on purely aesthetic grounds (the murals, three ivory figurines), to the mid-fourth century, *ca.* 350, and in any case not later than "the third quarter of that century." Even Hammond, a staunch defender of Andronikos's theories, was, understandably, moved by this to observe that "arguments for dating the murals are inevitably subjective as we have no contemporary frescoes for comparison."[5]

The case of Tomb III highlights the problem confronting us. Here we have a tomb that is dated to the mid-fourth century by an archaeologist, containing bones that, so a physical anthropologist claims (though we do not have access to his report), are those of a boy in early adolescence. Both assertions must be taken on trust, and the first, at least, on the face of it looks dubious.[6] The historian may well be forgiven for feeling that in such a case literary *testimonia* are preferable to so-called "hard" evidence. The only boy between twelve and fourteen eligible for a royal Macedonian burial in the fourth century was Alexander IV, murdered in prison by Cassander in 311/10. A second, highly marginal candidate would be Alexander III's bastard son by Barsine, Heracles. Born in 327 or 325, he emerged as a possible claimant to the throne in 323, but was rejected. In 310, after the execution of Alexander IV, Polyperchon, seeing in

---

[5] *RGV* 40 and 48: *The Times*, 5 Sept. 1978; *PM* 229-30, *Search* 37-38, cf. Hammond, PTHC 338 and n. 22.

[6] Nor, one might have thought, is the information to be extracted from burnt, shrunken, and in many cases pulverised bones — as regards their age or anything else — all that reliable.

The Royal Tombs of Vergina: A Historical Analysis

Heracles the sole surviving blood-descendant of the Argead dynasty, mustered an army to support him against Cassander. But Cassander made a deal with Polyperchon, and in 309 Heracles was strangled after a banquet. Diodorus gives his age the previous year as seventeen, and Justin as fifteen. At eighteen Heracles would be a little old as a candidate for Tomb III (if the bone-dating holds good); at sixteen he could pass. Even so, though the circumstances of his death do not rule out such a burial altogether, they do make it highly unlikely.[7]

At this stage we should, surely, concentrate on securing what external evidence we have — and it is a considerable amount — concerning the history and prosopography of the Macedonian royal house, and applying this to the Vergina finds. In the present test case, it should be possible, if the bones are confirmed as those of an adolescent boy, to say: This burial is that of Alexander IV (or, just conceivably, of Heracles), and no other hypothesis, given the facts of the case, is admissible. Such an approach has to be both ruthless and systematic, and the truth of the matter is that up till now the quest for evidence has been piecemeal.

Very early on, moreover, it became clear that Philip II was one obvious — indeed, the preferred — candidate for the occupancy of Tomb II; this possibility appeared, for various reasons, so immensely enticing that much of the work done has been, in effect, a *parti pris* search for evidence to clinch this claim. Diadem, larnax, ceremonial armor (the greaves in particular), ivory miniature heads, starbursts, gold wreaths, bones, pottery, silver vessels, murals — all have been used at one time or another by Andronikos or Hammond in support of this thesis. Yet cumulatively they have pointed rather to the condition of royalty than to a specific king. Hammond himself had to admit[8] that much of the evidence would suit Philip Arrhidaeus equally well. On the other hand, of the three main arguments advanced by advocates of Philip Arrhidaeus,[9] none carries anything

---

[7] For Alexander IV's death see Diod. 19.52.4, 105.1-2; Paus. 9.7.2; Justin 15.2.3-5. The evidence on Heracles is collected by Berve, *Alex* no. 353, p. 168. W. W. Tarn, *Alexander the Great* 2 (1948) 330ff., dismisses Heracles as a mere late romantic fiction, but the *testimonia* remain more circumstantial and convincing than Tarn will allow. See Curt. 10.6.11, Justin 11.10.3 and 13.2.6-14 for his consideration as a royal candidate in 323, and Diod. 20.20.1-2, 28.1-4, Justin 15.2.3-5, Paus. 9.7.2 for his death (and age).

[8] PTHC 337-38. Cf. now Giallombardo-Tripodi, 990.

[9] Adams, 67-72, PWL 527-31.

approaching complete conviction. The claim that the barrel-vaulting of Philip II's tomb could not have preceded Alexander's opening up of the East — where such vaulting abounded — rests on an *argumentum ex silentio*, which fresh discoveries could at any time refute; it also assumes a quite astonishing lack of prior communication between East and West. It is noteworthy that both Tomb II at Vergina and the vaulted stadium tunnel at Nemea were found as Boyd's article on the arch and the vault was in press. We also have to consider that passage in the *Laws* where Plato, writing about 350, refers to an underground tomb made in the form of an oblong vault (*psalida*) of porous stone, and covered with a tumulus.[10]

The assertion that the diadem, likewise, was an Oriental importation of Alexander's is highly debatable and, arguably, at variance with earlier numismatic evidence. Phyllis Williams Lehmann is obliged to explain away the gold medallion of Philip from Tarsus as an anachronism, and, further, makes no mention of several earlier coin-portraits (Archelaus, Aeropus, Alexander I) that appear to be furnished with a diadem.[11] Lastly, the supposition that Alexander

[10] See Thomas D. Boyd, "The arch and the vault in Greek architecture", *AJA* 82 (1978) 83-100, esp. 89 n. 24; cf. R. A. Tomlinson, "Vaulting techniques of the ancient Macedonian tombs," *AM* 2 (1977) 473-79, and for the Nemean tunnel S. G. Miller, (1) "Excavations at Nemea, 1977," *Hesperia* 47 (1978) 84-88 with fig. 7, and (2) "Excavations at Nemea, 1978," *ibid.* 48 (1979) 96-103. In the latter article Miller refers to a *graffito* in the tunnel naming Telestas of Messene, victor in the boys' boxing event at Olympia. This victory is normally dated *ca.* 340, on the authority of L. Moretti, *Olympionikai* (Rome 1957) no. 43, p. 125: see, e.g., *The Eternal Olympics*, ed. N. Yalouris (Athens/New Rochelle 1979) 292. It has thus been used to suggest a possible earlier date for the tunnel than the last quarter of the fourth century, where Miller firmly locates it, *loc.cit.* (2) 103. Unfortunately, our only evidence for Telestas is Paus. 6.14.4, which gives no date. Since he was a Messenian, Telestas must have competed after the liberation of Messenia from Sparta in 368 by Epaminondas; and since Silanion executed his statue, his victory must have fallen some time before 310, the date of Silanion's death. Within these limits, however, almost any Olympiad could plausibly be suggested. It follows, therefore, that Telestas cannot be used either to confirm or to deny the dating of the Nemea tunnel; and in any case there is no guarantee of how soon or late *post eventum* the *graffito* might have been inscribed. The relevant citation from the *Laws* (947D-E) runs: "Their tomb shall be constructed under ground, an oblong vault of porous stone. . .they shall heap a mound in a circle over it, and surround it with a grove of trees. . ." On the whole barrel-vaulting argument see now Fredricksmeyer 333-34, independently adducing further evidence that confirms the views expressed here. Andronikos' claim that the vaulting is later than the vertical walls was first published in "RTV" 170: see also his further arguments, *ibid.* 174-76.

[11] See PWL 529 with n. 21, and Giallombardo-Tripodi, 992-94, for the arguments: also Andronikos, "RTV" 177-78. Convenient reproductions of the relevant coins: C. M. Kraay and M. Hirmer, *Greek Coins* (London 1966) pl.169, nos. 556 and 557 (both of Alexander I, wearing the *kausia* and diadem, cf. p. 350), no. 559

The Royal Tombs of Vergina: A Historical Analysis

would never have accorded Philip's wife Cleopatra royal burial honors[12] out of respect for Olympias is mere speculation (in good fourth-century oratorical style) "from probability" and in any case implicitly contradicted by Plutarch, who says that Alexander was, understandably, "infuriated" by Olympias's murder of Cleopatra and her child the moment his back was turned. Better, at that tricky early point in his reign, to offend his mother than a powerful group of old-guard Macedonian barons.[13]

This seems as good a point as any to dispose of one piece of evidence that has had too long a run for its money: I mean the shortened and distorted greave that, it is hinted, got that way because Philip II was its owner, and had been lamed by a spear-thrust through the thigh.[14] We do not even need to argue, with Lehmann and Adams,[15] that such a wound would not shorten the leg. Especially since Philip sustained a further wound, in the shin, which might otherwise have clinched Andronikos's case (but which neither he nor anyone else cites), it is in a sense frustrating to have to report that Philip's wounds cannot possibly have any connection whatsoever with the ceremonial greaves in the antechamber of Tomb II. Our best source in general for those wounds, Didymus Chalcenterus,[16]

(Archelaus); M. Price, *Coins of the Macedonians* (London 1974) no. 53 (Aeropus: I owe this reference to Professor Borza). For a good reproduction of the Tarsus medallion, greatly enlarged, see *PM* 169. Further testimony undermining Lehmann's thesis in Fredricksmeyer 332-33, Calder 334-35 (who reminds us that, *pace* Andronikos, the so-called "diadem" is in fact a *stephanos* or crown).

[12] Adams, 69-70.

[13] Plut. *Alex.* 10.4: "...he showed his anger against Olympias for the horrible revenge which she took upon Cleopatra during his absence."

[14] Andronikos, *RGV* 46, "RT" 76, "RTV" 169, and esp. "RTP" 41, "the left one was 3.5 centimeters shorter than the right, a fact which reminded us that Philip was lame": cf. LF-*SA* 85. Most commonly cited sources for Philip's wounds: Demosthenes 18.67, Justin 9.3.2.

[15] PWL 528 n. 9; Adams, 70 and n. 37.

[16] Ed. H. Diels and W. Schubart (Teubner) 12.36-13.12. On the leg wounds see in particular 12.64-66: "Pleuratas the Illyrian charged him during an Illyrian campaign and wounded him with his lance in the right shin..." and 13.3-7, "he received a third wound during his attack on the Triballi when during a charge one of the enemy thrust a sarissa [*sic*] through his right thigh, laming him." The reading *klein* (collarbone) for *knēmēn* (shin) depends on the assumption that Demosthenes' report (18.67) is exhaustive, and that therefore the broken collarbone to which he refers must be the wound mentioned by Didymus, especially since Didymus does not refer to a broken collarbone himself. I see no reason for Philip not having suffered both wounds. It is interesting that Lehmann (supra n. 15) cites the second of these passages without drawing the obvious conclusion from it, while Adams' claim that Philip was *not* wounded in the tibia suggests either an unargued preference for the reading *klein*, or else unfamiliarity with Didymus' text.

reports spear-thrusts through the thigh and shin of the right leg, just as we might expect from normal cavalry encounters. Yet a glance at the greaves themselves, as Andronikos was well aware from the beginning,[17] shows that is it the *left* one that belongs to a shorter and in some way deformed limb. We are thus forced to the conclusion that, if these greaves *do* belong to Philip II, not only was his right leg virtually unaffected — except for the lameness Plutarch records (*Mor.* 331B) — by two major wounds, but, in addition, his left leg was malformed, perhaps congenitally.[18] This possibility cannot be ruled out, but it remains, if true, a striking physical trait mentioned in no surviving source.

Amid such a maze of ambiguities it is, surely, preferable to begin by establishing the facts on which scholars are in substantial agreement, and only then to see how this initial bridgehead may be extended. First and foremost we have Hammond's irrefutable demonstration, first made as long ago as 1968, that ancient Aigeai and modern Vergina are one and the same.[19] Since we possess ample evidence in our literary sources[20] that Aigeai was the traditional burial-place of Macedonian royalty, it was a natural inference from this identification that traces of such burials should be discovered *in situ*. In fact, Andronikos's excavations since 1977 have produced more startling confirmation for Hammond's thesis than anyone could have foreseen. The three tombs so far uncovered also enable us to take the argument a step further. The grave-goods found in these tombs — the diadem, the gold wreaths, the starburst, the fine frescoes (in particular the hunting scene), the ceremonial armor and

---

[17] See his remarks in *RGV* 46: " . . .measurement showed that the left greave is 3.50 cm. shorter. The greaves are also shaped differently: the left greave has a more pronounced bulge over the knee muscle."

[18] The opinion of an orthopaedic surgeon who examined photographs of the greaves is that their owner may well have suffered from the effects of a clubfoot or, more probably, polio in the left leg (personal information, Dr. George Kitzmiller). I recently had the opportunity to make a close personal examination of the greaves: the left one almost completely lacks that strong muscular "swell" so prominent in the right one, which would seem to offer support for the polio theory.

[19] First proposed by Hammond in *AM* 1 (1970) 65, and subsequently in his *Hist Mace* I 56-58 (cf. maps at 124 and 140), repeated *Hist Mace* II 13 and PTHC 331-32 with n. 2; accepted by Andronikos, *RGV* 5, "RTP" 35, "RT" 57, *PM* 188 (where he cites Fanoula Papazoglou as having first, in 1957, aired the difficulties of the equation Edessa = Aigeai), *Search* 26; cf. LF-*AG* 19 and 553, LF-*SA* 77-78. PWL 528 and n. 1, Adams 67 with nn. 4-5, G. Daux, "Aigeai: site des tombes royales de la Macédoine antique", *CRAI* (1977) 620-30.

[20] E.g., Plut. *Pyrrh.* 26.6, Justin 7.1.7-8,10; 7.2.1-4; Diod. 7.16.1, 19.52.5, 22.11.2-12.1.

furniture — clearly indicate royal burials.[21] It follows that the Great Tumulus of Vergina can be identified as the Macedonian royal cemetery, and that consequently any tomb found within it must be that of a Macedonian king or queen, prince or princess. Even the harshest critics of Andronikos's datings are agreed that the three tombs excavated so far can be placed within the second half of the fourth century (350 ± - 300 ±), with perhaps a certain extra upward latitude for the cist-grave of Tomb I. Now while a tomb may on occasion, as we have seen, be dated a little later than some of the artifacts in it, nevertheless, as Lane Fox rightly observes,[22] "any date after around 300 B.C. would require a belief that everything in the tomb was antique and that nothing contemporary had intruded."

We therefore have the task of providing candidates for the three tombs' occupants, from Macedonian royalty, within that half-century. While interest has mainly centered upon Tomb II, Adams is surely right to stress the importance of "the woman in the antechamber."[23] I would go further, and argue that the identification of all four burials must be considered part of a single, interdependent inquiry. It is my contention that our written *testimonia* provide us with a complete prosopography of the Argead dynasty and its marital affairs during this period (see tabulated chart, pp. 140-41). In particular, I am convinced that we know about every child of Philip II's, male or female, that survived past puberty; the enormous importance attached to all his recognized offspring makes it unlikely in the extreme that any claimant has been lost to posterity. Despite Justin's characteristically hyperbolic claim[24] that Philip had numerous sons by various marriages, the truth is that, even at the most liberal estimate,[25] on a total of seven wives and mistresses he sired no more than two sons and three daughters who reached maturity, plus one boy and/or girl murdered in infancy. All our candidates — with

[21] Cf. Hammond, PTHC 335 and n. 17.
[22] LF-*SA* 81.
[23] Adams, 69f.
[24] 9.8.3: *habuit et multos alios filios ex variis matrimoniis regio more susceptos, qui partim fato, partim ferro periere*. . .Alexander III is the only son of whom it could be said that he died *fato* (and even that claim has been disputed); if Justin can be trusted at all, he must here be speaking of still-births and infant mortality. As for *ferro*, the only possible candidates known are Philip Arrhidaeus and Caranus, the son of Cleopatra-Eurydice (cf. infra n. 25).
[25] That is, admitting (which presents problems, cf. Ellis, *PMI* 302 n. 4) both a son, Caranus, and a daughter, Europa, by Cleopatra; see Satyrus *ap.* Athen. 13.557e, Diod. 17.2.3, Justin 9.7.12, 11.2.3, Paus. 8.7.7.

the dubious exception of Amyntas IV son of Perdiccas[26] — are in direct line of descent from Philip himself. Careful scrutiny will not only sharply reduce the number of eligible occupants for the three Vergina tombs, but must also cast some doubt on the extent and universality of Macedonian royal polygamy, which has become an article of faith on surprisingly little evidence.[27] It scarcely seems to have extended, in any substantive sense, beyond Philip II himself; and the joke about Philip, that he "always married a new wife with each new war he undertook,"[28] both pinpoints the unusual nature of his practice, and, clearly, suggests how it might be exaggerated by critics. I hope I will not be regarded (however improbably) as a moralist in disguise[29] if I maintain that Philip was neither so polygamous nor so polyphiloprogenitive as modern scholars have sometimes assumed.

Our main (but not our only) source for Philip's marital and procreational activities is the famous passage excerpted from Satyrus by Athenaeus (13.557b-e = *FHG* 3.161 F5). It is my contention that this passage lists Philip's women (with one understandable exception) in chronological order, and, moreover, distinguishes between marriages — at least, those dynastically recognized in Macedonia, a crucial point — and mere local liaisons contracted in the interests of diplomacy.[30] While Philip was never averse to protecting his frontiers by means of a well-placed alliance, he (like every other Greek and Macedonian ruler) was acutely aware of the dangers involved in the

---

[26] Raised as a possible ("albeit remote") candidate for the occupancy of Tomb II by Adams, 68 and n. 16. Cf. Ellis *PMI* 44, 46-47, 250 n. 10 (with further literature therein cited). Though undoubtedly in the direct line of succession, it is debatable whether Amyntas ever occupied the throne of Macedon in any formal sense. Even if he did so, as a minor, in 360, or 359, by the time of his death he had long been replaced by Philip II, while the diadem and larnax of Tomb II indicate a reigning monarch. Since, furthermore, Amyntas was executed by Alexander in 336 on the (probably well-grounded) charge of aiming at usurpation of the throne (Plut. *Mor.* 327C, Ellis, "The Security of the Macedonian Throne under Philip II, *AM* 1 [1970] 68-75, and "Amyntas Perdikka, Philip II and Alexander the Great: a study in conspiracy," *JHS* 91 [1971] 15-24; Green *AM²* 111-12), it is scarcely to be credited that he would receive such lavish honors at his burial (cf, infra p. 148 and n. 56 for the incompatibility of Cynna's bones with those in the antechamber).

[27] See, e.g., *Hist Macc* II 153-54.

[28] Satyrus *ap*. Athen. 13.557b: "Philip always contracted a marriage with each new war."

[29] See, e.g., the comments of Ellis, *PMI* 212.

[30] The criticisms of Ellis, *PMI* 211-12, and n. 7, p. 302, against the similar position I took up in *AM²* 27f. and 515 n. 55, do not strike me as in any way cogent. For a similar conflation see now *Hist Macc* II 676.

indiscriminate begetting of sons.³¹ The troubles occasioned by his final, fatal Macedonian marriage offer a nice instance of this. It seems clear that his foreign liaisons, whether regarded in Macedonian eyes as marriages (Audata, Meda) or mere concubinage (Philinna, Nicesipolis), were in some sense distinct from his Macedonian and Epirote marriages (Phila, Olympias, Cleopatra). He was also lucky in that two of his relationships were without surviving issue, and two more produced only daughters. Yet in the last resort what conferred royal status, at least on his male children (and his daughters, we may note, all made royal marriages) was the simple fact of *Philip's paternity*: the grudging acceptance of Philip Arrhidaeus as king,³² albeit in an emergency, proves that beyond a doubt. Nevertheless, the status of these wives and mistresses remains important for us: it determines, *inter alia*, which of them was, and was not, entitled to burial in the royal necropolis at Aigeai.

Let us run quickly through the list as Satyrus presents it. The first name is that of the Illyrian, Audata, probably a niece or daughter of King Bardylis, whom Philip married in 359, immediately after the great disaster inflicted by the Illyrians on Perdiccas III, as a means of buying time to recoup Macedonia's fortunes.³³ By her he had one child, a daughter, Cynna or Cynane (Berve, *Alex* no. 456), who in 338 or 337 was married, at Philip's insistence, to Amyntas IV son of Perdiccas.³⁴ The one child of this marriage, a daughter again, Adea (later Eurydice), was born not earlier than 337, and not later than 336/5 (since Amyntas was executed by Alexander in mid-336). In 322 she married Philip Arrhidaeus, and was forced by Olympias to commit suicide in 317, when not more than twenty-one years old;

---

³¹ See, for example, the anecdote about Peisistratus's *mariage de convenance* with Megacles' daughter (Hdt.1.61) where the point is clearly stressed: "Since he already had grown male heirs . . . and had no wish for issue by his newly-wed wife, he had intercourse with her in abnormal fashion" [i.e. anally]. Though Philip's record in begetting children may be due to nothing but natural causes, I do not think we can rule out either exposure or primitive forms of birth-control such as that described by Herodotus in assessing his dynastic plans. It is noteworthy that when he clearly wanted another son, by Cleopatra-Eurydice, he duly got it, and without delay.

³² Though not without strong objections, precisely on the grounds of his birth: Ptolemy (Justin 13.2.11) complained that he was unfit for the succession, among other reasons, *quod ex Larissaeo scorto nasceretur*.

³³ See Ellis, *PMI* 47-48; *Hist Mace* II 214-15, regards her as "part of the settlement by which a marriage with Bardylis was made," and dates the marriage, less plausibly, to 358. In either case her daughter Cynna had to be of an age to marry in 338/7.

³⁴ Ellis, *PMI* 216-17 with reff.

Name	Birthdate	Status	Marriage	Date of death/repudiation	Age at death/repudiation	Eligibility for royal burial
Audata/Eurydice	ca. 380-77	foreign (Illyrian) wife of Philip II	359, to Philip II	?repudiated in 358	20-22	marginal/nil
Cynna/Cynane	359/8	daughter of Philip II and Audata	338/7, to Amyntas IV (q.v.)	executed ca. 322 by Alcetas; buried at Aigeai	ca. 36-37	*eligible by marriage
Adea/Eurydice	337-35	daughter of Amyntas IV and Cynna (q.v.)	322, to Philip III Arrhidaeus	executed Olympias; buried at Aigeai	ca. 19-21	*eligible by birth and marriage
Phila	ca. 378-75	daughter of Derdas and sister of Machatas of Elimiotis; wife of Philip II	358, to Philip II	died (?) without issue, 358/7	ca. 19-21	eligible by birth and marriage
Nicesipolis	ca. 372-70	Thessalian (?niece of Jason of Pherae) mistress of Philip II	——	351, 20 days after birth of daughter (Thessalonike, q.v.)	ca. 19-21	ineligible
Philinna	ca. 378-75	Thessalian from Larissa; dancing girl; mistress of Philip II	——	unknown, but probably repudiated before Oct. 357	ca. 19-21	ineligible
Olympias	ca. 378-75	Epirote wife of Philip II; daughter of Molossian King Neoptolemus	Oct. 357, to Philip II	316, executed by Cassander at Pydna; unburied (?)	ca. 60-62	†eligible by marriage
Meda	ca. 360	foreign (Thracian) wife of Philip II; daughter of King Cothelas	342, to Philip II	died (?) or repudiated without issue, ca. 340-38	?20-25	marginal/nil
Cleopatra/Eurydice	ca. 357-54	aristocratic Macedonian wife of Philip II	338, to Philip II	335; executed by Olympias, with her baby	?17-21	eligible by birth and marriage
Philip III Arrhidaeus	ca. 357/6	son of Philip II and Philinna (q.v.); king of Macedon 323-17.	322, to Adea/Eurydice (q.v.)	317; executed by Olympias; buried at Aigeai	40-41	*eligible by birth and status
Amyntas IV	ca. 365	son of Perdiccas III	338/7 to Cynna	336; executed by Alexander III (q.v.)	29-30	eligible by birth and status

The Royal Tombs of Vergina: A Historical Analysis

Name	Birthdate	Status	Marriage	Date of death/repudiation	Age at death/repudiation	Eligibility for royal burial
Alexander III	356	son of Philip II and Olympias; king of Macedon, 336-23.	327, to Roxane	323, in Babylon; body hijacked to Egypt	32	†eligible by birth and status
Cleopatra	?355/4	daughter of Philip II and Olympias	336, to Alexander of Epirus	309/8, executed in Sardis	ca. 46	†eligible by birth
Philip II	383/2	son of Amyntas III and Eurydice; king of Macedon, 359-36.	359, to Audata 357, to Olympias 342, to Meda 338, to Cleopatra/Eurydice	336, murdered at Aigeai, and buried there	ca. 46-47	*eligible by birth and status
Thessalonike	351	daughter of Philip II and Nicesipolis (q.v.)	316, to Cassander (q.v.)	295, executed by her son Antipater	56	eligible by marriage
Roxane	ca. 342-41	foreign (Bactrian) wife of Alexander III	327, to Alexander III	311/10, executed (with Alexander IV) by Cassander	31-32	eligible by marriage
Alexander IV	323	son of Alexander III and Roxane; king of Macedon, 323-11	—	311/10, executed (with Roxane) by Cassander	12-13	eligible by birth and status
Heracles (?)	327 or 325	son of Alexander III and Barsine	—	309, executed by Polyperchon	ca. 16 or 18	?eligible by birth (marginal)
Cassander	ca. 354	son of Antipater; de facto king of Macedon, 316-297	316, to Thessalonike (q.v.)	297, of disease	ca. 57	eligible by status

*denotes a person known to have been buried at Aigeai
†denotes a person known NOT to have been buried at Aegeai

subsequently (316) Cassander gave her, Philip Arrhidaeus, and Cynna a royal burial in Aigeai. Like her mother, and in all likelihood her grandmother before her, she was trained as a warrior.[35] We hear no more of that grandmother, Audata, after 359:[36] it seems clear enough that with his victory over Bardylis in 358 Philip felt that his Illyrian consort had served her purpose and could be repudiated. Besides, he urgently needed to strengthen his position at home, as a Macedonian dynast, by marrying into one of the always restive out-kingdoms. Thus it is that Satyrus next records his marriage to Phila, an Elimiote princess, sister to Derdas and Machatas, the father of Harpalus. Since we hear no more of Phila, despite her blue blood and impeccable Macedonian credentials, it is almost certain that she died soon after her marriage, probably of an illness (malaria was endemic to the Macedonian lowlands) without producing an heir. If she died in childbirth, which is possible (see p. 147), the child did not survive.[37] While Audata, as a foreign political consort, can probably be eliminated from the list of those eligible for a royal Macedonian burial, Phila, though eight years outside our provisional date-limit (but see above, p. 142), could, in theory, qualify.

At this point (358/7) Philip needed both a dynastic wife, and further territorial consolidation. His first move, according to Satyrus,

---

[35] Berve, *Alex* nos. 23, 61 and 456; Arrian, *Succ.* §22; Polyaen. *Strat.* 8.60; Diod. 19.11.1-7; Aelian *VH* 13.36; Justin 14.5.1-10. For the fighting tradition of Cynna and Adea see Duris *ap.* Athen. 13.560f. The royal burial at Aigeai: Diod. 19.52.5, cf. Diyllus *ap.* Athen. 4.155a.

[36] Hammond's thesis (PTHC 336) that Audata (who, to confuse matters, also took the name Eurydice on marriage) is said by Duris to have fought in single combat with Olympias (and was thus in evidence at least two years later) rests on a complete misinterpretation of the passage in question (supra n. 35). Duris refers not to a duel, but to a *war* (*polemon*), and makes it quite clear that the occasion was the confrontation in 317 between *Adea*-Eurydice and Olympias (Diod. 19.11.2), especially since the Eurydice mentioned by Duris is described as "being trained in martial arts by Cynna the Illyrian." A woman bred in a fighting tradition is, I would submit, more likely to learn such things from her mother than from her daughter.

[37] Satyrus offers our only ancient testimony to Phila's existence, let alone to her family background. For Machatas see Arrian *Anab.* 3.6.4, 5.8.3, and infra, p. 151. cf. Ellis *PMI* 38, *Hist Mace* II 215, and W. Hoffman, *RE* 19 (1938) 2086 , who writes that she "wurde wohl von Ph. gleich nach seiner Thronbesteigung geheiratet, muss aber bereits zur Zeit der Hochzeit mit Olympias im Oktober 357, die ebenfalls legitime Gemahlin war, tot gewesen sein oder von ihm getrennt gelebt haben . . . [no polygamous excesses there!]. Kinder aus dieser Ehe werden nicht genannt." On the prevalence of malaria in ancient Macedonia, especially in the central Emathian plain, see E. N. Borza, "Some observations on Malaria and the Ecology of Central Macedonia in Antiquity", *AJAH* 4 (1979) 102-24.

was to *beget children* (*epaidopoiēsato*) by two Thessalian women, Nicesipolis and Philinna, "wishing to put in a claim to the Thessalian nation as his own beside others." There is no mention of marriage.[38] Philinna of Larissa, variously described as a dancing-girl, a lady of ill repute, and a common whore (see n. 32), came into Philip's life in 358, while he was supporting the Aleuadae against Alexander of Pherae's relatives; the product of their brief union, born *ca.* 357/6, was Philip Arrhidaeus. I am suspicious of modern attempts to transform Philinna into an Aleuad or otherwise to improve her social status *via* a good marriage. Ptolemy son of Agesarchus includes her in a list of royal mistresses, which is precisely where she belongs.[39]

Nicesipolis, Satyrus's one divagation from strict chronological order, is clearly bracketed here with Philinna simply as Philip's second Thessalian mistress. This relationship can be dated to 352; an anecdote of Plutarch's (*Mor.* 141B-C) both emphasizes its non-marital nature, and describes how Olympias was charmed by the girl's good looks, wit, and elegance. A legitimate wife would have got much shorter shrift at Olympias' hands; and Satyrus is at pains to emphasize that it was only later, with Meda, his Thracian bride, that Philip brought home a *second wife* after Olympias (γήμας δὲ καὶ ταύτην ἐπεισήγαγεν τῇ Ὀλυμπιάδι). In other words, at the time of his marriage to Olympias, he was not contracted to any other official wife. Nicesipolis in 352/1 bore Philip a daughter, Thessalonike — who subsequently married Cassander — and then died, only twenty days after her confinement.[40] Neither she nor Philinna can on

---

[38] Ellis, *PMI* 302 n. 7, dismisses this distinction with the flip comment: "It is easier to take the whole passage at face value [*sic*] and to assume that Satyros was not interested in repeating a precise formula wife after wife merely to ease the task of future historians." But Ptolemy's *Histories of Philopator*, cited by Athenaeus (13.578a) would alone suffice to refute Ellis' assumption.

[39] For Philinna see, beside Satyrus, Arrian *Succ.* §§1a,1b, cf. §10; Justin 9.8.2, 13.2.11; Ptolemy *ap.* Athen. 13.578a. Ellis, *PMI* 61, and *Hist Macc* II 225 with n. 7, both apparently following Beloch, *Griech. Geschichte*³ III 2, p. 69, work hard to establish her status and respectability, though in my opinion with very little success. Much more to the point are H. D. Westlake's comments in *Thessaly in the Fourth Century B.C.* (London 1935) 168: "Philinna, far from being an aristocrat, is normally regarded as little better than a concubine." The dates of the relationship, and of Philip Arrhidaeus' birth, are secure: anything later would have run over into Philip's marriage with Olympias, and not have given Arrhidaeus time to be of marriageable age at the time of the Pixodarus affair (336).

[40] For Nicesipolis cf. Paus. 9.7.3, 8.7.7, and esp. Steph. Byz. s.v. *Thessalonike* (where she is described as Jason of Pherae's niece); also Westlake (supra n. 39) 181, Ellis, *PMI* 84-85, 261 n. 108, *Hist Macc* II 278-79 and 524. The latter authors' argument is uneasy over the relationship (they talk of a "marriage" in quotation-marks), and

any count be regarded as eligible for a royal Macedonian interment,[41] though their offspring, whether by marriage (Thessalonike) or by right of male descent (Arrhidaeus) undoubtedly were.

Philip's marriage to Olympias, which now follows on Satyrus's list took place in October 357 and produced two children: Alexander III in the summer of 356, Cleopatra perhaps a year later. Though all three were royal Argeads *par excellence*, by birth or marriage, none of them was buried in Aigeai, and indeed Olympias is said to have been denied burial of any sort: she was executed on Cassander's orders at Pydna in 316, aged about sixty, probably by stoning. Alexander, who met his end in Babylon (323), was removed to Alexandria by Ptolemy, where his embalmed remains were seen centuries later by Augustus and Caligula. Cleopatra survived until 309/8, being then in her mid-forties, when she was murdered, in Sardis, at the request of Antigonus; though he is said to have given her a funeral in royal style, there is no indication that her remains were returned to Macedonia for interment, and no extant bones, at present, of the right age-group to fit her.[42]

Nicesipolis apart, no extramarital liaisons are attributed to Philip between 357 and 342 — another hint that his appetite for marriage was not so indiscriminate as has been suggested, and was largely stimulated in 359-8 by the uncertain conditions prevailing at his accession. Either that, or his strong-willed Epirote queen was, from 357, riding him on an unprecedentedly tight rein, which (to judge from the anecdotes concerning her) is by no means impossible. At all events, in 342 he contracted a foreign, politically based marriage with a Thracian princess, Meda, daughter of Cothelas, who brought him

---

illogically supposes that, because Thessalonike "was evidently brought up at court, and eventually became queen herself" [by marriage, be it noted], *therefore* Philip's liaison with Nicesipolis, "though it did not make the bride a queen...cannot have been a mere association devoid of all honour and status". It was Philip's blood that counted; and if Nicesipolis *was* Jason's niece (which has been doubted), we can safely infer that her status, and the relationship, stood a good deal higher in Thessaly than it did in Macedonia.

[41] Lane Fox, LF-*SA* 93, is thus wholly mistaken in his assumption that Tomb I at Vergina could, in any circumstances, be occupied by Nicesipolis.

[42] For Cleopatra see Berve, *Alex* no. 433, pp. 212-13; her end is described in some detail by Diod. 20.37.3-6, where Antigonus, we are told, "took care that she got a royal funeral." For Olympias's birth-date see Berve, *Alex* no. 581 p. 283, and for her death, Diod. 19.51.4-6, Justin 14.6.4-12, Polyaen.4.11.3, Aelian *HN* 12.6. Ptolemy's hijacking of Alexander's body to Egypt: Diod. 18.28.2-4, Strabo 17.1.8, Paus. 1.6.3, Arrian *FGrH* 156.9.25, 10.1; visits to the tomb by Augustus, Suet. *Div.Aug.* 18.1, Dio Cass. 51.16.5; and Caligula, Suet. *Gaius* 52 and Dio Cass. *ibid.*

a substantial dowry and a useful alliance.⁴³ The status of this marriage in Macedonia is unknown; but we do not hear of Olympias raising any objections to it. This may have been because it had no dynastic implications, or simply because it did not last. Meda bore Philip no children who survived, and we never hear of her again. It is therefore a reasonable assumption that she either died — in childbirth or of an illness: again, malaria may be suspected — or else was repudiated and returned to Thrace, *ca*. 340. Like Philip's earlier foreign wife, Audata, she is unlikely to have been eligible for burial in the royal necropolis: at best she remains a borderline case. Her age is unknown, but we may assume that she was in her late teens or early twenties.⁴⁴

With Cleopatra-Eurydice⁴⁵ we are on far firmer ground. As the niece of Attalus she was a high-ranking Macedonian aristocrat, and the dynastic legitimacy of her marriage to Philip can be measured by the degree of reaction it produced in Olympias. The claim that Philip divorced or repudiated Olympias at this point on the trumped-up grounds of adultery rests only on Justin, but should not necessarily be disregarded on that account. Cleopatra had time on her side. She was young: unfortunately, we do not know how young. She could have been anything from seventeen to her early twenties when she was murdered, or made to commit suicide, in early 335, some months after Philip's assassination, together with the child she had borne him.⁴⁶ That she died as a regnant queen is certain, and that

---

⁴³ See Green, *AM²* 62 and Ellis, *PMI* 166.

⁴⁴ I am not including in this list — nor, indeed, did Satyrus — the putative daughter of the Scythian king Atheas, adduced as a candidate *ca*. 339 by Hammond, PTHC 336, on the basis of Justin 9.2.1-6, a passage which offers no evidence that Atheas even had a daughter, let alone bestowed her hand on Philip. He did, briefly, when hard-pressed by local enemies, offer to adopt Philip *in successionem. . .regni Scythiae*, but when the crisis was resolved (which took very little time), quickly sent the Macedonians packing (§3), and *nuntiari Philippo iubet, neque auxilium eius se petisse neque adoptionem mandasse*, a move that would have been quite pointless if he had already given his daughter away. In any case he was now extremely old (Lucian *Macrob*. 10), and unless he shared the propensity of Amyntas III for septuagenarian procreation, he is most unlikely to have had a daughter of marriageable age available. Griffith gives a sensible account of him: see *Hist Mace* II 557, 560-62 and 582-84.

⁴⁵ All relevant *testimonia* in Berve no. 434, pp. 213-14.

⁴⁶ Plut. *Alex*. 9.4 states that Philip fell in love with her *par' helikian*, and that she was *parthenos* at her marriage; but the unsuitability of age probably referred to him rather than her. For her dispatch by Olympias see Justin 9.7.12, cf. 12.6.14, and Paus. 8.7.7. For the problem of Caranus and Europa see above, n. 25, and for Philip's reputed divorce of Olympias, Justin 11.11.3-5.

Alexander overruled Olympias in the matter of her obsequies (supra p. 135 and n. 13) we have seen to be highly probable. The odds in favor of her burial in the Great Tumulus, together with at least one infant, are strong.

There remain one or two miscellaneous candidates for consideration. Amyntas son of Perdiccas, of the blood royal even though arguably never king, was executed by Alexander in 336 at the age of about twenty-nine or thirty; his wife Cynna, Audata's daughter, survived to be executed by Alcetas in 322 and buried at Aigeai six years later, which makes her roughly thirty-five at the time of her death.[47] Alexander's wife Roxane and his son, Alexander IV, were put to death in 311/10. Roxane at the time of her death was about thirty-two, and the boy-king twelve or thirteen, the last direct descendant (with the possible exception of Barsine's son Heracles, also executed a year later) of the Argead royal house.[48] Finally, we have the marginal figure of Cassander, *de facto* king of Macedonia, who died in 297, aged sixty-one, just outside our date-limits, but certainly not above ordering himself a royal funeral.[49]

This concludes our historical investigation.[50] It now remains to see which eligible candidates best fit the (still highly provisional) archaeological dating and other evidence from the Vergina royal tombs. Let me begin with Tomb III. This contains a mural depicting a two-horse chariot race (presumably indicating an interest of the occupant), as well as the remains of a gilded ceremonial spear, and a gold wreath hung round the silver hydria containing the bones. As we have seen, Andronikos reports these bones as being those of a boy between twelve and fourteen.[51] Now historically, if this bone-analysis is correct, the occupant of Tomb III can only be Alexander IV, or, just conceivably, Barsine's son Heracles. Andronikos, seemingly indifferent to this consideration, argues on what seem to be stylistic grounds (sculpture, silver, ceramics) that the tomb "should be assigned to roughly the middle of the fourth century and certainly cannot be later than the third quarter of that century" (*PM* 230).

---

[47] For Amyntas see Berve, *Alex* no. 61 pp. 30-31, and supra n. 26. Cynna's death: Diod. 19.52.2, Arrian *Succ.* §§23-4. Amyntas would be a little too young at death to match the bones in Tomb II.

[48] Justin 15.2.4-5, Paus. 9.7.2, Diod. 19.105.2-3.

[49] Stähelin, RE 10 (1919) 2312-13.

[50] Its results are conveniently tabulated above, pp. 140-41.

[51] Cf. *PM* 229-30 and *Search* 37-38.

The Royal Tombs of Vergina: A Historical Analysis

Nevertheless, I submit that Tomb III must, provisionally at least, be assigned to Alexander IV (or Heracles), and dated to 310 (or 309).[52] If the age of the bones should be revised upward to *ca.* 25 or 30, then Amyntas IV would at once become a likely, indeed the only possible, candidate (see tabulated chart, p. 140).

Tomb I offers a greater mystery.[53] As is well known, it was robbed, leaving only some bones, some pieces of pottery, and murals — a seated woman, the Rape of Persephone, possibly the Three Fates — the iconography of which, taken together, suggests a young girl cut off in her prime. As is not so well known, the bones were identified as those of a woman in her twenties, a baby, and a large man (the last explained, not too satisfactorily, as a grave-robber). On the basis of the pottery, Andronikos has dated this tomb to the mid-fourth century — "perhaps to about 340 B.C." Who fits the bill? Roxane, Thessalonike, Olympias, and Alexander's sister Cleopatra are all too old, and, if Andronikos' dating is correct, died too late for consideration in this context. Lane Fox (LF-*SA* 93) suggested Nicesipolis; but as we have seen she was clearly ineligible, and, further, to accommodate her Lane Fox was required to assume that she died bearing twins, of which only one (Thessalonike) survived. For this there is no evidence. Adea-Eurydice would be the right age; but if she had been executed with a new-born child, that fact would certainly have been preserved to add to Olympias's other enormities. In any case, we know that she was buried with Philip Arrhidaeus as his queen.[54] Meda is a marginal possibility. She could have died in childbirth, and the dates would fit (supra p. 145), but her eligibility for royal burial is dubious. Phila is certainly eligible, even if strictly speaking outside our date-limits (358). However, the slightly earlier style of cist-grave in Tomb I, parallel to similar burials at Dhervéni, might support her case. This is also true of Audata, though her eligibility is as questionable as Meda's.

---

[52] Lane Fox's speculation (LF-*SA* 93) that Tomb III may contain Philip II's murderer Pausanias rests on a very loose reading of Justin 9.7.11, and in any case completely ignores the stated age of the bones. Quite apart from the sheer improbability of a king's murderer being buried in the royal necropolis (whatever Olympias may have felt about him), the notion of a Bodyguard between twelve and fourteen, with a past history of rape victimisation, may have a certain bizarre charm, but scarcely carries historical conviction.

[53] See *RGV* 14-18, "RTP" 35, "RT" 70, *PM* 205, *Search* 27-30 (the only account in which Andronikos attempts to date this tomb), and LF-*SA* 80 (the only account hitherto to analyse the bones; see pp. 130-31 and n. 1 above).

[54] Supra n. 35.

The one remaining candidate who fits all the requirements for Tomb I is, of course, Cleopatra-Eurydice; age, date and baby are just right, even though the type of burial is, perhaps, arguably early for 335. For theorists who believe that Tomb II houses Philip III Arrhidaeus and Adea-Eurydice, Cleopatra-Eurydice must be the strongest candidate for Tomb I. Supporters of Philip II who place Cleopatra-Eurydice in the antechamber of Tomb II (with the bones of her murdered child either dispersed before formal burial or unrecognizable among her own through cremation) must fall back on Phila, or, less probably, Meda or Audata. If, on the other hand, they want to keep Cleopatra in Tomb I, they then have to provide a legitimate alternative queen for the antechamber, and their only available candidate is the marginally eligible Meda. This, however, involves the convenient assumption that Meda, like Cleopatra-Eurydice, died shortly after Philip, presumably of grief, or through a coincidental illness, or, as Hammond speculates, by *suttee* (for which there is no evidence, certainly not that which he cites), or obligingly sacrificed by the Macedonians over Philip's ashes in imitation of Thracian or Getic customs. Presumably in that case the mass of feathers found on her sarcophagus would be a kind of Indian-style native head-dress. This scenario cannot be ruled out altogether (Meda's marriage-date would fit the reputed age of the bones), but I nevertheless find it, to say the least, improbable.[55]

We must, I think, concede that Philip II and Cleopatra-Eurydice, or, alternatively, Philip III Arrhidaeus and Adea-Eurydice, are the only seriously viable candidates for the occupancy of Tomb II and its antechamber, and that though objections can be lodged against either pair, the cumulative weight of evidence, actual and circumstantial, favors the earlier burial. Adams (68) did, tentatively, raise the possibility of Amyntas son of Perdiccas for Tomb II, with Cynna being placed in the antechamber almost twenty years later; but Cynna, dead at thirty-five, would be too old for the bones in the antechamber, and from Andronikos's account it seems clear that the

---

[55] Hammond raised the possibility of Meda's self-immolation at PTHC 336, citing for this supposed Scythian or Getic custom Hdt. 4.71.4 and Steph. Byz. s.v. *Getia*. But neither passage bears out his contention. Both refer to the local practice of *sacrificing* (*episphazein, apopnixantes*) a king's wife at his funeral; there is no question of suicide. Herodotus also refers to the wholesale slaughter of household slaves, concubines, horses, etc., a practice reminiscent of the Royal Cemetery at Ur (CAH^3 I 2 282-86), but of which there is no trace in the antechamber to Tomb II. Herodotus further states that the Scythians use only gold vessels on such an occasion, not silver or bronze: but the latter metals are conspicuous by their presence in Tomb II.

The Royal Tombs of Vergina: A Historical Analysis

antechamber was added reasonably soon after the closing of Tomb II.[56] This remains one of the main arguments against identifying the burial as that of Philip Arrhidaeus and Adea-Eurydice: Cassander interred them at Aigeai together, with funeral games and proper ritual, *inter alia* as a formal means of claiming the throne for himself.[57] There was, in their case, no need for a quick, hugger-mugger burial, a vault roughly plastered, an absence of murals (*PM* 218); the circumstances of Philip II's death would make such disarray more than understandable.

Too much of the evidence remains tantalisingly indecisive. The diadem indicates royalty, but cannot identify the head that wore it; it may have been a copy, specially placed in the tomb, while the dead man's successors retained the original for official use. The Armenian version of the Alexander Romance (admittedly not the most reliable of sources) does state, however, that Philip II's "crown" was buried with him. The royal hunt depicted on the facade of Tomb II can be interpreted iconographically either as the commemoration of actual practice (in which case Philip II is the obvious candidate as its central figure, whereas the epileptic, physically handicapped Philip Arrhidaeus would be highly inappropriate), or, alternatively, as a symbolic appurtenance of Macedonian royalty *tel quel* (in which case the identity of the individual king would remain unimportant). The barrel-vaulting discussed above (see p. 134), could at any time be modified as an argument by further excavation (and has, indeed, already been implicitly challenged by Andronikos' new claim regarding the relative age of Tomb II's walls and vaulting). The significance of the twenty or more miniature ivory heads found in Tomb II remains a total mystery. While there is general agreement that the bearded head must represent Philip II, and a less certain consensus that one other head, with the characteristic Lysippan upward gaze and twist of the neck, portrays Alexander, the identity of the remainder (for the most part still unpublished, but reportedly all very like the "Alexander") remains quite uncertain, and the function of the group as a whole defies speculation. If, as has been suggested to me, they represent Philip II and his Royal Pages, that might add weight to the arguments claiming Tomb II for him (and, incidentally, explain the beardlessness of all heads except the "Philip"). On the other hand, the "Lysippan twist" suggests a date

[56] *RGV* 43 and 44; *PM* 212.
[57] Cf. W. W. Tarn, *CAH* VI 482.

later than 336. The Homeric elements in the burial ritual (gold casket, purple cloth, washing of bones in wine, sacrificial cremation, etc.) might apply equally well to Philip II or to Philip III, and Cassander knew his Homer no less well than did Alexander. Hammond in particular has argued that the presence of Scythian *gorytus* and ceremonial greaves in the antechamber testifies to the burial there of a Scythian warrior-queen; but Borza, observing correctly that greaves and *gorytus* were the only items missing from the ceremonial panoply in Tomb II, and that they were found leaning against the communicating door, argues that they were omitted from the main burial by an oversight. As Adams remarks, "after all, Andronikos has assumed that the greaves found [in the antechamber] actually belonged to the man in the main chamber, why not the bowcase and quiver as well?" Finally, there is the so-called heroön, the small marble edifice (destroyed except for its foundations) that was found close to the three tombs. Hammond reminds us that only two fourth-century Argead kings (apart from Alexander III) were paid divine honors: Amyntas III and Philip II. If we could be sure of this building's function, it might strengthen the case for Philip II; but Andronikos's identification of it rests, at best, on the flimsiest foundations. It could have been any kind of shrine.[58]

[58] The reference to Philip's diadem being buried with him I owe, along with much other useful discussion, to Dr. M. B. Hatzopoulos; see A. M. Wolohojian, *The Romance of Alexander the Great by Pseudo-Callisthenes* (New York 1969) §69, p. 45, cf. p. 166. At the symposium held at The Art Institute of Chicago in June 1981 Hammond tentatively identified three figures on the hunting mural as Philip II, Alexander III, and (his back to us in quasi-disgrace!) Amyntas IV. The case for symbolic representation was most persuasively argued, on the same occasion, by Dr. Jiří Frel. Andronikos at first selectively identified five of the ivory heads as Philip II, Alexander III, Olympias, Amyntas III and his wife Eurydice, and attempted to correlate this (essentially arbitrary) group with that of the same five portraits executed in gold and ivory by Leochares for the Philippeion at Olympia (Paus. 5.20.9-10; *RGV* 40, "RT" 75 — "possibly the work of Leochares himself," "RTP" 39-41 — "or his workshop"). This drew sharp, and well-justified, criticism from Lehmann (PWL 528 with nn. 5, 6, 7 and 13). Andronikos ("RTV" 169) has now, wisely, abandoned the comparison (cf. Fredricksmeyer 331-32), together with the identifications of Olympias, Eurydice, and Amyntas III (who seems in any case to have been bearded, if, as I suspect, the Heracles on the obverse of Kraay-Hirmer no. 560 is a royal portrait); all the other miniature heads, it is reported, are clean-shaven and probably male. The suggestion that these heads, collectively, may represent Philip II and his Royal Pages I owe to Prof. E. N. Borza. Giallombardo and Tripodi (1000), in support of Philip Arrhidaeus' candidacy, identify Andronikos' five original heads as portraits of Philip II, Alexander III, Philip III Arrhidaeus, the latter's wife Eurydice, and her mother Cynna. Their thesis (992) that a portrait of the living Alexander would not be included in a funerary collection has little to recommend it. (Nor am I wholly

The Royal Tombs of Vergina: A Historical Analysis

We see, then, that while the case for Philip II is circumstantially stronger than that for Philip III Arrhidaeus, it cannot, yet, be regarded as proven. Perhaps one tiny piece of evidence may help. The rim of a silver strainer in Tomb II is inscribed "MAXATA": Machatas. The name, a rare one (it does not recur till the 2nd cent. B.C.) is that of Phila's brother, Philip II's brother-in-law (supra p. 142).[59] That, together with the later completion of the antechamber, is about the strongest piece of specific evidence we have to go on until the final technical reports are out. If I lean, as I do, towards Philip II, it remains largely on circumstantial grounds — *apo ta eikota* — and in the full knowledge that fresh evidence may still tip the scales the other way. We can only hope that if, by some miracle, an epigraphical text does turn up, and mentions Philip, it makes it unambiguously clear just which Philip is in question.[60]

The University of Texas at Austin

---

convinced of this head's identification.) For Cassander's expertise in Homeric studies see Athen. 14.620b, and for Homeric elements in the Tomb II burial *RGV* 60-61, citing Hom. *Il.* 24.795-96, *Od.* 24.72-73. Greaves and *gorytus*: Hammond PTHC 335-37 and Adams 71. For the heroön see *RGV* 48, *PM* 204-5, *Search* 27, and Hammond PTHC 332-33. Andronikos excludes, without explanation, the theory "that it is a temple or other sacred building not associated with the graves," and claims that "the only possible explanation is that we have to do here with a "heroon" in connexion with the cult of the dead who are buried here." A possible explanation, indeed, but the *only* possible one? In "RTV" 169-70 Andronikos uses this identification to attack the likelihood of Philip Arrhidaeus being buried here, on the grounds that he (as opposed to Philip II) would not receive divine or heroic honors. But the argument remains circular.

[59] *RGV* 52 figure 31: this point was also picked up by Lane Fox, LF-*SA* 82.

[60] This paper was first presented, in somewhat abbreviated form, at the Art Institute of Chicago, and subsequently at Stanford (December 1981) as part of a plenary session of the American Philological Association and the Archaeological Institute of America. I am grateful to those many colleagues, in particular Lindsay Adams, Gene Borza, Jack Ellis, Jiří Frel, and Nick Hammond, whose comments, both formal and informal, helped to shed light on puzzling problems and to eradicate various errors and imperfections in my presentation. For those that remain (some in defiance of doubtless good advice) I of course take full responsibility.

The Search for Alexander's Portrait

ROBERT WYMAN HARTLE

Abstract

The search for Alexander's portrait is a continuing one because scholars disagree about what to look for. Some admit supposed portraits into the canon too easily, while others say we can never know what he looked like. The latter attitude resembles twentieth-century scientism more than the Hellenistic spirit.

Three apotheosized portraits of Alexander are examined, plus one unpublished portrait found in Egypt. The portrait found in Vergina Tomb II confirms the traditional view of Alexander's appearance, but presents stylistic problems because Alexander is represented in a style that, until now, was thought to have evolved considerably after 336. If the tomb is Philip's and was constructed in haste, the rapid sculpting of some twenty individual portraits found therein also presents practical problems.

The style of the tiny Vergina portrait cannot support the attribution of the tomb to Philip, but, if the tomb should be securely dated, the accepted chronology of Alexander iconography would be in doubt.

The search for Alexander's portrait is a continuing one for two reasons: in the first place there is no common agreement about what we are searching for, and, secondly, new portraits or alleged portraits keep popping up. As soon as one commonly received portrait is debunked, another attribution is made. For a long time it was thought that it was relatively easy to judge which examples could be admitted into the canon and which should be excluded, especially the former. One looked for a strong bull-like neck that twisted upwards in an inverted S-curve, and pointed sharply forward in profile, "melting" eyes turned upwards towards the heavens, an air of *pothos*, or *enthousiasmos*, and sometimes *pathos* in the expression, luxuriant hair standing up in a manner resembling a lion's mane, a fierce (*trux*) protrusion of the lower brow, and a transverse furrow of the brow that became more pronounced as time went on, not only as Alexander increased in age, but also as new styles evolved. All of these features were enough to call a head Alexander's, and sometimes merely one or two of these attributes sufficed. It seemed easy enough to recognize a head of Alexander even at quite a distance. The problem was where to draw the line, and, after a while, to keep from labeling all portraits representations of the hero.

Erkinger Schwarzenberg has pointed out the anachronism involved in assuming that "the aim of Greek art was an exact reproduction of a person's outward appearance instead of a rendering of man. . . . What the modern historian tends to look for in a likeness is the rendering of a particular moment in a person's life, rather than the definitive, the permanent expression of his character."[1] Schwarzenberg goes on to say that the "aim of the fine arts, and not only the art of portraiture, is to express the *ethos* of man," and not the "naturalistic rendering of detail unimportant except for passport identification."[2] He makes comparisons with the art of portraiture as practiced by Plutarch and with Aristotelean theory on the nature of art in general. In other words, portraiture is there to tell us about man and not about local color. What different styles *can* tell us about is the society that produced them, if not the (outer) reality of the person involved.

Some of this has always been assumed, for instance the Pergamon head of Alexander now in the Instanbul Museum may tell us more about the culture of Pergamon in its "baroque" period than it will about Alexander at any specific time of his life. The heads produced under the *diadochoi* give us more information about *their* political aspirations than they do about the reality of Alexander.

There is, however, a danger in carrying too far the notion that the ancient portraitists were concerned only with representing the *ethos* of the subject. There is a danger of falling into *too* scientific a frame of mind and thereby committing another kind of anachronism. Certainly it is true that Aristotle was seeking in art a kind of knowledge,

---

[1] Erkinger Schwarzenberg, "The portraiture of Alexander" in Fondation Hardt, *Entretiens* XXII, *Alexandre le Grand: Image et Réalité* (Vandoeuvres-Genève 1975) 224.
[2] *Ibid.* 227.

The Search for Alexander's Portrait

which he says all men hanker for; and to the moral end of poetry he says that in portraying the *ethos* the poet should keep in mind several criteria: the character should be good (*chrēsta*), appropriate (*harmotonta*), consistent (*homalon*), but he also adds that he should be *like* (*homoion*), that is, like the original. The artist must not take liberties with the character of the original.[3] Certainly enough people believed that one could learn something from the idiosyncrasies of individuals, otherwise there would have been no point to Octavian's having Alexander's coffin opened so that he could look at the original, warts and all. Otherwise he could have been content to gaze upon the original portraits by great artists, which he — fortunate man — could look upon in abundance.

Furthermore, history sometimes takes a capricious, if not malicious, pleasure in occasionally turning up evidence that turns the debunkers to confusion and confirms myths that have been passed on by the most dubious sources through long and murky traditions.

There is another kind of mistake that we can make by adopting too rigorous a scientific attitude towards portraits, asking: *Is this, or is this not*, a portrait of Alexander? By being so exclusionist and assuming that *the Truth* is somewhere ascertainable, we are betraying the scientism proper to the twentieth century, and thereby committing an ironically *unscientific* anachronism. The Hellenistic age was, as Aristophanes foresaw to his horror, a time in which old categories were becoming blurred, the old religion was softening, Euripides was becoming too familiar with the gods. . . . One can imagine the extent of his horror if he had survived to see the syncretism, the mysticism, and the profligate divinization of heroes and kings characteristic of the Hellenistic age. If we are going to look at Hellenistic works of art, we should try to look at them *in the spirit of Hellenism* and not with twentieth-century queries on our lips. Let me give three examples.

In the museum at Verria is a bust that has a very specific label on it, "Olganos" (Fig. 1). It is apparently a river-god. And yet it has many of the characteristics that would have no doubt led it to be labeled as Alexander if another label were not already on it. The mane is flowing and upstanding as would befit a river-god, as well as being typical of Alexander. All the rest is there, too: the brow, the melting eyes, the uplifted gaze, the twist of the neck.[4] We know that

---

[3] Arist. *Poetics*, xv. 1-6.

[4] The discovery of this head was first reported by V. Kallopolitis in *BCH* 71-72 (1947-1948) 438, described as "Un beau buste de jeune homme, du milieu du II᷄ siècle ap.

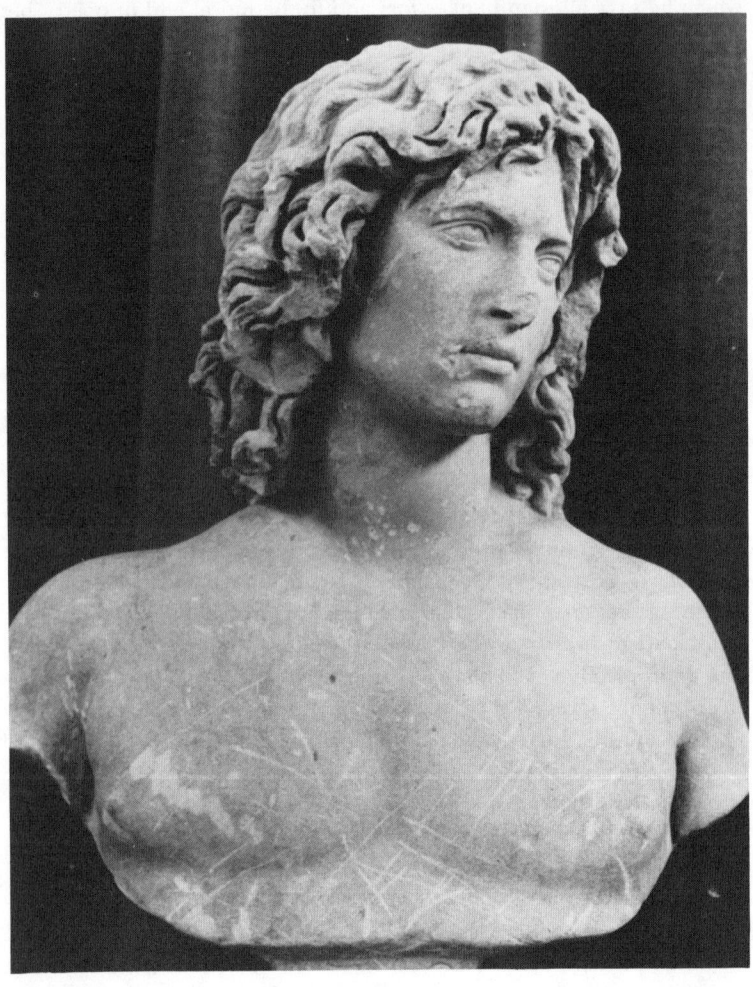

Fig. 1. The "Olganos" bust. Verria Museum

The Search for Alexander's Portrait

Fig. 2. The "Helios" bust. Rhodes Museum.

some of these characteristics considered idiosyncratic to Alexander — whether they *actually* were or not — influenced portraiture in general later on, and no doubt something of the sort was at work here. The admiration for Alexander influenced the canons of masculine beauty in general, and these characteristics were then given to those one wished to be admired. Evelyn Harrison has very wisely suggested that we not take a definite stand, but that we call this bust "Alexander-Olganos." In so doing we would no doubt be closer to the spirit of Hellenism than when we try to impose a twentieth-century taxonomy.

Similarly, there is a bust in the Rhodes museum that is labelled "Helios," (Fig. 2), yet to anyone practiced in looking at, and for, busts of Alexander, the resemblance to the traits of Alexander stands out sharply. This should not surprise us perhaps; Pliny notes, all in one breath, that Lysippos was made famous "above all by the four-horse chariot and the figure of the Sun made for the Rhodians. He also made a number of portraits of Alexander the Great, beginning with one of him as a boy. . . ."[5] They were associated in Pliny's mind, but how much more must they have been associated in the mind of the sculptor himself? In the catalogue of this exhibition (no. 8) Ariel Hermann suggests that the "assimilation [of Alexander and Helios] perhaps began with Lysippos' famous sculpture, made for the Rhodians, of Helios driving his sun chariot, and with the Colossus of Rhodes, a towering figure of Helios by Lysippos' pupil Chares of

---

J.-C., le visage encadré d'une abondante chevelure." Kallopolitis subsequently published a full article on the subject in *Monuments Piot* 46 (1952) 85-91. In this article he notes (p. 90): "Au point de vue iconographique, je serais tenté de voir en Olganos la survivance d'un type caractérisé par la chevelure épaisse et touffue. Créé à l'époque hellénistique, ce type représentait parfois des dieux-fleuves, mais il fut aussi fréquemment utilisé pour les portraits pathétiques de l'époque hellénistique; on y reconnaît en tout cas, semble-t-il, l'influence de l'iconographie d'Alexandre le Grand." On the mythological level, "Olganos était. . .fils du roi Bérès et éponyme d'un fleuve de la région" (pp. 85-86). This same king was the mythical founder of Verria and Mieza, named for his two daughters. Kallopolitis did some further excavating in the region where the head was found and uncovered the foundations for a large edifice, which he believes was the Nympheion of Mieza, where Aristotle taught Alexander. How appropriate, then, that a bust of the son should bear the traits of Alexander even after the passage of half a millenium!

I am grateful to Mrs. Maria Siganidou, Ephor of Antiquities for Western Macedonia, for permission to publish the head of Olganos and for the above references as well as two others which I was unable to consult.

[5] Pliny *NH* 34.63, trans. Jex-Blake, quoted in Franklin P. Johnson, *Lysippos* (reprint New York 1968) 266.

The Search for Alexander's Portrait

Lindos.'"[6] It would seem reasonable to include this bust in the Alexander-Helios group. Cornelius Vermeule, in speaking of no. 29, a silver didrachm, Head of Helios, is categoric on the subject: "As elsewhere when Helios was represented in Hellenistic art, the features of the patron god of the island of Rhodes were based on those of Alexander the Great." H. P. L'Orange says that "A number of representations of Helios have ... a type of face resembling Alexander to such an extent that one may feel uncertain whether it is the man or the god, where the distinction is not clear on other grounds."[7] This desire to be sure of whether it is one *or* the other is, I submit, anachronistic. I doubt that a person living in the second century B.C. would have felt the need for this kind of certitude. L'Orange puts it better in another passage when he says:

> In the portrait of Alexander ... the divine is fused with the human, the man transformed into the god. It is as though the mythical imagination of the Greeks is again at work here, conjuring up one of those beings that are outside nature's order and yet have nature's law in them.[8]

A third example concerns a statuette that was shown in the Thracian exposition from Bulgaria, which was labelled as a typical "Thracian Horseman" (Figs. 3 and 4). To anyone who is willing to see the statuette from the Naples museum (Fig. 5) as a representation of Alexander from the group done by Lysippos at Dion as a monument to the Companions fallen in the Battle of the Issus, the resemblance is striking.[9] There are also important differences, however. Most noticeably, the caparisons of the horses are quite

---

[6] *Search*, p. 102, no. 8. In the entries for numbers 8 and 39 (pp. 118-19) Hermann gives full bibliographical references for the Alexander-Helios type. (See Appendix.)

[7] H. P. L'Orange, *Apotheosis in Ancient Portraiture* (Oslo 1947) 34.

[8] *Ibid.* 38.

[9] Margarete Bieber, *Alexander the Great in Greek and Roman Art* (Chicago 1964) 36 (Figures 19-21).

In the supplement to *Search*, works added to the exhibition at the Art Institute of Chicago (Chicago 1981), Al. N. Oikonomides says of this statuette that because Alexander "wears simple sandals rather than greaves...he is represented in a hunting scene and not as a cavalry commander in battle" (Entry for Exhibit K). This is to introduce a realistic criterion which may be out of place. If one wishes to be *realistic*, then one would have to postulate a very complaisant beast being hunted, one that would be willing to stand up to the height of a man in order to be killed, given the length of the sword. Margarete Bieber (supra) assumes that the rudder used to support the weight of the horse is a symbolic representation of the fact that

Fig. 3   "Thracian Horseman." Archaeological Museum of Sofia

Fig. 4.   Rear view of Fig. 3.

The Search for Alexander's Portrait

Fig. 5. Equestrian figure. Naples Museum

Fig. 6. Bust of Alexander. Christos G. Bastis Collection, on loan to the Brooklyn Museum.

The Search for Alexander's Portrait

Fig. 7. Same as Fig. 6.

different; however it turns out that the horse and the rider were found very far apart and were put together merely because the size fit. The rider was found in Kjustendil (Ancient Pantalia), which a glance at a map tells us is actually a good bit closer to Dion than it is to Thrace. A second, presumably autochthonous detail, the long sleeves and long trousers, is extremely rare in statues of the Thracian Horseman; among the numerous stone votive plaques he is shown this way only three times. I am grateful to Professor Georgi Mihailov, of the University of Sofia, for these and other precisions. Professor Mihailov, who has written on the process of heroization or divinization characteristic of the process by which the dead became "typical Thracian Horsemen," agrees with me, I am happy to say, that it is perfectly consistent with that process for the same thing to have happened to Alexander, and he agrees with me that his horseman is an example of Alexander's being turned into a deity in this series.[10] Another example of how Alexander entered into the religions and the mythology of many diverse peoples.

Far to the south the process of divinization of Alexander was fomented by the Ptolemies to the point that it would appear that "every self-respecting Alexandrian household had a shrine dedicated both to the founder of the city and to its good genius."[11] This would account for the generally small size of the statuettes found in Egypt. Figs. 6 and 7 illustrate one from the Christos G. Bastis Collection, on loan to the Brooklyn Museum. So far, this head has been shown by me at the Symposium held at Thessaloniki in 1977, the papers from which are to be published in volume III of *Ancient Macedonia*, but otherwise it is unpublished. The provenance is unknown. It has been provisionally dated to the second century B. C., but this is not certain. The head is hollow cast with a patina that ranges from "copper" to brown to green. The height is 5.8 cm; width, 4.0 cm;

---

the battle being commemorated involved a river crossing. If one uses *realistic* criteria, what does one do about the rudder? Or for that matter the hunting scenes on the mosaics at Pella? One assumes that the Macedonians did not *really* hunt lions naked. Finally, theoretical questions aside, N. G. L. Hammond says, in his *Alexander the Great: King, Commander, and Statesman* (Park Ridge, N.J. 1980), that the Macedonian cavalrymen wore "sandal-type shoes" (p. 31), while the *infantrymen* wore "metal greaves" (p. 32).

[10] Professor Mihailov very kindly furnished me with a French translation from the Bulgarian of the original note on this rider by T. Gerasimov, *BIAB* 13 (1939) 327-28, n. 1, fig. 360.

[11] Schwarzenberg (supra n. 1) 235.

depth, 4.7 cm.[12] Though it is tiny, it is immediately recognizable as a head of Alexander, even at a distance. This is an example of how portraits of Alexander keep popping up all the time. In this case, there would seem to be no possible objection to the identification.

The latest bust of Alexander to show up, and the one that causes the most difficulties is the one found in Tomb II at Vergina and presented in this exhibition as Number 171 (Fig. 8).[13] Before discussing it, however, I should like to say a word or two about the head of Philip II in the context of the preceding discussion. First, there would appear to be no possible denying the identification of the head as Philip's. What is interesting is that in this case the sculptor, who was indeed a genius, succeeded in portraying the *ethos* of Philip in a manner that Philip himself might not have found too flattering, at least in comparison with the Copenhagen head, which is more idealized and in general nattier.[14] Secondly, the sculptor has portrayed quite clearly a scar which is rather more naturalistic and accidental than an essential part of Philip's *character*, unless one wished to say that his toughness in continuing to fight despite the loss of an eye tells us something essential about the character — an absence that is flaunted, like the late Moshe Dayan's eye-patch. The incision over the right eye is in exactly the same place as it is on the Copenhagen head, and is done quite deliberately.

As for the head of Alexander, if it had turned up any place else, one would no doubt have said that its features had been deformed in accordance with the so-called "baroque" art of the East, that it shows too much the expression of *pathos* and the heavenward gaze. (In the same way, we might be tempted to ascribe the portrait of Philip to late Hellenistic realism if it had been found under different circumstances.) Schwarzenberg says that "An attitude characteristic of Lysippan heroes was mistaken for the naturalistic rendering of Alexander's body. The level look of the victorious athlete was turned into the inimitable gaze of Alexander, privileged while alive to look up to Zeus as to his father. Callisthenes described Alexander looking

---

[12] From the Christos G. Bastis Collection, on loan to The Brooklyn Museum, Brooklyn no. L74.11.1. I am grateful to Mr. Bastis, The Brooklyn Museum, and to Dr. Robert S. Bianchi, Associate Curator of Egyptian and Classical Art, for permission to publish this head and to Dr. Bianchi for the technical details.

[13] *Search* p. 187, no. 171 and color plate 34. I am grateful to Professor Manolis Andronikos for permission to publish this plate.

[14] *Ibid.* p. 98, no. 1, for the Copenhagen head; p. 186, no. 170 and color plate 34 for the Vergina head.

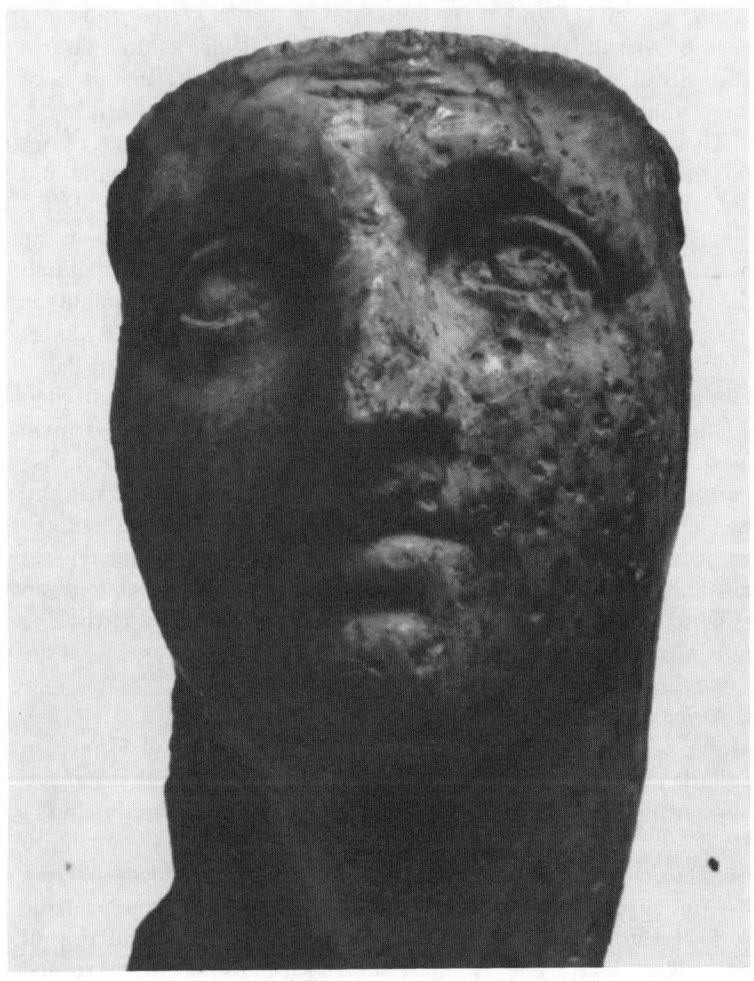

Fig. 8. The Vergina Alexander. Archaeological Museum of Thessaloniki

The Search for Alexander's Portrait

up in prayer to his Father in Heaven . . . [but] Plutarch was not fooled by these theatrical displays. He felt that Lysippus was not likely to have had recourse to external means (such as the direction of Alexander's look presupposing an object in Heaven) to express the *aretē* of his hero and to show that he was truly the son of Zeus. Alexander was not in the habit of raising his eyes to search for his father's celestial realm.''[15] This was all very scientific on Schwarzenberg's part, stripping away the accretions of legend, but is it not possible that, if it is true that Lysippos began to portray Alexander as a boy, he might have taken features of Alexander himself on which to model the gaze of his athletes, just as Vermeule suggests that he did for the features of Helios?[16] This suggestion is given more force by the fact that now we have a head showing precisely that characteristic, and the head was found in a place where inexactitude would not have been tolerated, especially given the fact that — as we have seen in the case of the portrait of Philip — we are not dealing with portraits that were meant to be any more flattering than *any* commissioned portrait is flattering.

In the past L'Orange, Schwarzenberg and others strongly asserted that we *could not* know what Alexander looked like, since Plutarch and the other writers were taking off from the portraits themselves and that thus any assumption derived from the writers as to what Alexander looked like would be circular. History sometimes has a strange way of validating tradition in spite of science. It now seems

---

[15] Schwarzenberg (supra n. 1) 251-52. See also H. P. L'Orange (supra n. 7) 19: "As allusions to Alexander's appearance go no further back than to Plutarch, whose characterisation rests entirely upon the portraits of Alexander, it is probable that the descriptions we have today are based upon the portrait tradition, that is, upon the dominating Lysippan type, which, according to the sources, first introduced the heavenward-gazing Alexander in art. In other words, we have to do not with the real Alexander, but with his representation in art."

[16] Cf. Professor José Dörig in the discussion following Schwarzenberg's presentation (supra n. 1) 277: "Le portrait du roi est préfiguré par les statues de Zeus que Lysippe a sculptées pour Sicyone, Mégare, Argos et Tarente. Si Alexandre a fait appel à Lysippe, c'est qu'il souhaitait être représenté par lui à l'image de Zeus, ce qui s'explique peut-être par le fait que les discussions concernant sa divinité ont commencé de son vivant." Without wishing to be unduly perverse, I might point out that this is a reversible argument: if Lysippos began to portray Alexander when he was still a child, perhaps he took Alexander's features when sculpting Zeus and not the other way around. Furthermore, one would doubt that discussions concerning his divinity began while he was still a boy, which is when Pliny said that Lysippos first sculpted him. The Vergina head may challenge a number of received opinions.

that we have known all along what Alexander looked like, perhaps without really knowing that we knew it. But scientific investigation itself was also at work on these suppositions.

In 1977, the same year coincidentally as Andronikos' finds, Heiner Protzmann argued that the reality, the personality, as well as the will of Alexander came through Lysippos' transmittals even in idealizing phases.[17] Perhaps more importantly, in 1979 Rüdiger Leimbach argued cogently that the readings of Plutarch on which these opinions were based were too hasty, and that a more careful reading of the text clearly indicated that Plutarch had at his disposal the means of control by which he was able to assert that Lysippos had *best* rendered the features of Alexander.[18]

I have heard some rumors of doubts expressed about the identification of the Vergina bust with Alexander, but I can see no reason for doubt. The emphasis on the powerful neck and throat, the turn of the head, the gaze, the forehead, are all typical of portraits of Alexander. The fleshy cheeks and the pointed chin are characteristic of portraits of the young Alexander, for example the one from the Acropolis Museum said to be an original by Leochares. For once we have a nose that is practically intact — aquiline and fleshy. Aquiline noses apparently were *de rigueur* in later antiquity, so we cannot be absolutely certain whether this one is portrayed as it was or as it should have been. All five of the heads so far shown by Andronikos have similar noses. The eyes are definitely looking up towards heaven in a way that is even more pronounced than in many of his other portraits. The head was apparently placed as a kind of cameo in a couch, bier, or trestle made of wood or other organic material that has subsequently disappeared.[19] As a result, there is no hair at all, consequently no *anastole*. The brows protrude somewhat, certainly more than Philip's. What is most striking is the expression of *pathos* and the extreme furrowing of the brow. This characteristic is even more pronounced than what we see on the Pergamon head. The obvious suggestion about the expression is that it is supposed to

---

[17] Heiner Protzmann, "Realismus und Idealität in Spätklassik und Frühhellenismus," *JdI* 92 (1977) esp. 196-97.

[18] Rüdiger Leimbach, "Plutarch über das Aussehen Alexanders des Grossen," *AA* no. 2 (1979) 213-20.

[19] Manolis Andronikos, *RGV* 59; "The Royal Tombs at Vergina" in *Alexander the Great: History and Legend in Art* (Thessaloniki 1980) 14-15; "The Royal Tombs at Vergina: A Brief Account of the Excavations" in *Search* 34.

The Search for Alexander's Portrait

represent grief, which would accord with the place where it was found, if Tomb II is indeed the tomb of his father.[20] This would not be the rendering of a momentary or trivial event but the expression of filial piety, which would represent character. (The same would be true of certain other events such as the taming of Bucephalus, the lion hunt, or the defeat of Darius.)

If the tomb is that of Philip Arrhidaios, as has been suggested by Phyllis Williams Lehmann and W. Lindsay Adams,[21] there would be no surprise in finding both Philip and Alexander therein, and art historians could say that the head of Alexander shows a certain orientalizing influence consequent upon Alexander's eastern campaigns and the development of portraiture during his lifetime. The inevitable problem in that case would be that Alexander is represented as rather young, whereas Philip is represented as being the age he was at his death. Why would one want to show a twenty-year old Alexander seven years after his death?[22] Perhaps these portraits were kept as heirlooms after the death of the subjects in preparation for just such an event. In that case, one could understand the discrepancy in age — perhaps they had been made many years before Cassander's burial of Philip Arrhidaios in 316.

---

[20] Andronikos has also published three other ivory heads in *RGV* 45 and 47, which also show twisted necks, a heavenward gaze, and a deeply furrowed brow. The head of Philip may exhibit a slight tendency in this direction, but the over-all impression is that of someone who is directing a straightforward gaze at the viewer. This observation might tend to support the theory that the expression of the others is one of grief at Philip's death. One would be curious to see what the other fifteen heads look like. Katerina Rhomiopoulou also found twenty-one heads in her Lefkadia tomb. She published one of them in "A New Monumental Chamber Tomb with Paintings of the Hellenistic Period near Lefkadia (West Macedonia)," *AAA* 6 (1973) 90. This head has a twisted neck and something of an expression of grief. There is no stylistic problem with her head (*vide infra*), however, since she dates the tomb provisionally to a period between 250 and 140 B.C.

[21] Phyllis Williams Lehmann, "The So-Called Tomb of Philip II; A Different Interpretation," *AJA* 84 (1980) 527-31. W. L. Adams, "The Royal Macedonian Tomb at Vergina: An Historical Interpretation," *AncW* 3 (1980) 67-72. Cornelius C. Vermeule III, in "Philip II, Alexander the Great, and Philip III," *Archaeology* 33 (1980) 52-55, mentions Lehmann's article in apparent agreement (esp. p. 52).

[22] Or an eighteen-year old, as Andronikos says in *RGV* 59. Cornelius Vermeule makes the suggestion rather diffidently in the *Search* caption for color plate 32 (catalogue no. 165), a silver alabastron from the main chamber of Tomb II at Vergina, that "The heads of Herakles in the skin of the Nemean lion, at the base of each handle, when viewed in profile, resemble such likenesses of Alexander the Great at the height of his career." Obviously if this is a portrait of Alexander at the height of his career, Tomb II could not be that of his father, whom he buried before his career had really begun.

One of the great puzzles of the many brought forth by the discovery of Tomb II is the heavenward gaze of the head of Alexander; it is curious to find it so early in his career if the bust dates from 336 B.C. The classic view of this phenomenon is best expressed by H. P. L'Orange in his justly famous study, *Apotheosis in Ancient Portraiture*:

> Our review of the material shows, then, that the effigies of inspired Alexander undergo — parallel with the development of Hellenistic baroque — a significant transformation: the heavenward gaze introduced for the first time in the Lysippan Alexander, becomes increasingly marked, and the heavenly emotion rises to ecstasy. This transformation corresponds to a definite change in the contemporary conception of Alexander himself. Starting with the heroic life of achievement, the emphasis is increasingly laid upon activity in the service of the Highest. Plutarch's Alexander feels that he is sent by God to save humanity. World-conquering Alexander is gradually transformed from a turbulent hero into an unresisting instrument of the gods, the inspired medium of an infinite world plan.[23]

All other things being equal, the head from Vergina would have to belong to the category of portraits classified as "emotional" rather than "ethical," or "Hellenistic" rather than "Classical." Concerning these distinctions Christine Havelock observes:

> No example of the so-called emotional . . . type can be dated with any real foundation before the second century B.C. . . . There is . . . [a] continuity between the two general types, but it is not the commitment to the special characteristics of Alexander's physiognomy for these are, after all, not very similar in any of the examples. Nor does it have anything to do with his biography. The continuity is based rather on an evolutionary principle, fundamental to Greek art, by which one style grows out of an earlier one.[24]

These carefully laid chronologies, long the mainstays of stylistic

---

[23] H. P. L'Orange (supra n. 7) 27. At the symposium where this paper was presented, Jiri Frel, Curator of Antiquities of the J. Paul Getty Museum, stated in his presentation quite simply that the portrait of Alexander is (1) posthumous and (2) a portrait of the apotheosis of Alexander. Presumably he was basing his statements on this chronology.

[24] Christine Mitchell Havelock, *Hellenistic Art: The Art of the Classical World from the Death of Alexander the Great to the Battle of Actium* (New York n.d.) 25.

The Search for Alexander's Portrait

analysis of the development of portraiture in Hellenistic times and after, may have to be completely reworked — or even discarded — if the attribution of the tomb to Philip II is correct.[25]

Two further intertwined and vexing problems are those of the realism and the individuality of the portraits of Philip and Alexander. Andronikos has insisted from the beginning, quite rightly in my opinion, on these two characteristics. He says that he recognized both portraits immediately from their features, in the case of Philip from the Tarsus medallion and in the case of Alexander from "his long stretched-out neck, the slight energetic turn of the head and the eyes looking upwards which we know about from the written sources and the faint echoes of Roman copies."[26] In the catalogue of this exhibition he states: "These heads have obviously individualized features and thus are some of the earliest and best portraits of Greek sculpture of the fourth century B.C."[27] He mentions that all of the heads he has found are "individual portraits."[28] "The figures are done in high relief and their heads have wonderfully rendered individual features, presenting us with some of the most authentic early portraiture of the 4th century B.C."[29] Until now it has been generally considered that traits of realism and individuality, or idiosyncrasy, in portraiture were traits that did not evolve until much later in the Hellenistic period, say, the second century or later. Professor Andronikos states that "The ivory heads and all other finds and the wall-painting and the architecture of the tomb are, with no use of special pleading, securely dated to the 4th century B.C., definitely in the third quarter of the century. And if one were to search for stylistic connexions, they are to be found in certain of the Mausoleum sculptures, such as Mausolus [?] himself or the heads

---

[25] Margarete Bieber's chronology (supra n. 9) is the *locus classicus* for the development of the styles of Alexander portraiture. Gisela M. A. Richter's review of the book in *Archaeology* 18 (1965) 297, summarizes it succinctly: "What makes this study particularly instructive is that in this succession of portraits one can observe the changing styles during the Hellenistic and Roman periods — first the soberer renderings during the early Hellenistic period, followed by those in the soft, "sfumato" style associated with the post-Praxitelean "Alexandrian" period, developing presently into the baroque renderings of the second century B.C. (admirably brought out in the head from Pergamon). . . ."

[26] Manolis Andronikos, *RGV* 59.

[27] Manolis Andronikos, *Search* 34.

[28] *Ibid.*

[29] Manolis Andronikos, "The Royal Tombs," *Alexander the Great* (supra n. 19) 14-15.

BM 1054 and 1055.³⁰ The example of the so-called Mausolus is unfortunate: at first thought to be from the middle of the fourth century, it was decisively assigned by Rhys Carpenter in 1960 to the middle of the *second* century B.C.³¹ As for BM 1054, it is a bearded male head, but the resemblance stops there: "its expression [is] neutral . . . the eyes are fairly deeply set, [and the] eyelids [are] not over emphatic,"³² none of which can be said about this head. And one can certainly not say of this head what Waywell further says about no. 1054, when he speaks of the "fifth-century classicising of this head, in particular the mild, dignified countenance"!³³ As for BM 1055, it does have a beard and an upward gaze, and it "appears to be a fourth century work,"³⁴ but, as Waywell says, the "rendering of the beard is rather impressionistic,"³⁵ which is not the case here, and the head is in such bad shape generally that it is hard to make any meaningful comparison between it and the beautifully finished work from Vergina, Tomb II. I can say nothing about the wall-painting, the other finds, or the architecture of the tomb, but the little heads do present us with an enigma. I rejoice in the thought that an original *Greek* bust of Alexander has been found, and I also rejoice in that it confirms the traditional notions of his appearance, but I can not agree that these portraits confirm the dating; rather it is up to the archaeologists and the historians to impose the convincing necessity for a reformation of art history.

If Tomb II is the tomb of Philip II, still another problem arises. Evidence presented by Professor Andronikos indicates that the tomb was constructed in haste, perhaps, he says, because Alexander was not yet in firm enough control of his kingdom to bury his father at leisure. Andronikos points to the workmanship and to the fact that a spear point was placed against the wall while the plaster was still wet.³⁶ If that was the case the mystery deepens. I have heard the

---

³⁰ Manolis Andronikos, *RGV* 60.

³¹ Christine Havelock gives a good bibliography of the subject in *Hellenistic Art* (supra n. 24) 36.

³² G. B. Waywell, *The Free-Standing Sculptures of the Mausoleum at Halicarnassus in the British Museum* (London 1978) 115.

³³ *Ibid.* 116.

³⁴ *Ibid.* 118.

³⁵ *Ibid.* 117.

³⁶ See Nicholas and Joan Gage, "Treasures from a Golden Tomb," *New York Times Magazine* (December 25, 1977) 19 (paraphrasing Andronikos): "Alexander would

The Search for Alexander's Portrait

estimate that the tomb could have been completed in three weeks. How then could these ivory masterpieces of portraiture have been produced in such a small space of time? It hardly seems credible that they could have been produced in such haste. Besides the heads that are here in the exposition, Andronikos first showed three other heads, much more idealized, and suggested that they were copies of the chryselephantine statues that Philip set up in the Philippeion at Olympia: statues of himself, Olympias, Alexander, and his parents, Amyntas and Eurydice. Since that time Professor Andronikos has found in all some twenty heads in the tomb, and he has not returned to the Philippeion theory. The question becomes more difficult: How could so many heads — "all . . . individual portraits," Andronikos assures us — [37] have been so finely sculpted in so short a time? If we assume that the heads were made in advance — for whatever reason — then we should have to re-interpret the expression of Alexander; it could not be one of grief. Could he in fact have had some kind of physical deformity, or has tradition been vindicated? Did he perhaps, after all, really hold his head in the way ridiculed by Schwarzenberg? Whatever the case, it hardly seems credible that a sculptor should have created in such a short length of time these heads which, as Cornelius Vermeule says in the catalogue of this exposition, "are impressive in their combination of incisive detail and overall monumental impact."[38] Andronikos further says of the heads: "Their exceptional quality indicates that they were made by a great master. Undoubtedly, these are the best and most authoritative

---

have been eager to bury his father as quickly as possible rather than remind everyone of Philip's death during the long time it would take to build a grand tomb." See also "RT" 69 (paraphrasing Andronikos): "The fact that the main chamber of the tomb was less lavish than might be expected has also sown doubts. Dr. Andronikos counters that, since Philip was assassinated with the possible complicity of Olympias, the burial may have taken place hastily, without time for the usual finishing touches on the tomb's inner walls."

[37] Manolis Andronikos, *Search* 34.

[38] Cornelius Vermeule, caption for color plate 34 in *Search*. One could say of these heads what Statius said of the Herakles Epitrapezios: "In so small a space what illusion of great size. What skill of hand, what deft craftsman's cunning. . . ." *Sylv.* IV.6, quoted in Gisela M. A. Richter, *The Sculpture and Sculptors of the Greeks*, rev. ed. (New Haven and London 1950) 290. This most famous statue is said to have belonged at one time to Alexander (*ibid.*). John Onians says in his *Art and Thought in the Hellenistic Age* (London 1979) 126, words about the same statue that could equally apply to these ivory heads: "There were two main attractions in smallness: first the opportunity to display technical skill in the most refined detail and second the possibility of persuading people that something that was physically tiny. . .could embody all the strength of something huge."

portraits not only of Philip but of Alexander as well."[39] Could they have been sculpted in three weeks? In the case of Philip's death, it would seem out of character for him to commission in advance a portrait of a grieving *young* Alexander to put in his tomb. Philip's actions prior to his death were never those of a man preparing for imminent death. One way or another, this little bust of Alexander is a pivotal find. Either the tomb is that of Philip and we must re-think the development of portraiture in the time of Alexander, or its presence is an indication that the attribution of the tomb to Philip is in error. Even in the latter case, recent thinking about the portraiture of *ethos* must be re-thought.

It is good for us not to become too complacent. Certainly no one could have foreseen the discovery of portraits that are certainly closer to the originals than anything else it has been our privilege to see. The search for Alexander's portrait is far from over and no doubt reserves for us more surprises. Christine Havelock's words, written thirteen years ago, were prophetic: "Although material evidence may be abundant, the study of the development of Hellenistic portraiture is baffling and difficult. We walk on a tightrope of conflicting theories, surmises, even guesses; a shred of new evidence can alter the balance overnight."[40] The Vergina head of Alexander is tiny in physical size, but it could never be called a "shred." The contrast between its small size and the impact of its find on scholarship is something that would have delighted the Hellenistic Age.

---

[39] Manolis Andronikos, "RTP" 41.

Professor N. G. L. Hammond very kindly pointed out to me a passage from Diodorus Siculus (17.115.1) concerning what happened after the death of Hephaestion. It seems that in accordance with Alexander's wishes all the generals and Friends made "likenesses" (*eidōla*) of Hephaestion out of ivory, gold, and other precious materials. Could it have been a Macedonian custom to carve these likenesses? Diodorus tells us nothing more than that, mentioning neither whether other members of the family were also sculpted, nor what was the disposition of the likenesses. Professor Hammond interprets the passage as implying a contest to make the most *realistic* likeness possible of Hephaestion. There are, however, two possible objections to this interpretation: in the first place, the passage, strictly speaking, does not say straight out that these *eidōla* were all of Hephaestion, nor that they were competing, merely that they did this in an effort to please the desires of the King. Secondly, one knows from experience that the portraits that please the most are seldom the most *realistic* ones. It is tempting to see in this episode the explanation of the heads in the Vergina tomb and in Miss Rhomiopoulou's tomb, but the notion of plural amateur authorship would make all the more puzzling the uniform excellence of the carvings as postulated by Andronikos.

[40] Christine Havelock, *Hellenistic Art* (supra n. 24) 21.

The Search for Alexander's Portrait

Appendix

The question of identifying the portrait of Helios with that of Alexander has created a polemic of alarming proportions and only politely muted intensity. Herbert Hoffmann, in "Helios," *JARCE* 2 (1963) 121, speaks disparagingly of the locution "Alexander-Helios" as a "convenient appellation," and adds that "there is not the slightest evidence in the writings of classical authors for Lysippos ever having represented Alexander in the guise of Helios." Later, speaking of Rhodian silver drachms of the early third century B.C., "The influence of the Alexander portrait is unmistakable." And, still later (p. 122), he says that the "iconography of Helios becomes inextricably intertwined with that of Alexander, and it is impossible to say for certain in every instance whether Alexander has been idealized as Helios, or whether Helios has been assimilated to the type established for Alexander." Gloria S. Merker, "The Hellenistic Sculpture of Rhodes," *SIMA* 40 (1973), states that the "head's resemblance to portraits of Alexander the Great has been noticed already, but any connection has been denied because of the presumed connection of Alexander, in Rhodes, with Dionysos rather than Helios. The Alexander-Dionysos is no longer fully accepted . . . but in any case, if the head need not represent Helios, it could be an idealized portrait of Alexander without reference to either deity" (p. 29, n. 64). She then goes on to suggest that the holes around the head, which had generally been thought to hold spikes representing the rays of the sun, were in reality too numerous, different in size and in spacing, and could perhaps have served to hold in place hair, a lion's pelt, or an elephant skin.

Ios. A. Zervoudakis, in "Helios kai haliea," [in Greek] *Deltion* 30 (1975) p. 12, n. 67, recognizes the undeniable similarity of the bust to the head of Alexander, and discusses the question of the holes in great detail, concluding that Laurenzi's original identification of the head as that of Helios is correct. Giorgio Gualandi, "Sculture di Rodi," *Annuario della Regia scuola Archeologia di Atene* (Nuovo serie) 38 (1976) 52 n. 2, calls Merker's suggestion "una ricostruzione ideale ancora più macchinosa di quella con la corona radiata." He continues: "la somiglianza con i tratti somatici di Alessandro va spiegata con la concezione politico-ideologica tendente a esaltare l'investitura divina e ciò può spiegare la diffusione di motivi legati a una immagine ispirata, ma non necessariamente riproducente i tratti personali di Alessandro" (*ibid.*). In the body of the text (p. 53), Gualandi says that the head merely documents the persistence of the Lysippan tradition, associated eclectically with other masters of the fourth century, especially Scopas. The importance of the solar divinity in the mythical history of the island frees the sculpture from any narrative relationship to the quadriga or to the person of Alexander. He concludes (*ibid.*): "Confermata appare la diffusione di un tema tipicamente rodio e anche il riconoscimento iconografico come Helios, *facendo cadere la ricorrente polemica*, tendente a privilegiare l'intenzione ritrattistica, sia pure con caratteri idealizzanti, collegabile al principe macedone" [emphasis mine]. Gualandi's certitude would not seem to be justified by the reasons alleged, nor does the certainty of others on either side of the controversy.

I am grateful to John Papachristodoulou, Director of Antiquities for the Dodecanese, for permission to publish the sculpture and for calling to my attention most of the articles cited above.

Queens College and the Graduate School,
City University of New York

Illustration credits:

Fig. 1. Photo Robert W. Hartle, reproduced through the courtesy of Mrs. Maria Siganidou, Ephor of Antiquities for Western Macedonia.

Fig. 2. Photo Robert W. Hartle, reproduced through the courtesy of John Papachristodoulou, Director of Antiquities for the Dodecanese.

Figs. 3 and 4. Archaeological Museum of Sofia. The rider is their inventory No. 7046; the horse is No. 6231. Reproduced through the courtesy of Professor V. Velkov, Director, Institut archeologique, Academie des Sciences de Bulgarie.

Fig. 5. Photo Alinari-Viollet.

Figs. 6 and 7. From the Christos G. Bastis Collection, on loan to the Brooklyn Museum; Brooklyn inventory No. L74.11.1. Photo courtesy of the Brooklyn Museum.

Fig. 8. Archaeological Museum of Thessaloniki. Copyright The Greek Ministry of Culture and Sciences/Prof. Manolis Andronikos. Reproduced through the courtesy of Prof. Manolis Andronikos.

Quintus Curtius Rufus: On His Historical Methods in the *Historiae Alexandri*[1]

LLOYD L. GUNDERSON

Abstract

Quintus Curtius, whose writing shows the proclivities of the Julio-Claudian Court, does not place Alexander in the center-stage of his Alexander-history to the same degree that Diodorus, Arrian, and Plutarch do. Personalities such as Antigonus, Polydamus, Nabarzanes, Bagoas, and Orsines interest Curtius. His decision to produce a rhetorical treatment of Alexander's career results in assigning to the Eunuch Bagoas influence over the King's last years far beyond what the actual record allows. That Nabarzanes gave Bagoas to Alexander and thereby won his pardon, and that the Eunuch procured the destruction of Orsines is fiction. Curtius' method is to bring personalities into the picture who will demonstrate Alexander's degeneration and the mounting "reign of terror" accompanying his last years. In doing so, Curtius ignores and obscures the facts about Nabarzanes' condemnation at Zariapsa, and that Alexander made his visit to the tomb of Cyrus on his initial arrival in Persia.

Tacitus,[2] in the course of telling an absorbing story about how the prominent Roman General Corbulo was prohibited from risking his legions in search of glory, observes that the disappointed campaigner nevertheless won a triumph for having compelled his idled troops to dig a twenty-three-mile canal from the Meuse to the Rhine River. Apparently inspired by this non-military and hence comparatively

---

[1] The sigula for the main sources are: A = Arrianus, *Anabasis*; C = Quintus Curtius Rufus, *Historiae Alexandri*; D = Diodorus Siculus, *Bibliotheca Historica*, Book 17; J = M. Junianus Justinus, *Epitoma Historicarum Philippicarum*; P = Plutarchus, *Vita Alexandri*.

[2] Tac. *Ann.* 11.20-21.

riskless means of obtaining a triumph, a Curtius Rufus set his soldiers in upper Germany to digging for silver. To them the undertaking seemed so onerous and unprofitable that it caused Curtius' troops to petition the emperor to the effect that henceforth he award his general a triumph on the same day he gave out the commission as a means of relieving them of useless effort. Having introduced Curtius Rufus on this mirthful note, Tacitus apologizes for speaking of his subject's origins: about them, Tacitus says, he is left with the dilemma whether to lie, of which he didn't approve, or to tell the truth which, in this case, would be equally shameful. On the same matter, Tacitus tells, when Curtius attained the praetorship, Tiberius, concealing some disgrace left unrevealed about his appointee's birth said, "Curtius Rufus seems to me to have been self-generated." Finally, his consular career was alleged to have been prophesied to Curtius in the mid-day heat during his service in Africa in the town of Adrumentum, when in a vision a woman in an enlarged form appeared to him and said, "You are Rufus, and you will come to this province as pro-consul."

Perhaps the uncertainties about identifying this Curtius Rufus with Quintus Curtius Rufus, author of the *Histories of Alexander*, has obfuscated the Tacitean humour. Indeed, an individual described in those terms would seem to be an unlikely candidate for the authorship of one among the four surviving lives of Alexander written during the Roman Imperial period. But in spite of Tacitus' derisive description of him, a consensus appears to be settling on the conclusion that Curtius Rufus, suffect consul in A.D. 43 is the author of our *Historiae Alexandri*, and has rightly come to possess the *praenomen* Quintus.[3] Thus our author would have lived through the reigns of Tiberius, Caligula, and Claudius, and as has been widely observed, would reflect in his views of the central characters in Alexander's story and sometimes in Alexander's behavior the proclivities of the Julio-Claudian principate and the atmosphere of its court. And should better evidence than we have now lead scholarship to a Quintus Curtius Rufus dated to the first year, or years, of the Flavian Emperors, it would only mean the addition of Nero to the list of Julio-Claudians whose demeanor is so often mirrored in Curtius' *Historiae Alexandri*.

In addition to the times-coloring which gives the Julio-Claudian

---

[3] The latest with references to past literature, A. M. Devine, "The Parthi, the tyranny of Tiberius, and the date of Q. Curtius Rufus," *Phoenix* 33 (1979) 142-59.

patina to his work, Curtius has a focus that makes his history of special interest to Alexander research. In sharp contrast to Curtius, Arrian, drawing on Ptolemy and Aristobulus, but especially Ptolemy, concentrates his narrative almost entirely on Alexander. Other characters are of secondary interest and usually come into play only if they are in court or directly involved in Alexander's movements. This is equally pronounced in Plutarch's "Life" though for the obvious reason that Plutarch was writing not history but biography. Diodorus XVII does show some tendency to see events in a broader perspective but since Alexander's Age comprises but a book in this universal history, its sources are summarized to such an extent that the narrative tends nevertheless to center on Alexander. From these Curtius' history differs in that situations and characters alluded to or suggested in our other Alexander-histories play significant roles in his narration.[4] To detect what and how much narrative material he took from his sources and what must be attributed to Curtius' inventiveness and imagination in composition is an issue that needs to be explored.

Clues to Curtius' commitments emerge from the text itself. In an important instance Curtius called his entire history the *oratio*.[5] In calling it an oration Curtius obviously does not mean that his work is a long speech possessing the divisions of a classical oration. The great number of speeches introduced in the *Histories of Alexander* shows how well Curtius knew standard and traditional rhetorical form. Rather he means that his history is from end to end a narration, a major division of an oration. This is then a synedoche, but also in the sense that his total work possesses the narrative quality bestowed on an oration by virtue of the narration. And hence, in the passage where he calls his history the oration, when he says he digressed from his oration he means that he is diverging from that part of the *oratio* in which the history of the events under consideration is grouped: he is digressing from the *narratio*. In an offhand and indirect way, Curtius is acknowledging that he understands that historical writing belongs to the rhetorical arts. That is hardly surprising to those who have studied his books, but it is well to recall Curtius' own statement on his procedures. This concept of his writing can be interpreted to mean that he has the freedom to adapt his materials to attaining the

---

[4] Among several noting these tendencies, cf. P. A. Brunt, "Persian Accounts of Alexander's Campaigns," *CQ* 12 (1962) 151.

[5] C. 10.6.1.

goals of the rhetorical arts while still writing history. Thus historians need to know when Curtius expands on a character's role to heighten interest in his narrative, and when a fuller picture has won its place in Curtius' story because his sources and/or the historical circumstances dictated it.

The difference is sometimes not hard to detect. For example: Curtius offers us the most detailed rendition of Antigonus' activities, beginning with his appointment as satrap of Phrygia, his siege of the satrapy's capital Celaenae, and his subsequent contributions to defeating the Persian counteroffensive after the Battle of Issus.[6] As it turns out it is only from Curtius that we have some idea of Antigonus' achievement and a sketch of the campaigns that he, as well as Calas and Balacrus, carried out in Asia Minor.[7] The importance to Alexander that the possession of these areas of western Asia had before he moved eastward is obvious. Briant's vigorous and detailed analysis concludes that Curtius used a digression on Antigonus' activities in Asia Minor under Alexander found in Hieronymous' *History of the Successors*.[8] Whatever one decides on the source, it is clear that Curtius required one; although Curtius may have possessed a strong imagination, what happens in a satrapy such as Phrygia could hardly have been written up from mere names.

The name Polydamas calls attention to passages nearly at the opposite pole. The reality of the individual is not in doubt. Arrian cites him as the *hetairos* Alexander selected to bear the death-note concerning Parmenio to Ecbatana.[9] Curtius introduces him far earlier. Polydamas appears at Gaugamela as Parmenio's assistant carrying a message from the left wing requesting Alexander's aid.[10] Those events had already been well embroidered with comments about Parmenio's competence in Plutarch's source which Curtius follows in outline but not in detail since the unfavorable remarks on

---

[6] C. 4.1.35 (A. 1.29.3); on Celaenae, C. 3.1.6-8; on the counter-offensive, C. 4.1.34-35.

[7] C. 4.5.13.

[8] P. Briant, *Antigone Le Borgne* (Paris 1973) 114.

[9] A. 3.26.3.

[10] C. 4.15.6-7; cf. J. E. Atkinson, *A Commentary on Q. Curtius Rufus' Historiae Alexandri Magni: Books 3 and 4* (Amsterdam 1980) 439: " . . . it is . . . natural to ask whether Polydamas was introduced into the story (Gaugamela) because of the role he later played in Alexander's attack on Parmenio."

Parmenio would not suit his larger design.[11] In his source Curtius probably found the name and kept it with design since it would bring Polydamas on stage in a way he could exploit to elicit pity when he would describe Parmenio's murder. And so when Curtius introduces Polydamas in his role as Alexander's designated messenger, we have an element added to the drama. We are reminded by Curtius of their long association and that Polydamas customarily serves at Parmenio's side.[12] That they are near in age is likely,[13] for Justin lists Polydamas among the *senes* sent home with Craterus from Babylon. Polydamas might have been sixty years or more in 330.[14] But at this juncture Curtius invents too much to mislead us, for he says that Polydamas has brothers in the army, *iuvenes*, unknown to the King because of their youth. This is, of course, incredible! At any rate, in Curtius' story these Alexander makes hostage to insure that Polydamas will faithfully carry out his dreaded duty. How could Alexander's conduct be made to seem worse than to have him suborn Parmenio's best friend to deliver the kiss of death! Nor does Curtius forego the embrace just as Polydamas hands Parmenio the king's dissembling note. This is Curtius at his shabbiest, or his most perverse. Indeed, it is not unreasonable to conjecture that the whole scene was constructed for the gleeful irony Curtius injected into Parmenio's observation upon reading Alexander's treacherous letter about his plans: "The king is preparing an expedition against the Arachosii. How active he is and never resting! But it is the right time for him to look after his own safety after having gained so much glory."[15] For such compositions Curtius required no source beyond the pen in his hand. Moreover, he had opened Book Seven with observations about Parmenio based on feelings his soldiers had for him, ironically adding that Alexander at the time of his accession had selected Parmenio to carry out the murder of Attalus.[16] Curtius must have changed what he knew was the truth. Diodorus twice names Hecataeus as Alexander's chosen agent in eliminating Attalus,[17] and

---

[11] P. 32.3-4; cf. J. R. Hamilton, *Plutarch. Alexander: A Commentary* (Oxford 1969) 83. Atkinson (supra n. 10) 447-48; the source was primarily Callisthenes with modifications.

[12] The whole episode of Parmenio's death is described in C. 7.2.11-32.

[13] Berve, *Alex* no. 448.

[14] J. 12.12.8.

[15] C. 7.2.26.

[16] C. 7.1.3 and 8.7.4.

[17] D. 12.2.5-6 and 17.5.2.

it is known and can be demonstrated that Curtius and Diodorus much of the time followed the same source.[18] Curtius would have known the name no matter the extent of Parmenio's involvement in removing Attalus. His special interest in Parmenio would have insured that.[19] Curtius may have named Hecataeus in one of his lost first two books, where he would have described the murder of Attalus, and thoughtlessly or perversely have contradicted himself as he prepared the ground for the parallelism he exploits in describing Polydamas' mission.

Such expansion on Polydamas' role in Parmenio's murder may appear to be justified, even an appropriate and harmless means of emphasizing the enormous treachery to a man who had loyally served Alexander. It may seem to be quibbling to complain against Curtius for taking such liberties with his material since what he has done carries essential truth: Curtius decorates to convey an impression of Alexander's menacing brutality. Here Polydamas' role was chosen for analysis with the deliberate purpose of illustrating Curtius' less pernicious adornment of an historical event; nor does it extend so far that it affects much of Curtius' narrative. It is a borderline case; through the characterization of leading figures judgment is passed on Alexander's ruthless dealings with the Macedonian nobility that he has for one reason or another come to distrust. But other passages which Curtius injects with suspense and striking action lead his readers astray not only by directing their attention from Alexander's efforts at statecraft, but concealing decisions which show how he tried to govern his new conquests.

The name "Bagoas" provided for Curtius the web upon which to spin a tale which, I believe, has misled his readers on Alexander's decisions in two adversary situations. Those are his efforts to develop a policy to deal with the rebellious nobility of eastern Iran and to maintain the governance of Persia as a satrapy. The Bagoas story has been examined from the standpoint of Tarn's rejection of it as inconsistent with Alexander's character, and that it was a fabrication produced by the "peripatetic" school in revenge for Alexander's treatment of Callisthenes. Badian's article is too well known to

---

[18] E. Schwartz, *RE* 4 (1901) *s.v.* "Q. . . ." (no. 31) 1871-1891. Also A. B. Bosworth, *A Historical Commentary on Arrian's History of Alexander* I (Oxford 1980) 30 and n. 52, with reference to others. Hereinafter referred to as: Bosworth, *Commentary*.

[19] Cf. H. Strassburger, review of E. Kornemann's *Die Alexander-geschichte des Königs Ptolemaios I*, in *Gnomon* 13 (1937) 491, with reference to passages in Curtius.

require recapitulation.[20] Although it will inevitably touch on it, the main purpose of this essay is not to dispute Badian's contention that an atmosphere of terror developed in Alexander's court after the death of Darius. That issue deserves separate treatment. It is rather the case that little discussion of the details of the Bagoas matter in Curtius has taken place since Badian's article;[21] indeed his article has stimulated much reaction on the positive side, especially his characterization of Alexander's court after his return from India. There have been few dissenting voices.[22] It is thus a desideratum to test the coherence of Curtius' version and examine it against the entire tradition about the events in which Bagoas is a factor. Here the procedure will be first to examine Nabarzanes' career, since he allegedly gave Bagoas to Alexander, and then the desecration and looting of Cyrus' tomb, an affair in which Curtius assigns Bagoas a sinister role.

Nabarzanes was the chiliarch of Persia, a position that placed him in second command to Darius.[23] Curtius introduces him as Darius' *praetor* and in that role author of a letter to a Persian Sisines who had deserted from Persian service in Egypt to the Macedonian court in Philip's time and now was a loyal member of Alexander's entourage. This letter urged him to do something worthy of his notoriety and his character, promising that he would win high office with Darius. Presumably Nabarzanes suggested assassination, for Sisines, treating this offer in the same dilatory fashion as Philotas later did the intelligence of the plot against Alexander's life, was murdered by Cretans after Alexander had secretly read the letter.[24] Now this has nothing to do with the Lyncestian's arrest in which connection Arrian names another Sisines, a confidant of Darius, carrying a letter promising the Macedonian kingship and a thousand talents for the assassination of Alexander the son of Philip.[25] Curtius himself says later that he narrated the arrest of Alexander the Lyncestian and that

---

[20] E. Badian, "The Eunuch Bagoas: A Study in Method," *CQ* 8 (1958) 144-157.

[21] The most extensive and approving discussion in Reimer Egge, *Untersuchungen zur Primartradition bei Q. Curtius* (Freiburg 1978).

[22] A vigorous dissent on Bagoas, N. G. L. Hammond, *Alexander the Great. King, Commander, and Statesman* (Park Ridge, N.J. 1980) 322, n. 114. Now on the "Reign of Terror," W. Heckel, "The Conspiracy Against Philotas," *Phoenix* 31 (1977) 9-21.

[23] Cf. F. Schachermeyr, *Alexander in Babylon* (Wien 1970) 31-33. Also Bosworth, *Commentary* (supra n. 18) 243.

[24] C. 3.7.11-15.

[25] A. 1.25.3.

he was charged by two informers.[26] This discussion must have been in the now lost Book Two. It is too much to believe that two Persians with the same name within a matter of months should be involved in plots against Alexander. What is revealing is that Arrian and Justin have the Lyncestian Alexander arrested in 334/333 before Alexander went to Gordium.[27] Since Curtius put it in Book Two, he had the same date; in fact, he refers to Darius' offer of bribes later, showing that he knew the story in roughly the same terms we find in Arrian.[28] But Diodorus, whose source Curtius again proves to know, dates the arrest in 333 before Issus on the basis of Olympias' warnings. When confronted with the conflicting traditions about offers of money from Darius Curtius avoided making a clear-cut choice between them. He decided to inflate the tradition, leaving in his history that the Lyncestian Alexander was arrested before Alexander went to Gordium on Olympias' charges that Darius had offered money, and then made a separate vignette of the offer to Sisines just before Issus. Atkinson, for other reasons, says that "Sisines is — a symbol of the collaborator for a romantic tale invented by Curtius."[29] Not quite invented but altogether reshaped! In the immediate context Alexander believes Nabarzanes' letter to Sisines but disbelieves Parmenio's warning about his physician, Philip the Acarnanian, simultaneously calling attention to Alexander's *ingenium* for judging the *fides* of his associates.[30] But in the economy of Curtius' whole narrative it is not the name of Sisines that interests him; the tale provides Curtius the appropriate vehicle to introduce the chiliarch of the Persian Empire.

Arrian and/or his sources ignore Nabarzanes until the arrest of Darius. This neglect of the Persian Empire's second-leading figure might justify complaint against Arrian and/or his sources. To Curtius' credit he identifies him as the leader at Issus of the Persian cavalry on the right wing[31] which both Arrian and Curtius describe as the most hotly contested sector of the fighting.[32] Arrian, again in a compressed and sketchy version of Darius' arrest, has Bessus playing

---

[26] C. 7.1.6.
[27] At Phaselis in A. 1.25.1, and before Gordium, J. 11.7.1.
[28] C. 4.1.12.
[29] Atkinson (supra n. 10) 187.
[30] *Ibid.* 187.
[31] C. 3.9.1.
[32] A. 2.2.3; C. 3.11.14-15.

the leading role[33] while Curtius, taking us back to the plotting before the arrest, puts Nabarzanes on the same level with Bessus; Nabarzanes becomes the chief spokesman if not the actual instigator of the plot. Curtius has attributed to him a speech which greatly enhances his role; most dramatic of them all is a provocative speech followed by a scene in which Darius draws his sword and would have killed his chiliarch had not Bessus intervened.[34] Curtius' story with plots and counterplots most resembles a novelette;[35] in succession there is a feigned reconciliation with Darius,[36] a report of Darius' suicide,[37] and finally Nabarzanes and Bessus arrest the harried king.[38] What is fact and fiction we may never know. But the great king died of wounds the conspirators inflicted. Arrian has Satibarzanes and Barsaentes committing the deed.[39] Curtius, more vague, includes them all with Bessus taking the lead.[40] In the aftermath Bessus returns to his satrapy while he appears to have assigned Nabarzanes the satrapy of Parthia-Hyrcania.[41] Curtius initially says Nabarzanes simply went there but later affirms he went there to take up his appointment.[42] We shall return to this matter and its probable basis in fact in a moment.

At this juncture we need to note that in the large lacuna at the end of Book Five Curtius described the death of Darius. That is the plan he outlines at the beginning of Book Five when he says he will return to European affairs in the next book after dealing with Darius' flight and death.[43] By proceeding in a topical rather than annalistic manner he was able to supply a dramatic climax to each book. The fate of the conspirators remained for the next book, and became available to form subsidiary episodes to the larger theme in Book Six about how

[33] A. 3.21.1-5.
[34] C. 5.9.2-11.
[35] C. 5.9.12-12.10.
[36] C. 5.10.12-15.
[37] C. 5.12.12-13.
[38] C. 5.12.14-17.
[39] A. 3.21.10.
[40] C. 5.13.16-17.
[41] In Strab. 11.9.1-2 Parthia-Hyrcania was one administrative unit. Cf. Bosworth, *Commentary* (supra n. 18) 349-50, and A. 3.23.4. Once A. 3.21.5 assigns Parthia-Hyrcania to Bessus.
[42] In C. 5.13.18 we are told that Nabarzanes goes there; in C. 6.3.9 *Hyrcaniam Nabarzanes occupavit*. The latter must mean that he took the satrapy.
[43] C. 5.1.1-2.

Lloyd L. Gunderson

Alexander's character changed during his campaigns in eastern Iran. Arrian's narrative detours into Parthia-Hyrcania before resuming the eastward thrust; during the Parthian-Hyrcanian campaign Arrian tells us that Nabarzanes surrendered, and apparently nothing more is heard of him.[44] Berve suggested that he met his death as did the other conspirators.[45] Tarn, it is well known, denied that any who surrendered was punished.[46] However, this may not be the end of the matter in Arrian nor what actually happened.

It is not necessary for our purposes to recount all the horrors of rebellion and insurrection Alexander met with in Areia, Bactria, and Sogdiana. Autophradates in Tapuria,[47] Satibarzanes in Areia,[48] and Satibarzanes' successor, Arsakes, rebelled.[49] Spitamenes and Dataphernes handed over Bessus,[50] but they took over his command, proceeding thereupon to oppose Alexander with still greater vigor. The fierceness of their revolt, now supported by the Sogdianians, drew support from areas of Bactria thought reconciled to Alexander's new regime.[51] In this context we are told Alexander had ordered the Hyparchs of Bactria to a meeting at Zariapsa; this summons had inspired the revolt, Arrian says, because they knew or feared that it would not be for their benefit.[52] Curtius also knows of this meeting since he refers to the summons, speaks specifically of Spitamenes and Catanes as recipients of it, and the contents of their reaction: according to Curtius they said it was Alexander's intent to kill off the entire Bactrian cavalry at such a meeting, and to avoid committing an unforgivable crime against their own people they would not attend.[53] They said "the savagery of Alexander was no more

---

[44] A. 3.23.4.

[45] Berve, *Alex* no. 543; Barsaentes Alexander caught up with in India, C. 8.13.3; about Satibarzanes Bosworth, *Commentary* (supra n. 18) 344-45, lists the problems of his status as an assassin; perhaps Nabarzanes is the correct reading at A. 3.21.10 as Schmieder suggested.

[46] W. W. Tarn, *Alexander the Great* 2 (Cambridge 1948) 321.

[47] Autophradates' (Phradates) refusal to hear a summons; A. 4.18.2 and C. 8.3.17; executed at Persepolis, C. 10.1.39.

[48] Satibarzanes' revolt; A. 3.25.5; D. 17.78.1 and 83.3; C. 6.6.20.

[49] Arsakes' willful neglect; A. 3.29.5.

[50] A. 3.30.1-2.

[51] A. 4.1.5.

[52] A. 4.1.5.

[53] C. 7.6.14-15.

endurable than the outrageous treachery of Bessus."⁵⁴ Surely Alexander contrived and announced this meeting to reach a settlement with the local nobility that continued to cause him concern and casualties.⁵⁵ The fact that he had not been able to bring his military force back to full strength at the time he announced the meeting would have added to its feasibility as an alternate means of pacification.⁵⁶ Moreover, since Alexander had claimed to be King of Asia and was now asserting his claim to succeed Darius this sort of conference would have on its agenda the fate of those who had participated in the latter's murder, and what should be done with Bessus who had claimed the throne and called himself Artaxerxes.⁵⁷ Since no source other than Arrian tells us about the meeting itself, and he in a most sketchy way, we can only certify that it voted to punish Bessus in the traditional Persian manner.⁵⁸ But Alexander would have exploited such a meeting for settling with other prominent rebels, a purpose alluded to in Curtius' explanation of the announcement. Iranian nobility compelled to vote to punish their rebellious associates would be co-opted from revolting. It was neither conceived nor conducted as a democratic assembly. But it would reduce the number of those to whom Spitamenes might appeal, and he was still at large. Presumably Alexander had delayed any action about Bessus that he might deal with the regicide at the Zariapsa conference. Arrian also tells us that, in the same winter at Zariapsa, "Phrataphernes the satrap of Parthyaea came to him [Alexander] with Stasanor who had been sent to Areia to arrest Arsaces, bringing him in chains along with Brazanes whom Bessus had made satrap of Partyaea, and others who had revolted with Bessus."⁵⁹ The arrival of these is reported in the context of the Zariapsa conference, and the purpose of Phrataphernes' long journey from Parthia cannot be other than to bring prisoners whose fate was to be the leading topic for discussion.⁶⁰

---

[54] C. 7.6.15.

[55] C. 7.6.14. On Alexander's effort to gain cooperation from the locals Curtius is explicit.

[56] A. B. Bosworth, "Alexander and the Iranians," *JHS* 100 (1980) 6, with all the references.

[57] A. 3.25.3; C. 6.6.13.

[58] A. 4.7.3; Curtius only tells us that Alexander ordered Bessus sent from there to Ecbatana. C. 7.10.10.

[59] A. 4.7.1 (Brunt's trans. in the Loeb Classical Library).

[60] W. Heckel, "Some Speculations on the Prosopography of the Alexanderreich,"

Aside from Arrian the name Brazanes does not occur in the Alexander-histories. His appointment also causes difficulty, and we can only suppose Bessus managed to raise a revolt in the west, as Bosworth does,[61] or with Schachermeyr, speculate that Bessus sent out satraps to non-existent satrapies.[62] Unless, of course, this is not an unknown and unaccounted-for satrap but Nabarzanes whom Bessus had appointed to Parthia-Hyrcania and whose appointment to that satrapy Curtius noticed.[63] This would solve the problem of a crowded office since, as our sources stand, there is Nabarzanes who held it from Bessus, Phrataphernes who held it before Nabarzanes and again after him as Alexander's appointment, plus the unknown Brazanes. Waldemar Heckel has recently offered the speculation that Brazanes is simply a corruption of Nabarzanes, "A common occurrence with Persian names transliterated into Greek."[64] Heckel assumes that the Volcanius reading (and widely printed thereafter) "Barzanes" has equal validity with Brazanes, this being a simple case of inversion as in Atraphrenes and Artaphernes. As an additional reason for conjecturing that a prefix is missing, Heckel calls attention to the quality of the transmission of this passage which has two other corrupt names.[65] The likelihood that Brazanes is Nabarzanes, coupled with the fact that this conference was conceived to eliminate Bactrian-Sogdianian resistance to Alexander's regime, would make it the appropriate panel to try Darius' former chiliarch into whose office Hephaestion had now been installed.[66] The reality

---

Liverpool Classical Monthly (March 1981) 66. Heckel regards A. 4.7.1 a doublet of 4.18.1. This seems inconsistent with the purpose of Phrataphernes' arrival, which must coincide with the Zariapsa meeting, and the fact that Autophradates survives until 324.

[61] Bosworth, "Alexander and the Iranians" (supra n. 56) 6.

[62] F. Schachermeyr, *Alexander der Grosse* (Wien 1973) 339.

[63] C. 6.3.9.

[64] W. Heckel (supra n. 60) 66. Heckel handles the details of Nabarzanes' appointment in a different way: he conflates Arrian and Curtius by having Nabarzanes return to Hyrcania with an appointment from Bessus because he became dissatisfied with his pardon, pp. 68-69.

[65] *Ibid.* 66. Heckel reads Menidas for Melamnidas, and Brunt n. 3, pp. 360 and 361, on A. 4.7.2 Menes for Bessus. Heckel follows J. R. Hamilton, "Three Passages in Arrian" *CQ* 5 (1955) 217.

[66] The consensus seems to be that Hephaestion became chiliarch shortly after his appointment to the command of Companion Cavalry in 330 (A. 3.27.4); cf. Bosworth, "Alexander and the Iranians" (supra n. 56) 5. It should not be assumed the title held the same powers under Alexander as it did in the Achaemenid Empire. On changes, cf. Schachermeyr (supra n. 23) 33-37.

of the Zariapsa conference offers no problem; as an instrument for the pacification of the Bactrian-Sogdianian nobility its efficacy must be doubted; its failure to do more than punish assassins and rebels may account for its obscurity in our sources.

That Alexander should have dispensed with a man of Nabarzanes' importance for no more advantage than a eunuch, whom he could have had anyhow, appears to be in conflict with the personal qualities attributed to him by those who believe the Bagoas story. It has been lately proposed that Arrian's source (Ptolemy) suppressed the negotiations with Nabarzanes and the Bagoas story in the cause of portraying a victorious king.[67] The corollary to that premise is that Curtius supplies us with details from sources that are rich in material about the king's change in character and his developing reign of terror. All of that is an oversimplification. It is really a matter of which details are to be believed. Curtius provides us with useful material which supplements our other sources about Alexander's military operations in eastern Iran. But Alexander's negotiations with the local nobility are confused and obscure in Curtius; he really does not give us any hint about the Zariapsa conference. Instead Curtius strains his readers credulity in summarizing a letter Alexander allegedly received in Hyrcania in which Nabarzanes denies that he was ever an enemy to Darius, pleading that he risked death at Darius' hand in return for good advice.[68] Such contemptible sophistry would not have won him Alexander's *fides*. Nor do we have any reason to believe there was avarice in Alexander's character which Nabarzanes' gifts satisfied to obtain the pardon Alexander supposedly gave him at Zadracarta.[69] Finally, however much Curtius has preserved of useful material in Book Six and elsewhere, it must be part of our consideration that this book devotes considerable space to providing exempla which give colour to Curtius' generalizations in Book 6.2 and Book 6.4 about the degeneration of Alexander's character.

While Curtius chose Bagoas as the instrument of salvation in his first appearance in the *Historiae Alexandri*, in the second he made the eunuch the sinister avenger. The gift-giving and gift-receiving episodes join Alexander's private iniquity to the more serious

---

[67] R. Egge (supra n. 21) 154-55.

[68] C. 6.4.8-14.

[69] A. 3.23.6 gives this as the area's chief city. This was Alexander's *stativa* in C. 6.5.22.

allegations about his mounting peccability in public policy. These concepts about Alexander's character Curtius finds needing amplification as the biography moves to its conclusion, hence another novelette.

Orsines first appears in Curtius at Gaugamela, prominent in Darius' battle order.[70] A descendant of Cyrus and a member of the seven families, he would be no stranger to Alexander.[71] At Pasargadae, Curtius says, Orsines met the king with gifts for him and his companions; among the items enumerated are 3000 talents.[72] Bagoas, playing the role of Potiphar's spurned wife, since he was conspicuously excluded from receiving anything out of Orsines' bounty, devises the ruin of a man described as "most noble and innocent."[73] Orsines excused the insult on the grounds that he was "honouring the king's friends but not his prostitutes."[74] Him Bagoas convinced Alexander to punish for the depredation of Cyrus' tomb. Just coincidently Bagoas credits Darius with the intelligence that 3000 talents had been buried in that very tomb. Striking at the quality of Alexander's Asian victories (recalling Cleitus' insult which seems inappropriate coming from a Persian prince) as well as his current administration of the empire, to Orsines Curtius gives this parting epigram: "I had heard that women once reigned in Asia; this, however, is something new, for a eunuch to reign."[75]

Curtius is emphatic about Orsines' innocence and loyalty to Alexander, referring to the charges as altogether false. It is most remarkable that in the tradition which survives about the tomb of Cyrus all agree that Orsines did not rob the grave. In fact the report of Aristobulus as preserved in Strabo, specifically calls attention to the fact that the satrap did not rob the tomb; it was the work of

---

[70] C. 4.12.8-9; cf. Bosworth, *Commentary* (supra n. 18) 290-91 on the difference between C. and A., and the possible lacuna in A. That Orsines was over Ariobarzanes, whom he succeeded in the satrapy, may be questionable; cf. Atkinson (supra n. 10) 405; "Orsines merited mention as a member of one of the Seven Families and because he featured in the story of the despoliation of Cyrus' tomb."

[71] Most likely because of his family and prominence at Gaugamela; Hedicke's emendation "Orsines" from "Orsilos" of the codices at C. 5.13.9 would entail Alexander having met him during the pursuit of Bessus; Hedicke's correction does not seem justified.

[72] The whole story of Bagoas and Orsines in C. 10.1.22-38.

[73] C. 10.1.26.

[74] C. 10.1.26.

[75] C. 10.1.37.

Quintus Curtius Rufus: Historical Methods

plunderers.[76] As we have a specific denial, we must deduce that someone writing before Aristobulus did indeed write that Orsines robbed the grave.[77] Does this also lead one to conclude that Curtius knew the tradition which held Orsines responsible, noticed the denial in Aristobulus (in whatever form he had him), and made this an ingredient of his narrative?

Certainly nothing in the confused and contradictory tradition we have now about Cyrus' tomb gives a hint of anything resembling Curtius' story. Another factor to be weighed is the absence from Arrian of Aristobulus' specific denial that the satrap robbed the tomb. This is not a serious omission since the description in Arrian of the damage done to the tomb agrees well with the reasoning in Strabo's version of Aristobulus that the thievery was furtive, resulting in the loss of those specific objects that could be easily carried off. One must also reckon with Arrian's narrative (after he stops quoting Aristobulus and, presumably, resumes Ptolemy) which reports that among the crimes of which Orsines was accused, there was looting of tombs. Again the Arrian and Strabo versions of Aristobulus do not really contradict one another. It looks as though Arrian, in excerpting Aristobulus, left out the specific reference to Orsines' innocence in the matter of Cyrus' tomb because he thought the magi's refusal to accuse anyone sufficient denial of the satrap's guilt.[78] From Arrian's version it can only be concluded that Alexander never found the thieves. But there is one notable difference between Arrian and Strabo's version of Aristobulus: the explicitness with which Strabo's Aristobulus tells us that Alexander visited the tomb on his first visit of Pasargadae. Arrian only implies Alexander saw the tomb on his first arrival in Pasargadae for he said parenthetically, that "It was always Alexander's intention to visit the tomb of Cyrus whenever he conquered Persia."[79]

Jacoby[80] noticed that this first visit is also reflected in Curtius' implication that "By chance Alexander ordered the tomb of Cyrus to be opened in which the famous king's body was buried to which he

---

[76] *FGrH* 139 (Aristobulus) F 51b = Strabo 15.3.7 (C730); F 51a = A. 4.29.4-11.
[77] *FGrH* IID, p. 522. Jacoby has written some nonsense when he asserts that Aristobulus' denial that the Satrap robbed the tomb corrects Cleitarchus (that is, Curtius) forgetting that Curtius also declared Orsines innocent.
[78] A. 6.29.11.
[79] A. 6.29.9.
[80] *FGrH* IID, p. 522.

wanted to pay honours.'"[81] That this must refer to the first visit seems eminently reasonable; it is then that Alexander had great leisure for he stayed in Persepolis and its environs some months in the winter of 331-330.[82] It is to one's first visit that the paying of honours belongs and that is also the force of Arrian's remark that it was always his intention to visit the tomb after conquering Persia.[83] To which it may be added that, on Alexander's initial contact with the center of the Persian Empire, the novelty of those monuments belonging to the figures of legend must have had considerable fascination for him; their attraction would have dimmed after seven more years of campaigning. The scene in which Curtius has Alexander making a personal visit to the tomb on his return from India is burdened with a lack of plausibility.

But on the importance of that first visit Aristobulus is crystal clear: Alexander knew from it how the tomb should look because it was then that he made a personal inspection of it. The implications for the coherence of Curtius' story are crushing. Bagoas becomes the informant on the tomb's contents. From Darius the eunuch had learned of its contents, and without Bagoas, the story goes, Alexander would have concluded that the tomb's modesty should be attributed to the Great King's austerity about which he conceivably read in Xenophon.[84] But, of course, Alexander knew the tomb, and Curtius is asking his readers to nod. One cannot easily construct a story that forever confounds historical reality unless one is in the position to destroy all the conflicting evidence. Curtius could not even expunge it altogether from his own pages; it slipped in that Alexander had been at the tomb before. For this composition Curtius would not require any sources.[85]

There is yet the matter of Orsines, his high position, and his removal from office. He had usurped it after the natural death of Phrasaortes, Alexander's appointee.[86] For the sake of vividness

---

[81] C. 10.1.30.

[82] E. Badian, "Agis III," *Hermes* 95 (1967) 188-189; E. N. Borza, "Fire from Heaven: Alexander at Persepolis," *CP* 67 (1972) 233-245; Peter Green, *Alexander of Macedon* (Harmondsworth 1974) 314-321.

[83] In Ps.-Call. II. 18 (Recension A) he also visits the tomb on his first arrival in Persia.

[84] Xen. *Cyr.* 8.7.25.

[85] Egge (supra n. 21) 150-151 believes Curtius had a source other than Aristobulus on the tomb.

[86] Berve *Alex* no. 813.

Quintus Curtius Rufus: Historical Methods

Curtius avoided mentioning that in order that nothing should cloud Orsines' innocence and Bagoas' complete domination of Alexander. Such matters must be assessed when we rely on Curtius for our knowledge of Alexander. His silence about Orsines' appointment is some indication of Curtius' inability to relate events to Alexander's development of policy; his failure as an historian in this respect also calls attention to his commensurate obsession with proving that Alexander's structure of character (*natura*) could not withstand success (*res secundae*).[87] Surely we can agree that the historian must, in as much detail as possible, analyse the structure of any leading figure's character and the changes in it might affect the making of policy. But Curtius, in search of the striking incident that will reveal his leading character's true nature, and while writing as though he were creating a Hellenistic literary *bios*, looses track of the balance. His history, by tracing institutional modifications back exclusively to detectable changes in single individuals, earns our suspicion. Historical explanations must assess varied forces in accounting for change. To some extent our sources permit us to infer that not one but diverse factors influenced Alexander to remove and execute the Persian satrap.

Judging by the anxiety Alexander shortly made public when he ordered the satraps to disband their mercenaries,[88] he feared a revival of Persian feudalism of which kind Orsines' usurpation was a species. That would call for removal from office. Then there is the matter of the law of the land. Orsines was charged. Unless we are prepared to assert that Alexander was incapable of righteous indignation, it must be conceded that Orsines may actually have committed the thievery which merited the punishment he got. But assuming that his downfall was a matter of arrogation of office and misconduct, there were still other considerations. We can be certain that administering Persia, the center of the Achaemenid Empire, as a satrapy posed some special problems. Surely in 324, the time of his transactions with Orsines, Alexander did not view those issues from the same perspective he held when he appointed Phrasaortes the satrap of Persia in 331-330. Diodorus and Curtius associate two atrocities with the Macedonians' initial visit to Persia, first the plundering of the city, and then the firing of the palace.[89] These acts may have been

---

[87] C. 10.1.40.
[88] D. 17.106.3.
[89] Plundering, C. 5.5.1-8 and D. 17.70.1-5; burning of the palace, C. 5.7.1-11 and

premeditated and hence regretted years later, or done on impulse and regretted immediately.[90] Whatever their nature, it is not hard to imagine their effect on the local population. Orsines' pillaging of tombs and killing of people without due process must have reminded Alexander of what he had permitted to happen on his previous visit to Persepolis. As Schachermeyr observes, Orsines behaved as if he were a Macedonian.[91] Similar thoughts about Orsines' conduct of office would probably have occurred to Alexander on returning to Persepolis, as Arrian says, for he expressed regret about burning the Persian palace.[92] Our best evidence that Alexander took exceptional care with the governance of Persia as a satrapy, and drew some negative lessons from Orsines' two-year conduct of the office, comes from his appointment of Peucestas.[93] Peucestas, according to Arrian, was an exception among the Macedonians in learning Persian and adopting Median dress;[94] in Diodorus there is the additional information that Alexander made an exception of Peucestas for the purpose of pacifying the Persians and gaining their cooperation.[95] That the exception would cost him the morale, and worse, open criticism from many of his Macedonian troops was probably anticipated by Alexander. Difficult situations require hard decisions; harsh realities dictated that he reach back to the failed and discarded experiment of mixing conquerors and the vanquished. The appointment of Peucestas represents Alexander's improvisation in governance; not an exemplum of highminded blending of the nations.

Bagoas' frivolous machinations as a means of explaining Orsines' dismissal and execution altogether obscure the political exigencies Alexander met after a long absence in the east. Nor was the satrap's demise an event in a generalized atmosphere of repression and violence;[96] the accommodation of the local population with the

---

D. 17.72.1-6; also P. 38 who stresses Thais' role; A. 3.18.11 has a different source. Cf. Bosworth, *Commentary* (supra n. 18) 331.

[90] The plundering appears to be premeditated. Only Arrian seems to be clear that the burning of the palace was planned; cf. Bosworth, *Commentary* (supra n. 18) 331-32.

[91] Schachermeyr (supra n. 23) 477.

[92] A. 6.30.1.

[93] Bosworth, "Alexander and the Iranians" (supra n. 56) 12: "Doubtless Alexander had laid to heart the lesson of Orsines' usurpation and concluded that in Persia his satrap had to conform and to seem to conform to the local *mores*."

[94] A. 6.30.1.

[95] D. 19.14.5.

[96] cf. E. Badian, "Bagoas" (supra n. 20) 148.

appointment of Peucestas runs counter to that proposition. There has been special pleading that Peucestas was a compliant toady whose loyalty to Alexander was his greatest distinction; that does not square with the fact that he successfully governed his satrapy until 317.

In sum, from a scrutiny of the details, it emerges that the actual fate of Nabarzanes was different from what Curtius tells us, nor can we rely on his explanation of Orsines' execution. Nabarzanes with Bessus betrayed Darius whose murder Alexander vowed to punish. In the course of events the king arrested both assassins. Their disposition he postponed for a politically opportune occasion. During the bitter struggle for northeastern Iran Alexander nearly in despair of a military solution to the subjugation of Bactria and Sogdiana decided on the expedient of a Council at Zariapsa at which he tried to reach a settlement with the Iranian nobility and to secure recognition of his hegemony as King of Asia. Included on the agenda was the trial of Bessus and Nabarzanes along with other rebels. By obtaining the Iranians' assent to the punishment of his predecessor's murderers, Alexander hoped for a form of cooptation. The vote to execute the regicides he got, but events proved that the Iranians refused the colleagueship. The story that Bagoas provided Nabarzanes' ransom is a fiction. No matter what his sexual preference, Alexander could not at one of the more desperate junctures in his career have sacrificed matters of policy to frivolity.

Of Orsines, the Persian satrap, Curtius says, Bagoas falsely accused him of robbing Cyrus' tomb. All our sources agree that Orsines was innocent; Aristobulus, as preserved in Strabo, specifically says that the satrap did not rob the tomb. Aristobulus also says that Alexander visited the tomb on his first visit to Pasargadae, and thus knew how the tomb was furnished. This last information is shattering to Curtius' story, for he presents Alexander making his first visit after his return from India in the company of Bagoas who describes the tomb as it would have appeared before it was plundered. Curtius' story lacks coherence. Worse, he ignores the fact that Orsines had usurped his satrapy in Alexander's absence in India. Finally, by appointing Peucestas the satrap of Persia, Alexander was accommodating the Persians who had experienced the worst of Macedonian savagery when Alexander first called at Pasargadae and Persepolis. Orsines had not robbed Cyrus' tomb, but in other respects his conduct toward his own people recalled the atrocities of the Macedonians. Alexander had to find a way to make them forget if he was to govern effectively. Again, Curtius, by introducing Bagoas, misleads his readers by obscuring an issue of governance which tested Alexander's statecraft.

There is no direct route leading to the core of useful and valid historical tradition in Curtius. Stripping the veneer of rhetoric may reveal no more core than does peeling an onion. Not that the names and events have no reality; there is no need to deny the reality of a Bagoas in Alexander's court.[97] But an examination of the details prove their lack of coherence and that Curtius has constructed a tale with a mere tissue of plausibility. He represents Bagoas as the darling of Alexander's affections whose influence pervades the king's later years. He alleges that Bagoas, due to Alexander's sexual attraction for him, obtained the salvation of his former master Nabarzanes and the murder of Orsines who insulted him. The moralist position (as Badian's), that a general degeneration took place in Alexander, and that an atmosphere of terror prevailed in the last days of his reign, draws on Curtius' fabrication that Bagoas' influence through Alexander's erotic tendencies could secure the deliverance or destruction of important individuals. Curtius' elaboration of the Bagoas episode is the veneer of rhetoric. Strip it away and nothing Curtius tells us about Bagoas has any reality. Nor is Bagoas circumstantial to Curtius' narration. He is, in fact, the personality necessary to maintain the dramatic interest and tension with which Curtius imbues his history. To Curtius must be applied the most rigorous analysis if we are to avoid the folly of allowing the bad to drive out the good tradition. If we strip away Curtius' invention we see that Bagoas stands in the way of the clear light the Council at Zariapsa sheds on Alexander's struggle in Bactria, and that the eunuch conceals the negative behaviour of Orsines that caused Alexander to make the exceptional decision to appoint Peucestas.

St. Olaf College

---

[97] P. 67 and Dicaearchus (Athen. 13.603a b).

Arsinoe II Philadelphos: A Revisionist View

STANLEY M. BURSTEIN

Abstract
Arsinoe II (316-270 B.C.), wife successively of Lysimachus, Ptolemy Ceraunus and Ptolemy II, is one of the most striking figures in the history of the third century B.C. Of the unusual position she held in the long line of Ptolemaic queens there can be no doubt. Her incestuous marriage to her brother Ptolemy II and the well-documented posthumous honors awarded to her confirm it. Scholars, however, have claimed more, namely that during the 270's she was the *de facto* ruler of Egypt. This paper analyzes the evidence adduced in support of this thesis. Particular attention is devoted to the prominent role assigned to Arsinoe in the determination of the royal succession and the formulation of Ptolemaic policy in the Chremonidean War. After reviewing the evidence, the paper concludes that the claims made for her dominance in the political life of Egypt in the 270's are exaggerated.

Plutarch despairingly begins his life of Lycurgus with the remark that "concerning Lycurgus the lawgiver, in general, nothing can be said which is not disputed."[1] A modern Plutarch might well make the same confession at the beginning of a study of the life of any Hellenistic king or queen. With the loss of virtually the whole of Hellenistic historiography, the would-be biographer must build up the picture of his subject from brief notes in late epitomes and occasional allusions in often fragmentary and insecurely dated literary and epigraphical texts. A particularly serious example of the problem is provided by the life of Arsinoe, wife and *basilissa* (queen)

[1] Plut. *Lyc.* 1.1.

successively of Lysimachus, Ptolemy Ceraunus and Ptolemy II between 300 and 270 B.C. and, according to modern scholars, one of the central figures in the history of the early third century B.C.[2]

The sources for the biography of Arsinoe are meagre in the extreme. Only for the period of her brief and tragic marriage to her half-brother Ptolemy Ceraunus in late 281 or early 280 after the death of Lysimachus does a connected account survive in a few sensational chapters of Justin's *epitome* of Pompeius Trogus' *Philippica*. Otherwise, except for her involvement in the execution of Lysimachus' son Agathocles in the late 280's, little explicit information survives in the sources. Still, enough remains to permit an outline of her life to be sketched.

Arsinoe was born in 316, the daughter of Ptolemy I and his mistress (and later wife and queen), Berenice. Nothing is known of her life before 300 when, about the age of 16, she married Lysimachus, the 61-year-old king of Thrace.[3] According to Memnon of Heraclea Pontica, the marriage was a love match,[4] but this is unlikely. The marriages of Hellenistic princesses were counters to be played in the game of diplomacy and Arsinoe's was no exception. The death of Antigonus the One-Eyed at the battle of Ipsus in 301 shattered the alliance of his enemies, leaving Ptolemy and Lysimachus facing a greatly strengthened Seleucus. Common fear led to an alliance and Arsinoe's marriage was the cement that sealed it.[5]

Thereafter, however, little is known of Arsinoe before the 280's. A questionable tradition maintains that Ephesus was renamed Arsinoea by Lysimachus in her honor at the time of its refoundation in the second half of the 290's; more likely it was named for Lysimachus' similarly named daughter by Nicaea, his first wife, just as he

---

[2] Studies devoted to Arsinoe alone are rare. The most important are: Grace Harriet Macurdy, *Hellenistic Queens: A Study of Woman-Power in Macedonia, Seleucid Syria, and Ptolemaic Egypt* (Baltimore 1932) 111-30; Ernst Kornemann, *Grossen Frauen des Altertums im Rahmen zweitausendjähriger Weltgeschens*, 4th ed. (Bremen 1958) 110-34; Gabriella Longega, *Arsinoe II* (Rome 1968); and Hermann Bengtson, *Herrschergestalten des Hellenismus* (Munich 1975) 111-38. Hereafter all dates are B.C.

[3] OGIS 16, once thought to commemorate the dedication of a shrine to Ptolemy I at Halicarnassus by Arsinoe before her marriage, was shown by Nelly Greipl, "Über eine Ptolemäerinschrift," *Philologus* 85 (1930) 159-74, to refer to the foundation of a temple of Arsinoe II by Ptolemy II after his wife's death.

[4] Memnon, *FGrH* 3B, 434 F 4.9.

[5] Plut. *Dem.* 31.3. Paus. 10.3; cf. Jakob Seibert, *Historische Beiträge zu den dynastischen Verbindungen in hellenistischer Zeit*, Historia Einzelschriften 10 (Wiesbaden 1967) 74, for the date and circumstances.

Arsinoe II Philadelphos: A Revisionist View

renamed Smyrna Eurydicea in honor of her sister Eurydice.[6] In the 280's, however, her prominence at court is clear. By then Nicaea was dead and Arsinoe was *basilissa*.[7] The Arsinoeion on Samothrace, the largest known Greek round building, bears witness to her piety and wealth at a shrine traditionally patronized by the kings of Macedon,[8] wealth that was increased by Lysimachus' gift to her of the city of Heraclea Pontica about 284.[9] But her emergence as queen also

---

[6] Ephesus: Strabo 14.1.21, C 640. Stephanus of Byzantiun *s.v.* Ἔφεσος, and Eustathius, *Comentarii in Dionysium Periegetem*, *GGM* 2, 363, line 19, are independent of Strabo, but seem to derive from a similar source. Smyrna: Strabo 14.1.37, C. 646. Nicaea: Stephanus of Byzantium *s.v.* Νίκαια. Strabo 12.4.7, C 565. Until *SIG*³ 368, line 24, revealed that the refoundation of Ephesus dated to the 290's and not the 280's as had previously been believed (and, curiously, still is by Longega [supra n. 2] 30-33), there was no reason to doubt Strabo's statement that it was renamed for Arsinoe, given her influence in the 280's. The suggestion offered in the text is based on the clear evidence provided by Lysimachus' actions in the cases of Nicaea and Smyrna of his desire to honor the members of his existing family in the 290's and the close association between the refounded cities of Ephesus and Smyrna in the 290's as evidenced by Strabo 14.1.4, C 633 and Vitruvius 4.1.4, with the comments of U. v. Wilamowitz, "Panionion," *Kl. Schr.*, 5,1 (Berlin 1937) 128; and of the similar images of a veiled woman on the coins issued by the two cities under their new names, cf. *Cat. Coins Brit. Mus.* 15 (1892) pl. x, Nrs. 5 & 7 (Barclay V. Head, *Historia Numorum*, 2nd ed. [Oxford 1911] 575, 592; and Ulrich Kahrstedt, "Frauen auf antiken Münzen," *Klio* 10 [1910] 266), which, if intended to be portraits, are more compatible with the individuals represented being Arsinoe I and Eurydice than Arsinoe II and Eurydice. In this situation, it would be tempting to suggest on the basis of the reading θυγατρὸς in Eustathius recorded by Mueller (*GGM* 2, 363, *app. ad* 19) that the received text of Strabo is corrupt, but Professor Aubrey Diller has informed me by letter that this reading lacks manuscript support.

[7] The date of Nicaea's death is unknown, but as Lysimachus was polygamous (Plut. *Comparison of Demetrius and Antony* 4.1), she may have been alive at the time of Arsinoe's marriage. Arsinoe is not certainly attested as *basilissa* before *SIG*³ 381 which dates to the 280's (for the date see below note 55). *OGIS* 14, which Dittenberger dated to *ca.* 299 and which does refer to Arsinoe as *basilissa*, is of doubtful authenticity (cf. Franco Ferrario, "Arsinoe — Stratonice: a proposito di una iscrizione ellenistica," *RendIstLomb* 96 [1962] 78-82). For the importance of her position as *basilissa* see Justin 24.2.9, 3.2-3. The conferring of the title meant recognition as a legitimate royal wife with the privileges connected with that status, presumably including her own household (cf. E. Bikerman, *Institutions des Séleucides* [Paris 1938] 26, for the privileges of the Seleucid queens), but no official role in the government (Longega [supra n. 2] 65; and Hans-Werner Ritter, *Diadem und Königsherrschaft: Untersuchungen zu Zeremonien und Rechtsgrundlagen der Herrschaftsantritts bei den Persern, bei Alexander dem Grossen und im Hellenismus*, Vestigia 7 [Munich 1965] 115-20).

[8] *OGIS* 15. For the most recent text see P. M. Fraser, *Samothrace*, 2,1, *The Inscriptions on Stone* (New York 1960) Nr. 10. For the connection of Samothrace with Macedon and the rotunda see Karl Lehmann, *Samothrace: A Guide to the Excavations and the Museum*, 4th ed. (Locust Valley, NY 1975) 18 and 54-58.

[9] Memnon, *FGrH*, 3B, 434 F 5.4-5. For the date and circumstances see Stanley Mayer Burstein, *Outpost of Hellenism: The Emergence of Heraclea on the Black Sea*,

divided the court between her supporters and Ptolemy's (the eldest of the three sons she had borne Lysimachus and whose favor in his father's eyes is revealed by a Theban inscription[10]) and the supporters of Agathocles, Lysimachus' eldest son and heir. Given Lysimachus' age and the fact that Agathocles also had children, the danger to Arsinoe and her sons should Agathocles come to the throne was acute. Tragedy followed. The details are obscure, but the sources all agree that Arsinoe was instrumental in accusing Agathocles of conspiring against his father. Whatever the truth of the charge — and the recent studies of the sources by Gabriella Longega and Heinz Heinen leave no doubt that the truth of the matter was unknown even in antiquity — Lysimachus was sufficiently convinced of his son's guilt to order his execution.[11] Arsinoe's triumph, however, was brief. Roused by the pleas of Agathocles' widow Lysandra (Arsinoe's half-sister) and the hope of exploiting the political confusion in Lysimachus' kingdom, Seleucus invaded Anatolia. Battle was joined at Corupedium in Lydia where the Thracian monarch fell in February, 281. In the wake of the disaster Arsinoe and her sons managed to salvage only the fortress city of Cassandrea; and even that was lost within a year when her desperate attempt to regain (through marriage to her half-brother Ptolemy Ceraunus) her position as queen of Macedon and recognition of her sons' claims to their father's throne failed. Her efforts resulted instead in the murder of her two younger sons and her own exile, first to Samothrace and then to Egypt, where she probably arrived seeking asylum at her brother Ptolemy II's court sometime in 280 or 279.[12]

The decade between Arsinoe's arrival in Egypt and her death in mid-270[13] was undoubtedly the most dramatic and eventful of her 46-

University of California Publications: Classical Studies 14 (Berkeley and Los Angeles 1976) 86 and 93-94.

[10] L. Moretti, *Inscrizioni Storiche Ellenistiche*, I (Florence 1967) 67. For the interpretation of this inscription see Louis Robert, "Notes d'épigraphie hellénistique, XL. Inscription de Ptolémée, fils de Lysimaque," *BCH* 57 (1933) 485-91.

[11] Longega (supra n. 2) 44-55; and Heinz Heinen, *Untersuchungen zur hellenistischen Geschichte des 3. Jahrhunderts v. Chr.*, Historia, Einzelschriften 20 (Wiesbaden 1972) 3-20. For factionalism at Lysimachus's court see Paus. 1.10.4; Strabo 13.4.1, C 623; Athen. 14.616c; Justin 17.1.6. Note the reference to Arsinoe's "friends" in Justin 24.2.7.

[12] Justin 24.1.3. Cf. Longega (supra n. 2) 59-67; and Heinen (supra n. 11) 75-83. Beloch's assumption *Greich. Gesch*² 4. 2, 340) that Arsinoe fled to Samos instead of Samothrace is arbitrary.

[13] More precisely, July, 270. For translations of the relevant portions of the Mendes stele see S. Sauneron, "Un document égyptien relatif à la divinisation de la reine

Arsinoe II Philadelphos: A Revisionist View

year life. From exile she rose again to the status of a queen, this time of Egypt as the wife of her younger brother Ptolemy II, eight years her junior,[14] following the divorce and exile to Coptus on a charge of conspiracy of his first wife, Arsinoe's former step daughter Arsinoe.[15] Her image appeared on her brother's coins, alone on copper, and jointly with him on gold and silver.[16] She received a throne name similar to that of a king[17] and gloried in the intimacy of her incestuous relationship with her brother by taking the surname Philadelphos, "brother-lover."[18] She shared public honors with her brother at Olympia where the Nauarch Callicrates erected columns in honor of each of them[19] and at Athens where her statue stood next to Ptolemy's in the agora.[20] Following her death she received unprecedented honors: deification with her own priestess, the *kanephoros*, a temple (the Arsinoeion) at Alexandria, another at Memphis, and yet another at Cape Zephyrium where, assimilated to Aphrodite, she protected sailors. In addition, her cult was established in all the temples of Egypt. A festival, the Arsinoeia, was established in her honor, and she received co-divinity with her brother as the gods Adelphoi,[21] while a nome and a boulevard in Alexandria as well

---

Arsinoé II," *BIFAO* 60 (1966) 96; and Dorothy Burr Thompson, "A Portrait of Arsinoe Philadelphos," *AJA* 59 (1955) 201.

[14] *FGrH* 2B, 239 B 19.

[15] *Schol. ad. Theocritem* 17, line 128.

[16] Kahrstedt (supra n. 6) 17.

[17] On the Pithom Stele as noted by U. Wilcken, "Arsinoe II," *RE* 2 (1896) 1284.

[18] The title, without obvious divine implications, is clearly alluded to at Theocritus 17, lines 128-130.

[19] *OGIS* 26, 27. For these columns see Hans Hauben, *Callicrates of Samos: A Contribution to the Study of the Ptolemaic Admiralty*, Studia Hellenistica 18 (Louvain 1970) 34-36.

[20] Paus. 1.8.6.

[21] The posthumous character of the personal cult of Arsinoe Philadelphos is clear from the Mendes Stele (supra n. 13) and the new inscription from Memphis published by Sauneron which specifically refers to it (Cf. Sauneron [supra n. 13] 91 for the relevant passages in translation). For comprehensive lists of the posthumous honors to Arsinoe see Edwyn Bevan, *The House of Ptolemy* (London 1927) 129-30; and Longega (supra n. 2) 109-22. For the Memphite temple see Jan Quaegebeur, "Documents Concerning a Cult of Arsinoe Philadelphos at Memphis," *JNES* 30 (1971) 239-70. Temple at Cape Zephyrium: Athen. 7.318d and Hauben (supra n. 19) 42-46. Cult in Egyptian temples: A. D. Nock, "ΣΥΝΝΑΟΣ ΘΕΟΣ," *HSCP* 41 (1930) 204-207; Sauneron (supra n. 13) 94; and Dorothy Burr Thompson, *Ptolemaic Oinochoai and Portraits in Faience: Aspects of the Ruler Cult* (Oxford 1973) 57-59, with a list of the Egyptian goddesses with whom Arsinoe was identified. Arsinoeia: Thompson, *Oinochoai*, 56-57, 71-75. Controversy still exists only about the cult of the *theōn adelphōn* attested as *synnaos* with Alexander in year 15 of Ptolemy II, in

as ports throughout the Aegean and Red Seas were named after her.[22] Finally, a special law authorized even private citizens to sacrifice to her; evidence of the popularity of her cult is found throughout the Ptolemaic empire in the form of small plaques dedicated to Arsinoe Philadelphos or Arsinoe Thea Philadelphos.[23] New discoveries continually add to the list which well testifies to the unique position she held in the long line of Ptolemaic queens. Yet hardly a single datable event can be associated with her. Instead, the sources provide only random allusions: to her visit with Ptolemy to inspect the re-excavated Nile canal in 274/3,[24] to her adoption of his first wife's children,[25] and to her patronage of a festival of Adonis at Alexandria.[26] Not even her incestuous marriage, which so outraged Greek public opinion and whose justification so taxed the talents of the court poets, can be dated more closely than to the decade of the 270's.[27]

That Arsinoe was a significant force at the court of Ptolemy II cannot be gainsaid. Hellenistic kings ruled relatively unfettered by

---

P. Hibeh 199 and dated, therefore, either before Arsinoe's death (e.g. Longega [supra n. 2] 95-103; P. M. Fraser, *Ptolemaic Alexandria* [Oxford 1972] I 217; II 367, n. 228) or after (Alan Edouard Samuel, *Ptolemaic Chronology* [Munich 1962] 25-28; and Sauneron [supra n. 13] 83-109), depending on how you calculate year 15 (for the chronological problems see most recently Ludwig Koenen, *Eine agonistisches Inschrift aus Ägypten und frühptolemäische Königsfeste* [Meisenheim am Glan 1977] 43-45); and especially Michael Wörrle, "Epigraphische Forschungen zur Geschichte Lykiens II: Ptolemaios II und Telmessos," *Chiron* 8 (1978) 212-16.

[22] See now Louis Robert, *Hellenica*, XI-XII (Paris 1960) 154-59.

[23] *P. Oxy.* 27 (1962) Nr. 2465 with the analysis of Louis Robert, "Sur un decret d'Ilion et sur un papyrus concernant des cultes royaux," *Essays in Honor of C. Bradford Welles*, ed. A. Samuel (New Haven 1966) 192-210.

[24] Attested by the Pithom Stele. For translation see Édouard Naville, "La stèle de Pithom," *ZAeS* 40 (1902) 72, lines 12-16.

[25] *Schol. ad Theocritem* 17, line 128. For the correct interpretation of the scholion see Macurdy (supra n. 2) 121-22.

[26] Theocritus, *Idyll* 15. There is no reason to doubt the historicity of this event.

[27] As Fraser notes (supra n. 21) II 367, n. 228, where a comprehensive list of proposed dates is given, only the *terminus ante quem* of year 12 (274/3) provided by the Pithom Stele is certain. I have omitted from consideration Strabo's claim (10.2.22, C 460) that Arsinoe refounded the village of Conopa in Aetolia as an Arsinoea for two reasons: first, because it is not clear if the reference is to the reign of Lysimachus (V. Tscherikower, *Die hellenistischen Städtegründungen von Alexander dem Grossen bis auf die Römerzeit*, Philologus, Supp. 19 [Leipzig 1927] 5) or that of Ptolemy II (Peter M. Fraser, "Two Hellenistic Inscriptions from Delphi," *BCH* 78 [1954] 60, n. 3); and, second, because, as Tscherikower noted, there is something wrong with the Strabo passage since Arsinoe cannot have been responsible for colonizing activity within the territory of the Aetolian League.

Arsinoe II Philadelphos: A Revisionist View

the constraints of tradition or bureaucracy. Their personal decisions were law. Great power belonged to those able to influence those decisions, and pride of place among such individuals belonged to their queens. Evidence of their power is common in inscriptions of third-century Greek cities. Thus, an inscription of 279 from Telmessus expresses the city's fear of the possibility of a queen hostile to its interests.[28] More common, however, are those honoring queens for using their influence with their husbands and sons on behalf of the cities. So Miletus praised Apama, wife of Seleucus I, for aiding Milesian citizens serving in Seleucus' army and for her involvement in her son Antiochus's decision to build a stoa for the city.[29] An inscription from Troezen seems to allude to Stratonice, Antiochus I's queen, arranging for the release of Troezenians captured during Demetrius' ill-fated invasion of Asia in 286.[30] Laodice, queen of Antiochus III, was honored for the benefactions she brought Teos while a recently published inscription from Iasus contains a letter from her to the *boulē* and *dēmos* of Iasus outlining the initiatives she had taken to provide the city with grain and the daughters of the poorer citizens with doweries.[31] In view of her extraordinary honors and the popularity suggested by them and the skill at court politics evidenced by her during the reign of Lysimachus, it would be idle to deny that Arsinoe must have been able to exercise influence similar to that attested for other queens during the years she reigned as Ptolemy II's queen.[32]

Despite or, perhaps, because of the paucity of direct evidence, historians have made far-reaching claims for the extent of her influence while queen of Egypt. It has been suggested, for example, that Arsinoe, "a typical Hellenistic tigress queen in the formidable tradition of Olympias and Cleopatra,"[33] and not Ptolemy II was the

---

[28] Michael Wörrle (supra n. 21) 202, line 30.

[29] *SEG* 4, 442, lines 4-14.

[30] *IG* 4, 750, lines 21-25.

[31] Peter Hermann, "Antiochos der Grosse und Teos," *Anadolu* 9 (1965) 37-40 *passim*; and Giovanni Pugliese Carratelli, "Supplemento epigrafico di Iasos," *ASAtene* 45-46 (1967-1968) Nr. 2.

[32] The exercise of this kind of influence by Arsinoe is perhaps implied in the title "the great benefactor" in line 2 of the hieroglyphic inscription on a base for a statue of Arsinoe from Thebes published by P. M. Fraser, "Inscriptions from Ptolemaic Egypt," *Berytus* 13 (1959/60) Nr. 2.

[33] Eleanor Huzar, "Egyptian Influences on Roman Coinage in the Third Century B. C.," *CJ* 61 (1966) 337.

true ruler of Egypt during their marriage.³⁴ Thus, in her classic study of the lives of the Hellenistic queens, Grace Macurdy wrote that "Arsinoe was, of course, absolutely a managing woman; she was the directing power in the government" and the "spur in all the action, political and military, of her indolent and pleasure-loving brother."³⁵ Not surprisingly, her influence has been detected everywhere: behind the charges of conspiracy that destroyed Arsinoe I and the remainder of the family of Ptolemy I by his first wife Eurydice,³⁶ in the decision of Ptolemy II to marry her,³⁷ in the determination of the royal succession and the stimulation of the cultural life of the court,³⁸ but, especially, in the guidance of the foreign affairs of Egypt. Hers, it is claimed, was the decision to begin the First Syrian War or, alternatively, the ability that saved the Egyptian forces from total defeat;³⁹ hers was the responsibility for the initiative establishing relations between Rome and Alexandria in 273;⁴⁰ and, most important of all, hers was the plan to contain the power of Antigonus Gonatas in Greece by championing the freedom of the Greeks that Ptolemy II ineptly tried to implement in the 260's when he joined Athens and Sparta in the Chremonidean War. This plan, had it

---

[34] E.g., W.W. Tarn, *Antigonos Gonatas* (Oxford 1913) 262-63; Beloch (supra n. 12) 4, 1, 242 and 582; Macurdy (supra n. 2) 119; and Bevan (supra n. 21) 60-61, who well expresses this interpretation: "It seems to have been an understood thing in the Greek world that the line henceforth followed by the Egyptian court was drawn by the firm hand of Arsinoe Philadelphus."

[35] Macurdy (supra n. 2) 118 and 120.

[36] E.g. Wilcken (supra n. 17) 1283; Macurdy (supra n. 2) 110 and 116; Beloch (supra n. 12) 4,1, 582; Longega (supra n. 2) 72. Again Bevan (supra n. 21) 61, best expresses the interpretation: "With Arsinoe in command one never knows whether such charges were true or fabricated."

[37] E.g. Wilcken (supra n. 17) 1283-1284 and Kornemann (supra n. 2) 124. Others tend to emphasize his psychological weakness to account for the marriage as Beloch (supra n. 12) 4, 1, 582; or W. W. Tarn, "The First Syrian War," *JHS* 46 (1926) 161: "Ptolemy married her after his defeat in Syria because things were going badly for him, and he needed her strength and brains to manage the war he was going to lose. . . ;" or Longega (supra n. 2) 73-74: "Ptolemy, hostile by nature to the cares of state, with an energetic and capable wife like Arsinoe II, would have been able to cultivate in peace his love for the arts."

[38] This theory is most fully developed by Rudolf Pfeiffer, "Arsinoe Philadelphos in der Dichtung," *Die Antike* 2 (1926) 161-74; but see also Kornemann (supra n. 2) 125, who gives her credit for creating the Museum.

[39] Responsible for the war: Huzar (supra n. 33) 337. For saving the Egyptian forces from defeat: Macurdy (supra n. 2) 119; and W. W. Tarn, *Hellenistic Civilisation*, 3rd ed. by G. T. Griffith (London 1952) 16-17.

[40] H. Mattingly, "Zephyrites," *AJA* 54 (1950) 126-28. Longega (supra n. 2) 91-92. The weaknesses of this theory were pointed out by Huzar (supra n. 33) 337-46.

Arsinoe II Philadelphos: A Revisionist View

succeeded, would have allowed Arsinoe "to say that she possessed the whole Greek Mediterranean and had realized in great part the dream that had tormented all the Diadochoi; to weaken their adversaries and reunite in the hands of only one, the great empire of Alexander."[41]

Occasional protests have been raised against this picture of an ineffectual Ptolemy II dominated by his "tigress queen" who influenced him even after her death.[42] Ptolemy's intellectual interests, his sensuality and his physical weakness are all matters of record,[43] but nowhere is there evidence of any weakness as a ruler. The contrary is suggested by the record of his thirty-seven-year reign as a whole and in particular by the evidence pointing to the conduct by him of an active and successful foreign policy in the years before his marriage to Arsinoe, a foreign policy that brought him significant gains in the Aegean, western and southern Anatolia and Nubia.[44] In ignoring the implication of these facts, biographers of Arsinoe rely essentially on the alleged implications of her admittedly unusual position and her honors and two specific pieces of evidence which, it is claimed, prove her dominance, namely, (1) that Ptolemy the Son, co-regent with Ptolemy II for a number of years after 267, was a son of Arsinoe and (2) that IG II^2 687 and SIG^3 381 indicate that in the Chremonidean War Ptolemy II followed a plan to contain Macedon by supporting Greek freedom formulated by Arsinoe and reflecting ideas held by her already while she was Lysimachus' queen. On these contentions the case for Arsinoe's power rests and none withstands careful scrutiny.

Much the weakest of these propositions is the identification of Ptolemy the Son with a son of Arsinoe. Originally he was identified with Ptolemy, the son of Arsinoe by Lysimachus, who, it was argued,

---

[41] Longega (supra n. 2) 93. This theory is too generally accepted for selected references to be useful, but note Tarn (*Antigonos Gonatas* [supra n. 34] 313) who remarks that "it must be borne in mind that the Chremonidean War was Arsinoe's war."

[42] First strongly by Walter Otto, "Zu den syrischen Kriege der Ptolemäer," *Philologus* 86 (1931) 413-14, and more recently by Édouard Will, *Histoire politique du monde hellénistique (323-30 av. J.-C.)* (Nancy 1966) 198-99; and Heinen (supra n. 11) 99 n. 14.

[43] Intellectual interests and physical weakness: Strabo 18.5, C 789; Aelian, *VH* 4.15. Sensuality: Ptolemaios VIII Euergetes II, *FGrH* 2B, 234 F 4.

[44] Cf. Theocritus 17, lines 85-92 for the achievements of the early part of his reign. Their significance in this connection was pointed out by Otto (supra n. 42) 412-13, and Wörrle (supra n. 21) 216.

after escaping the trap prepared for him by Ptolemy Ceraunus, eventually came to Egypt and was adopted as his heir by Ptolemy II in 267 in deference to the wishes of his deceased wife. This identification has had to be abandoned following the demonstration by Holleaux that Ptolemy, the son of Lysimachus by Arsinoe, was to be identified with Ptolemy, the son of Lysimachus, attested under Ptolemy III (after the death of Ptolemy the Son) as ruler of the city of Telmessus in Lycia and founder of a dynasty that lasted into the second century.[45] It has been replaced by a new claim, namely, that Ptolemy the Son was an otherwise unattested son of Ptolemy II by Arsinoe.[46] Implicit in this view, however, are two further propositions: first, that the evidence of Pausanias[47] and the scholiast on Theocritus (17, line 128) to the effect that the marriage of Arsinoe and Ptolemy II was childless is to be rejected; second, that Ptolemy II disinherited, even if only briefly, after Arsinoe's death the children of his first marriage in contradiction to the scholiast's explicit statement that he had compelled Arsinoe to adopt them as her own. In a field where evidence is so scarce, it is a bold course indeed to reject the little we have, especially when it is supported by such circumstantial evidence as does exist. Hitherto, little attention has been paid to the probable age of any son of Ptolemy II and Arsinoe although it is, in fact, a crucial consideration. The fact that Ptolemy II cites reports by him concerning political conditions in Miletus about 262 in *I.Milet.* 139 strongly suggests an individual of adult age, but on the most generous calculation a son of Ptolemy II and Arsinoe would have been at the most in his middle teens in 262.[48] Taken together with the explicit evidence of the scholiast on Theocritus and Pausanias, this would seem to exclude the identification of Ptolemy's co-regent with any son of his by Arsinoe II. If correct, this conclusion has important implications for the whole question of Arsinoe's assumed influence

---

[45] Maurice Holleaux, "Ptolémée de Telmessos," *Etudes d'épigraphie et d'histoire grecques* 3 (Paris 1942) 365-404. Cf. Mario Segre, "Iscrizioni di Licia," *Clara Rhodos* 9 (1938) 181-208. For the current state of the problem see A. G. Roos, "Remarques sur un edit d'Antiochos II Roi de Syrie," *Mnemosyne*, Ser. 4,3 (1950) 54-63; Jonas Crampa, *Labraunda, Swedish Excavations and Researches*, Vol. 3,1, *The Greek Inscriptions Part I: 1-12 (Period of Olympichus)* (Lund 1969) 97-120; and Wörrle (supra n. 21) 218, n. 85.

[46] H. Volkmann, *s.v.* "Ptolemaios," *RE* 23,2 (1959) 1666.

[47] Paus. 1.7.3.

[48] *I. Milet.* 139, lines 8-9. The significance of this was recognized by Tarn (supra n. 37) 160, who, however, used it to support his dating of *I. Milet.* 139 to the 270's, and more recently by Crampa (supra n. 45) 100-101. For the date in the text see Hauben (supra n. 19) 52-57.

over her brother, since it means that Ptolemy II, far from regulating the succession in favor of her progeny, compelled her to accept the exclusion of her son by Lysimachus from the succession to the throne by forcing her to adopt his children by his first wife as her own.

Apparently better supported is the claim that Ptolemaic policy in the Chremonidean War reflected policies devised by Arsinoe with the ultimate goal of regaining for her son by Lysimachus his father's kingdom of Macedon which had been, in her opinion, usurped by Antigonus Gonatas. Recognition that her son had been excluded from the Ptolemaic succession only strengthens the plausibility of the goal ascribed to her. Furthermore, the recently published decree in honor of Kallias of Sphettos, Ptolemaic governor of Halicarnassus in 270, attests to relations between Egypt and Athens in the 270's,[49] while Pausanias' report (1.8.6) of the existence of statues of both Ptolemy II and her in the Athenian Agora suggests that Arsinoe was somehow involved in those relations as does the friendly reference to the two of them in a fragment of a comedy by Alexis.[50] Decisive proof of the theory, however, has been seen in lines 16 to 18 of *IG* II² 687, the decree moved by Chremonides in the summer of 268/7 urging other Greeks to join the alliance of Athens, Sparta and Ptolemy II against "those attempting to abolish the laws and the ancestral constitution of each [city]," that is, against Antigonus Gonatas.[51] After briefly alluding to the past struggles of Athens and Sparta on behalf of Greek freedom and the glory they had gained from them, Chremonides adds that in the present crisis they have as their ally King Ptolemy who "in accordance with the attitude of his ancestors and of his sister is openly zealous for the common freedom of the Greeks."

References to a king's actions being in accord with those of his ancestors are frequent in Hellenistic inscriptions; not so a reference to them being in accord with the views of his sister. Striking though the allusion to Arsinoe is, a close reading of *IG* II² 687 gives pause. If the goal of Asinoe's plan was to regain the throne of Macedon for her son, then a war directed at Antigonus in Macedon was required, but that is precisely what is not envisioned in *IG* II² 687. Instead, the

---

[49] T. Leslie Shear, Jr., *Kallias of Sphettos and the Revolt of Athens in 286 B.C.*, Hesperia, Supp. 17 (Princeton 1978) 2-4; cf. Frank J. Frost, "Ptolemy II and Halicarnassus: An Honorary Decree," *Anatolian Studies* 21 (1971) 167-72.

[50] Alexis *apud Athenaeus* 11.502b.

[51] For the Chremonides' decree see now Hatto H. Schmitt, *Die Staatsverträge des Altertums* 3 (Munich 1969) Nr. 476 for the text, and Heinen (supra n. 11) 102-10.

decree clearly pre-supposes less ambitious goals, namely, the frustration of Antigonus' attempt to expand his influence in Greece through a common alliance "in order that, there being a common unity of feeling among the Greeks, they shall be with King Ptolemy and each other enthusiastic fighters against those who have now wronged the cities and violated treaties, and in the future they shall with unity of feeling save the cities" (lines 31-35). In other words, the decree suggests that Ptolemaic policy in the Chremonidean War had the limited goal of containing Antigonid power in Greece by supporting the still-independent Greek states in the name of Greek *homonoia* and freedom; and this is borne out by the little we know of the course of the war which indicates that fighting was concentrated near Athens and the Isthmus of Corinth.[52] Since such a policy is the reverse of that needed to achieve the ambitious goal ascribed to Arsinoe, her biographers assume that Chremonides, Ptolemy's agent, invoked her name in the decree while his master retreated from her grand design because "his weak and irresolute nature did not permit him to continue so audacious an undertaking without the support of his extraordinary sister-wife."[53]

But even in retreating from her more ambitious plan, Ptolemy still may have been following the lead of his wife since sympathy for Greek freedom, it is claimed, had been characteristic of her even when she was Lysimachus' wife and queen. In support of this thesis reference is made to *SIG*³ 381, a Delian decree honoring a Spartan agent of Lysimachus named Demaratus.[54] After recounting the benefactions conferred by Demaratus and his ancestors on Delos and the influence he exerted on the Delians' behalf with Lysimachus, the decree continues (lines 17-22): "and he also reported the good will which King Lysimachus has for the temple and he promised to make clear to King Lysimachus and Queen Arsinoe the complete good will of the *dēmos* of the Delians." Again, however, the thesis does not survive close reading of the text. Demaratus is praised for his influence with Lysimachus, not Arsinoe, and, as the Delians note, it was only Lysimachus' good will of which he informed them. Why then the reference to Arsinoe if no service to hers to Delos is being

---

[52] For the details of the war see Heinen (supra n. 11) 142-202.

[53] Longega (supra n. 2) 95. Cf. Bevan (supra n. 21) 67-68: "The Chremonidean War was a miserable exhibition of incapacity or timidity or dilettantism on Ptolemy's part. Perhaps, if Arsinoe had still been alive to supervise her brother's carrying out of her policy---!"

[54] Longega (supra n. 2) 29-30. Macurdy (supra n. 2) 119.

commemorated? Chronology provides the answer. Although originally dated to the 290's, Irwin Merker has shown in a still unpublished paper that it actually dates to the 280's.[55] Delos was then a Ptolemaic possession, and in the 280's relations between Lysimachus and Egypt were generally close. The alliance of 300 was reaffirmed in 288 and with it probably also recognition of Ptolemy II as the legitimate heir to the throne of Egypt.[56] In 284 Lysimachus' alliance with Ptolemy I was renewed with Ptolemy II and sealed by the diplomatic marriage of Ptolemy to Lysimachus' daughter Arsinoe[57] while Ptolemy, for his part, gave to the shrine of Samothrace a fine propylon situated close to the rotunda dedicated by his sister.[58] In these circumstances, what would be more natural than that the Delians, subjects to Ptolemy II, should have included in the message that Demaratus was to bring to Lysimachus a courteous greeting to their sovereign's sister? *SIG*[3] 381 provides no proof, therefore, that Ptolemy II was influenced by Arsinoe in seeking to disrupt Antigonid influence in Greece by adopting the policy of supporting Greek freedom, nor, indeed, was there any need for such influence since that had, in fact, been traditional Ptolemaic policy, particularly in dealing with Macedon, long before Arsinoe's return to Egypt. Ptolemy I had used it against Antigonus the One-Eyed in 314,[59] against Cassander and Lysimachus in 310,[60] and probably against Demetrius Poliorcetes in 287/6.[61] Ptolemy II reaffirmed it

---

[55] Théophile Homolle, "Inscriptions de Delos," *BCH* 20 (1896) 508-509, dated it to 295. Convincing evidence for the later date was provided by Irwin Merker in a paper entitled "Lysimachos and the Cities of Greece" delivered to the annual meeting of the Association of Ancient Historians, May 2, 1980, at the University of Cincinnati.

[56] Plut. *Demetrius* 44.1.

[57] For the marriage see Pausanias 1.7.3 and *Schol. ad Theocritem* 17, line 128. For Arsinoe I see Macurdy (supra n. 2) 109-11. For the date see F. Lassere, "Aux origines de l'anthologie I: L'papyrus P. Brit. Mus. Inv. 589," *RhM* 102 (1959) 236-37.

[58] *OGIS* 23. For the most recent text see Fraser, *Samothrace* (supra n. 8) Nr. 11 with his comments at 6, n. 19 for the date. For the propylon itself see Lehmann (supra n. 8) 88-90.

[59] Diod. 19.62.1.

[60] Diod. 20.19.4. Cf. Diod. 20.37.2 for Ptolemy's abortive plans along these lines in 308.

[61] *IG* II[2] 650 records honors for the assistance in supplying Athens with food rendered by the Ptolemaic naval officer Zenon at this time. The full extent of Ptolemy's involvement was made clear by the decree in honor of Kallias of Sphettos (supra n. 49) 2-3, lines 11-43.

shortly after his father's death[62] and, as the new decree from Plataea honoring Chremonides' brother Glaucon reveals, he continued to employ it even after the setback of his defeat in the Chremonidean War.[63] Arsinoe's name was invoked in *IG* II² 687, therefore, not to cover a retreat from a grandiose scheme to overthrow Antigonus Gonatas but in support of a policy that was, as Chremonides claimed, truly that of Ptolemy and his ancestors.

As was true with regard to the determination of the royal succession, the allusion to Arsinoe in *IG* II² 687 does not indicate that Arsinoe exercised a dominant influence on the policy of her brother Ptolemy II. Édouard Will, therefore, was probably correct in characterizing it as "un formule de courtoise" inspired by the dynastic cult and Arsinoe's recent deification.[64] Clearly, a new interpretation of Arsinoe's relationship to her brother in general is required.

Because of the obvious benefit to Arsinoe of her marriage to Ptolemy II, there has been an understandable tendency to ascribe to her the initiative in the decision to enter into it on the basis of the argument *cui bono*. The sources, however, credit it to Ptolemy himself,[65] and they are supported by the insubstantial nature of the evidence hitherto adduced as proof of his subjection to Arsinoe's will. Memnon[66] noted that such marriages were customary in Egypt. Moreover, the posthumous identification of Arsinoe with Isis[67] and her becoming *synnaos* in the temples of the Egyptian gods, suggest a hope that the marriage would be popular with the native Egyptians, even though such popularity would be gained only at the price of shocking and outraging his Macedonian and Greek subjects. Appeals to Egyptian practice or precedents would not impress them as Theocritus' citation of Zeus and Hera as appropriate models for the

---

[62] *SIG*³ 390, lines 11-20.

[63] Roland Étienne and Marcel Piérart, "Un décret du koinon des Hellènes à Platées en l'honneur de Glaucon, fils d' Étéocles, d'Athènes," *BCH* 99 (1975) 51-53 with the editors' remarks on page 62.

[64] Will (supra n. 42) 199.

[65] *Schol. ad Theocritem* 17, line 128, Paus. 1.7.1; *P. Haun*, 6, F 3, lines 2-3.

[66] Memnon, *FGrH* 3B, 434 F 8.7 *apropos* of her marriage to Ptolemy Ceraunus. On this subject see now the exhaustive study by Keith Hopkins, "Brother-Sister Marriage in Roman Egypt," *Comparative Studies in Society and History* 22 (1980) 303-354.

[67] *OGIS* 31. Quaegebeur (supra n. 21) 245 notes the close connection of the posthumous cult of Arsinoe at Memphis with the cults of the Egyptian kings.

royal couple indicates.⁶⁸ The brutal punishment meted out to the poet Sotades⁶⁹ for expressing what many must have thought is evidence enough of Ptolemy's awareness of the problem and his determination to silence opposition to his plans.

Unfortunately, the exact nature of those plans must remain matters for speculation, but several indications point to dynastic considerations as an important part of them, that is, a desire to strengthen the claim of Ptolemy's immediate family as a group to be the only legitimate descendants of Ptolemy I. Certainly, his introduction of a cult with its own festival and temple in honor of Ptolemy I and his mother Berenice as *Theoi Soteres* suggests this.⁷⁰ But even more striking in this connection are the various public declarations of family solidarity attested in the sources. Such declarations are most notable in the case of Arsinoe herself not only in the epithet *Philadelphos* ("brother-lover"), taken by her after her marriage and under which she was deified after her death, but also in her adopting at Ptolemy's behest his children by his previous marriage. Most especially we recall the numerous instances of her sharing honors with her brother alone or together with their deified parents as on the gold and silver coins minted during her lifetime,⁷¹ in the Chremonides' decree, and especially in the Arsinoeion, the temple to her built by Ptolemy in Alexandria immediately after her death which, as Giulia Ronchi has shown, she originally shared with her deified parents.⁷² When these items are taken together with the fact that Ptolemy II conferred virtually identical honors on their only sister Philotera also in the 270's,⁷³ there can be little doubt that one of his goals in marrying Arsinoe was the unification of the royal family — past, present and future — around himself.

A reason for such action is readily apparent. The basis of Ptolemy

---

[68] Theocritus 17, lines 131-134.

[69] Athen. 14.620f. For traces of the shocked response of the Greeks in later sources see Longega (supra n. 2) 74 n. 14.

[70] *Schol. ad Theocritem* 17, line 121-123d. Theocritus 17, lines 121-123.

[71] Kahrstedt (supra n. 6) 267; Head (supra n. 6) 851.

[72] Giulia Ronchi, "Il papiro cairense 65445 (vv. 140-154) e l'obelisco di Arsinoe II," *Studi classici e orientali* 17 (1968) 56-75. For the Arsinoeion see *Schol. ad Theocritem*, 17, lines 121-23d; and Pliny, *NH* 36.64.

[73] Title *basilissa*: *OGIS* 35, line 1. Deification with shrines: *Schol. ad Theocritem* 17, lines 121-123d; Quaegebeur (supra n. 21) 246; Callimachus, F 228, lines 43-45 (Trypanis). Cities named after her: Tscherikower (supra n. 27) 13, 72-73. For Philotera in general see Johannes Regner, "Philotera," *RE* 20, 1 (1941) 1285-1294.

II's claim to the throne was the disinheritance by Ptolemy I of his children by Eurydice, his first wife, in favor of those by Ptolemy II's mother Berenice.[74] The death of Ptolemy Ceraunus in early 279 at the hands of the Galatians eliminated the chief rival claimant, but not the problem. Pausanias records the execution by Ptolemy in the 270's of one, or possibly two, further sons of Eurydice on charges of conspiracy, one named Argaeus and another, who attempted to stir up a rebellion on Cyprus, events soon to be followed by the revolt of his own half-brother Magas in Cyrene.[75] In such circumstances the desire to unify the members of his own line around his person and to assert their right to the throne even at the expense of the shock and dismay his marriage to Arsinoe created would be understandable.

In the absence of new evidence, however, any explanation of Ptolemy's motives for entering into an incestuous marriage with his sister must in the end remain tentative. Be that as it may, the evidence discussed in this paper does point toward a significant revision of the accepted view of Arsinoe's role in the government of Egypt in the 270's. Hitherto, the history of the reign of Ptolemy II has been made to pivot around his marriage to her. The years during which she was queen and ruled Egypt through her brother have been seen as years of greatness flanked by periods of weak and ineffectual government. Of the importance of Ptolemy's marriage to Arsinoe there can be no doubt. The extraordinary honors she enjoyed before and after her death are sufficient evidence of the prominent and popular role she played in the life of Egypt during her brother's reign and of his determination to benefit from that prominence and popularity.[76] But they do not prove that her influence in the actual governing of Egypt and its empire was significantly greater than that attested for other third-century queens, a conclusion that is strikingly confirmed by her inability to secure a place in the succession to the throne of Egypt for Ptolemy, her son by Lysimachus. Alexander is reported to have said that his mother was wise to leave Macedon because Macedonians would never endure being ruled by a woman.[77] In third-century Egypt, at least, that was still true.

California State University, Los Angeles

---

[74] Appian, *Syriaka* 62. Memnon, *FGrH* 3B, 434 F 8.2. Cf. Justin, 17.2.9.

[75] Paus. 1.7.1-2.

[76] Cf. Athen. 11.497b-c for the personal role Ptolemy took in determining the iconography of statues in honor of Arsinoe.

[77] Plut. *Alex.* 68.3.

Sea-power and the Antigonids

F. W. WALBANK

Abstract

The article discusses the importance of sea-power to the Antigonids from Demetrius Poliorcetes to Perseus. It distinguishes between the limited use of the sea to maintain communications with Macedonian outposts in southern and central Greece and the periodic attempts by Antigonid kings to assert a more aggressive policy by building larger fleets. It examines the naval position during and just after the Chremonidean War and the results of the battle of Cos, the Carian expedition of Antigonus III and Philip V's successive incursions into the Adriatic and the Aegean. Its conclusion is that after 277 Macedonia was not at risk from any of the other Hellenistic monarchies; that those Antigonid kings who adopted an active naval policy were pursuing expansionist aims; that the arrival of Rome put paid to all such aims; and that when embraced they had invariably proved disastrous.

I.

An anecdote recorded by Phylarchus[1] relates how Patroclus, who is known from other sources as the admiral of Ptolemy II at the time of the Chremonidean War,[2] once sent a present of large fish and green figs to Antigonus Gonatas "as a hint at what would happen to him, just as the Scythians did to Darius when he was invading their country. For the Scythians, Herodotus tells us, sent a bird, an arrow

---

[1] Ath. 8.334a; *FGrH* 81 F 1; cf. H. Heinen, *Untersuchungen zur hellenistischen Geschichte des 3. Jahrhunderts* (Wiesbaden 1972) 191-92.

[2] See H. Volkmann *s.v.* "Patroklos" (2), *Kl. Pauly* 4 (1975) 558-59.

and a frog."[3] Antigonus was quick to solve the riddle: "either we must be masters of the sea (*thalassokratein*) or else we must eat figs," that is, go short of food.[4] But was the choice a real one? The answer to that question depends on whether Patroclus' point was a general one — that Macedon must be a sea-power or starve — or a particular one, in the sense that at the time of the incident Antigonus had for instance got himself caught in an awkward situation without access to supplies of food. Oddly enough, some sixty years later his grandson Philip V was to find himself in that very plight. Confined within the Gulf of Bargylia in Caria and unable for several months to make an easy getaway through the Rhodian and Pergamene fleets, he was compelled to furnish an illustration of Patroclus' riddle by feeding his troops throughout the winter of 201/200 largely on figs provided by the Seleucid general Zeuxis and by Greek cities like Magnesia which were short of corn.[5] It is not unlikely that it was in some such situation that Patroclus sent his riddling message; and by comparing it to the one the Scythians sent to Darius, Phylarchus may be implying that Antigonus too was engaged in aggression, in this case against the Ptolemaic empire. Without knowing more of the context of the anecdote — which certainly implied a challenge to a naval battle, and equally implied that when it was fought Antigonus was the victor — one can not however be sure of this. On the whole, a limited context for the challenge rather than a more general statement about Macedonian sea-power seems the more likely. Nevertheless the story raises in a sharp form the question of how important sea-power was to Antigonid Macedonia, and I offer a brief discussion of this question as a tribute to the memory of a friend and a colleague much of whose own published work was concerned with Macedonia and with naval matters.

The word (*thalassokratein*) is probably not to be taken in a very wide sense. Patroclus was simply challenging Antigonus to meet him at sea: the verb would apply to whichever won. As Tarn observed,[6] thalassocracy has a limited meaning in Hellenistic times; until the Romans came on the scene no one power controlled more than a part of the Mediterranean, and even within a limited area the word

---

[3] Hdt. 4 131, where this riddle is elucidated: a mouse was also included in the gift, but omitted by Athenaeus.
[4] So rightly W. W. Tarn, "Two notes on Ptolemaic history," *JHS* 53 (1933) 68.
[5] Polyb. 16.24.5 (= Ath. 3.78e-f).
[6] W. W. Tarn, *Antigonos Gonatas* (Oxford 1913) 79-80.

merely implied the ability to meet a challenge (such as Patroclus was making to Antigonus) rather than to exercise a permanent control of the seas and police them. Short of even that restricted kind of thalassocracy there were, of course, many reasons why a state might need to possess ships for certain defined needs, and the question to be asked in connection with Macedonia is to what extent the Antigonids were content to restrict their naval activity to such limited ends — or whether they in fact chose to build up a fleet to expand their power; and if they did, whether that was to the advantage or disadvantage of Macedonia. One must distinguish Macedonia from the dynasty controlling it, because until Antigonus Gonatas made himself master of Macedonia naval power was self-evidently of more vital importance to the Antigonids than it was later.

For Antigonus I, facing a coalition of Ptolemy, Cassander and Lysimachus, a strong fleet was essential to drive a wedge between his opponents, to debar Cassander from access to Greece proper and to secure his own position there. The League of the Islanders, a Macedonian creation (though it was later to be taken over by the Ptolemies),[7] served to reinforce Antigonid power in the Aegean; and Demetrius Poliorcetes affirmed his mastery of eastern Mediterranean waters by his decisive victory over the Ptolemaic fleet off Salamis in Cyprus in 306 B.C.[8] Demetrius continued to dominate the eastern Mediterranean even after the defeat and death of his father Antigonus at Ipsus in 301. As king of Macedonia between 294 and 288 he possessed perhaps 300 ships and in 289 he planned to build a further 500 in various shipyards.[9] Even after losing most of these (the ones being built at Pella) to Pyrrhus, he still retained a substantial navy, and it was primarily the desertion of Philocles, the king of Sidon, from his cause that put an end to his naval preponderance.[10]

Until he gained Macedonia Antigonus Gonatas was in a similar position. A fleet was essential to link together his scattered possessions, Corinth, Piraeus and Euboea, and his control of such a fleet is

---

[7] E. Will, *Histoire politique du monde hellénistique (323-30 av.J.-C.)*² I (Nancy 1979) 58.

[8] Diod. 20.47-52; Just. *Epit.* 15.2.6-9; Plut. *Dem.* 15-16; App. *Syr.* 54; Will (supra n. 7) 73.

[9] Plut. *Dem.* 43; Tarn (supra n. 6) 83.

[10] It was not, as Tarn (supra n. 6) 80 supposed, by virtue of his naval preponderance that Demetrius was able to cross over to Asia unchallenged in 287, for it is now known that a peace had already been concluded with Egypt; see C. Habicht, *Untersuchungen zur politischen Geschichte Athens im 3. Jahrhundert v. Chr.* (Munich 1979) 62, 63, n. 79.

attested for 283 or 282, when he sailed to meet Seleucus in order to receive his father's ashes.[11] Though he was defeated at sea in 281 by Ptolemy Ceraunus, who had taken over Lysimachus' fleet,[12] his ships, drawn up on shore as a bait to the enemy, played an important part in his victory over the Galatians near Lysimacheia, which led to his final conquest of Macedonia.[13] How big his fleet was at this time is unknown.

II.

As king of Macedonia Antigonus was now established with a land base and naval power no longer of such fundamental importance. Macedonia was largely self-supporting and so was not normally concerned with the policing of vital corn-routes which played so large a role in Athenian history. Included within the boundaries of Macedonia in Hellenistic times were some of the richest corn-producing lands in Greece, and Macedonia was an exporter of grain.[14] This is attested from Delos, where honours were voted to Demetrius II's *sitōnēs*, Aristobulus, and to Admetus, both citizens of Salonica and the latter probably a private business-man;[15] and in 227, when following a devastating earthquake at Rhodes, there were many royal gifts to the city, those from the royal house of Macedonia included 100,000 medimni of corn donated by Chryseis, the wife of Antigonus Doson, and probably grown on the royal estates.[16] This does not of course exclude the occasional need of imported corn, especially at times when a full mobilisation might interfere with production. In 168, for example, after three years warfare against the Romans and the loss to them of the rich corn-growing plains of Thessaly, Perseus had to send out a fleet to Tenedos *ut inde sparsas per*

---

[11] Plut. *Dem.* 52-53.

[12] Memnon *FGrH* 434 F 8 (13); Just. *Epit.* 24.1.8: cf. Heinen (supra n. 1) 65-66 (on the date and the site), 190.

[13] *SIG,* 401; Just. *Epit.* 25.2.6; Trogus *Prol.* 25; Diog. Laert. 2.141; Heinen (supra n. 1) 190.

[14] For Macedonian prosperity in Hellenistic times see M. Rostovtzeff, *The Social and Economic History of the Hellenistic World* I (Oxford 1941) 251-53. According to A. Jardé, *Les céréales dans l'antiquité grecque* (Paris 1925) 203, in 1921 41.33% of the area of Macedonia was given over to wheat and 23.48% to barley; the yield per hectare of wheat was the highest in Greece except for Arcadia. Similar figures are given in the British Admiralty Geographical Handbook *Greece* II (1944) 58-60.

[15] *IG* XI, 4, 666 (Aristobulus); 664, 665, 1053 (Admetus).

[16] Polyb. 5.89.7.

Sea-power and the Antigonids

Cycladas insulas naues, Macedoniam cum frumento petentes, tutarentur.[17] But in general the continuing need for a fleet rested mainly on political rather than economic grounds.

It was of course still essential to maintain communications with the military outposts in Greece. But the danger confronting Macedonia from the other major powers was limited and can easily be assessed. Either just before or just after the victory at Lysimacheia Antigonus Gonatas had made a peace with Antiochus I, Seleucus' successor in Asia, which was to last for many decades.[18] In fact, there was never to be any real threat to Macedonia from a Seleucid king again (for though Antiochus III invaded Europe, there is no reason to think that his plans included the invasion of Macedonia).

Later in the third century and still more in the second Pergamum was to become the leading power in western Anatolia and its rulers were persistent enemies of the Antigonids; but as yet the power of Pergamum still lay in the future. The other kingdoms of Asia Minor were small powers and no threat to Antigonus. Indeed for some time his main rival was Ptolemy II Philadelphus. Ptolemy II's foreign policy has aroused considerable controversy. According to Polybius,[19] it was based on the possession of Coele-Syria and Cyprus, on the exercising of strong pressure on the dynasts of Asia Minor and on the control, through the Egyptian fleet, of the islands and the main cities, strongpoints and harbours on the Asia Minor coast from Pamphylia to the Hellespont, together with a number of places like Aenus and Maronea on the European coast which enabled Ptolemy to keep watch over Thrace and Macedonia; but in Polybius' opinion this "fence of client states" was designed to protect Egypt and was defensively conceived. In short, like his father, Ptolemy II did not aim at attacking Macedonia. In this passage Polybius perhaps oversimplifies the situation. Ptolemy was clearly not above fishing in troubled waters, especially in Greece, where he had a footing at Methone in the Argolid, and where he was always ready to cause embarrassment to the Macedonians. Still, there is a *prima facie* case for thinking that Egypt represented a danger of very limited proportions to Macedonia and that the construction of anything more than the small naval force needed to secure communications and the

---

[17] Livy 44.28.1-2.

[18] Just. *Epit.* 25.1.1; cf. Will (supra n. 7) 109. Justinus dates the reconciliation before the battle of Lysimacheia, but that is by no means certain.

[19] Polyb. 5.34.2-9.

safe passage of men and materials between Macedonia and the strongpoints of southern Greece can be taken as evidence of a more forward policy on the part of the Antigonids themselves. In short, with the Seleucids occupied in Asia and the Ptolemies interested primarily in protecting Egypt by means of their outposts in Greece, Anatolia and the Aegean, any breach of the equilibrium was likely to come from Macedonia.

Family traditions were not against that assumption. It was a belief in Greece (attested by Polybius writing in the second century)[20] that the Antigonid house had always cherished ambitions for universal dominion. Certainly Antigonus I had fought tenaciously to maintain the unity (and the control) of Alexander's empire; and Demetrius I had used his powerful fleet to the same end, though with diminishing hope of success. For their descendants any such ambitions are harder to believe in. But the persistence of the tradition indicates that the Antigonids were at any rate not regarded as pursuing a defensive policy.

Evidence for the reign of Antigonus II is still most inadequate. Three events are relevant to the present enquiry: the Chremonidean War and the battles of Cos and Andros. The real causes of the Chremonidean War remain uncertain.[21] It has generally been thought that it was provoked by Ptolemy II, and discussion has concentrated on his motives. But the help which he gave to Athens and Sparta was meagre, and Habicht has recently argued[22] that he was drawn in reluctantly by the Athenians, who took the initiative as the main instigators of the war. It is hard to assess Ptolemy's degree of commitment in Greece so long as we are ignorant of what he had to face elsewhere. His admiral Patroclus was active in Ceos, at Itanus in Crete and at Thera, and he landed some troops at Rhamnus in Attica.[23] Otherwise the Ptolemaic contribution was slight. This can be explained (on Habicht's theory) as due to lack of interest in a war he had not sought. Yet the alliances between Ptolemy and Athens and between Ptolemy and Sparta both preceded the Spartan-Athenian

---

[20] Polyb. 15.24.6; cf. 5.102.1.
[21] See Heinen (supra n. 1) 189-97.
[22] See Habicht (supra n. 10) 95-112.
[23] See Heinen (supra n. 1) 142-52; Will (supra n. 7) 226.

alliance which led to the war,[24] and it is therefore hard to believe that that alliance was not encouraged, if not sponsored, by Ptolemy; in which case he was presumably behind the war. Will has argued plausibly that he was provoked into promoting the war by Gonatas' decision to build a fleet and that the Chremonidean War was therefore the Ptolemaic reply to a new phase of Macedonian expansion.[25]

What in fact is known of Macedonian naval activity at this time? On the whole very little. According to Pausanias,[26] Antigonus moved on Athens *pedzō te kai nausin*. Tarn argued[27] that these ships were transports; but elsewhere Pausanias asserts[28] that Antigonus shut off the Athenians from the sea, and despite Tarn's rejection of this statement it could well be true, implying the presence of warships off Attica.[29] The size of Gonatas' fleet is unknown. Heinen quotes[30] Beloch and Will for the view that "at the beginning of the Chremonidean War the Macedonian fleet was numerically weak"; but Will in fact asserts that only for 272, and his view of what caused the war implies that since then Antigonus had been building new ships. If so, one must suppose that most of these were active elsewhere, not to have left a greater impression on the tradition. They may have been operating somewhere off Asia Minor, as they must have been shortly afterwards when the battle of Cos was fought (see below). Unhappily these are decades for which evidence is still scanty. That some Macedonian ships were active off Attica is suggested by the fact that Athens had serious food problems, as we know from an inscription from Rhamnus,[31] containing a decree honouring the *strategos* Epicharēs for getting in the grain. This inscription also reveals the fact that Gonatas employed pirates against Athens, but this does not exclude the use of Macedonian ships as

---

[24] *SVA* (= H. Bengtson and H. H. Schmitt, *Die Staatsverträge des Altertums* II-III [Munich, 1962-1969], 476; H. Heinen, reviewing Habicht (supra n. 10) in *GGA* (forthcoming).

[25] Will (supra n. 7) 219-21.

[26] Paus. 3.6.4.

[27] Tarn (supra n. 6) 300.

[28] Paus. 1.1.1 ναυσὶν ἅμα ἐκ θαλάσσης κατεῖργεν.

[29] Heinen (supra n. 1) 190 n. 303, who observes that *kateirgen* could also mean "he threatened them."

[30] Heinen (supra n. 1) 190 n. 301, quoting K. J. Beloch, *Griechische Geschichte* IV 1 (Berlin-Leipzig, 1925) 587 and Will (supra n. 7) 193 (= I² 216).

[31] *SEG* XXIV. 154; cf. Heinen (supra n. 1) 152-59.

well. The use of pirates was a well-established practice with the Antigonid dynasty as a way of contracting out (for one reason or another) some of one's military obligations. Examples are the Glaucetas who operated under Antigonus I and was captured by the Athenian Thymochares of Sphettus in 315/14,[32] Timocles who fought against Rhodes in the interest of Demetrius I and was captured by the Rhodians in 304,[33] and Ameinias, a Phocian "archpirate" who had earlier helped Antigonus Gonatas himself to take Cassandreia.[34] Later, in 205 or 204, Philip V was likewise to employ the Aetolian pirate Dicaearchus to plunder the Aegean islands and cities of the Troad and to help the Cretans against Rhodes.[35] The custom was not of course confined to the Antigonids.[36] There is therefore some, but not a great deal, of evidence for Macedonian naval activity in Greece at this time.[37]

The question cannot, however, be left without some mention of the battles of Cos and Andros. A new treatment of this ancient crux is promised by H. Heinen, who has already discussed Cos in a recent work.[38] Here I need say only that on present evidence the most likely context for the naval battle of Cos, in which an Antigonus (probably Gonatas) won a victory over the Egyptian fleet, which he commemorated with the dedication of his flag-ship to Delian Apollo,[39] is in my view the end of the Chremonidean War. It most likely occurred in the spring of 261, since it must have followed the capitulation of Athens (where Gonatas received congratulations on his victory) but will have preceded the setting up of an inscription at Delos in the archonship of Tharsynon (261) which refers to peace existing in the Aegean.[40] It

---

[32] *SIG*. 409, lines 10-14.

[33] Diod. 20.97.5. In 302 Demetrius employed a large force of "light-armed troops" and "pirates" on land against Cassander (Diod. 20.110.4), but these were perhaps freebooters.

[34] Polyae. *Strat.* 4.6.18; he was later in Antigonus' regular service and helped save Sparta from Pyrrhus (Plut. *Pyrrh.* 29.6).

[35] Polyb. 18.54.8; Diod.28.1; see infra p. 228.

[36] See for example Tarn (supra n. 6) 86; H. A. Ormerod, *Piracy in the Ancient World* (Liverpool and London 1924) 122-24, 126.

[37] Tarn (supra n. 6) 300 quotes Livy 35.26.5 as evidence for Macedonian naval weakness at the time of the Chremonidean War; see against this Heinen (supra n. 1) 192-93.

[38] Heinen (supra n. 1) 193-97.

[39] Plut. *de seipsum laudando* 16; *apophth.reg.* 183c; Ath. 5.209e; the story told here is referred to the battle of Andros in Plut. *Pel.* 2.4.

[40] *IG* XI. 2. 114.

was perhaps followed immediately by the Macedonian attack on Miletus known from an inscription from that city.[41] If this dating is correct[42] — and it cannot be regarded as certain — it follows that by this time Macedon possessed a powerful fleet.

When that fleet was built is less certain. Tarn, who dated Cos to the Second Syrian War and (probably) 258,[43] believed that it was not built until well after the Chremonidean War was over. But that war provides the only likely context for a clash with Ptolemy, since there is no evidence at all that Antigonus was involved in the Second Syrian War. (As for Tarn's belief that Gonatas was inspired to build a fleet by the news that "a great landpower, by the adoption of a few simple expedients, had taken to the water with instantaneous and overwhelming success,"[44] surely the son of Demetrius Poliorcetes did not need the Roman performance in the First Punic War to teach him lessons in naval warfare.) If Cos was in 261, there had been plenty of time since the outbreak of war in 268 to build a fleet; all the materials were to hand in Macedonia and could easily be transported to Demetrias or Corinth. Indeed, if we accept Will's view concerning the origin of the war, the fleet was already built or being built before 268, since it was this that provoked Ptolemy to war. Nearer than that we cannot get. Nor does it help to bring the obscure battle of Andros into the picture.[45] Its date is uncertain; and indeed the Antigonus involved in it could as well be Doson as Gonatas.

The results of Cos were less important than has often been

---

[41] A. Rehm in Th.Wiegand, *Milet: Ergebnisse der Ausgrabungen und Untersuchungen seit dem Jahre 1899 I* (Berlin 1914) 3 n. 139 = C. B. Welles, *Royal Correspondence in the Hellenistic Period* (New Haven 1934) 71-77, no. 14.

[42] If, as seems likely, Plut. *Quaest.conv.* 676d, with its story of parsley springing spontaneously out of a ship's prow, refers to Antigonus' flagship at Cos, its name was *Isthmia*; according to Moschion (Ath. 5.209e) it was dedicated to Apollo. Plutarch's story need not imply that the battle was fought in a year of the Isthmian games (i.e., one with an even number in the Julian calendar) as argued by Will (supra n. 7) 225 and by W. W. Tarn, *CAH* VII (1928) 862. As Tarn had himself suggested earlier ("The dedicated ship of Antigonos Gonatas," *JHS* 30 [1910] 218-21), the ship could have been built at Corinth and so named as a compliment to that city.

[43] *CAH* VII 862-63; earlier (supra n. 6, 461-66) he had made it 246.

[44] Tarn (supra n. 6) 342.

[45] Trogus, *Prol.* 27; Plut. *Pel.* 2.4. The relevance of *P. Haun.* I, 6 (cf. A. Momigliano and P. Fraser, "A new date for the battle of Andros? A discussion," *CQ* 44 [1950] 107-18) is doubtful. For possible dates of the battle see Will (supra n. 7) 237-38.

supposed.[46] It was the fall of Athens rather than the naval encounter that brought Gonatas his main advantage from the war. Moreover, though Cos was a Macedonian victory, it did not displace Ptolemy from his position as dominant naval power in the Aegean and eastern Mediterranean. The evidence adduced by those who believe it did is indecisive or, in some cases, misinterpreted. Delos, it has been pointed out, was at this time the recipient of Antigonid dedications;[47] but it is now generally agreed that no political conclusions are to be drawn from such dedications, which possess a purely religious and social significance.[48] That Egypt continued to dominate the Aegean is clear from the continued existence of the League of Islanders at least until the Second Syrian War; and this view receives some support from the evidence of the Alexandrian historian Appian, who tells us that at the time of Ptolemy II's death in 246 the royal register recorded a substantial Egyptian war-fleet in commission.[49] The possibility is not to be ruled out that Antigonus acquired control of certain islands. Several inscriptions from Syros, Ios, Amorgos, Cimolos and Cos mention a king Antigonus as influential there; and a similar inscription without a king's name visible comes from Ceos.[50] But until it is clear whether the Antigonus in question is Gonatas or Doson, one may not use these as proof of a Macedonian thalassocracy in the Aegean at this time. New evidence may bring more light to an area and a period of great obscurity. But so far there is nothing to indicate that the victory at Cos brought substantial naval advantages to Antigonus Gonatas. During the next decade his interest was directed rather to central Greece and the Peloponnese,

---

[46] See Will (supra n. 7) 231-32, 239. For the view that Cos led to a Macedonian control of the Cyclades see F. Durrbach, *Choix d'inscriptions de Délos I* (Paris 1921) 42; W. W. Tarn in *CAH* VII 713; W. Huss, *Untersuchungen zur Aussenpolitik Ptolemaios' IV.* (Munich 1976) 215, n. 288.

[47] Antigonus founded the *Antigoneia* and the *Stratoniceia* (named after Stratonice, the bride of his son Demetrius) in 253; cf.*IG* XI, 2, 287 B lines 124-25.

[48] Cf. P. M. Fraser, *Samothrace II, Part 1: The Inscriptions on Stone* (New York 1960) 4-5; Ph. Bruneau, *Recherches sur les cultes de Délos* (Paris 1970) 579-80; and more generally L. Robert, "Smyrne et les Sôtéria de Delphes," *REA* 38 (1936) 18 n. 1; Will (supra n. 7) 232-33. For an interesting passage showing the strictness with which Delian neutrality was observed see Livy 44.29.1-2.

[49] App. *praef.*10. A papyrus (*SB* 9215) refers to the building of new warships by Ptolemy II early in 250; cf. Huss (supra n. 46) 216, n. 288.

[50] *IG* XI, 4, 1052 (Syros); XII, 5, 1008 (Ios); XII, 7, 221-23 (Amorgos); *SGDI* 3611 (Cos); T. W. Jacobsen and P. M. Smith, "Two Kimolian dikast decrees from Geraistos in Euboia," *Hesperia* 37 (1968) 184-99 (Cimolos); *IG* XI, 5, 570 (Ceos).

where his main concerns lay; and it was here in about 249 that he sustained a serious blow when Alexander, who had succeeded his father Craterus, Antigonus' half-brother, as governor of Corinth, declared himself independent, thus depriving his uncle of two vital naval bases and garrison towns, Chalcis and Corinth. Piraeus fortunately continued loyal to Antigonus under an independent command and of course maintained its sea links with Macedonia; but we hear of no large-scale naval operations for the rest of Gonatas' reign.

If Will is right, Antigonus precipitated the Chremonidean War by building a fleet. His purpose in building it can only have been to challenge Egypt, as indeed he did at Cos. If Habicht is right (and for the reasons already indicated this seems less likely) the Chremonidean War was forced on a reluctant Macedonia and a reluctant Egypt by the enthusiasm of Athenian patriots. In that case Gonatas built his fleet in response to the revolt, and his main purpose was to subdue Athens and to restore the *status quo*. In either case, however, the results were unimpressive and brought no positive gain to Macedonia.

III.

Gonatas' successor, Demetrius II, succeeded him in 239 and reigned for ten years. There is no evidence of naval activity throughout his reign; and though the alliance which he made with Gortyn and Crete[51] might seem to indicate a widening of political interest beyond Greece proper, it is probably mainly concerned (like the similar treaties made by his successor Antigonus III with Eleutherna and Hierapytna)[52] with raising useful light-armed troops either as allies or as mercenaries. In the main Demetrius was kept busy in central Greece by his war against the Achaean and Aetolian leagues; but obviously he must have maintained his sea connections with Euboea and Chalcis (which Gonatas had recovered along with Corinth in 245)[53] and with Athens. It was a reign in which Macedonia was mostly on the defensive.

His son Philip was a child when Demetrius died; and the

---

[51] *SVA* (supra n. 24), 498.

[52] *SVA* (supra n. 24), 501, 502. That these belong to Doson is conjectural. Huss (supra n. 46) 139-42 reverts to the view that the Antigonus of these inscriptions is Gonatas, but his arguments fall short of being decisive.

[53] He had lost Corinth again, to Aratus and the Achaeans, in 243.

succession went to Antigonus Doson, his cousin. Doson's reign interests our present enquiry on account of an expedition which was long regarded with scepticism, but is now too firmly attested to be dismissed as imaginary. Antigonus' naval expedition against Caria in south-west Asia Minor[54] took place in 227 after he had re-established the Macedonian hold on Thessaly, which had been largely overrun by the Aetolians on the death of Demetrius. It was clearly a reaffirmation of Macedonian naval interests for the first time since the reign of Antigonus II. Trogus asserts that Doson conquered Caria; and a Rhodian arbitration between Samos and Priene, recorded on an inscription from Priene, shows that city accepting Macedonian authority, and mentions both Antigonus and the "heir to the throne, Phi. . ." (who must be Philip). Another inscription from a dossier concerning a local Carian dynast, Olympichus, mentions Antigonus' presence in Mylasa. Thus the effects of the expedition were fairly widespread. But it is not clear at whose expense the gains were made. There is no evidence that Ptolemy was the enemy (unless the battle of Andros took place now);[55] more probably Antigonus had seized opportunities presented in Caria following the defeat of Antiochus Hierax by Attalus I of Pergamum — both had been interested in Caria — to reaffirm an Antigonid concern with Asia Minor which went back to Monophthalmus and Poliorcetes. Just how Attalus came into the picture is not clear. Antigonus' gains may have been partly to his detriment or, more probably, given the distance between Pergamum and Caria, made in collusion with him. If that is so, the Carian expedition would be the first break between Macedonia and the Seleucids since the beginning of the reign of Antigonus Gonatas, though Doson could fairly have

---

[54] Trogus, *Prol.* 28; Polyb. 20.5.7-11; F. Hiller von Gaertringen, *Die Inschriften von Priene* (Berlin 1906) no. 37 lines 136-37; J. Crampa, *Labraunda: Swedish excavations and researches*, VIII, 1: *the Greek inscriptions*, Part I: 1-12 (period of Olympichus) (Lund 1969) no. 7, line 12 (presence of Doson in Mylasa). Cf. F. W. Walbank, *A Historical Commentary on Polybius* I (Oxford 1957) 621-22; II (1967) 645; III (1979) 70-71.

[55] Supra n. 45. W. Otto *s.v.* "Hippomedon," *RE* 8 (1913) 1885-87, argued that in the course of Doson's expedition an attack was made on the Ptolemaic island of Samothrace; but the enemy mentioned in *SIG*, 502, like the one in the inscription published by A. Bakalakis and R. L. Scranton in *AJP* 60 (1939) 452-58, is not Antigonus Doson but barbarians from the mainland (either Thracians or Gauls from Tylis) (cf. M. Rostovtzeff and C. B. Welles, "A note on the new inscription from Samothrace," *AJP* 61 [1940] 207-208; Rostovtzeff [supra n. 14] III, 1645), nor has that inscription anything to do with the Carian expedition. On the expedition see Walbank (supra n. 54) III 70-71.

claimed that he was setting foot in areas which had already escaped from legitimate Seleucid control. The size and composition of Antigonus' fleet is not known, nor yet its origin. It can hardly be an inheritance from his predecessor, for there had been, so far as we know, a gap of about thirty years since the last (recorded) major naval activity, the battle of Cos. So probably Doson had built the ships, at Demetrias or Cassandreia, in the winter of 228/7; we know from Polybius[56] that they sailed south through the Euripus (where they temporarily ran aground) before crossing the Aegean. On their financing we have no information. The real scope of Antigonus' ambitions cannot however be assessed, since unexpected developments in the Peloponnese gave him an opportunity to recover Corinth from the Achaeans, and he abandoned his Carian plans, leaving an area under loose Macedonian control for his successor Philip V, who acceded in 221. This control lasted (to our knowledge) until the third year of Philip's reign, but thereafter there is a gap in our records until Philip resumed an Asiatic policy in the final years of the century. The Carian expedition is perhaps to be regarded as a quick response to an opportunity presented by events across the Aegean. It accorded with the traditions of the dynasty; and in addition such a demonstration may have proved very useful to a king who was something of a stop-gap (the obvious heir being still a child) and who had taken over a kingdom which was militarily at a low ebb.

IV.

It is unlikely that a substantial Macedonian war-fleet remained in commission after the Carian expedition. During the first few years of his reign Philip V was involved, as a leader of a new Hellenic alliance created by Antigonus Doson, in a war against Aetolia and her allies, and he needed ships mainly for communication with and inside Greece. From the outset he showed himself awake to the importance of the sea for this purpose. A campaign in Ambracia and Acarnania in 219 culminated in the seizure of Oeniadae, an excellent naval base for operations against either Aetolia or the Peloponnese; and in 218 he planned a new programme of naval action, partly under the influence of the Illyrian, Demetrius of Pharos, who had joined him in flight from the Romans the previous summer. But this remained on a rather small scale. Philip mustered his fleet from old vessels already available and amounting in all to no more than twelve decked ships

---

[56] Polyb. 20.5.7.

and forty light craft.⁵⁷ They were to be used for the transportation of troops between various points in the west of Greece, from Lechaeum to Patrae and thence to Cephallenia. In fact, in a war against Elis, Sparta and Aetolia, the only real function for naval craft was to facilitate quick movement and to drive a wedge between these enemy states.

The first signs of a more ambitious naval policy came in the winter of 217, when Philip built a new fleet of 100 *lembi* at Demetrias using Illyrian shipwrights.⁵⁸ These *lembi* were light craft, much used by the Illyrians on piratical expeditions;⁵⁹ they were quick-moving and could carry each at least fifty men — more, if necessary.⁶⁰ "Philip," says Polybius,⁶¹ "was about the first king of Macedonia to build such a fleet," evidently in reference to the type of ship rather than the numbers. The war with Aetolia was now over, and Philip's purpose was first to attack Scerdilaidas in Illyria and then perhaps the Roman "allies" on the Adriatic coast and on the islands off Epirus and Illyria; later, we are told, he proposed to invade Italy.⁶² But the sudden approach of a Roman squadron of a mere ten ships from Sicily caused him to beat a hasty retreat to the Aegean; and two years later, in 214, having conveyed a force of 6,000 men to Oricum in 120 *lembi*, he was trapped by the Roman commander Laevinus in the river Aous and forced to burn all his ships and retreat overland to Macedonia.⁶³ The whole enterprise had collapsed disastrously, the reason evidently being that Philip was banking on his Carthaginian allies organising a diversion against Laevinus, which never in fact took place.

---

[57] Cf. M. Holleaux, *Rome, la Grèce et les monarchies hellénistiques au IIIe siècle av.J.-C. (273-205)* (Paris 1921) 158, n. 6, 159, n. 1; F. W. Walbank, *Philip V of Macedon* (Cambridge 1940) 51.

[58] Polyb. 5.109.3; the ships sailed through the Euripus to round C. Malea the next summer.

[59] See L. Casson, *Ships and Seamanship in the Ancient World* (Princeton 1973) 125-27, for full references and discussion of *lembi* and *pristeis*.

[60] Polyb. 2.3.1; Holleaux (supra n. 57) 176 n. 1. These figures are based on the likely assumption that Philip's *lembi* resembled the Illyrian. But variations in size and arrangement are found; cf. Livy 34.35.5 for *lembi* with only sixteen rowers. And some of Philip's in 214 were biremes: Livy 24.40.2.

[61] Polyb. 5.109.3, σχεδὸν πρῶτος τῶν ἐν Μακεδονίᾳ βασιλέων; why σχεδόν?

[62] Polyb. 5.108.4 (Scerdilaidas); cf.101.8 (Italy), 101.10 (world dominion). How far Philip believed Demetrius' rhetoric about world dominion is a moot point; but the Illyrian's influence was strong.

[63] Livy 24.40; Zonaras 9.4.4: Plut. *Arat.* 51.1.

Sea-power and the Antigonids

These incidents and his treaty with Hannibal (215) had brought Philip into open collision with the Romans. Any plans to invade Italy (if indeed they were ever seriously conceived) now quickly disappeared with the loss of his fleet. It is unnecessary to follow the details of the First Macedonian War. Philip now had to abandon the western waters to Laevinus and very soon found himself under pressure from the combined Roman and Pergamene fleets. In 209 we find him borrowing five Achaean ships in the hope of making contact with Bomilcar, the Punic admiral — who failed to turn up;[64] and the next year, this time using six Achaean ships, he linked up with seven quinqueremes and over twenty *lembi* of his own at Anticyra and, after a plundering expedition in Aetolia, dragged his own ships over the Isthmus and made his way back to Demetrias.[65]

The events of 209 and 208 had demonstrated that there was nothing to be hoped for from the Carthaginians. In addition it looks as if Bomilcar had sustained a decisive defeat at the hands of the Romans.[66] This would help to explain Philip's decision in the winter of 208 to build a new fleet of 100 warships at Cassandreia.[67] The keels were laid down, but when the Romans now virtually withdrew from Aegean waters, Philip evidently shrank from the expense and the ships were left unfinished.[68] Soon afterwards the war ended in the Peace of Phoenice (205). As regards naval activity, the years 217-207 had shown little but misguided effort and even disaster. Once the overambitious plan to invade Italy alongside Hannibal had been abandoned (as it must have been as early as Cannae in 216), the main use for Macedonian ships remained what it had been in the previous war, a means of conveying troops expeditiously from point to point or carrying out small plundering expeditions. The fleet of *lembi* was really a *residuum* from the ambitious plans of 217 and no longer essential. Once it was lost, Philip continued to attack Illyria successfully by land. Indeed his main effort and not inconsiderable achievement in this rashly precipitated war against Rome was on the land.

---

[64] Livy 27.30.15; cf. Holleaux (supra n. 57) 240, n. 2.
[65] Livy 28.8.7-13. Whether the quinqueremes were dragged across the *diolkos* or (more probably) left at Lechaeum, we are not told.
[66] See Holleaux (supra n. 57) 244, n. 2.
[67] Livy 28.8.14, *nauium longarum*.
[68] See Holleaux (supra n. 57) 246, n. 2, 285, n. 5.

V.

Between 205 and 200 Philip turned from Illyria and western Greece to take up the threads which Doson had let fall when he saw the chance to re-establish Macedonian power in Corinth. An expansionist policy in the Aegean, in the approaches to the Straits and in Asia Minor required both ships and money to pay for their construction (and to hire the crews).[69] It was largely because of the methods he adopted to get this money that Philip won himself so evil a reputation during these years. His reversion to a plan for Aegean expansion seems to have been partly a reaction against an Illyrian policy which had brought no lasting results, partly a move away from areas in which Rome had a declared interest, partly a return to aims pursued by his forebears (including most recently Antigonus Doson) — and the Antigonids had a strong family feeling — and partly the determination to get in first before Antiochus, who had just got back with some prestige from his eastern *anabasis*; no doubt too he was encouraged by the manifest weakness of the third great power, Egypt, a weakness which was even more patent following the death of Ptolemy IV in the summer of 204 and the accession of a child to the throne.

About the same time (205) war broke out[70] between Rhodes and a group of Cretan cities allied to Philip, and since Rhodes was the Greek state with the strongest interest in policing the seas and putting down piracy, it was in Philip's interest to encourage this war (which he may even have provoked).[71] The most recent studies of this Rhodo-Cretan war[72] suggest that the island was at this time divided into two camps, one led by Gortyn, the other by Cnossus, and that the former group was supported by Philip, while the latter was allied to Rhodes and enjoyed some support from Nabis of Sparta.[73] Despite the involvement of Rhodes, both groups of Cretan cities seem to have practised piracy. In order both to help those Cretans allied to him (since about 217 he had been *prostates* of the Cretan *koinon*) and to

---

[69] Cf. Polyb. 16.7.5 for a distinction between Macedonian troops and non-Macedonian crews.

[70] Diod. 27.3; *SIG*, 567,673.

[71] Polyb. 13.4.2. P. Brulé, *La piraterie crétoise hellénistique* (Paris 1978) 44, points out that the Rhodian offer to help make peace between the Aetolians and Macedonia in 207 indicates fairly amicable relations: had some special incident occurred since then to cause a rupture?

[72] R. M. Errington, *Philopoemen* (Oxford 1969) 34-48; Brulé (supra n. 71) 29-56.

[73] Polyb. 13.8.2.

undermine the power of Rhodes Philip employed an Aetolian, Dicaearchus, to sail with twenty ships and indulge in piracy against the rich cities of the Troad and the Cyclades, and also to lend a hand in the Cretan War;[74] and he succeeded in introducing an agent, Heracleides of Tarentum, into Rhodes, where he burnt part of the dockyards.[75] By the early months of 203 Philip could use the proceeds of Dicaearchus' piracy to start the building of a new fleet;[76] and just as earlier he had found it useful to make an alliance with Hannibal to coordinate action against Rome, so now (probably in the winter of 203/202) he made an agreement with Antiochus of Syria to act in consort at the expense of young Ptolemy V.[77]

In 202 the fleet was ready. Its numbers are not recorded but in 201 Philip had forty to fifty decked ships, a few light vessels and 150 *lembi*,[78] so presumably he had about the same in 202, since he is not known to have suffered any losses during that year. His campaign led to the seizure of Lysimacheia, Calchedon (both Aetolian), Perinthus (Byzantine) and Cius (Aetolian).[79] Cius was sacked and its population enslaved, a profitable operation, and the same treatment was meted out to the free city of Thasos. Whether he took Lemnos now or possessed it earlier is uncertain.[80] The object of the campaign seems to have been mixed. In the light of his conviction that the Antigonid house was bent on universal rule,[81] Polybius interprets it as a first step in that direction. But Philip's real aims were probably much more modest. On the one hand he was clearly seeking what he achieved, an extension of Macedonian-controlled territory along the

---

[74] Diod. 28.1.

[75] Polyb. 13.5.1-3; Polyae. *Strat.* 5.17 (2).

[76] Cf. Holleaux (supra n. 57) 285, n. 5.

[77] Polyb. 15.20; see Walbank (supra n. 54) II 471-4; III 785 (discussing R. M. Errington, "The alleged Syro-Macedonian pact and the origins of the second Macedonian war," *Athenaeum* 49 [1971] 336-54, who rejects its authenticity). The compact was probably less precise than the sources suggest. The initiative will have been Antiochus's.

[78] Polyb. 16.2.9; the 53 decked ships which Philip commanded at Chios will include some Egyptian vessels incorporated at Samos.

[79] Polyb. 15.23.8-9 (Lysimacheia and Calchedon), 18.2.4, 44.4 (Perinthus), 15.21-23 (Cius), 15.24 (Thasos). It has been argued that he also took Sestus this year (Polyb. 18.2.4); but despite the absence of any mention of it in Livy 31.16.4-6 it seems more likely that Philip seized it in 200 (cf. Polyb. 16.29.3: Walbank [supra n. 54] II 539 *ad loc.*).

[80] Walbank (supra n. 54) II 611 on Polyb. 18.44.4.

[81] Supra n. 20.

Thracian coast towards the Hellespont and the Bosphorus. This was highly reminiscent of the policy of Philip II, and its similar effect on Athens, always sensitive to any threat to its corn-supply, can be detected in the appointment of Cephisodorus as *tamias tōn sitonikōn*.[82] But in addition the expedition furnished rich plunder, including the proceeds of enslaving the populations of Cius and Thasos, which would go towards the cost of manning the fleet.

The next year (201) he sailed out again with a fleet which, after the seizure of a number of Egyptian vessels stationed at Samos, came to over 200 ships.[83] Polybius gives a fullish account of the campaigns of this year, but the order of the main events is controversial owing to the fragmentary character of his narrative. I have argued elsewhere that Philip was defeated by Attalus and the Rhodians off Chios, invaded the territory of Pergamum, gained a victory over the Rhodians at Lade, and finally sailed south to campaign in the Rhodian Peraea and Caria,[84] in that order; but the details do not concern us here. That Philip was acting against Pergamum and Rhodes is clear; but in Caria he was also moving against Egypt, which he deprived of Samos.[85] The campaign of 201 harks back to earlier Antigonid pretensions, for in seizing the Cyclades Philip was looking to Antigonus I's creation of the Island League, and by invading Caria he was taking up Doson's interrupted project. The positive character of this programme weighs against Holleaux's view[86] that his main objective was the Straits, but that he was diverted by his defeat at Chios (a view which links with his contention that Philip had no designs on Egyptian possessions).[87] Holleaux

---

[82] L. Moretti, *Iscrizioni storiche ellenistiche* I (Florence 1967) no. 33. Three were elected annually, the earliest recorded being in 267/266: *IG* II-III², 1272; but Cephisodorus' appointment clearly links with the crisis of this year, as appears from his funerary monument, the gist of which is summarised by Pausanias 1.36.5-6. The inscription says συνδιεξηχὼς τρίτος which Moretti rightly takes to mean that he served along with two others ("assieme ad altri due"), not necessarily with superior authority.

[83] Polyb. 16.2.9. For details see supra n. 78.

[84] See Walbank (supra n. 54) II 497-500.

[85] Supra n. 83.

[86] M. Holleaux, *Études d'épigraphie et d'histoire grecques*, ed. L. Robert, IV (Paris 1952) 334.

[87] See C. Habicht, "Samische Volksbeschlüsse der hellenistischen Zeit," *AthMitt* 72 (1957) pp. 233-41 no. 64 (especially p. 239 n. 109), an inscription which refers to the Ptolemaic recovery of Samos in the face of Macedonian resistance. It shows that Philip had seized and retained the city by violence and so renders Holleaux's belief in a friendly occupation of the island untenable.

explained the Carian campaign as an improvisation to take revenge on Rhodes for her intervention at Chios. Certainly in 200 Philip again moved in the direction of the Straits; but that could itself have been the result of a general setback in his plans for 201. What Philip's real object was in that year is bound to be somewhat obscure, since his defeat at Chios (like any major defeat) must have caused a modification of plan; and the invasion of Pergamum and perhaps that of the Rhodian Peraea were both motivated at least in part by anger. What is clear is that Philip was prepared to attack free cities like Thasos, Iasus, Bargylia, Euromus and Pidasa, Ptolemaic cities such as Samos, Miletus and Myus and, after the battle of Chios, Rhodian possessions on the mainland;[88] and of course the territory of Pergamum. W. E. Thompson has detected[89] in this campaign a policy of breaking up links between cities and larger units, but his thesis is not proved. On the whole to recover control of the islands and to acquire enough booty to help pay the costs of the operation seem the most likely objects of the campaigns of 202 and 201.

In the later autumn of 201 Philip found himself trapped by the Rhodian and Pergamene fleets in the Bay of Bargylia in Caria, and it was only after spending the winter there that he slipped out by means of a trick the next spring and returned to Macedonia.[90] From there he sent out some Macedonian ships to carry off four Athenian warships from the Piraeus, but they were soon obliged to surrender these to Attalus, whose fleet along with that of the Rhodians had followed Philip across the Aegean. Philip spent the summer of 200 in a combined land and sea operation in the north-east. He took Maronea, and Aenus was betrayed to him by its Egyptian governor.

---

[88] For the political alignment of these cities see Huss (supra n. 46) 197 (cities in Caria), 201 (Miletus and Myus), 232-33 (Samos), 235 (Thasos). *SIG*, 572 is a letter from Philip to Nisyros (an island forty miles off Rhodes) together with a Nisyrian decree. It indicates that Philip had seized the island but now granted it the right to use its ancestral laws.

[89] Cf. W. E. Thompson, "Philip V and the Islanders," *TAPA* 102 (1971) 616-20. He argues that Philip detached Nisyros from Rhodes (to which it certainly belonged in the second century) and treats this as typical of a general policy of breaking up larger units, e.g., between Perinthus and Byzantium, between Lysimacheia and the Aetolian League. He also postulates the rupture of a union between Cos and Calymna (M. Segre, *Tituli Calymnii* (Bergamo 1952) 9-17: the use of the word *apokatastasis* implies the restoration of a *homopoliteia* which could only have existed briefly before and been broken by Philip). But there is no evidence that Nisyros was Rhodian before 201, the date of *SIG*, 572. Thompson does not suggest why Philip sought to break up larger political units.

[90] Polyae. *Strat.* 4.18.2.

These were followed by a series of small towns and forts, Cypsela, Doriseon, Serrheum and then, in the Chersonese, Elaeus, Alopeconnesus, Callipolis, Madytus and others,[91] perhaps including Sestus.[92] Most of these places were Egyptian. Philip then crossed the Hellespont to mount a combined military and naval siege of Abydus. It was here that Roman ambassadors found him and delivered what was in effect a declaration of war. Philip now took the city after most of the men had perished or committed suicide; and returning to Macedonia he learnt *en route* of the landing of a Roman army at Apollonia.

The purpose of this season's campaign is hard to detect. A fragment of Polybius from the *Suda*[93] has been placed by editors at xvi.29.1, just before the siege of Abydus. It states that "Philip wished to deprive the Romans of the resources and stepping stones in those parts." But Philip will hardly have attacked Abydus to deprive the Romans of its use. Why he did attack Abydus is stated in the next sentence (xvi.29.2), also from the *Suda*: it was in order to have a bridgehead if he wished to cross over into Asia again. Clearly xvi.29.1 does not belong here and is irrelevant to Philip's intentions. In De Sanctis' opinion[94] these were to establish a land route to Asia by conquering the Thracian Chersonese and the Straits and then with the help of his allies in Asia to crush his enemies on land and "to prepare the destruction of their fleets as Alexander had prepared the destruction of the Persian fleet." This ambitious programme seems to forget that Rhodes could not be reached by land (though her Peraea might); and the reluctance Zeuxis showed in providing supplies in 201 suggests that Philip would have been ill advised to look for much help to his "allies in Asia." On the other hand, he had acquired a substantial province in Caria (which was to remain Macedonian until after Cynoscephalae) so perhaps his ambitions looked beyond gaining a foothold in north-west Asia, to forestall Antiochus, whose interest in western Anatolia was already apparent.[95] His ultimate aims, however, must remain a matter of speculation, since his campaign was abruptly terminated by the

---

[91] Livy 31.16.4-6.

[92] Supra n. 79.

[93] I hope to discuss this fragment elsewhere.

[94] G. de Sanctis, *Storia dei Romani* IV 1 (Turin 1923) 34.

[95] For his possession of Teos by 204/203 see P. Herrmann, "Antiochos der Grosse und Teos," *Anadolu* [*Anatolia*] 9 (1965) 29-160.

Sea-power and the Antigonids

Roman ultimatum delivered to him at Abydus.[96] For the present enquiry we need only note that the campaign of 200 represents a reduction in the active role of the fleet. The defeat off Chios and the embarrassment of a winter spent at Bargylia had cooled Philip's enthusiasm to become a naval power. The advance to the Straits had taken the traditional form of a land campaign (with 2,000 light armed troops and 200 cavalry) relying on the fleet (under Heracleides) for support and provisioning; the assault on Abydus was a joint operation. It was to be almost the last serious naval action carried out by an Antigonid.

VI.

Throughout the Second Macedonian War the fleet never ventured out of Demetrias.[97] At the outset Philip had destroyed Sciathos and Peparethos to deprive the enemy of booty and useful bases off the north coast of Euboea.[98] He realised that his fleet of perhaps twenty-five warships and some eighty galleys and light vessels could not face the united fleets of Rome and Rhodes, which together with some Illyrian galleys came to seventy warships and twenty lighter craft.[99] After his defeat at Cynoscephalae, the Romans restricted him to possessing five *skaphē* and a single vessel, a "sixteen" (*hekkaidekērēs*), which he was perhaps allowed to keep as a craft of prestige.[100] Naval power played no part in Philip's subsequent policies. As for Perseus, his successor (in 179), we hear of an attack with *lembi* on Oreus, early in the Third Macedonian War, in which thirty Roman transports were captured;[101] and in 168 he carried out a lively and successful raiding cruise with forty *lembi* and ten *pristeis* commanded by Antenor and Callippus, designed to protect grain convoys proceeding from the Black Sea and Asia Minor to Macedonia and to intercept ships

---

[96] His general Nicanor had already conveyed to Philip a warning delivered to him by the Roman embassy at Athens, when Philip sent him to ravage Attica (Polyb. 16.27.1-5). Whether Philip was aware of the rejection of the war-motion by the centuries when it was first put to them (Livy 31.6.3) is uncertain and must depend on the chronology of this year. For one view see Walbank (supra n. 57) 313-17, and for other views Will (supra n. 7) II 116.

[97] Half Livy's statement (31.33.1, referring to 200) that *Philippus impigre terra marique parabat bellum* must be taken with a pinch of salt.

[98] Livy 31.28.6.

[99] See Walbank (supra n. 57) 147, n. 6.

[100] Polyb. 18.44.6.

[101] Plut. *Aem*.9.3.

bringing corn to the Romans.[102] But the Roman victory at Pydna put an end to the war and with it to the kingdom of Macedonia.

VII.

It is clear that once the Romans had intervened decisively east of the Adriatic in the Second Macedonian War, one can no longer speak of a meaningful Macedonian naval policy. Before then naval policy has to be assessed against a general political background in which the three major monarchies in practice operated a balance of power which, however, was never accepted in principle.[103] None of the three had any hope of reconquering the whole empire of Alexander, yet each was alert to threats from its rivals and ready in turn to press any advantage to increase its own security and area of influence; the possible exception was Ptolemaic Egypt, whose rulers seem to have themselves accepted certain limits on expansion. In general, the situation is one not unfamiliar in our own time. Looked at objectively, the Antigonids seem at no moment to have been in serious danger from the Seleucids and the Ptolemies. The latter, as we saw, regarded as defensive their ring of possessions in the Aegean, in Greece (Methana-Arsinoe perhaps from the time of the Chremonidean War)[104] and towards the Straits,[105] though at the same time they were ready to subsidise any potential trouble-maker in Greece such as Sparta or, later, Achaea. The Seleucids were mainly neutralised by the treaty made between Antigonus II and Antiochus I.[106]

In this context an active Antigonid naval policy indicated a resumption of expansionist aims; and in each case that these were pursued the results were negative. The first example is in the

---

[102] Livy 44.28-29; App. *Mac*.18.4: ἐς δὲ τὴν Ἰονίαν ἔπεμπε κωλύειν τὴν ἀγορὰν τὴν ἐκεῖθεν αὐτοῖς (*sc.* the Romans) φερομένην. See J. H. Thiel, *Studies on the History of Roman Sea-power in Republican Times* (Amsterdam 1946) 402, n. 787.

[103] See H. H. Schmitt, "Polybios und das Gleichgewicht der Mächte," in *Polybe*, ed. E. Gabba: Entretiens Hardt (Vandoeuvres-Geneva 1974) 65-102; P. Treves, "Balance of power politics in classical antiquity," *Thirteenth International Congress of Historical Sciences: Proceedings* (Moscow 1970).

[104] Cf. Heinen (supra n. 1) 131, 210, n. 465, who points out that Methana was directed towards Ptolemaic control of the sea, not towards domination of the mainland; L. Robert, "Sur un décret des Korésiens au musée de Smyrne," *Hellenica* XI-XII (1960) 159 compared it with Gibraltar.

[105] Supra p. 217.

[106] Supra p. 217.

Sea-power and the Antigonids

Chremonidean War. As we have seen,[107] there is disagreement as to whether the building of a Macedonian fleet precipitated the war or (as Habicht implies) occurred in the course of it. But the war was really decided on land with the surrender of Athens, and the battle of Cos cannot be shown to have changed substantially the Egyptian dominance in the Aegean. The next attempt at naval expansion was Doson's Carian expedition. It brought some acquisitions lasting at least until the early years of Philip's reign and perhaps contacts which persisted in a somewhat dormant form until the Carian policy was revived by Philip in 201. But it was for his achievements in Greece, not in the Aegean, that Doson was remembered. Philip twice took to the sea, in Illyria and then again in the Aegean. Both episodes were failures and ended in the destruction or curtailment of his navy; and the Aegean enterprise could only be maintained by a programme of plunder and terror which made Philip enemies everywhere and eventually provided the Romans with an excuse to resume the struggle against Macedonia, the first round of which had ended indecisively in 205. Further, this led to the collapse of the Hellenic alliance created by Doson and the permanent expulsion of Macedonia from southern Greece. Philip's more substantial achievements were in the north, where he consolidated the frontiers, and in his internal strengthening of the land itself, though the latter was carried out with typical brutality. Perseus, as we saw, could have no naval policy.

That the Antigonids sought world dominion is an exaggeration;[108] but their repeated attempts to create a fleet for objects beyond the minimum needs of communication and security indicated their determination to challenge the Ptolemies and (in the case of Philip's Aegean campaign) perhaps the Seleucids too. In Illyria Philip made the even greater mistake of encroaching on an area pre-empted by Rome. One is tempted to correlate these repeated failures to establish or maintain a naval preponderance with the relative poverty of Macedonia compared with the rival kingdoms. But despite the manifest difficulty which Macedonia experienced in financing a fleet over any considerable period of time, when one looks at the details, it is the human factor that stands out, along with the element of pure chance; the unexpected appeal by the Achaeans to Doson, Philip's poor intelligence at the Aous, his policy of sheer terror in the Aegean

---

[107] Supra p. 218.
[108] Supra p. 218.

(and the resentment it induced), his being faced with the combined navies of Rhodes and Pergamum at Chios. As regards Antigonus II and the battle of Cos (and Andros?) we know too little to say why his success brought so small a return. But looked at together, one fact emerges clearly from this brief survey, the consistency with which Antigonid naval policy proved a mistake and a disaster.

Cambridge

Perseus and the Third Macedonian War

W. LINDSAY ADAMS

Abstract

Scholarship concerning the origins of the Third Macedonian War has revolved around particular aspects of the relations with Rome (the Demetrius affair, social unrest in Greece, the Macedonian revival and its challenge to the status quo) rather than the context for those actions. Perseus did his best, virtually from his accession onwards, to allay Roman fears, to settle questions by negotiation, and to submit to arbitration long after Rome had decided on a new war. He did so in an attempt to avoid a conflict he could not win. The reasons for Perseus' failure in this regard are twofold: 1) the atmosphere of distrust inherited from Philip V's two wars with Rome, as well as Perseus' role in the death of his brother Demetrius; and 2) the changing nature of both the Roman *nobilitas* and consequently the Senate itself to a more proprietary view of the Hellenistic East and the aggravation of these factors caused by Eumenes II of Pergamum and his ambitions. Perseus was caught between them.

The origins of the Third Macedonian War and the role of King Perseus in those events have held the attention of scholars from Polybius to the present. The most prevalent theory in antiquity, and the least likely, was that Perseus inherited the war from his father, Philip V.[1] The provenance for this idea came from the widely held view that Philip was planning a new war with Rome during the last years of his reign. Polybius, in particular, argues for its acceptance

---

[1] For example, Livy 42.5.1; 40.57; 40.52.3; Polyb. 22.18.10; Justin 32.3.5; and App. *Mac.* 11.1 (frgm.). For Perseus' direct involvement in the war plans, see Livy 40.5.9, most of which is derived from Polybius. See, also, F. W. Walbank, *A Historical Commentary on Polybius* III (Oxford 1979) 205-209.

on the grounds of analogy with Philip II's legacy of the Persian war to Alexander.[2] The chief problem with this interpretation is that, while Philip V may very well have been planning a new war in theory, in fact Perseus did everything possible to avert the real war.[3]

There are other causes traced to various acts on the part of Perseus: the expulsion of Abrupolis from his Thracian kingdom;[4] the Dolopian campaign and Perseus' subsequent "march" through northwestern Greece to Delphi;[5] and the attempt on the life of Eumenes II of Pergamum.[6] Another more general cause put forward is the ill will and distrust engendered with Rome following the death of Perseus' brother, Demetrius, and Perseus' role in that death.[7] Finally, there is Appian's generalization that the Roman Senate "did not choose to have on their flank a sober-minded, laborious, and benevolent king, a heredity enemy to themselves . . . ."[8]

Recently, Adalberti Giovannini added a new twist to this last interpretation: that Perseus tried to increase his popularity and power in Greece by playing on the interests of the lower classes, thereby forcing Rome to respond in order to protect the *status quo*.[9] Giovannini's ideas have not been well received. E. S. Gruen effectively challenged Giovannini's reading of the sources and Giovannini's overall interpretation.[10] Passerini, in an earlier work, demonstrated that Rome did not rely on a government based on a single class, something Giovannini failed to take into account.[11] F. W. Walbank has taken exception, as well, with Giovannini over the idea of social motivation as the chief catalyst for the war. Yet he comes to the same general conclusion as Giovannini that it was the

[2] Polyb. 22.18.10 for the analogy; cf. Polyb. 22.18.11 for his refutation of the other causes.

[3] The major demonstration of this is below; for now, see Livy 42.14.3-4; 42.39.1; and 42.48.3.

[4] Polyb. 22.18.2. Abrupolis was the king of the Sapaei, from the Nestus River region on the extreme eastern border of Macedonia; see Walbank (supra n. 1) 206.

[5] Polyb. 22.18.4-5; Livy 41.22.4-5.

[6] Polyb. 22.18.5; App. *Mac.* 9.11.4.

[7] See C. F. Edson, "Perseus and Demetrius," *HSCP* 46 (1935) 191-202.

[8] App. *Mac.* 11.3.

[9] A. Giovannini, "Les Origines de la 3ᵉ Guerre de Macédoine," *BCH* 93 (1969) 853-61.

[10] E. S. Gruen, "Class Conflict and the Third Macedonian War," *AJAH* 1 (1976) 29-60.

[11] A. Passerini, "I Moti Politico-Sociali della Grecia e Romani," *Studia di Storia Ellenistico-Romana* VI, *Athenaeum*, n.s. 11 (1933) 326.

challenge to the Roman settlement, however unwitting, that prompted the Third Macedonian War.[12] This still leaves open the question of how to interpret Perseus' conduct *ante bellum*. Here it is best to follow Polybius' advice, if not his reasoning in this instance, to seek "the difference between a pretext and a cause . . ."[13] Since Polybius and virtually all the sources at least consider the matter of Perseus' inheriting the war, that is the best place to start.

Three general features characterize the end of the reign of Philip V: the expansion to the north which occupied the military energy and concern of Philip following the end of the Syrian War; Philip's deteriorating relations with Rome, which center on the embassies and arbitrations of the period; and the death of Philip's younger son, Demetrius.

Philip was limited by the treaty which ended the Second Macedonian War to "the ancient boundaries of his kingdom."[14] Although he tried to expand to the southwest and east, in his last years Philip looked north. He was involved with the plans of just such a campaign when he died in 179 B.C.[15] In this regard, Philip enlisted the aid of a Germanic tribe, the Bastarnae, which gave rise to the Annalistic suspicions that he was plotting a new war with Rome.[16] According to Livy the plan would allow the Bastarnae free passage through the kingdom and a free hand in dealing with a troublesome Illyriote people, the Dardani, whom Philip claimed rather loosely as a dependency. A seemingly plausible offer of the Dardanian lands went with the scheme.[17]

Livy adds a second motive to Philip's plan: namely that once this tribe had settled into its new lands it would be a simple matter to direct their attention west *ad populandam Italiam possent mitti*.[18] In this tradition, Philip was to add the Scordisci to his plans, but at this point Livy's imagination or his sources fail him, for his only course following the juncture of the two tribes is to state: *Inde in omnem*

---

[12] F. W. Walbank, "The Causes of the Third Macedonian War: Some Recent Views," *AM* 2 (1977) 81-102.

[13] Polyb. 22.18.6

[14] For the terms of the treaty ending the Second Macedonian War, see Polyb. 18.44 and Walbank, *A Historical Commentary on Polybius* II (Oxford 1967) 609-12.

[15] Livy 40.56.8-10.

[16] Livy 40.57.

[17] Livy 40.57:4-6.

[18] Livy 40.57.6.

eventum consilia accommodabantur.[19] Livy, however, has neglected to get Philip's motley alliance to Italy. One thing is clear: the possibility of such an alliance did concern the Romans. An embassy was sent to observe the Bastarnae, but not until long after Perseus had been king and a new Macedonian war was imminent.[20] Their concern, then, did not come until long after Livy's scenario, and basically revolved around fears which Eumenes of Pergamum played upon in 172.[21]

In any event, Philip's plans were about to come to fruition when he died. Indeed, the Bastarnae led by Cotto and Antigonus were almost at Amphipolis when news reached them of Philip's death.[22] As Philip had no intention of committing any of his own forces to such a venture, the actions of the Bastarnae in the beginning of Perseus' reign are telling in regard to Philip's plans. The Bastarnae, after some initial trouble in Thrace which reduced their numbers considerably, proceeded to follow the initial portion of the scheme: to move into the Dardanian territory.[23] Nothing further materialized as far as the invasion of Italy was concerned. A Roman commission under Aulus Postumius was sent to investigate the ensuing war between Dardani and the Bastarnae, and reported that Perseus was not involved.[24] Strictly speaking, this was true both in terms of actual aid to the Bastarnae and in that he had nothing to do with the planning or execution of it.

Postumius' commission made its report to the Senate in 175, and Livy could already state that there was "anxiety" over the possibility of another Macedonian war.[25] Livy's assumption that Perseus was stirring up the Dardanian conflict probably reflects an annalistic source, and is certainly reminiscent of the origins of the first two Macedonian wars.[26] There was, however, a considerable lapse of time between Philip's scheming and the outbreak of the new war with Rome, which ultimately came at Rome's insistence, and, of course, the invasion never took place. The origin of the invasion tradition

---

[19] Livy 40.57.8.

[20] App. *Mac.* 11.1.

[21] Livy 42.11.5; App. *Mac.* 11.2.

[22] Livy 40.57.3.

[23] Livy 40.58.8.

[24] Polyb. 25.6.2-6. Cf. Walbank, *Commentary* III (supra n. 1) 282 and P. Meloni, *Perseo e la Fine della Monarchia Macedonia* (Rome 1953) 38-40 (Perseus' marriage to a Bastarnian princess) and 78-85.

[25] Livy 41.19.4.

[26] *Ibid.* Compare this to Polybius' statement (25.6.2-6).

probably results from the real possibility of such a thing in the Second Punic War and from their own propaganda of the Second Macedonian War. The Roman populace had become accustomed to this threat as part of the traditional Macedonian menace. What lent it credence was the strained relations between Philip and Rome in the last years of the king's reign.

Philip's policy of expansion did not sit well with the Senate, but in two areas — the southwest and east — it brought Philip up against the Thessalians and, more importantly, Eumenes of Pergamum. Though Philip saw these as undefined areas, clearly the Thessalian *koinon* and Eumenes did not. A stream of embassies to Rome with their continual complaints against Philip caused one commission after another to be sent out from Rome to investigate.[27] As for Philip, he complained with some justice that he had not adequately rewarded for his services to Rome in the Syrian War, especially for his active campaigns against the Aetolians.[28] In those arbitrations the Senate rather monotonously decided against Philip.[29] In particular, concerning the occupation of the Thracian coastal towns of Aenus and Maronea, the commission on a complaint from Eumenes ordered Philip to evacuate them.[30] In addition, there were charges from the Thessalians, Perrhaebians, Athamanians and Thracians made at the same time. Nor did the manner of the commissions soften the blows for Philip. Livy states that Philip was summoned "to hear the charges almost as a criminal."[31]

Philip was not at pains to hide his feelings, nor did he hesitate to take revenge by massacring the anti-Macedonian party among the citizens of Maronea.[32] As a result, the final catastrophe of Philip's reign was set in motion. The commission, outraged at Philip's

---

[27] For a full discussion of the problems with these commissions, see F. W. Walbank, *Philip V of Macedon* (Cambridge 1940) 225-46.

[28] See Livy 39.38 for Philip's complaints in general; and Livy 36.25.7 for the problems with the Aetolians. The existence of a formal alliance, and therefore obligation on the part of Rome, has been convincingly challenged by E. S. Gruen, "The Supposed Alliance Between Rome and Philip V of Macedon," *CSCA* 6 (1973) 123-36.

[29] For a complete treatment of this, see E. Badian, *Foreign Clientelae (264-70 B. C.)* (Oxford 1958) 92-96.

[30] On the commission, see Livy 39.24.13-14; for the decisions in these cases, see Livy 39.26.14; Polyb. 22.11.2 and Walbank, *Commentary* III (supra n. 1) 195-97.

[31] Livy 39.25.1. Badian (supra n. 29) 93 points out that we should be skeptical in that virtually all these rulings went against Philip.

[32] Livy 39.34.; Polyb. 22.13 and Walbank, *Commentary* III (supra n. 1) 197-99.

action, demanded that it be answered in Rome by those responsible for the massacre.³³ The fact that the Romans "advertised" their displeasure did not reduce Philip's anxiety, and he chose a dramatic gesture to reassure Rome of his fidelity: he dispatched his younger son, Demetrius, as ambasssador to Rome in 184. Demetrius had been in Rome before, as a hostage for peace in 194, and Philip sent him now *simul ad purganda crimina, simul ad deprecandam iram senatus*.³⁴ Philip felt that his young son would be well received by the Senate, and unfortunately he was correct in that assumption.³⁵

The Senate virtually invited complaints against Philip, and Polybius states that the list was so long that it took three days merely to introduce the embassies.³⁶ The charges involved everything from cattle theft to loss of territory and the claim that justice could not be gotten from Philip "in some [cases] as Philip surpressed the proceedings, and in others, finding fault on the grounds that the decisions were unfair, Philip having bribed the judges."³⁷ Livy is even harsher in the charge that *de jure aut dicto per libidinem aut non dicto, de rebus per vim gratiam indicatis*.³⁸ Even Livy, however, had to admit that many of the charges were "trivial in the extreme."³⁹

By all accounts, Demetrius did not cover himself with glory in his defense of Philip. The Senate, "as they were well disposed towards him," decided that Demetrius would not have to answer all of the charges.⁴⁰ Instead, Demetrius merely read a notebook of Philip's which answered the major points by stating that he "had executed the orders for the Romans."⁴¹ The details of the defense need not concern us; it barely concerned the Romans. The Senate accepted it in all respects, not because Philip had proven his points, but "that he met with this indulgence owing to Demetrius."⁴² This was adding

---

[33] Livy 39.34.6; Polyb. 22.14.1.

[34] Livy 39.35.2-3; for Demetrius' period as a hostage in Rome, see Polyb. 18.39.5 and Livy 33.13.14.

[35] Livy 39.35.3; Polyb. 22.14.10. Cf. Walbank, *Commentary* III (supra n. 1) 199.

[36] Polyb. 23.1.9 and Walbank, *Commentary* III (supra n. 1) 114-120. See, also, Livy 39.46.7-8, and 47.1-3. The Senate made it known "that the Romans were ready to listen to complaints against [Philip]," Polyb. 23.1.1.

[37] Polyb. 23.1.12.

[38] Livy 39.47.3.

[39] Livy 39.47.2.

[40] Polyb. 23.2.1. Cf. Livy 39.47.3-5.

[41] Polyb. 23.2.5.

[42] Polyb. 23.2.10; 23.7.1-4; and Livy 39.47.11.

insult to injury, and both Philip and his older son, Perseus, were "gravely offended" by the action.[43] Apparently, however, the Senate went further. In a blatant attempt at influencing the succession in Demetrius' favor, Flamininus "deluded [Demetrius] into cherishing the idea that the Romans were about to secure the throne for him at once."[44] C. F. Edson has best evaluated this as "an absolutely unwarranted interference in the private dynastic affairs of an independent and technically free state."[45] The impact of this on Demetrius was profound, and his return to Macedonia in 183 signals the beginning of a campaign of innuendo and propaganda designed to undermine Perseus' position. Most of it can be seen in Livy's account, where he refers to Demetrius' mother as *iusta matre familiae*, and Perseus' mother as a concubine, states that Demetrius more than Perseus resembled Philip, and asserts "that Romans would establish Demetrius upon his father's throne."[46] One certainly could not be more direct in terms of Rome's influence and if, as Livy states, this was being said by *vulgus Macedonum*, it certainly smacks of treason.[47]

The relations between Perseus and Demetrius rapidly deteriorate from this point on. Perseus adroitly fought back by emphasizing the very Roman connection Demetrius touted, drawing him onto Roman subjects, implicating him totally with pro-Roman sympathies.[48] Polybius makes it clear that both "young men were plotting against each other," though Livy's account follows the annalistic tradition and emphasis Perseus role only.[49] In 182 Perseus made his accusations open, and produced a letter from Flaminimus urging Philip to send Demetrius to Rome, and charging that Flamininus *nunc est auctor omnium rerum isti et magister*, while Demetrius *cupit*

---

[43] Polyb. 23.3.6.

[44] Polyb. 23.3.7-8; Livy is silent on what Polybius obviously accepts as fact, and oddly enough so is Appian, as Gruen (supra n. 10) has pointed out. See Walbank, *Commentary* III (supra n. 1) 216. Gruen accepts the Polybian account of the conversations between Flamininus and Demetrius, but doubts that it was done deliberately to stir up trouble in Macedonia, "The Last Years of Philip V," *GRBS* 15 (1974) 234-35. Nevertheless, it is difficult to see how they could have had any other effect, despite Flamininus' intention.

[45] Edson (supra n. 7) 193. Edson is still the best authority on this problem, especially in terms of its implications within Macedonia. Cf. Meloni (supra n. 24) 29-60, *passim*.

[46] Livy 39.53.3-4.

[47] Livy 39.53.1-4; Edson (supra n. 7) 194.

[48] Livy 40.5.7-8.

[49] Polyb. 23.10.12 and Walbank, *Commentary* III (supra n. 1) 229-35.

regnum.[50] Philip was reluctant to condemn either of his sons, and postponed any action *inquirendo in utriusque vitam ac mores.*[51]

Philip was serious about the investigation and despatched two ambassadors, Philocles and Apelles, to make inquiries in Rome about Demetrius' actions and conversations, in particular with Flamininus and concerning the kingship.[52] In the meantime, Demetrius was sent back to Macedonia proper, according to Livy because of Philip's preparations to invade Italy, and the young prince "contemplated flight to the Romans."[53] His plans were discovered and he was held in arrest pending the return of the embassy to Rome.[54] Apelles and Philocles did return in 181, bearing a letter from Flamininus to the effect that if Demetrius had held conversations with him, *quid adulescens cupiditate regni,* that they should not be misinterpreted; that Demetrius meant no harm and that Flamininus would not sponsor such a scheme.[55] In other words, Demetrius had held such conversations with Flamininus and Livy admits: *Hae litterae fidem Persei criminibus fecerunt.*[56] No sentence was ever passed on Demetrius, but Philip had him poisoned at a banquet.[57]

The importance of this whole incident lies in that it predisposed the Senate to distrust Perseus, and that it foiled their own plans. It is clear from Livy's account that they held Perseus fully accountable for their candidate's death. In summing up the affair, Livy states: *Haec maxime . . . semina iacta sunt Macedonici belli.*[58] Whether or not Demetrius was innocent in reality is not as important as the fact that

---

[50] Livy 40.11.1 and 11.7, respectively. For the letter, which Flamininus has sent on Demetrius' return to Macedonia, see Polyb. 23.2.8.

[51] Livy 40.16.2.

[52] Livy 40.20.3. Livy also states that Demetrius' popularity with the Romans made him suspect to Philip (40.16.3). Though Livy tries to claim that Apelles and Philocles were prejudiced because they were followers of Perseus, he also lets slip that Philip chose them precisely because they were *nec in alterius favorem inclinatos* (40.20.4).

[53] Livy 40.23.2.

[54] Livy 40.23.2-5. Livy does not bother to deny the charge.

[55] Livy 40.23.8.

[56] Livy 40.23.9. The authenticity of the letter was questioned even in antiquity. One Xychus, secretary to the ambassadors, later confessed it a forgery. Philocles and Apelles were arrested; the former died under torture maintaining its authenticity, while Apelles confessed to forgery and retired to an estate in southern Italy (which surely must rouse our suspicions concerning his veracity). See Livy 40.55. For a full discussion of the problem, see Edson (supra n. 7) 199-200.

[57] Livy 40.24.2-8; Cf. Polyb. 23.7.10-11 and Diod. 29.25.

[58] Livy 40.26.3.

the Senate thought he was the victim. Such an atmosphere made the Senate more than willing to believe the worst about Perseus; when Eumenes laid his charges before them in 172 there could be, *de facto,* no defense, no answer, and no negotiation. The two major factors then influencing the origins of the Third Macedonian War have nothing to do with the actual events leading up to the outbreak of hostilities: the aura of distrust of Macedon in general left by Philip from two previous wars, and the specific distrust of Perseus. When Philip died in 179, Perseus came to the throne amid preconceived Roman suspicions and prejudices. Nevertheless, it is clear from Perseus' record that his anti-Roman role was just that: a role forced on him by dynastic politics. His actions reverse that portrait and instead show a king desperately trying to avoid conflict at almost any cost.

Perseus took over the reins of government quickly and easily. His first official act, as one would expect, was to have his position confirmed by Rome. Though Livy states that this was a gesture *dum firmaret res,* the fact is that Perseus despatched an embassy to Rome almost immediately both to renew the treaty of friendship and *ut rex ab senatu appellaretur.*[59] The latter request was not required but highly diplomatic, and shows Perseus' cognizance of his position in the eyes of the Senate. The treaty would have been enough to confirm him and provide formal recognition. By requesting from the Senate his title, Perseus was acknowledging his dependency on Rome's good will. It was a remarkable admission for an ultra-nationalist, and clearly designed to inaugurate a new era of friendly relations with Rome.

Roman confirmation was forthcoming, though the specific date is unknown.[60] Perseus, in the meantime, carried on the activities one would expect from a king in a vulnerable position. Polybius reports that immediately after renewing the treaty with Rome, Perseus "began to aim at popularity in Greece, calling back to Macedonia fugitive debtors and those who had been banished from the country

---

[59] Livy 40.58.8.

[60] Livy 41.24.6; Polyb. 25.3; and Diod. 29.30. No reference appears before this, though Livy (41.19.5) reports the arrival of an embassy from Perseus to discuss the question of the Bastarnae. One presumes that a treaty of *amicitia* was then in effect. Polybius speaks of the renewal just prior to discussing Perseus' first acts as king, but it is unclear whether he is referring to Perseus' request or actual confirmation. There is no doubt that *amicitia* is all the treaty involved, see Walbank *Commentary* III (supra n. 1) 275.

either by sentence of the courts or for offences against the King."[61] A general amnesty was declared and lists of those concerned were published at Delos, Delphi, and the temple of Itonian Athena.[62] As both Gruen and Walbank point out, it was an internal measure designed to secure his position with Macedonia. It proclaimed Perseus' consistent policy of maintaining his father's friends and settling differences with his father's enemies.

Perseus' actions in the realm of foreign policy reflect the same principles. He entered into a number of dynastic marriages, the most important of which was his own marriage to Seleucus IV's daughter, Laodice.[63] This not only was designed to cement friendly relations with the Seleucids, but also to secure the good will of the Rhodians. In return for escorting his bride, Perseus refitted the Rhodian navy and rewarded its crews.[64] His final diplomatic move in the east was the marriage of his sister to Prusias II of Bithynia.[65] The marriages, ostensibly peaceful, could be and were seen by Rome as raising the spectre of a coalition of kings. Dynastic marriages, however, were common and no one presumed that the frequent intermarriages between the Seleucids and the Ptolemies presaged a coalition. Further, the Rhodians would hardly have fallen in with such a scheme, as it was the possibility of Seleucid and Antigonid cooperation which had led them to seek Roman aid in 201. The point of all of this was to isolate diplomatically the archenemy of Philip's last years: Eumenes of Pergamum. It was a point not lost on Eumenes.

One did not have to go far in that regard. Eumenes' popularity in Greece began to decline in 185, with the war against Prusias II.[66] After 179, it plummeted. Not the least of the actions here being the assassination of Seleucus IV in 175, and the subsequent support for and alliance between Eumenes and Antiochus IV.[67] This real

---

[61] Polyb. 25.3.1. and Walbank, *Commentary* III (supra n.1) 274-77.

[62] Polyb. 25.3.2-3. Cf. Meloni (supra n. 24) 94-130.

[63] Polyb. 25.3.4. Polybius goes on to praise Perseus in the highest terms. Considering Polybius' bias, that is saying quite a bit.

[64] Livy 42.12.3-4; Polyb. 25.4.8; *SIG*³ 639 (inscription from the Delians to "Queen Laodice").

[65] Polyb. 25.4.10.

[66] Livy 42.12.3.

[67] App. *Syr.* 45; *OGIS*, 248, lines 17-20. For the decline in Eumenes' popularity, see E. V. Hansen *The Attalids of Pergamum*² (Ithaca 1971) 108-109; and R. B. McShane, *The Foreign Policy of the Attalids of Pergamum* (Urbana 1964) 164.

coalition of kings brought no concern to Rome, for they seemed to trust Eumenes as a matter of course.

One final foreign policy venture of Perseus needs to be mentioned. In 174, he sent envoys to Carthage, though the outcome and purpose of the mission remains obscure. It was injudicious at best, and Massinissa of Numidia used it for his own purposes by revealing their presence to a Roman embassy.[68] The Romans immediately confronted Carthage, which promptly denied that any such embassy existed.[69] Massinissa was the chief beneficiary of the resulting ill will, and some speculation exists that he may have fabricated the incident altogether. Still, it fits into Perseus' general policy of renewing old friendships, and Rome dispatched another embassy to Macedonia to check into the matter.[70]

Internally, aside from the debt relief already mentioned, Perseus saw through to completion his father's plan for the Bastarnae, giving them safe passage through Macedonia proper and a free hand in dealing with the Illyrian Dardani. He had nothing further to do with the scheme, as indeed Aulus Postumius duly reported to the Senate in 175.[71] In 174, however, Illyria was again the center of controversy for Perseus. In that year he campaigned against the Dolopi, but Perseus quickly brought them to heel. On his return from this campaign, Perseus decided to swing through Delphi to consult the Oracle.[73] His sudden appearance caused a stir, but he left in three days and marched through Thessaly *sine damno iniuriaque eorum per quorum fines inter fecit*.[74] While one may suggest that Perseus was naive, his actions in themselves were not siniter, though he was pressing his luck by taking the army outside the borders of the kingdom, however friendly a gesture was meant.

To recapitulate from the Roman point of view, so far Perseus had tried to establish an alliance with the Seleucids, to isolate Eumenes of

---

[68] Livy 41.22.2. Cf. Meloni (supra n. 24) 127-30.

[69] Livy 41.22.3.

[70] *Ibid.*

[71] Polyb. 25.6.2-6; Livy 41.19.4-6.

[72] Livy 41.22.4-5; Cf. Meloni (supra n. 24) 131-34.

[73] Livy 41.22.6. For Perseus' intentions regarding the potential of the Delphic Amphictiony largely surmised from Philip's policy, see A. Giovannini, "Philipp V., Perseus und die delphische Amphiktyonie," *AM* 1 (1970) 147-54. Giovannini, however, assumes too much of a continuation of Philip's policies by Perseus on almost no evidence.

[74] *Ibid.*

Pergamum, an avowed friend of Rome, to conduct or condone campaigns on the northwestern borders of his kingdom against Illyrian tribes over which he had dubious authority, and he may have tried to establish contact with Carthage. As a whole, these actions assumed more significance and Rome rightly paid attention to them. Seen in the light of Perseus' later activity when confronted with war, these incidents clearly were not intended as acts hostile to Rome.

Perseus continued to curry favor in Greece. Shortly after his visit to Delphi, Perseus made a concerted effort to resolve old quarrels in Greece and *ad instituendam fideliter amicitiam*.[75] He made special effort with the Achaean League, hoping to get them to rescind anti-Macedonian legislation forbidding them entry into Achaea. As a gesture of friendship, he offered to return Achaean slaves who had sought refuge in Macedonia.[76] The first step was to be a simple exchange of refugees. After lengthy debate, however, the matter was deferred, so that the only result was to fuel Rome's suspicions.[77]

The embassy sent to review Perseus' activities following the incident at Carthage reported back in 173.[78] Perseus had declined to see the envoys on the grounds of both illness and absence, excuses under the circumstances as impolite as they were false. The report was even more damaging for "it had become easily apparent to [the envoys] that preparations for war were being made and that Perseus would not long put off his resort to arms."[79] Livy states directly that a Macedonian war seemed likely, and the proper religious rites were begun. Yet, the charges are easily disproved because Perseus did put off war for three more years, and then fought only when he failed to divert Rome from a war she had already declared. Before returning the embassy had foiled Perseus' attempt at reconciliation with Achaea.[80]

---

[75] Livy 41.22.7-8.

[76] Livy 41.23. Cf. Meloni (supra n. 24) 135-140.

[77] Livy 41.24.20. Livy's account shows that quite a lot was made of Demetrius' death in the debate, which reflects a good deal of Roman influence.

[78] Livy 42.2.1.

[79] Livy 42.2.2.

[80] M. Claudius Marcellus, who apparently went on a separate commission to Aetolia, took the opportunity to call a meeting of the Achaeans at Aegium, where a debate on Perseus' offer was held (Livy 42.5.7-6.4). Another five-man commission, led by Ap. Claudius Pulcher, was looking into civil strife in the area at the same time. One is inclined to think that Livy may have made a mistake in the list of the commission and that Marcellus is part of the Claudian group. See T. R. S. Broughton, *Magistrates of the Roman Republic* I (Cleveland 1951) 405 and 409.

The political atmosphere in Rome could not have been worse. In the praetorial elections for 173, no fewer than three of the candidates had held the office before, which suggests not only a shortage of experienced people in the face of the eastern troubles that were brewing, but also a certain distrust of the younger *nobiles*.[81] The general character of the Roman politician of the period is exemplified by the consulate of L. Postumius Albinus in 173. He had managed to outrage the allies, specifically at Praeneste, where he required special marks of honor and "burdensome" service.[82] His colleague, M. Popillius Laenas, was even more excessive. Having attacked the Ligurian town of Statellae without provocation, and accepted their surrender, Laenas sacked the town anyway and sold the population into slavery.[83] This proved too rapacious even for the Senate, which censured Laenas and ordered him to restore both freedom and property to the Statellians. Laenas ignored the order.[84]

The elections for 172, the crucial year for Perseus, reflected the same attitudes of arrogance and ambition. Laenas' brother, C. Laenas, was elected consul despite his brother's flagrant behavior, and openly desired the province of Macedonia even though no war had been declared and Macedonia was still officially a friend.[85] Nor were those that followed the next year much better. C. Cassius Longinus became so blatant and sarcastic about the coming war that he demanded Macedonia as his province without the lot.[86] As it turned out, Italy fell to Longinus, but he did not consider that the end of the matter. In the summer of 171, he attempted to leave his province and attack Macedonia through Illyria.[87] The Senate was incensed and shocked that a consul would so exceed his constituted authority and ordered him back to Italy on pain of prosecution.

This was the tenor of the new age of politics and the generation which was coming to power. The personal desire for *gloria* and *fama* had become paramount. Nor were the acts of Cassius Longinus and the Popilii isolated. Similar incidents continually cropped up during

---

[81] See H. H. Scullard, *Roman Politics, 220-150 B.C.* (Oxford 1951) 193.

[82] Livy 41.1.7-12.

[83] Livy 41.8.

[84] Livy 41.9.1.

[85] For the election, see Livy 42.9.8; for the "province" of Macedonia, see Livy 42.10.12.

[86] Livy 42.32.1.

[87] Longinus attempted to move from Istria, at the head of the Adriatic Sea, along the Dalmatian coastal route, into Macedonia. Livy 43.1.4-12.

the course of the war, and were only mitigated by the fact that they were failures.[88] It was the beginning of the changes which, a generation later, would precipitate the Roman Revolution. Into this climate of ambition Eumenes of Pergamum arrived in Rome on a special embassy in 172.

The Senate, concerned with Perseus' activities and unsatisfied with the report of the embassy of 174, was equally ill at ease with the general situation in the rest of Greece. It had found civil strife in Aetolia, Thessaly, and Perrhaebia in particular.[89] In addition, Postumius' embassy reported that "the sympathies of a large portion of the people were for [Perseus] and they were more inclined to favor him than Eumenes."[90] This rivalry prompted both Eumenes' visit to Rome in 172 and a third senatorial commission to investigate the civil disturbances which the Senate seemed to link with Perseus and the cancellation of debts.[91]

In any event, Eumenes arrived in Rome in 172 specifically "to lay charges against Perseus and to give an account of [Perseus'] preparations for war."[92] Eumenes was received with splendor, granted honors, and given a private audience with the Senate. He set forth his accusations after first disclaiming that he did so not out of any personal wish for gain, a bit of dissembling the Senate accepted at face value.[93] He accused Perseus of inheriting the war from Philip V, and that it involved the Bastarnae; that Perseus was too "strong in the number of his young men and in the resources of his kingdom;" and finally he stated that Macedonia was accustomed to war with Rome, neatly raising the spectre of past Macedonian sins.[94]

Eumenes then moved on to Perseus' actions in Greece itself. First of all, Perseus was more successful with the Greeks than had been

---

[88] For a general characterization, see Scullard (supra n. 81) 198-201. For examples of conduct, Livy 43.5.1-2 (Longinus, who finally made it legitimately to Macedonia) and 43.4-8.13 (Hortensius' sack of Abdera).

[89] Livy 45.5.8.

[90] Livy 42.5.2. They, also, reported that Perseus had killed his wife and recalled Apelles from Italy in order to execute him: Livy 42.5.4-5. Even at worst, however, these were purely internal matters and there is considerable doubt that they go beyond rumor in the case of the wife.

[91] Diod. 29.33; Livy 42.13.9-10 (from Eumenes' charges).

[92] Livy 42.11.1; App. *Mac.* 11.1. Cf. Meloni (supra n. 24) 150-65.

[93] Livy 42.11.2-3. The honors to Eumenes were so excessive that Cato was openly disgusted at their behavior (Plut. *Cat. Mai.* 8.7).

[94] Livy 42.11.6; 42.11.7-8; and App. *Mac.* 11.1.

Perseus and the Third Macedonian War

Philip, which is hardly surprising considering both this conciliatory diplomacy and the fact that Macedonia no longer posed the same threat to Greece as in Philip's day. Eumenes turned this, for his own purposes, to anti-Roman propaganda:

> In consideration of what services or what generosity such respect was being paid to [Perseus], Eumenes could not see, or say for certain whether this was happening by reason of a certain good luck or whether — and Eumenes feared to suggest this — the ill will felt for the Romans won men over to his cause.[95]

To emphasize his point further, Eumenes brought up the dynastic marriages and in so doing deftly turned all of the activity directed against himself to the appearance of anti-Roman activity. This was pure chicanery, and the Senate should have known it as such since their own commission had reported the rise in Perseus' popularity measured against the fall in Eumenes' support.

Eumenes then became more specific, and one can get a better view, albeit biased, of Perseus' activities between 178 and 175. He established relations with the Boeotians, attempted détente with the Achaeans, and it was to Perseus that some of the Aetolians looked in their own civil strife.[96] Finally, of actual war preparations, Eumenes attested to an alarming level: Perseus had gathered a ten-year supply of grain for an army of 35,000 men, pay for 10,000 mercenaries for ten years, and weapons for an army three times that size. Eumenes declared that these were obviously not intended for internal security and that Perseus "was not preparing war, but almost waging it."[98] No possible accusation was left unmade; Eumenes even attacked "the industry and sobriety of life he showed at such an early age."[99] In short, as Appian puts it, "Of the things that could excite [the Senate's] jealousy, envy, and fear even more strongly than direct accusations, Eumenes omitted nothing."[100] It was the work of a consummate diplomat who knew his audience well. Only a few Senators, the most notable of which was M. Porcius Cato, were

---

[95] Livy 42.12.2-3; for the dynastic marriages, see Livy 42.12.3-4 and App. *Mac.* 11.2.
[96] Livy 42.12.5-7.
[97] Livy 42.12.9-10.
[98] Livy 42.13.5.
[99] App. *Mac.* 11.2: for less "back-handed" praise of Perseus, see Polyb. 25.3.
[100] App. *Mac.* 11.2. It was, also, Eumenes who raised the vision of possible invasion; Livy 42.13.11.

unconvinced. In general, Eumenes' address made a "profound impression" on the Senate, which voted to keep the contents of the speech a secret.[101] This is hardly surprising since the consuls had been quarreling for well over a year about who would get the command against Perseus. The Senate was already convinced; Eumenes was simply telling them what they wished to hear.

When Perseus' ambassadors, led by Harpalus, replied to the charges a few days later, "The Senators' feelings even more than their ears having been prepossessed by King Eumenes, every plea and every excuse of the ambassadors was rejected."[102] It is clear from this that nothing Harpalus could have said would have done any good. Harpalus must have sensed this, for he soon lost his temper, and Livy reports that his arrogance at this point exasperated the Senate. In effect, Harpalus told the Senate the truth, however unpalatable it was to them:

> He said that the King really wished and exerted himself that he should be believed when he pled in his defence that he had neither said nor done anything with hostile intent; but if he saw that a pretext for war was being all too eagerly sought, he would defend himself with resolution.[103]

Other embassies, fearing that Eumenes' charges might implicate them in some way, were in Rome as well. The Rhodians, in particular, were upset with Eumenes' accusations.[104] Much later, Livy reports, "Many Senators blamed Eumenes for causing so great a war on account of his own private grudges."[105] By then, of course, it was too late. For the time being, if the Senate needed a confirmation of their distrust, they soon had it. While on his way to Delphi, Eumenes was assaulted and, rightly or wrongly, Perseus was blamed.[106] The attack was traced to Evander, a Cretan mercenary,

---

[101] Livy 42.14.1. For Cato's reaction, see Plut. *Cat. Mai.* 8.7-8.

[102] Livy 42.14.2.

[103] Livy 42.14.3-4. Harpalus wanted to refute Eumenes' charges to his face, but was denied admittance until after Eumenes left the Senate: App. *Mac.* 11.3.

[104] App. *Mac.* 11.3 (which may anticipate later events). As a result, the Rhodians refused admittance to Eumenes' representative to the festival of Apollo Helios.

[105] *Ibid.*

[106] Livy 42.15.3-16; App. *Mac.* 11.4. The first steps toward war were taken when Rome despatched an embassy to Macedonia to demand reparations and denounce the treaty (Livy 42.25.1), as well as a campaign to isolate Perseus diplomatically (App. *Mac.* 11.4 and Livy 42.19). For the success of these missions, see Livy 42.26.7-9 and Meloni (supra n. 24) 166-84.

and it put just the right emphasis on Eumenes' charges. Other rumors soon became rife, and Livy's account is filled with them. Among the more spectacular and patently ridiculous was that Perseus suborned one Ramnius of Brundisium to poison the Roman generals and envoys on their way to Greece.[107]

Perseus, surprised at the quick march of events, sent another embassy to Rome to mediate. Unfortunately, it too met with rebuff, and the charge of Eumenes' attempted assassination was added to the list of accusations.[108] Perseus tried to answer the charges by stating that the driving of Abrupolis from Thrace, one of Eumenes' earlier points, was done only after Abrupolis had attacked Macedonia and that the whole incident had been fully explained prior to the renewal of the treaty with Rome, that the Dolopi were his subjects, who were punished for killing their governor, and that his only involvement in the death of Arthetaurus, the Illyrian dynast, from another of Eumenes' specifications, was to grant asylum to his assassins, and these he expelled upon hearing of Rome's displeasure.[109] He had been accused of aiding the Aetolians, the Boeotians and the Byzantines, which was true, but in doing so he had notified Rome of his actions.[110] Finally, as for the attempted assassination of Eumenes: "How many Greeks, how many barbarians have sent ambassadors to [the Senate] to complain against Eumenes, to all of whom he is an enemy because he is so base a man."[111] It is the picture of a loyal ally, submitting almost every policy decision, save internal ones, to Rome and deferring to Rome on every point. Further, it was all argued from points made to the Senate itself, and from evidence they could confirm themselves. The Senate's answer was to move for war.[112]

Preparations began almost immediately, and Cn. Sicinius was ordered to prepare a force to leave no later than the Ides of February

---

[107] Livy 42.17.3-9; and App. *Mac.* 11.7 (where the erstwhile assassin is called Erennius).

[108] App. *Mac.* 11.5.

[109] App. *Mac.* 11.6.

[110] App. *Mac.* 11.7.

[111] *Ibid.*

[112] App. *Mac.* 11.9. The Senate began preparations for war almost immediately; Livy 42.27. The chronology of the actual declaration, necessary by fetial law, is uncertain. See F. W. Walbank, "A Note on the Embassy of Q. Marcius Philippus, 172 B.C.," *JRS* 31 (1941) 91 and Meloni (supra n. 24) 176-84.

(which was autumn of 172 by Walbank's calculation).[113] Sicinius was to hold positions in Illyria against any possible Macedonian attack. Meanwhile, a few days after the initial orders to Sicinius, the Senate despatched Q. Marcius Philippus to conduct a diplomatic campaign to isolate Perseus within Greece.[114] During the course of this mission, which was highly successful, Perseus again made an attempt to open negotiations. He sent a letter to Philippus asking why he had come with troops (evidently the escort) and was occupying cities.[115] Philippus refused to answer in writing but verbally stated that Rome was "acting for the protection of the cities themselves."[116] Perseus, nevertheless, persisted in his attempts to open negotiations; when the envoys came to Larisa, he relied on the guest friendship between Philippus and his house to appeal personally for a conference.[117] The meeting took place in the Vale of Tempe.

Perseus, with "a faint breath of hope presenting itself," exhibited a great deal of deference to Philippus.[118] Philippus, however, took a hard line by stating that Perseus' only wise act had been to renew the treaty with Rome.[119] Perseus repeated his defense and capped it with an acute observation: "It does not so much matter what I have done or with what intent as how you will receive the action."[120] At this point, Philippus suggested that Perseus send envoys to the Senate to open up negotiations, an opportunity which Perseus seized. To insure peace in the meantime, Philippus granted, with a show of

[113] Walbank, "Philippus" (supra n. 112) 82. For the preparations and instructions see Livy 42.18.2-3, and for the orders to hold the Illyrian *castella*, 42.27.6. Walbank attributes these, along with the assignment of forces (Livy 42.27.3-6) to annalistic sources.

[114] For the interpretation of "a few days," see Walbank, "Philippus" (supra n. 112) 83-86. For the Philippus embassy, see Livy 42.37; Polyb. 27.1 and Walbank, *Commentary* III (supra n. 1) 294-99.

[115] Livy 42.37.5-9; and Walbank, (supra n. 112) 83-84.

[116] Livy 42.37.6.

[117] Livy 42.38.8. According to Walbank, the meeting took place in October of 172, "Philippus," (supra n. 112) 86.

[118] Livy 42.39.1; for the courtesies shown, see Livy 42.39.4-6. On the conference in general, see Meloni (supra n. 24) 185-90. Dio Cassius (20.22 and Zonaras 9.22) suggests that Perseus needed the delay, but clearly has misinterpreted his sources. See Walbank, "Philippus," supra n. 112) 91-93, where he points out the problems of following the fetial law.

[119] Livy 42.40. Among his claims, Philippus stated that any alliance with Boeotia was forbidden by the treaty, which is demonstrably false. See Livy 33.30 and Polyb. 28.4.4.

[120] Livy 42.42.8.

reluctance, a truce which had been his real purpose in holding the conference in the first place.[121] Livy states directly that the truce and the third embassy to Rome were canards "for the Romans had nothing thoroughly ready for war at this time."[122] Perseus was fully prepared for a war he clearly did not want and, Livy admits, could have begun advantageously. Instead, Perseus seized on "this idle hope for peace."[123] It was another blatant bit of chicanery, and one which held Perseus "immobilized throughout the winter months, in the vain hope of a peace the Senate had not the slightest intention of granting."[124] This has been characterized as *nova sapientia*, and there was a sharp reaction to it among the older members of the Senate.[125] Perseus' envoys were heard, perfunctorily, and ordered to depart Italy within thirty days.[126]

Clearly, Perseus had done his best to avoid the war. No fewer than three embassies were sent to Rome, and a conference was held at Larisa in which he offered reparations. Nor did Perseus' efforts cease there. Even during the war, when he had outmaneuvered this same Philippus, Perseus fell for exactly the same ploy: the hope for peace. He granted Philippus a truce by which the Roman extracted his army from its predicament.[127] In the face of these attempts, continued almost beyond reason by Perseus, it is impossible to maintain either that Perseus inherited the war from Philip V or that he had plotted the war on his own from the beginning.

The majority cf the accusations were excuses rather than causes for the Third Macedonian War. Perseus' actions in trying to isolate Eumenes and to raise his own prestige in Greece diplomatically, rather than by force, can be accepted on face value. Further, it seems clear that Perseus understood his limitations from the very beginning of his reign, judging from his attempts to avoid confrontation in

---

[121] For Perseus' eagerness to continue the negotiations in Rome, see Livy 42.43; Polyb. 27(frgm.).5.8. For Philippus' true intentions, see Livy 42.43.2 and note 118 supra.

[122] Livy 42.43.3.

[123] *Ibid.*

[124] Walbank, "Philippus," (supra n. 112) 86; Livy 42.47.1-3. Dio Cassius reports that the embassy was not even permitted to enter the City (20.22; Zonaras 9.22).

[125] Livy 42.47.4-12, which is particularly damning.

[126] Livy 42.48.1-3. P. Licinius was ordered to muster an army immediately; Livy 42.48.3. Cf. Meloni (supra n. 24) 191-210.

[127] For a full discussion of this incident, see J. Briscoe, Q. Marcius Philippus and *Nova Sapientia*," *JRS* 54 (1964) 66-77.

general and war in particular. What Perseus inherited, or perhaps engendered himself in the Demetrius affair, was an atmosphere of distrust within which each separate act, however well intentioned, was viewed as hostile. The ambitions of the rising *nobiles* in Rome, and of Eumenes in the Aegean, played on what were at worst somewhat naive attempts by Perseus to act properly. The origins of the Third Macedonian War lie not so much in the actions of Perseus, or of Rome, but in the changing nature of Rome's relationship to the Hellenistic East and the change in the attitudes of the *nobilitas*. Perseus was merely caught up between them.

University of Utah

Macedonia and the Settlement of 167 B.C.

ERICH S. GRUEN

Abstract

In the opinion of Polybius, the Third Macedonian War decisively established Roman control and authority over the Hellenic world. The fate of Macedonia is often taken as emblematic of Rome's new role as mistress of the eastern Mediterranean.

Yet the public posture of Rome, in fact, had not altered markedly. She withdrew her forces from Macedonia in 167 and retained the conventional sloganeering of "freedom and autonomy." The governmental changes were designed to develop a new political class which could run affairs, thus to dispense with any further Roman intervention. Closing of the Macedonian mines grew out of a Roman internal conflict and proved to be temporary in application. The peculiar nature of the revenue payments is explained by the traditional requirement of war indemnity, complicated by the fact that the monarchy which would normally be held responsible for it had now been deposed. Neither the political nor the economic measures imply a Roman intent to supervise and control the nation.

Macedonia suffered calamitous defeat in her third war against Rome. Polybius reckoned the conflict as a decisive turning point in the history of Hellas: Rome's power had now reached its zenith, all peoples in agreement that no recourse remained except to obey her behests.[1] So it certainly seemed to the victims of Roman might in 168 and 167, Polybius himself among them. The Republic would not

---

[1] Polyb. 3.4.2-3: ὁμολογούμενον ἐδόκει τοῦτ' εἶναι καὶ κατηναγκασμένον ἅπασιν ὅτι λοιπόν ἐστι Ῥωμαίων ἀκούειν καὶ τούτοις πειθαρχεῖν ὑπὲρ τῶν παραγγελλομένων; cf. 1.1.5, 6.2.3.

abide Hellenic recalcitrance any longer; she would take the eastern world in hand.

The Polybian perspective derives from bitter experience. That lends immediacy, but prevents detachment. Had Roman leaders, in fact, determined to subjugate eastern powers to their will? Did the Third Macedonian War mark the key division in Roman attitudes, a fateful turn toward active dominance in the East? Polybius' affirmative answer still holds the field. Yet the matter is not so simple and the "turning point" is not so sharp. Macedonia herself, three times a beaten foe of Rome, provides the most appropriate test case. Penalties inflicted upon her after the third contest were severe indeed. And they have elicited some immoderate statements.[2] The matter can profit from closer scrutiny.

The Third Macedonian War had shaken Roman confidence and provoked Roman retribution. At its conclusion the Republic took action against Macedonia and Illyria in ways unprecedented through the history of her eastern diplomacy. Rome had made a point of sparing kings who had opposed her in the past, even confirming them on their thrones, and acknowledging them as *amici populi Romani*.[3] Not this time. Perseus, last of the Macedonian monarchs, was dragged to Rome in fetters and humiliation, paraded in his conqueror's triumph, then cast into a dismal dungeon to exacerbate his torment.[4] The penance demanded of Perseus served as symbol for the larger settlement now imposed on his nation. The Senate put an end to the institution of monarchy itself in Macedonia. Henceforth, four separate republics would constitute the political geography of the land. The arrangements, formulated on senatorial instructions, were

---

[2] The treatment of Macedonia has commonly been taken as exemplary of a Roman shift toward a forceful suzerainty; e.g. B. Niese, *Geschichte der griechischen und makedonischen Staaten seit Chaeronea* III (Gotha 1893) 180, 312: "ganz Makedonien und Hellas . . . mussten sich gewöhnen römische Untertanen zu sein"; J. A. O. Larsen, *Greek Federal States* (Oxford 1968) 297-98: "they were expected to be ready to listen to directives coming from Rome"; R. M. Errington, *The Dawn of Empire: Rome's Rise to World Power* (London 1971) 222: "From now on, Rome was not only the acknowledged mistress of the Mediterranean world, but she was also prepared to act the part . . . a decisive change, a turning point, in Rome's whole attitude to . . . the development of the empire." The same interpretation now in the recent study of W. Dahlheim, *Gewalt und Herrschaft: Das provinziale Herrschaftssystem der römischen Republik* (Berlin 1977) 117-20.

[3] Cf. Polyb. 21.11.5-10; Livy 37.25.8-12; Diod. 31.8.1.

[4] Livy 45.40.6; Diod. 31.9; Plut. *Aem*. 33.3-34.2, 37.1-2. The king's advisers, Macedonian military commanders, and those closest to the throne were also deported to Italy; Livy 45.32.3-6.

Macedonia and the Settlement of 167 B.C.

implemented by Rome's victorious general L. Aemilius Paullus and the commission of ten legates dispatched by the *patres*.[5] They fixed the boundaries of the four districts and authorized installation of the governing bodies for each district. The regions were to be kept strictly separate, only minimal contact between them permitted, no marriages or commercial intercourse across the frontiers.[6] The Roman ruling class had evidently resolved to assure fragmentation, that they might never again have to face a united Macedonia.

The economic resources of the nation left a deep impression in Rome. Booty brought to Italy from the treasury of the king astounded observers, the more astounding as they reckoned up the sums. Captured loot did not even include the moneys spent on the war itself or lost in Perseus' desperate flight before surrender. The state had evidently accumulated staggering wealth in a mere thirty years since the close of the Second Macedonian War.[7] Such accumulation could not be tolerated again. The Senate took aim at the Macedonian economy. A decree of the *patres* cancelled the leasing of revenues from the mines and from the rural properties of the crown. Paullus and the *decem legati* subsequently closed down the gold and silver mines altogether, while allowing the continuance of the iron and copper mines.[8] Other directives prohibited traffic in salt and the cutting of ship timber.[9] And, most significant, half the *tributum* which Macedonians had previously remitted to their king would now be due to the Roman treasury.[10] The Senate had seen to it that Macedonia could never again amass resources on the scale that Perseus had commanded.

Comparable measures were directed against Illyria. Genthius, ruler of the Ardiaeans and ally of Perseus in the latter stages of war, suffered a fate akin to that of his Macedonian counterpart. He rode before a Roman triumphal chariot, was then interned with his family and entourage at Iguvium, and subsequently disappears from history.[11] The Ardiaean monarchy disappeared as well. A commission of five did the Senate's work in Illyria. They dismantled the

---

[5] Livy 45.17.1-3, 45.29.1-3; Diod. 31.8.6.
[6] Livy 45.18.6-7, 45.29.5-10, 45.32.1-2; Diod. 31.8.8-9.
[7] Livy 45.40.1-3.
[8] Livy 45.18.3, 45.29.11; Diod. 31.8.7.
[9] Livy 45.29.11, 45.29.14.
[10] Livy 45.18.7, 45.29.4; Diod. 31.8.3; Plut. *Aem.* 28.3.
[11] Livy 45.43.6, 45.43.9.

monarchy and divided up Illyria into three independent districts.[12] Financial arrangements also followed the lines of the Macedonian settlement. The Illyrians would hereafter send to Rome half the sums they normally provided to their kings — with the exception of those communities which had defected to Rome in the war and now enjoyed immunity.[13]

The import of these enactments seems clear enough. Rome had determined to strip Macedonia and Illyria of the military and financial resources that might sustain any future war. The Illyrian fleet was confiscated and awarded to Roman allies on the Hellenic coast of the Adriatic. Three of the four Macedonian republics were permitted to retain border guards to fend off the barbarian, but Rome eliminated the national army of the kingdom.[14]

A larger question now needs to be faced. Did these arrangements signal a new direction in Roman policy — a move toward more direct supervision and the conversion of Macedonia into a Roman dependency? The inference would be hasty and misleading. Despite the Polybian analysis, Roman behavior lends itself to a different interpretation. The Republic hoped to institute stable political circumstances in Macedonia that would dampen the nation's external ambitions but promote its internal vitality.

Rome's armies withdrew from Macedonia in 167, just as they had withdrawn from the East after all previous wars. The reluctance to extend administration to that part of the world remained unshaken. And the removal of troops also gave public sign of Rome's confidence in the new Macedonian regimes. The Senate's official pronouncement set the tone: Macedonians and Illyrians would be free, thus to demonstrate to the world that Roman arms bring liberty to the enslaved rather than servitude to the free.[15] Aemilius Paullus then applied the tried and true formulas, long familiar to Hellenistic diplomacy: Macedonians would be autonomous, retain possession of their cities and lands, operate under their own laws, and choose their own officials.[16] To be sure, this was propaganda. None will mistake

[12] Livy 45.17.1, 45.17.4, 45.18.1, 45.26.15; Diod. 31.8.6.

[13] Livy 45.18.7, 45.26.13-14; Diod. 31.8.3, 31.8.5.

[14] Livy 45.29.14, 45.43.10; Diod. 31.8.9.

[15] Livy 45.18.1: *liberos esse placebat Macedonas atque Illyrios, ut omnibus gentibus appareret arma populi Romani non liberis servitutem, sed contra servientibus libertatem adferre*; cf. 45.22.3, 45.26.12, 45.32.3-4; Diod. 31.8.1-3; Plut. *Aem.* 28.3; and see Polyb. 36.17.13: μεταλαβόντες ἀπὸ δουλείας ὁμολογουμένως ἐλευθερίαν.

[16] Livy 45.29.4; Diod. 31.8.4-6; Plut. *Aem.* 29.1.

Macedonia and the Settlement of 167 B.C.

the Roman attitude for philanthropy. "Freedom and autonomy" were catchwords, understood and acceptable, even when, indeed especially when, enforced by the great powers. It does not follow, however, that they lacked content, mere sloganeering without substance.

The new political arrangements suggest a serious effort to install working governments. Details are obscure and disputed. The evidence simply does not suffice to reconstruct the actual machinery. But it is clear that each of the Macedonian districts was to have its own governing body and its own capital, to collect its own revenues, and to elect its own magistrates.[17] Whether those governing bodies were primary assemblies or representative organs remains beyond recovery — and unimportant for our purposes. Nor can we ascertain to what extent the four districts were independent political units rather than part of a larger Macedonian entity.[18] They were, in any case, independent of Roman direction. Aemilius Paullus left the country, admonishing its citizens to remember their benefactors but to preserve their own liberty through order and concord.[19] The words recall those of T. Quinctius Flamininus a generation earlier, on the eve of his departure from Hellas: the *libertas* which Rome has restored

[17] Livy 45.29.9: *capita regionum, ubi concilia fierent . . . eo concilia suae cuiusque regionis indici, pecuniam conferri, ibi magistratus creari* [Paullus] *iussit*; Diod. 31.8.8-9; see also Livy 45.18.7. The officials are perhaps to be distinguished from the annual magistrates elected by individual communities; Livy 45.29.4; Justin 33.2.7. The latter are identified by C. Schuler, "The Macedonian Politarchs," *CP* 55 (1960) 90-100, with politarchs, known from later inscriptions. But the office may well have existed before 167, not necessarily a Roman creation; see B. Helly, "Politarques, Poliarques et Politophylaques," *AM* 2 (1977) 531-44; cf. F. Gschnitzer, *s.v.* "Politarches," *RE*, Suppl. 13, 483-500.

[18] The case for primary assemblies was argued by M. Feyel, "Paul-Émile et le synedrion macédonien," *BCH* 70 (1946) 187-98; challenged by J. A. O. Larsen, "*Consilium* in Livy xlv. 18.6-7 and the Macedonian *Synedria*," *CP* 44 (1949) 73-90, who reckoned the *concilia* (*consilia*) as representative bodies; cf. T. Frank, "Representative Government in the Macedonian Republics," *CP* 9 (1914) 49-59. The matter should be left open; cf. A. Aymard, "L'organization de la Macédoine en 167 et la régime représentatif dans le monde grec," *CP* 45 (1950) 96-107; F. W. Walbank, *A Historical Commentary on Polybius*, III (Oxford 1979) 467. Livy elsewhere speaks of *senatores quos synhedros vocant*; 45.32.2; cf. Polyb. 31.2.12: δημοκρατικῆς καὶ συνεδριακῆς πολιτείας; 31.17.2. But that is not enough to establish the existence of a federal body administering all four republics, as argued by Feyel, *loc. cit.*; so also, more recently, F. Papazoglou, "Quelques aspects de l'histoire de la province de Macédoine, *ANRW* II.7.1 (1979), 305, who stresses that the individual units did not have separate names; they were simply μερίδες, i.e. *partes*. Papazoglou, *op. cit.*, 353-54, even postulates a Macedonian *koinon* that preceded the Roman intervention. The speculation does not advance understanding.

[19] Plut. *Aem.* 29.1: παρακαλέσας τοὺς Μακεδόνας μεμνῆσθαι τῆς δεδομένης ὑπὸ Ῥωμαίων ἐλευθερίας σώζοντας αὐτὴν δι' εὐνομίας καὶ ὁμονοίας.

is now left to Greeks to defend and secure.[20] Rome's posture had thus undergone no radical change. Establishment and endorsement of the new governments had as a principal aim effective management by the Macedonians themselves — thereby to permit Roman withdrawal and render needless any future intervention. The Romans still shunned administration in the East.

The economic measures seem at first glance more devastating. A closing of the gold and silver mines and the exaction of annual tribute, half of what had been paid to Macedonian rulers, might suggest that the relationship was now placed on an entirely new footing: rigorous exploitation of Macedonian resources and reduction of the land to a Roman dependency. The issue needs reconsideration.

First, the mines. A decision to close them down would have severe repercussions on the Macedonian economy. Was this Rome's intent? It is generally overlooked that the initial resolution of the senate said nothing about shutting off the operations of the mines. The *senatus consultum* declared rather that farming out of the revenues from the mines, as well as from the rural estates of the crown, should be terminated.[21] This places the episode into a context different from that of mere exploitation. Livy offers reasons for the senatorial decree: the leasing of contracts to operate the mines would mean recourse to the *publicani* whose involvement inevitably erodes public law and the liberty of Roman allies, whereas to have Macedonians themselves administer the revenues runs the risk of stirring sedition and upheaval.[22] The motives need not be doubted. Livy very probably reproduces the substance of senatorial argument against

---

[20] Livy 34.49.11: *redditam libertatem sua cura custodirent servarentque*.

[21] Livy 45.18.3: *metalli quoque Macedonici, quod ingens vectigal erat, locationes praediorumque rusticorum tolli placebat*. M. H. Crawford, "Rome and the Greek World: Economic Relationships," *Economic History Review* 30 (1977) 44, incorrectly takes this to mean that "the senate originally wished to close the mines in Macedonia, apparently without exception." The text does not warrant any such conclusion. Nor are there grounds for the assertion of Larsen, (supra n. 2) 299, that "the mines and royal estates were confiscated and became the property of the Roman state." Similarly, Papazoglou (supra n. 18) 305, n. 8: "les mines et les domaines royaux ont été confisqués par les Romaines en 168." Some Macedonian lands were in Roman possession by 63 B.C.; Cicero ascribes their acquisition partly to Flamininus, partly to Paullus; *De Lege Agrar.* 1.5. That hardly suggests widespread confiscation in 168/167 — there certainly was none at the time of Flamininus — and it says nothing about the mines.

[22] Livy 45.18.4-5: *nam neque sine publicano exerceri posse et, ubi publicanus esset, ibi aut ius publicum vanum aut libertatem sociis nullam esse*. Diodorus 31.8.7 does not mention *publicani* explicitly but his explanation parallels closely that of Livy.

Macedonia and the Settlement of 167 B.C.

Roman management of the mines. The background to that decision can be reconstructed without difficulty. *Publicani* surely lobbied for the system of letting contracts for mines and public estates, a system comparable to that already in effect in Spain. They could make a case for transferring that mode of operation to Macedonia, thereby bringing profit both to the state treasury and to the *societates publicanorum*. The senate, however, did not buy their argument. Resistance to the *publicani* materialized for reasons readily comprehensible. Two years earlier, an altercation between the censors and representatives of the *veteres publicani* led to public disputes, tribunician interference, and the near condemnation of a censor. The fierce conflict, stemming from disagreements over the letting of contracts, had reverberations that still echoed in 167.[23]

Domestic politics had thus intervened to shape senatorial opinion. Precisely how the *patres* envisioned the operation of the mines without awarding contracts to *publicani* and without leaving it in the hands of Macedonians is unclear. L. Paullus, in any case, found a solution: the silver and gold mines were to be shut down completely, while the iron and copper mines would continue to function, evidently under Macedonian supervision, with half of the taxes previously paid to the king now due to the Roman *aerarium*.[24] Greed for Macedonian revenues and desire for subjugation of the land do not explain Roman policy. Internal political circumstances played the predominant role. Thwarting the *publicani* took precedence over any intent to control Macedonia and her resources. The sequel to these events bears out the conclusion. A decade later, when conflict between *publicani* and *patres* had lost its relevance, the mines of Macedonia were quietly reopened.[25] The evidence fails to specify whether Romans or Macedonians were to administer them. In view of the fact that Macedonians had operated the iron and copper mines for a

---

[23] Livy 43.16; cf. 44.16.8. The connection is rightly discerned by E. Badian, *Publicans and Sinners: Private Enterprise in the Service of the Roman Republic* (Ithaca, N.Y. 1972) 39-42. A more elaborate analysis, also accepting the association, can now be found in G. Calboli, *Marci Porci Catonis Oratio Pro Rhodiensibus* (Bologna 1978) 150-81, who observes that the censor under fire in 169, C. Claudius Pulcher, was one of the *decem legati* in Macedonia in 167; Livy 43.16, 45.17.2. Coincidence is unlikely. The conjecture of L. Perelli, "La chiusura delle miniere macedoni dopo Pidna," *RivFC*, 103 (1975) 410-12, that the mines were closed because an over-supply of metal depressed its value and fed inflation, lacks concrete testimony.

[24] Livy 45.29.11: *Metalla quoque auri atque argenti non exerceri, ferri et aeris permitti. Vectigal exercentibus dimidium eius impositum quod pependissent regi.*

[25] Cassiodorus, *Chron.* s.v. 158 B.C.

decade without incident allows the inference that Rome was content to have them run the gold and silver concessions as well.[26]

Next, the collection of tribute. This would appear to have broader ramifications. On the face of it, the exaction of regular payments to the Roman treasury implied enduring subjection to the western power. Such is the construction placed upon it by most scholars.[27] Rome's settlement obliged the conquered Macedonians to supply the *aerarium* half of what they had customarily rendered to the Antigonids.[28]

Must this be understood, however, as a permanent, regular levy signifying a state of dependency? No source affirms that the tax was established in perpetuity. Burdens imposed by victor upon vanquished were, of course, standard practice. Rome conventionally demanded indemnity payments to cover the expenses of war — and to penalize her defeated foes. The Macedonians fully expected such exactions. Advisers of Perseus had recommended that the king agree to them in advance in 171, in order to avert war.[29] Perseus himself expressed willingness to indemnify the Romans on the same terms imposed upon his father a quarter-century earlier — although the Macedonians had recently secured a victory on the battlefield.[30] Rome naturally would not consider ending a war upon the heels of a defeat. Arrangements would have to await a Macedonian surrender. When that came, infliction of an indemnity was inevitable.

This time, however, a different situation imposed itself. The distinction, overlooked though obvious, needs to be stressed. It

---

[26] Perelli (supra n. 23) 408-409, argues that the Macedonians must have administered the mines, on the grounds that Roman *publicani* could only operate in a Roman province. The argument, however, founders on the facts; see Diod. 36.3. Badian (supra n. 23) 128, n. 41, takes the opposite line, assuming that Rome still considered it too dangerous to allow Macedonians to control the gold and silver deposits. But Macedonian quiescence since 167 may have allayed those fears. And senatorial suspicions about the *publicani* probably still lingered. Crawford (supra n. 21) 45, suggests that the reopening of the mines was connected with the resumption of silver coinage at Rome in 157; cf. Crawford, *Roman Republican Coinage* I (Cambridge 1974) 47-48, 74; II, 635. A possible, but unverifiable, conjecture.

[27] E.g. Niese (supra n. 2) 180; E. Will, *Histoire politique du monde hellénistique* II (Nancy 1957) 236; Larsen (supra n. 2) 298; Crawford (supra n. 21) 44; J. L. Ferrary, in C. Nicolet, *Rome et la conquête du monde méditerranéen* 2 (Paris 1978) 759-60; W. H. Harris, *War and Imperialism in Republican Rome, 327-70 B.C.* (Oxford 1979) 73.

[28] Livy 45.18.7, 45.26.13, 45.29.4; Diod. 31.8.3. One hundred talents, according to Plut. *Aem.* 28.3.

[29] Livy 42.50.2.

[30] Polyb. 27.8.2; Livy, 42.62.10.

Macedonia and the Settlement of 167 B.C.

reintroduces a point made earlier. Rome had treated conquered kings with generosity in the past — at least to the extent of permitting retention of their thrones. As a by-product of that policy, of course, the surviving monarchs had responsibility for discharging the indemnity payments. Those circumstances no longer held in the wake of the Third Macedonian War. Rome had deposed Perseus and terminated the Antigonid dynasty. And the Senate made it clear that their quarrel had been with the king, not with the Macedonian populace. The latter had now been "liberated."[31] Rome's international posture rested on projection of that image. Who then would defray the costs of war? An intriguing dilemma. The form of reimbursement shouldered by the new Macedonian republics here receives its explanation. The *patres* hit upon a scheme consonant both with their *dignitas* and with their propaganda. Macedonian citizens would continue paying the same taxes they had always paid — hence, not technically a penalty. Half the funds would remain in the country, presumably to finance the new governments and promote smooth administration. The other half would revert to Rome as reimbursement for war expenditures. The people were free, so it could be affirmed, for their resources no longer went to support a monarchic autocracy.[32]

How long these payments continued or were expected to continue cannot be determined. The sources make no further reference to them.[33] Once they provided the sums to recover Rome's outlay in the war, they may, for all we know, have been allowed to lapse.[34] To be sure, Rome suspended in 167 the collection of *tributum* which she had

---

[31] See, especially, Diod. 31.8.1-4; Livy 45.18.1-2, 45.32.3-7.

[32] Polyb. 36.17.13; cf. 30.31.9. It is noteworthy that the payment of half their taxes is directly associated with the "freeing" of Macedonians and Illyrians; Livy 45.29.4; Diod. 31.8.3, 31.8.5. In fact, some of the Illyrians were tax exempt, others required to pay half to Rome, but all were "free"; Livy 45.26.12-14; cf. L. Robert, "Inscriptions hellénistiques de Dalmatie," *Hellenica* 11-12 (1960) 509-14.

[33] One may bring into the reckoning I *Macc.* 8.4, which mentions annual tribute paid to Rome by the "kings." In all probability, however, this refers to indemnity exactions. It cannot, in any case, apply to Macedonia after 167, which no longer had a monarchy.

[34] That the payments were indemnities, rather than permanent tribute, was suggested long ago by Frank (supra n. 18) 58, who, however, needlessly saw the hand of an "anti-imperialistic party." The suggestion was endorsed by Badian, *Roman Imperialism in the Late Republic* (Oxford 1968) 18-19; and Dahlheim (supra n. 2) 255-61. In the most recent discussion, however, Harris (supra n. 27) 73-74, again finds Rome's purpose to be that of enriching herself, the taxation "set at the maximum level possible."

periodically demanded of Italians, not to be revived for more than a century. It is natural to connect this with an annual income derived from Macedonia.[35] Yet the connection nowhere appears in the evidence. Rather, the release of Romans and Italians from *tributum* is consistently associated with the windfall of booty from the East.[36] The only explicit testimony, in fact, late though it be and largely ignored, specifies that Macedonia became tributary not in 167 but in 148.[37] That testimony, in light of circumstances and attitudes outlined above, deserves more respect than it has customarily been accorded. One need not embrace the standard proposition that Rome transformed Macedonia and Illyria into tax-paying vassal states in the wake of the Third Macedonian War.

The Romans would neither occupy nor administer those lands. They carried back captured booty, as always after conquest. They set up a schedule of payments to recover losses incurred in the war. They unseated the monarchs, fragmented the kingdoms, and reduced the economic power of those nations in order to render them militarily harmless. But they fostered new governments that could run themselves without Roman supervision and that could maintain concord without (it was hoped) Roman intervention. The Republic evidently promoted the prospects of success for the post-Antigonid regimes. Reopening the gold and silver mines in 158 very probably represents a move to ease economic pressure and perhaps facilitate remission of the indemnity. The move would also strengthen the new leadership and serve the interests of stability.

The results, of course, did not sustain expectations. In retrospect, it is plain that the expectations were naive from the start. To permit Macedonians to "live under their own laws" while abolishing the monarchic system that had been in force for centuries amounts to a contradiction in terms. Polybius alleges that the settlement of 167 relieved the Macedonians of civil strife and internal disorders.[38] That may have been the purpose, but it did not prove to be the outcome. Within four years of the settlement Macedonians were already quarreling among themselves. The people had not yet adjusted, so

---

[35] So, most recently, Crawford (supra n. 21) 44; Ferrary (supra n. 27) 760.

[36] Cic. *De Off.* 2.76; Pliny, *NH* 33.56; Plut. *Aem.* 38.1; Val. Max. 4.3.8.

[37] Eusebius, *Chron.* 424 (Helm): Μακέδονας . . . ὑποφόρους ἐποίησαν. The same in Porphyry, *FGrH* 260, 3, 19; Jerome, *Chron.* 143C (Helm): *Romani interfecto Pseudofilippo Macedonas tributarios faciunt.*

[38] Polyb. 36.17.13.

Polybius put it, to democratic and republican institutions.[39] Deep-seated sentiments for monarchy endured in the land, even persistent loyalty to the house of the Antigonids. Those feelings would eventually culminate in the revolt of Andriscus and doom the settlement of 167.

The consequences bely Rome's foresight but do not comdemn her intent. The *patres* had resolved to leave Macedonia with functioning polities that would obviate the need for external interference. Rome turned her attention elsewhere.[40] The alternative would have been a burdensome and unwelcome administration. In 167, as before, the Republic rejected that alternative. Some may have argued for it. The *publicani* certainly hoped for a share of the profits, and their advocates in the senatorial class had a case to make on their behalf. But Cato spoke for the majority: since the Macedonians cannot be defended, best to leave them free.[41]

University of California, Berkeley

---

[39] Polyb. 31.2.12, 31.17.2.

[40] When upheaval occurred in 163, Rome did no more than send an "investigatory" commission — an embassy with a broad range of duties in the East for whom a stop in Macedonia was but a sidelight; Polyb. 31.2.9-14. A dozen years later, in 151, Macedonian leaders, still plagued with internal *stasis*, ceased even to make official appeal to Rome, calling instead upon Scipio Aemilianus, son of the man who had implemented the settlement of 167. But Scipio too declined to intervene; he found campaigns in Spain more to his taste; Polyb. 35.4.10-12.

[41] *SHA*, "Hadrian," 5.3: *Macedonas liberos pronuntiavit, quia tueri non poterant.*

Polybius, Pliny, and the Via Egnatia

JOHN PAUL ADAMS

Abstract

Old and new epigraphical material, referring to property and highway marking, offers the means to investigate statistics and literary sources which refer to distances on the Via Egnatia. A new milestone of Cn. Egnatius gives a firm distance to Thessalonike from Dyrrachium or Apollonia of 267/268 mp. Pliny's confusions can be resolved by emendation in the light of the new *datum* and by an appreciation of his method. Strabo's reports of Polybius indicate that the road was dealt with in segments, that geometrical calculation provided intermediate and long distances, that Polybius certainly knew some Roman distances, and that he had a unique method of converting from Roman miles to Greek stadia.

The full extent of Polybius' knowledge is obscured by losses in Strabo VII. Strabo's Vatican Epitomator produced two monstrous and misleading confusions, which can however be rectified to restore sense to Strabo and thus Polybius. Polybius did have Roman distances at least as far as Cypsela, and he could have had (geometrical) distances to the Bosporus, if not (perhaps) Roman distances. Thus, reconciliation of statistics found in epigraphical and literary texts is possible, leading to a more correct understanding of the methods of geographers of the Via Egnatia.

The lands of northern Greece, the homeland of Philip II and of Alexander III, as well as the land in which they campaigned, is not a land which accommodates itself easily to the army, the administrator, the merchant or the traveller. Lofty mountain ranges, deep gorges, swift and rocky torrents, lakes, swamps, and other barriers not only break up Macedonia into a considerable number of discrete regions, but also canalize the pedestrian and vehicular traffic which must

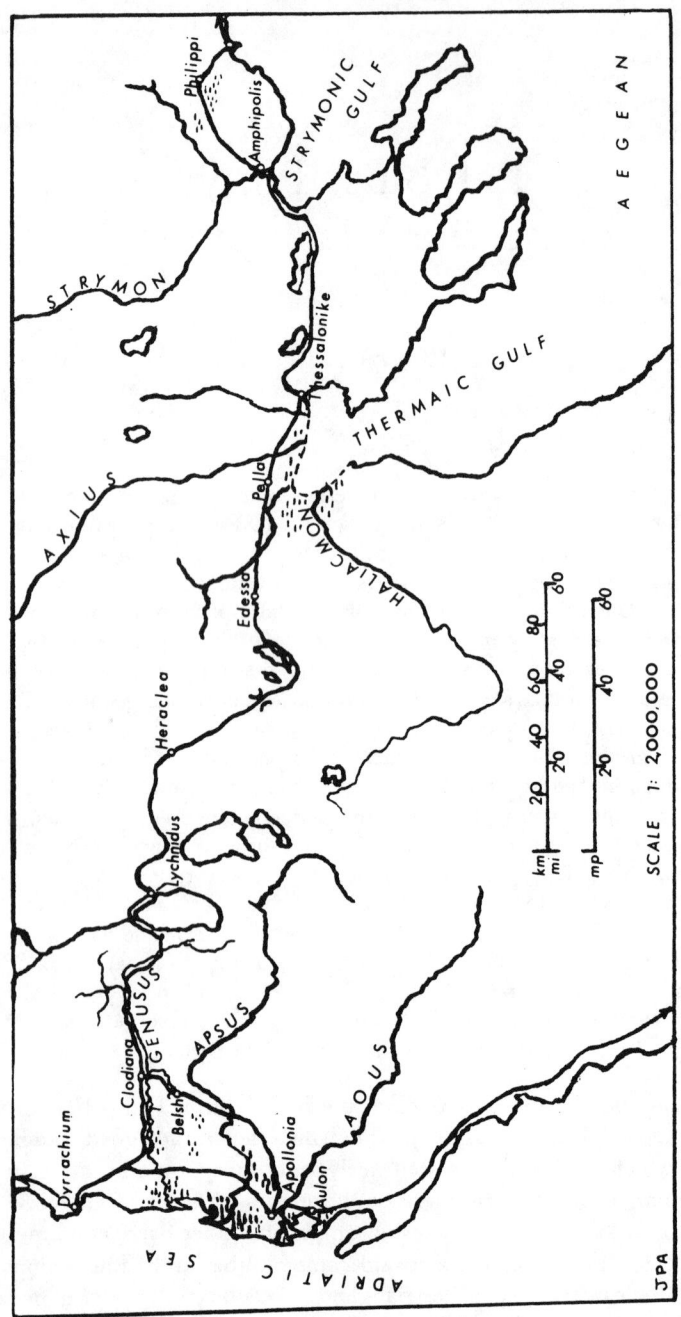

Fig. 1 The Via Egnatia in Macedonia

Polybius, Pliny, and the Via Egnatia

make its way across them.[1] In the east-west direction, there is only one clear, natural and convenient road. Though it was known from time immemorial,[2] we are accustomed (following Strabo, if not perhaps Polybius) to give it the name Via Egnatia. It has, Strabo says, two western termini on the Adriatic Sea,[3] and it proceeds by way of Lichnidus, Heraclea Lyncestis, Edessa, Pella, Thessalonike, Apollonia, Amphipolis and Philippi towards the east, ultimately terminating (as Cicero informs us[4]) at the Hellespont, or (as Polybius and Pliny state[5]) at Byzantium.[6]

---

[1] Geography of Macedonia and Thrace: N. G. L. Hammond, *Hist Mace* I 19-58, 142-49, 195-96; N. G. L. Hammond, *Epirus* (Oxford 1967) 425-83; Dimitrios Sampsaris, *Historikē geōgraphia tēs anatolikēs Makedonias kata tēn archaiotēta* [in Greek] (Thessaloniki 1976) especially 43-59, 143-64; Stanley Casson, *Macedonia, Thrace, and Illyria* (Oxford 1926) 13-19, 21-24, 40-44; Velizar Velkov, *Cities in Thrace and Dacia in Late Antiquity* (Amsterdam 1977).

Much useful information of various sorts — some of it unreliable — can be found in Konrad Miller, *Itineraria Romana* (Stuttgart 1916), 516-27, and exceedingly useful testimonia and bibliography in Jaroslav Šašel (ed.), Tabula Imperii Romani, K34: Naissus, Dyrrhachion, Scupi, Serdica, Thessalonike (Ljubljana 1976), though the map of the area does not take into account some of the important modifications of the route of the Via Egnatia in the valley of the Skhumbi River due to N. G. L. Hammond, "The Western Part of the Via Egnatia," *JRS* 64 (1974) 185-94 (hereafter, Hammond "Western . . . Via Egnatia"), or in the neighborhood of Lake Begorritis (Lake Ostrovo), suggested by Pierre A. MacKay, "The Route of the Via Egnatia around Lake Ostrovo," *AM* II 201-10.

[2] N. G. L. Hammond, *Migrations and Invasions in Greece and Adjacent Areas* (Park Ridge, N.J. 1976) 29-33, and Hammond, *Epirus* (supra n. 1), 409, 439, 449. The old standard work on the Via Egnatia, that of Gottlieb Lukas Friedrich Tafel, *De via militari Romanorum Egnatia, qua Illyricum, Macedonia et Thracia iungebantur* (Tubingen /Berlin 1837-41) is still useful. See also Ch. Makaronas, "Via Egnatia and Thessalonike," *Studies presented to David M. Robinson* I (St. Louis 1951) 380-88; Charles Edson, "The Location of Cellae and the Route of the Via Egnatia in Western Macedonia," *CP* 46 (1951) 1-16; G. Radke, "Egnatia Via," *RE* Supp. XIII (1973) 1666-67; Paul Collart, "Les milliaires de la Via Egnatia," *BCH* 100 (1976) 177-200 (hereafter, Collart, "Milliaires"); Paul Collart, "Une réfection de la 'Via Egnatia' sous Trajan," *BCH* 59 (1935) 395-415; and Georges Daux, "Le milliaire de la Via Egnatia au musée du Louvre," *JS* (Juillet-Septembre 1977) 145-63.

[3] Polybius 34.12.4 = Strabo 7.7.4 C322.

[4] Cicero *de prov. cons.* 2.4; Pliny *NH* 4.11(18).50.

[5] Polybius 34.12.9-10 = Strabo *Epitome* VII F 57 Meinecke (*Epitome Vaticana*); Pliny *NH* 4.11(18).46. Cf. Strabo *Epitome* VII F 10 (*Epitome edita*).

[6] Caution is necessary in assessing the details of geography. The statistics in Strabo (*Epitome* VII F 57) are a bone of contention (*infra*, n. 43 and Part V of this paper). A distance from Perinthus to Byzantium of 630 stadia is given; a distance from the Hebrus and Cypsela to the Cyanean Rocks of 3100 stadia is attributed to Artemidorus; a distance from Apollonia to Byzantium of 7320 stadia is alleged; and a statement is made that Polybius adds 180 more stadia (to the 7320?). Demetrius of

The exact course of this roadway, and the exact sites of towns situated on it, is not only a concern to the topographer, but is of critical importance to the archaeologist, the epigraphist, and the historian. The total distance of the Via Egnatia, as well as the relative distances between the intermediate points on it, can have considerable significance, especially as we attempt to understand the methods and the narratives of our literary sources. The evidence of epigraphy, however, is of more immediate concern, for it not only reveals something valuable about pre-Roman habits of marking highways in Macedonia, but also presents us with an important new datum for our study of the Via Egnatia.

I

There are a number of indications that some care was given to this east-west highway even before it became the Via Egnatia in the third quarter of the second century B.C.[7] In his excellent study of the Roman *mansio* at Cellae, Charles Edson republished the evidence for the existence of road markers of a far earlier period.[8] The texts are much the same in form, and are engraved on four-sided pillars about three feet high (0.95 m H, 0.32 m W, 0.17 m D in the case of #1):

Skepsis gives the distance from Perinthus to Byzantium as 600 stadia, and other (irrelevant) data are recorded. The Epitomator is condensing the text of Strabo, now missing, where a summary of various statements on the length of Macedonia and Thrace from the Ionian Sea to the Bosporus were being tabulated. Polybius was one of these, it seems, but it is obvious that Artemidorus and Demetrius belong to a later time, and that the testimonia are a compilation (of Strabo). Two questions arise. Whose is the distance of 630 stadia? What did Polybius write in his text — if anything — to which Strabo makes reference? The Epitomator is obviously interested in the statistics, and not in the explanation. It needs to be explained, in any case, that the Cyanean Rocks to which Artemidorus calculates are some 30 mp beyond Byzantium, at the edge of the north entrance to the Bosporus, a distance which can be supplied from Arrian, *Periplus Maris Euxini* 25 (G. Marenghi, *Arriano, Periplo del Ponto Eusino* [Naples 1958] 108; Roos-Wirth, Edd. *Flavii Arriani Quae exstant omnia* II [Leipzig 1968] 128; *GGM* I 423, and cf. 424-26).

[7] See, e. g., Dietrich Müller, "Von Doriskos nach Therme, Der Weg des Xerxes-Heeres durch Thrakien und Ostmakedonien," *Chiron* 5 (1975) 1-11. A new boundary stone was reported recently from the excavations being conducted by Dimitrios Lazaridis at Amphipolis, *Praktika* 1975 (1977) 65-66 #5, with Plate 57 γ; *SEG* 27 (1977) 255. Lazaridis expresses uncertainty, however, as to whether this small stone (0.65m H and 0.18m W) is a road marker or a property marker. The text reads simply ΟΡΟΣ.

[8] Edson (supra n. 2) 11-12.

#1 Philippi	#2 Drama, in a house	#3 Drama, in a house
(Collart, 1933)	(Heuzey, 1861)	(Giannopoulos, 1893)
ΟΡΟΣ	ὅρος	ὅρος
ΤΗΣΟ	τῆς ὁ	τῆς
ΔΟΥ	δοῦ	ὁδοῦ

There is a question, first of all, about the actual number of stones. #1 certainly exists, and Edson dates it (by letter forms) "not later than the third century B.C."[9] Louis Robert is quoted by Paul Collart in the *editio princeps* as agreeing "qu' elle peut être du IVe siècle avant notre ère."[10] Collart himself speculates that the stone might go back as far as the decade 360-350 B.C., when the Thasians founded the colony at Krenides and when Philip II drove them out and created Philippi.[11] With regard to #2, however, there is uncertainty. Collart believed that #1 is the same as #2, although the stone had been moved between the time it had been seen by Léon Heuzey in a house at Drama in 1861 and Collart's rediscovery of it on a hill behind the Acropolis at Philippi in the 1930's.[12] Giannopoulos also saw a stone in a house in Drama (#3) and published it in 1893;[13] but the *omicron* of the word ὁδος is not in line two, as it is on #1 and #2, but rather on line three. There is therefore some question as to whether #3 is actually the same as #2.

Edson saw no reason to doubt the accuracy of Giannopoulos' report, but he did believe that #1 was not the same as #2; for him there are three stones.[14] For Collart, there can be no more than two,

---

[9] Ibid. 11.

[10] Paul Collart, "Inscriptions de Philippes," *BCH* 57 (1933) 363-65 #23, with photograph (hereafter, Collart "Inscriptions"). Paul Collart, *Philippes, ville de Macédoine* II, Planches (Paris 1937) Plate XXVII.2.

[11] Collart "Inscriptions" (supra n. 10) 365. Hammond, *Hist Mace* I 56-57.

[12] Collart "Inscriptions" (supra n. 10) 363-64. Cf. M. G. Demitsas, *Sylloge Inscriptionum Graecarum et Latinarum Macedoniae (E Makedonia en lithois* . . . [in Greek]) II (Athens 1896) 783 #1016.

[13] N. Giannopoulos, reported *per litteras* in *BCH* 17 (1893) 633: "MACÉDOINE. *Drama* et région voisine. Inscriptions communiqueés par M. Giannopoulos. — avec des copies nouvelles, sans variantes utiles, de *CIL* . . . Heuzey . . . *Drama*. . . . Maison de Pantélaki Pantazidis. Marbre blanc, formant marche d' escalier.ΟΡΟΣ | ΤΗΣ | ΟΔΟΥ."

[14] Edson (supra n. 2) 12: "If the line divisions have been correctly reproduced, which there is no reason to doubt, this roadmarker was different from the one seen by Heuzey at Drama. It is probably to be dated to the same general period as the other two texts."

for he theorizes that #1 was removed from a house in Drama, and carried some 20 km to Philippi. But this is only a theory, without a reason; and despite the well known phenomenon of *pierres errantes,* it seems unlikely that a stone would be carried from a house in an inhabited city to a rather inaccessible place in uninhabited ruins. While #1 cannot confidently be stated to be the one from Drama, therefore, neither can it be said to be *in situ,* and consequently Collart's assertion that it came from a route which united Philippi to the sea, "soit à l'époque de son fondateur [Philip II, 356 B.C.] soit à l'époque plus ancienne de la colonie Thasienne établie par Kallistratos à Krenides [Philippi] en 360," cannot be more than another theory.[15] Likewise, since the stone or stones at Drama are in a house or houses, they can offer no help in establishing a route, for they are not *in situ* or indeed anywhere near a road built in the 350's between Neapolis and Krenides. These stones do, however, bear witness to an interest (perhaps on the part of a *polis,* perhaps on the part of a Macedonian king; perhaps a local interest for purposes of communication, perhaps a local interest asserting power over a newly subjected *polis,* perhaps a wider imperialistic interest which had a view toward both consolidation and advancement). In any event, there is no doubt that both Philip and Alexancer travelled the highway eastward from Pella as far as Byzantium. But the situation to which these stones testify is actually much more fluid and speculative than either Collart or Edson would have it, and we must not be so bold as to state that they actually stood on the old traditional route which the Romans were to turn into the Via Egnatia.[16]

---

[15] Collart "Inscriptions" (supra n. 10) 365. Edson (supra n. 2) 12, appears to favor the time of Philip II rather than the period of the Thasian colony or earlier. But Athenians, whose presence in the general area goes back much earlier, used milestones (in Attica) from the time of Hipparchus at least (M. Guarducci, *Epigrafia greca* II [Roma 1969] 440-41), and a fifth-century stone, giving distances, has been found at Thasos itself (Guarducci, 442-43).

[16] The *horos* stone from Amphipolis (supra n. 7) complicates the issue perhaps. Collart and Louis Robert canvassed the idea that the stones from the neighborhood of Philippi were markers delimiting private property from public property, and thus not *miliaria* in the sense of stones placed at a regular interval along a public highway. Even if the stones are *miliaria,* however (as they believe), there is an important distinction in purpose between a route from Krenides to the sea at Neapolis (some 12 mp away) built by a *polis* for commercial and imperialistic purposes, and a road from Pella to Philippi and points further east built by a Macedonian king for imperialistic and military reasons. Macedonia also knew of the territorial *horos*; see B. D. Meritt, "Inscriptional and Topographical Evidence for the Site of Spartolus and the Southern Boundary of Bottice," *AJA* 27 (1923) 334-39 = *SEG* 2 (1924) 408.

Polybius, Pliny, and the Via Egnatia

A more suggestive indication of the involvement of the Macedonian kings in the roads of this same area is at hand. In 190 B.C. the consul L. Cornelius Scipio (Asiaticus)[17] obtained as his province both Greece and the conduct of the Syrian War which was soon to end at the Battle of Magnesia. He crossed from Italy to Aetolia to take command of his army, and marched from Amphissa (by way of Lamia, Thaumaci, Thessaly, Macedonia, and Thrace) to the Hellespont; from there his army was carried across to Asia, though his brother P. Cornelius Scipio chose to delay on the European side. To facilitate this movement of troops the Scipio brothers had sent an envoy, Ti. Sempronius Gracchus, to King Philip V at Pella, to demand passage through Macedonia as well as assistance.[18] "It would have been a very hard march for P. Scipio had not Philip of Macedon repaired the roads (*hōdopoiei*), entertained him, escorted him, bridged the streams sometime before, and furnished provisions for him."[19] Naturally this was not simple *philanthropia* or loyalty to the recent peace terms and alliance, for Philip V had had interests of a military nature in the Cheronesus and Hellespont for more than a decade, and Antiochus III of Syria had recently been provisioning Sestus, Abydus, and Lysimachia against an anticipated Roman invasion of Asia by that route.[20] But Philip's actions are, more or less, what any of his predecessors or successors or generals would have had to do if they were to embark on campaign in Thrace or Asia.[21] Military necessity, therefore, saw to it that the road which ran to the Hellespont from Pella was being maintained with elaborate installations in the first decade of the second centrury as least. And Cicero's characterization of the highway is more than apt: *via illa nostra quae per Macedoniam est usque ad Hellespontem militaris.*[22]

---

[17] T. R. S. Broughton, *The Magistrates of the Roman Republic* I (New York 1951) 356.

[18] Livy 37.7.11-14.

[19] Appian *Syr.* 9.5.23.

[20] Appian *Syr.* 9.5.21.

[21] See Donald W. Engels, *Alexander the Great and the Logistics of the Macedonian Army* (Berkeley 1978) 8-30.

[22] Cicero *de prov. cons.* 2.4. On the classification of the *via militaris*, see Thomas Pekary, *Untersuchungen zu den römischen Reichstrassen* (Bonn 1968) 10-13; and on the general subject of the importance of military considerations in Roman road building, Heinz Herzig, "Probleme des römischen Strassenwesens," *ANRW* II.1(Berlin/New York 1974) 615-17.

II.

There is evidence as well from the pre-Roman period for the western course of what was to become the Via Egnatia. A milestone, which was found in 1893 *in situ* (at a depth of 2 m) at a point one-half km south of the railway station at Tserovo in the Kirli Derven pass, and which (again on the basis of letter forms) is "not later than the middle of the third century B.C." (Edson),[23] carries an inscription which is considerably different from those which we have just been discussing:

#4 Tserovo (now Klidhi)   0.94 m H
                            0.40 m W
ΕΓ ~ ΒΟΚΕΡΙΑΣ   0.16 m D
ΣΤΑΔΙΟΙ   Ε
ΚΑΤΟΝ

This inscription names a town, Bokeria, from which the distance is being counted, and also a distance, one hundred stadia (18.3 km; 12.3 mp). But here is no longer simply the designation of a road, but rather something more informative and specific. Bokeria has been placed on the eastern shore of Lake Begorritis (which may have derived its name from the town, at a point a little north of the village of Kelemesh,[24] but it is worth asking why a distance should be computed from that place. The name occurs nowhere else in ancient literature or in epigraphy, and it is difficult to imagine why such an insignificant town should be the starting point. It is not impossible that the 100th stadion stone marked the town's territorial boundary, but it is far more likely that Bokeria is being used, not as a *caput viae*,[25]

---

[23] J. H. Mordtmann, "Inschriften aus Edessa," *Ath Mitt* 18 (1893) 419 = Demitsas (supra n. 12) I, 393 #4. Margaret Hasluck, "The Archaeological History of Lake Ostrovo in West Macedonia," *Geographical Journal* 88 (1936) 454-55. The fourth-century date is apparently Edson's (supra n. 2), 4 and 13 n. 25, but not based on autopsy: "I have Mordtmann's manuscript from the files of *IG*, which seems very accurately to reproduce the letter forms. . . . Mordtmann does not give the height of the letters." In 1893, Mordtmann wrote, "In Ekschisu befindet sich eine Inschrift, von welcher ich durch die Güte des Herrn Meissner folgende Abschrift des H. Meyer erhielt. . . ." Is Mordtmann's manuscript this *Abschrift*, or perhaps only a copy of it? If so, how do we know that Meyer reproduced the letter forms "very accurately"?

[24] Hasluck (supra n. 23) 454-55. Cf. Ph. Petsas, "Βοκκεριος καὶ Βοκκέριος," *AAA* 4 (1971) 115-18; L. and J. Robert, *Bull. épig.* (1971) 392.

[25] See Gordon J. Laing, "Roman Milestones and the Capita viarum," *TAPA* 29 (1908) 15-34. On the stone from Bokeria, the seriph in the first line is worth

but as a convenient reference point for short distances in an area where there were not *poleis* on a highway which would have led from Edessa to the west to Heraclea Lyncestis. Some support for this may perhaps be derived from the items in the *Itinerarium Burdigalense,* which is much more detailed in noting each *mutatio, mansio* and *civitas* than the other itineraries. As the traveller moves westward from Edessa, he comes to a *mutatio* called *ad Duodecimum,*[26] from which it is 16 mp to the next installation, the *mansio* at Cellae (note that Bokeria is passed by in silence). One hundred stadia from Edessa would amount to about 12 mp, and it may be that the *mutatio* was established there (where there was no town) at a traditional place, perhaps where a convenient marker stood.[27] While this speculation may not convince, it cannot be denied that Macedonia was familiar with road markers which bore an indication of distance (intermediate distance) no later than the mid-third century. Whether this is a purely local phenomenon in Eordaea, or a project of wider application we do not yet know; whether the distances marked were purely and entirely local ones, or were perhaps cumulative after a certain number of stones, we cannot say; whether there was a *caput viae* besides Bokeria for an entire lengthy section of road, cannot be determined. For, between the time of the Bokeria stone and the

considering. Was there, perhaps, a standard layout for stones of that type, ΕΓ_____, the carving of the name of the *caput* to begin at the right, and the extra space in the middle to be filled in with a seriph?

[26] *Itinerarium Burdigalense* 606,5 Wessely.

[27] Designations of locations using the form *ad* (with or without an ordinal number) are rare on the Via Egnatia:

ad Novas	*Itin. Ant.* 329,6
ad Quintum	*Itin. Burd.* 608,3
ad Duodecimum	*Itin. Burd.* 606,5
ad Decimum	*Itin. Burd.* 605,5
ad Duodecimum	*Itin. Burd.* 604,2

Both designations ad Duodecimum (*ad XII*) are to the west of the place from which the distance is being computed — an intermediate *caput* (Edessa, Philippi). Ad Novas is approximately 48 mp in the westerly direction from Clodiana in the itineraries, and this might conceivably represent four times the distance ad XII (that is, 400 stadia). Castra (also called Nicaea) might perhaps be added to the list as well, for it is 12 mp to the west of Heraclea Lyncestis (*Itin. Ant.* 308,5 and 330,2; *Itin. Burd.* 607,1). Raymond Chevallier, *Les voies romaines* (Paris 1972) 213, points out that the average distance between *mutationes* on Roman highways was 8 1/3 mp, and that the most frequent intervals were between seven and twelve mp. Between *mansiones* (which were more extensive installations than *mutationes*) the interval is usually between thirty and thirty-three mp, that is, three *mutationes*.

John Paul Adams

Roman activity which created the Via Egnatia, there is no evidence at all for the development of this route.

It is only after the Battle of Pydna, the end of the Macedonian kingship, followed by the period of the independent *merides* (167-148), and ultimately with the war against Andriscus (150-148), that we reach a point where we are able to add to the picture. By that time, of course, a Roman magistrate or promagistrate was regularly being sent to Macedonia as his *provincia*.[28] It is in such a context that we meet Cn. Egnatius, the builder of the Via Egnatia.

III.

A new milestone from the Via Egnatia (published by K. Romiopoulou in 1974) has provided an important new datum and a distance. It was discovered deep in the alluvium on the eastern bank of the Gallikos River, some four km south of the old Athens-Thessalonike highway bridge, a site which is approximately 10 km west of the Vardar Gate.[29] The stone is bilingual, with the Latin text given precedence:

CC ↓ X
CN EGNATI C F
PRO COS

ΓΝΑΙΟΣ ΕΓΝΑΤΙΟΣ ΓΑΙΟΣ
ΑΝΘΥΠΑΤΟΣ ΡΩΜΑΙΩΝ
Σ Ξ

---

[28] See Fanoula Papazoglou, "Quelques aspects de l' histoire de la province de Macédoine," *ANRW* II.7.1 (Berlin/New York 1979) 302-69, especially 303-307. Normally, but not inevitably, Macedonia was governed by a propraetor, but it was not a "Praetorian province." For the governors of Macedonia, the short list of Papazoglou, 310, can be completely documented in Theodoros Sarikakis, *Rōmaioi archontes tēs eparchias Makedonias, A'* (Thessaloniki 1971), *B '* (Thessaloniki 1977) [in Greek]. Papazoglou tentatively places Cn. Egnatius *ca.* 146-43 B.C., though there is no positive evidence, and there are many unknown governors down to 115 B.C. and a few blanks down to the end of the century. If the milestones on the Via Egnatia mentioned by Polybius are Egnatius', then they were erected before Polybius' death — though that unhappy event is undatable. It may be as early as 133 B.C. or as late as *ca.* 120-18.

[29] C. Romiopoulou, "Un nouveau milliaire de la Via Egnatia," *BCH* 98 (1974) 813-16 (*Bull. épig.* [1976] 456). Collart, "Milliaires" (supra n. 2) 187-88 and 197 #1. The stone is cylindrical, like the usual Roman milestone and unlike the Greek stones which we have been discussing; its dimensions: 1.31 m H, diameter at top 0.365 m, diameter at bottom 0.335 m. Georges Daux (supra n. 2) 145-47 (*Bull. épig.* [1978] 291). An epigraphical date of the third quarter of the second century B.C. is adopted by all three scholars.

Polybius, Pliny, and the Via Egnatia

Gnaeus Egnatius, the Roman proconsul, built the road; the milestone is Number 260. The Greek version confirms the accuracy of the Latin text, and it is an easy deduction that the *civitas* of Thessalonike was only seven (or eight) Roman miles further along the Via Egnatia to the east (that is, some 10 km). This secure fact on a Roman milestone confirms the statement of Polybius (34.12.8) as reported by Strabo (7.7.4 C323), that the length of the road to Thessalonike was 267 mp. It likewise suggests that a parallel passage in Pliny (*NH* 4.10(17).36), which reports a distance from Dyrrachium to Thessalonike is incorrect:

> In ora sinus Macedonica oppidum Chalastra et intus Pyloros, Lete medioque litoris flexu Thessalonice liberae condicionis (ad hanc a Dyrrhachio CCXLV), Therme in Thermaico sinu [etc.].

Gabriel Brotier noticed this in his edition of Pliny (1779), and corrected the text in such a way that it agrees with the datum given by Polybius: CCLXVII. There can now be no doubt that this is the correct distance, and that Polybius was reliable, but this does not mean that Pliny should be emended so quickly. It may be that Pliny, whose work habits are known,[30] wrote something incorrect, or had his secretaries copy something which was incorrect (or copy incorrectly something which was correct); in that case, an emendation of the text of Pliny will produce something which Pliny did not write. On the other hand, it is completely likely that the carelessness of generations of scribes corrupted what was a correct statement, as they have actually done time and time again in the manuscripts of the *Naturalis Historia*. Some further consideration is necessary before a decision is possible.

An emendation of the numeral reported by the *mss*. of Pliny (CCXLV *A*, CXIIII *R d*, CXV *B*) to the numeral desired by Brotier is not an easy business in terms of palaeography. Moreover, the Procrustean method must take into account several other passages. At *NH* 4.11(18).42, a distance between Dyrrachium and Philippi is inserted (and here there are no *ms*. variants):

---

[30] The *locus classicus* is Pliny the Younger *Epistulae* 3.5. See R. Syme, *Tacitus* (Oxford 1958) 60-63, and "Pliny the Procurator," *HSCP* 73 (1969) 201-36. A. N. Sherwin-White, *The Letters of Pliny* (Oxford 1966) 223-25. For the text of the *Naturalis Historia*, I have consulted the editions of J. Sillig (Gotha 1851), L. Jan (Leipzig 1854), C. Mayhoff (Leipzig 1906), D. Detlefsen, *Die geographischen Bücher der Naturalis Historia des C. Plinius Secundus* (Berlin 1904), and H. Rackham, Loeb Classical Library (London and Cambridge, Mass. 1942).

...Neapolis, Datos — intus Philippi colonia (absunt a Dyrrachio CCCXXV) — Scotussa, Topiros civitas, Nesti amnis ostium...

This numeral, 325 mp, is as widely wrong as the numeral of 245 mp from Dyrrachium to Thessalonike, for the distance from Thessalonike to Philippi is only 100 or 101 mp,[31] and this, when added to the now secure figure of 267 mp, would yield a total distance of 367 mp or 368 mp to Philippi from Dyrrachium. Likewise another passage, *NH* 4.11(18).46 (also without *ms.* variants):

> ...promunturium Chryson Ceras in quo oppidum Byzantium liberae condicionis antea Lygos dictum — abest a Dyrrachio DCCXI p...

The numeral, 711 mp, is also far too low. Even on a modern map with regularized routes, it can be seen that the distance from Dyrrachium to Byzantium would approach 1071 km, or some 723 mp (though, to be sure, the distance would have been greater in antiquity). And yet it can be verified that Pliny actually did intend this numeral of 711 mp, since he repeats at *NH* 4.11(18).50 (again without variants):

> Macedoniae, Thraciae, Hellesponti longitudo est supra dicta, quidam DCCXX faciunt.

Now 720 mp may seem to be close enough to the modern estimation of 723 + adduced earlier, but it is in grave disagreement with the ancient road maps. The *Itinerarium Antonini* (317,7 Wess.) offers 754 mp. A variant route in the same itinerary (322,10 Wess.) extends the route to Aulona in the west, but apparently gives the distance from Apollonia of 756 (as it does also at 329,4 Wess.). The *Itinerarium Burdigalense* records a total distance from Aulona to Heraclea Perinthus of 688 mp, but if the distance from Aulona to Apollonia (24 mp) is subtracted, and the distance from Heraclea Perinthus to Byzantium (65 mp) supplied from the *Itinerarium Antonini* (332,4-9 Wess.), then a total distance from Apollonia-Dyrrachium to Byzantium of 753 mp is suggested by the Pilgrim. All the itineraries, therefore, insist that the correct length of the entire highway is about 754 mp, not Pliny's 711 mp.

---

[31] 101 mp: *Itin. Ant.* 320,1-5 and *Tabula Peutingeriana*. 100 mp: *Itin. Burd.* 603,10-605,4. See Paul Collart, "Une réfection de la Via Egnatia sous Trajan," *BCH* 59 (1935) 405, and Hammond, *Hist Mace* I 55 n. 1.

Polybius, Pliny, and the Via Egnatia

There is perhaps an explanation, one which can satisfy both topography and all the Plinian passages adduced, but it requires *both* understanding and emendation. The total distance of 711, when placed against the *itineraria*'s distance of 754, suggests an error of 43. The distance from Dyrrachium to Philippi of 325 mp, when placed against the calculation (derived from the new milestone of Cn. Egnatius and the *Itineraria*, as well as Polybius) of 368 mp, also suggests an error of 43. What is the significance of the number 43? As Hammond has shown,[32] it is the distance between the two *capita viae*, Apollonia and Dyrrachium, and the place where they meet to form a single highway, *mansio Clodiana*. Now, if the error of 43 has also occurred in the Plinian passage giving the distance from Dyrrachium to Thessalonike, we might expect to read some numeral like 224 (that is, 267 − 43 = 224). It happens that only one of the manuscript variants can accommodate such a numeral under this hypothesis, *CCXLV* (which is in fact the numeral commonly printed in our texts). There is, of course, evidence in the *mss.* that *X* and *L* were easily confused with one another.[33] Thus, we should not hesitate to emend the text of Pliny at *NH* 4.10(17).36 to read *CCXXV* instead of *CCXLV*. When this has been done, Pliny can stand as a perfectly reliable witness to the distances on the Via Egnatia, as computed from Dyrrachium to Thessalonike, Philippi, and Byzantium. We might note that Pliny's source for these statistics apparently had information for the entire route, not just as far as the Hebrus River and Cypselus as did Polybius (it would seem).[34]

[32] Hammond, *Hist Mace* I 21-24, and "Western . . . Via Egnatia" (supra n. 1) 188-89. Cf. F. W. Walbank, *A Historical Commentary on Polybius* III (Oxford 1979) 626.

[33] In the *mss.* of Pliny *NH*, the following confusions (selected from Books 3-6) are relevant:

X for *V*:	4.12(20).60	A MALEO PELOPONNESI LXXX/LXXV.
	6.26(30).119	LXX/LXV
V for *X*:	3.25(28).147	CXV/CXX
	5.31(39).140	TOTA INSULA CIRCUITER UT ISIDORUS CCLXVIII/CCLXXIII
X for *L*:	6.17(21).62	XXIX/XLIX
I for *L*:	6.17(21).59	CCCCLI/CCCCII

The confusion of *V* and *II* is very frequent, and the appearance of *XL* [for XXXX?? at 4.7(11).24] is sometimes not above suspicion; e.g. 6.17(21).62 (XXIX/XLIX). Perhaps *X* and *II* are confused at 6.27(31).130 (LXX/LXII).

[34] With the addition of the 43 mp, Pliny attests to the following data:

4.36:	Dyrrachium to Thessalonike	267/268 mp
4.42:	Dyrrachium to Philippi	367/368 mp
4.46:	Dyrrachium to Byzantium	754 mp
	Dyrrachium to Byzantium (others)	763 mp

John Paul Adams

With the accuracy of Pliny's statistics established, we may next ask why he (or his source, or his secretaries) chose to misrepresent the place from which the count of Roman miles was being made, Clodiana rather than Dyrrachium (the true *caput viae*[35])? In part, it may be that the sources themselves lend their assistance to this confusion. It was common to treat the entire highway in segments, with distances given to intermediate points (as the Bokeria stadion stone might suggest). Polybius (34.12.2-8 = Strabo 7.7.4 C322), for instance, appears to have divided the highway into three or four parts, the first of which ran from Apollonia and Dyrrachium to Thessalonike (267),[36] and the second of which ran from Thessalonike

---

[35] Polybius reckoned from Apollonia (34.12.2 = Strabo 7.7.4 C322), and probably also from Dyrrachium-Epidamnus (34.7.2 = Strabo 2.4.4. C106). Strabo also testifies that the roads from the two *capita* (if we may use the Roman word loosely in a disputed situation) meet at a point equidistant from each (7.7.4 C323), and speaks about "the Via Egnatia from Epidamnus and Apollonia," using the older Greek name for what was, in his day, a Roman colony. The *Epitome edita* of Book VII (F 10), however, talks about "the Via Egnatia which runs from the *polis* Dyrrachium towards the east as far as Thessalonike," and we may well wonder how closely the actual words of Strabo are being reproduced — or for that matter those of Polybius to the effect that the Via Egnatia was delimited with milestones as far as Cypsela and the Hebrus. Cicero is not explicit in his famous remark about the Via Egnatia, but it may be that the rhetoric at *de prov. cons.* 3.5 suggests that the two termini of the highway were Dyrrachium and Byzantium: *cum interea quis vestrum hoc non audivit, quis ignorat, Achaeos ingentem pecuniam pendere L. Pisoni quotannis, vectigal ac portorium Dyrrachinorum totum in huius unius quaestum esse conversum, urbem Byzantinorum vobis atque huic imperio fidelissimam hostilem in modum esse vexatam?* So the commentary, H. E. Butler and M. Cary, *M. Tulli Ciceronis de provinciis consularibus oratio ad Senatum* (Oxford 1924) 51; cf. S. J. DeLaet, *Portorium* (Brugge 1949) 71. Pliny, of course, consistently names Dyrrachium (supra n. 34).

Despite the statements of scholars (supra n. 29: Romiopoulou 85 and Collart 188; Daux [supra n. 2] 146 n. 4; but cf. Walbank [supra n. 32] 642), the new milestone of Cn. Egnatius does *not* state that the distance is computed from Dyrrachium (or from Apollonia). The earliest epigraphic testimony to that fact dates from the reign of Trajan (Collart, "Milliaires" [supra n. 2] 197-98, #2 and #3). The essential question is whether *miliaria* were erected on the Via Egnatia by Cn. Egnatius between Dyrrachium and Clodiana, or between Apollonia and Clodiana, or on both routes which led to Clodiana. The evidence which would settle this point has not yet appeared.

[36] Polybius 34.7.2-3 = Strabo 2.4.4 C106. The third part may have been the distance from Cypsela to Byzantium (as Polybius 34.12.9-10 = Strabo *Epitome* VII F 57 [*Epitome Vaticana*] and F 10 [*Epitome edita*] might suggest), or it may have been from Cypsela to Perinthus in Thrace, making a fourth part out of the distance from Perinthus to Byzantium (infra, Part V). Note that Thessalonike is exactly halfway between Apollonia-Dyrrachium and Cypsela; the halfway point between Dyrrachium-Apollonia and Byzantium would be some 9 mp to the east of Philippi (to which place, a colony, Pliny provides a distance), and the three-quarter point about 30 mp (a day's journey) beyond Cypsela.

to the Hebrus River and Cypselus (268),[37] making a total elapsed distance for these equal portions of 535 mp. There is also evidence which suggests that the first part of the highway, before the road entered the mountains above Elbasan, was treated as a separate segment. Polybius (34.12.7) says that the whole road is called the Via Egnatia, but the first section passing through the town of Lychnidus and through Pylon, the point on the road which separates Illyria from Macedonia, derives its special name Candavia from Mt. Candavia in Illyria. Strabo too (7.7.8 C327) speaks of the Via Egnatia which begins at Epidamnus and Apollonia and the "road to Candavia," as does Pliny himself (*NH* 3.23.145). This passage is of interest,

> A Lisso Macedonia provincia. gentes Partheni et a tergo eorum Dassaretae, montes Candaviae a Dyrrachio LXXVIII p., in ora vero Denda civium Romanorum, Epidamnum colonia propter inauspicatum nomen a Romanis Dyrrachium appellata, flumen Aous a quibusdam Aeas nominatum, Apollonia quondam Corinthiorum colonia IV [or X] p. a mari recedens. . . .

since it shows Pliny treating of a portion of the Via Egnatia (or rather an aside about the Via Egnatia) while he is moving geographically south along the coast highway.[38] For Pliny, as for his sources, it would be easy to allow these separate intermediate areas to be detached for reasons of geometrical geography[39] or ethnographical description, and then to misunderstand through carelessness in the process of composition that a portion had been treated previously.

---

[37] Strabo (7.7.4 C323) makes the Strymon River and the Pontus natural boundaries of the Macedonians and the Thracians, not of the Via Egnatia. Others, he says (*Epitome* VII F 33-35), make the Nestus River an ethnic boundary. Cf. also Epitome VII F 9, F 10, and F 47, where the Hebrus River is treated as a boundary of political and ethnic significance.

[38] The coast was described as early as the works of Hecataeus of Miletus, and the information may ultimately go back to explorations made by Phocaeans (W. A. Heidel, *The Frame of Ancient Greek Maps* [New York 1937] 36). Hammond, *Epirus* (supra n. 1) 443-69, examining the sources of Strabo, finds a large residue of the work of Hecataeus still in circulation in discussions of the Adriatic and of northwest Greece; and Strabo himself quotes and criticizes Dicaearchus, Eratosthenes and Polybius with regard to this area.

[39] Dicaearchus had apparently made the distance from the Peloponnesus to the head of the Adriatic greater than the distance from the Peloponnesus to the Pillars of Hercules, which he estimated at 10,000 stadia. Polybius (= Strabo 2.4.1 C105) took him to task for this, and by a model geometrical argument showed Dicaearchus' statements to be absurd. Strabo then took Polybius to task, using a geometrical proof as well (though with different distances postulated); the latitude which was believed to run from the Pyrenees through Massilia (Dicaearchus' native

In the case of Pliny the detachment of the area from Dyrrachium to Clodiana was consistent throughout, as was the misrepresentation of the place from which the computation was being made. This treatment of intermediate distances and our observation about the possible significance of the *mansio Clodiana*, however, raises a separate problem. The geographical location of *mansio Clodiana* has within the past decade been moved several times by various scholars, and consequently it is necessary to inquire into the various grounds on which such changes have been made.[40]

IV.

The measured distances of Polybius in the western part of the Via Egnatia, as we have seen, are perfectly acceptable: 267 Roman miles to Thessalonike from Apollonia, and another 268 miles to Cypsela and the Hebrus River, but Strabo,[41] in reporting these Polybian

---

city) and Byzantium is mentioned (cf. Strabo 2.5.41 C134), and Strabo has a distance from Rhodes to Byzantium, which are on the same longitude (or were believed to be). It was possible in antiquity to arrive at a reasonably accurate estimate of the latitude of a place through the observation of celestial phenomena — as Eratosthenes did in his famous experiment with the well at Syene (see Heidel [supra n. 38] 122-28), and even earlier Dicaearchus is said to have done for Massilia (Heidel 107). But the determination of the latitude of many points was not in fact done observationally, and the accurate determination of longitude was a problem not seriously tackled until the early modern period (Galileo), nor satisfactorily solved until the eighteenth century, when John Harrison made his famous clocks which made possible accurate observations using J. D. Cassini's work on the transits of the satellites of Jupiter. See L. A. Brown, *The Story of Maps* (Boston 1949) 208-40.

The question of Pliny's sources in the geographical books of the *Naturalis Historia* is like the Schleswig-Holstein question, the intricacies of which had been mastered only by three men: one was dead, one was mad, and Lord Palmerston had quite forgotten it. One must be deeply grateful to Klaus Günther Sallmann, *Die Geographie des älteren Plinius in ihrem Verhältnis zu Varro* (Berlin 1971), for his clear exposition of the many problems and theories. Pliny certainly knew the work of Marcus Agrippa, at least on the Illyrian areas, from which he quotes at *NH* 3.26.150 (Sallmann 91-107); but in Book I, the index for the entire work names fifty-four authors whose work is alleged to have contributed (directly or indirectly). For Agrippa's map, see A. Klotz, "Die geographischen Commentarii des Agrippa und ihre Überreste," *Klio* 24 (1931) 38-58, 386-466. The arrangement of data may also have been affected, in some authors at least, by political considerations, especially the Roman conventus-district system.

[40] In 1974 Hammond ("Western . . . Via Egnatia" [supra n. 1] 189) removed Clodiana from the neighborhood of Ziberrakë to the Albanian town of Mafmutaga, approximately 4 km east of Peqin and a total distance of 45 km (that is, 30.3 mp) east of Dyrrachium.

[41] Strabo 7.7.4 C322 = Polybius 34.12.3-4.

Polybius, Pliny, and the Via Egnatia

numbers for the Via Egnatia, remarks that Polybius had been using a different means of calculating the relative values of the Roman mile and the Greek stadion. "If we reckon the Roman mile as most people do, at eight stadia to the mile, this makes 4280 stadia to the Hebrus; but if, as Polybius does, we add to the eight stadia two plethra, that is a third of the number of miles, we must add 178 stadia." N. G. L. Hammond[42] applied this remark to the Polybian distance from Apollonia to the Hebrus and Cypsela, concluding that the actual distance used by Polybius was reckoned in stadia ("evidently, 4,458 stades"); these stadia were then converted into Roman miles, for the reader's convenience, but at an unusual conversion factor of 8 1/3:1 rather than 8:1 — a 4.16% difference. For Hammond, then, the numerals 267 and 535 of Polybius, as reported by Strabo, do *not* represent actual known numbers, but are rather calculations derived *from stadia* (and perhaps from a putative Macedonian *itinerarium* in Polybius' possession). These "Polybian miles," however, are dubious. Suspicion exists, of course, when we notice that a very similar statement is made by Strabo (according to the *Epitome Vaticana*) at the eastern end of the Via Egnatia at Byzantium and the Cyanean Rocks, and a similar conversion number is reported as a calculation of Polybius, this time 180 stadia.[43] The statistics offered for Byzantium are wrong, to be sure, and I shall have more to say about them presently, but in the matter of the 178 stadia which are to be added to the Polybian stadia at the Hebrus, we are able to state that they are superfluous. The milestone of Cn. Egnatius, which guarantees the distance to Thessalonike of 267 mp, proves that it is unnecessary, and the itineraries suggest strongly that the distance of 535 mp to the Hebrus is also a Roman mile numeral.

Now Hammond has used the Strabonian theory of conversion to allow himself to recalculate the intermediate distances between Dyrrachium and Thessalonike, and to assign the names of the highway's *mutationes, mansiones*, and *civitates* to particular places, in some cases ancient ruins. His total distance, which includes more than a few emendations of the itineraries (whose numerals are confused, and do not often agree precisely), amounts to 277-279 mp. But this conclusion is wrong, and again the intermediate distances

---

[42] Hammond, *Hist Macc* I 56.
[43] Strabo *Epitome* VII F 57 = Polybius 34.12.10.

and topographical identifications must be reworked.[44] In the 1960's, moreover, Albanian archaeologists made a number of interesting discoveries, including several milestones and what appears to be a *mutatio* from the Roman highway; Hammond also visited the area in 1972, and produced a revision of his theories which had been expressed in *A History of Macedonia* I (1972) in an article which appeared in the *Journal of Roman Studies* in 1974.[45] The discovery of the *mutatio* on the northern (right) bank of the Skhumbi (Genusus) River at Bradashesh indicates that the Via Egnatia from Dyrrachium did *not* cross from the right bank to the left (south) bank in the flood plain of the Skhumbi at all, but only when it reached the gorge of the river at Mirakë,[46] the site of the *traiectio* of which the *itineraries* speak, some 9 mp above Scampi.[47] This correction of the route will, as F. W. Walbank pointed out,[48] somewhat shorten the actual route of the Via Egnatia in the "Candavian" section, and, with a judicious reemendation of the figures in the itineraries,[49] will produce the desired total figure of 267 mp (though in truth, as Walbank admits, it produces a figure of 269 or 272) without having recourse to Strabo's principle of recalculation, as applied by Hammond in his *History of Macedonia* I. Unfortunately, this manipulation of statistics and topography has meant that the *mansio Clodiana* has been situated in three separate places within the last decade. In 1972 it was 43 mp from Dyrrachium; in 1974 it was at 79 mp; and today it is at 31 mp. Moreover, in order to take into account the alleged statement of Polybius reported by Strabo to the effect that the roads from Apollonia and from Dyrrachium met at a point which was equidistant from the two cities (Strabo 7.7.4 C322 = Polybius 34.12.4),

---

[44] Polybius (34.12.8) is made by Strabo (7.7.4 C322) to give a distance of 267 mp, and the milestone of Cn. Egnatius implies that this number is correct.

[45] Hammond, "Western . . . Via Egnatia" (supra n. 1) 185-94.

[46] Ibid. 187-88, revising the view expressed in *Hist Mace* I 32-35, that the crossing was at the Albanian village of Cotaj.

[47] *Itin. Burd.* 608,1. For the *Tab. Peut.* see Hammond, *Hist Mace* I 20, Map 2 (where the crossing is called *Genesis fl.*). Hammond finds that "the numbers of Roman miles in the Itineraries are consistent for the stretch from Clodiana to Scampis. . . . Thus there is every reason to regard the numbers as correct and not corrupt for this stretch" ("Western . . . Via Egnatia [supra n. 1] 188; *Hist Mace* I 29-30).

[48] Walbank (supra n. 32) 626.

[49] Ibid.: "The *Tab. Peut.* has two sections, probably dividing at Genusus (modern Shtodhër), and given as 15 and 26 *m.p.* The first of these is correct, but 26 must be emended to 16 to fit the new location of Clodiana at Ad Quintum."

Hammond has recourse to a new topographical description of the Roman roads in the flood plain of the Skhumbi (Genusus) River and the Semeni (Apsus) River in Albania.[50]

He describes three roads from Apollonia toward the north besides the coast highway, and decides that the easternmost of these (Apollonia-Stephanapha-Apsus-Belsh), which joined the Via Egnatia from Dyrrachium between the *mutatio ad Quintum* and the *mansio Scampi* (*Hiscampis*), a little below the modern Elbasan, is *the* Via Egnatia. While there may indeed have been an ancient road which followed this course outlined by Hammond, it must be noticed that the *Itinerarium Burdigalense* and the *Itinerarium Antonini* both include the *mansio Clodiana*,[51] and thus apparently do not follow Hammond's main Via Egnatia to Apsus by way of Belsh. The Bordeaux Pilgrim, in fact, was travelling from east to west, and was heading for Aulona; yet he goes to Clodiana before he turns to the south, crosses the Skhumbi (Genusus), and makes for *mansio Apsus*. Indeed, no ancient source knows about Hammond's route from Apsus via Belsh to the Via Egnatia, and we might be surprised that no installation existed at the place where the Via Egnatia from Apollonia crossed the Skhumbi (Genusus) and joined the highway from Dyrrachium. Likewise, it must be noted that there is no way of referring to this important confluence of the highways, except by the vague term "the road to Candavia," despite the fact that Polybius already had specific material about the Roman road in the third quarter of the second century B.C. Clodiana would have been familiar to Polybius, of course, for it was there that the armies of Appius Claudius camped in the Spring of 168 B.C., while he awaited the arrival of the praetor Anicius (who was at Apollonia, within a three-days' march).[52] This camp was *circa Genusum flumen* (as Hammond himself has argued[53]) in the territory of the Parthini. Consequently, it had to be "near Ziberrakë or further east," rather than where Hammond and Walbank now wish to put Clodiana, at 31 mp from Dyrrachium (4 km east of Peqin). One may well be dismayed at this repeated movement of bridge and *mansio*, and since I have already suggested

---

[50] Hammond, "Western . . . Via Egnatia" (supra n. 1) 189-92 with Fig. 6, abandoning the position taken in *Hist Mace* I 21-24.

[51] *Itin. Ant.* 318,1 and 329,7. *Itin Burd.* 608,4. Hammond, "Western . . . Via Egnatia" (supra n. 1) 191.

[52] Livy 43.23.6; 44.30.10; cf. 44.46.3.

[53] Hammond, *Hist Mace* I 23 n. 3.

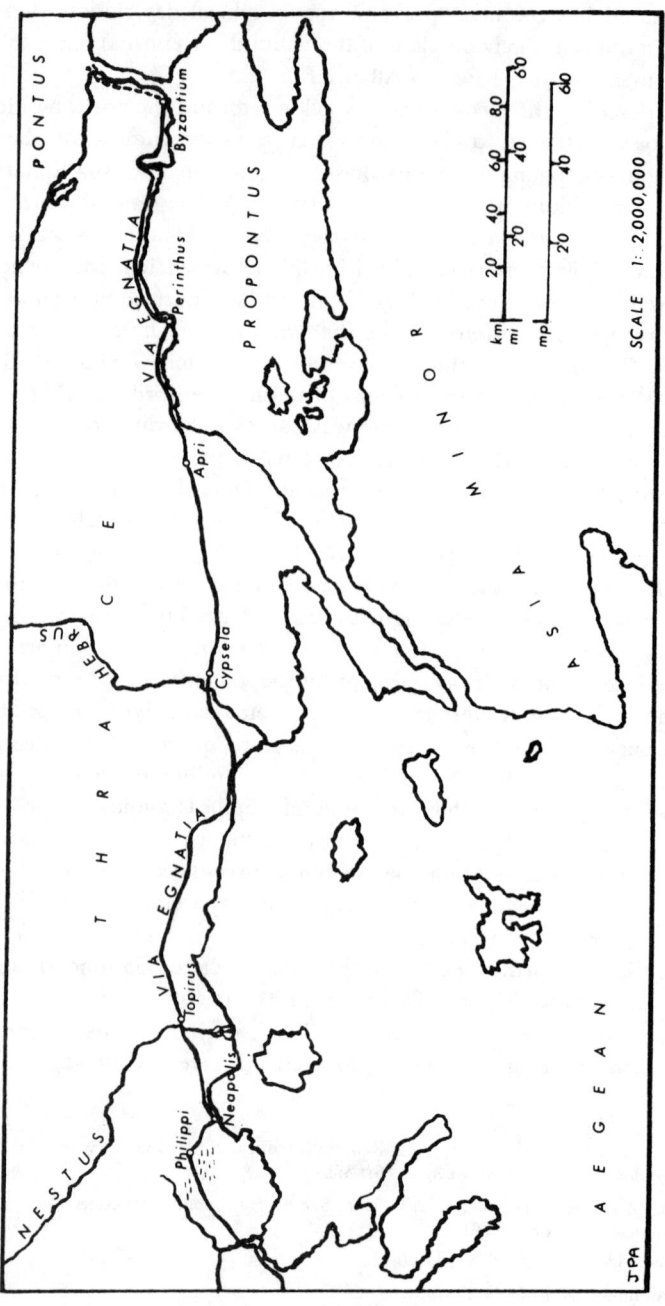

Fig. 2 The Via Egnatia in Thrace

that 43 mp meant something (to Pliny at least), it may be useful to reconsider this problem and the identification of ancient sites. It may be suggested that the Via Egnatia from Apollonia did indeed go by way of Apsos and Belsh, as the itineraries indicate, but that it arrived at the road from Dyrrachium at the 43rd milestone — where Clodiana may again be placed.

V.

Let us return now to the texts of Strabo concerning distances on the Via Egnatia. There is, as we have indicated,[54] no compelling argument to apply Strabo's remark about Polybius' conversion of Roman miles into stadia to the portion of the Via Egnatia between Apollonia-Dyrrachium and Thessalonike, for the *exemplum* (which we attribute to Strabo) refers only to the distance to Cypsela (reported by Polybius as 525 mp). There is something more, however, to be said about the various numbers — both of the distance to Thessalonike and the distance to Byzantium, and these need to be seen in the light of the method of composition and analysis used by Polybius and Strabo. It can be seen that Polybius, the earliest of our sources which survives in any quantity (however fragmentary), was already treating the Via Egnatia and the land of Macedonia in sections. His predecessor, Eratosthenes of Cyrene (*ca.* 275-196 B.C.) had already pronounced that the distance between Epidamnus (Dyrrachium) and Thessalonike was 900 stadia (= 112.5 mp),[55] though evidently Polybius had a more accurate figure or figures at hand, and Strabo reports that Polybian figure as "above 2000 stadia" (250 + mp), congratulating Polybius on being correct.[56] This does not mean, of course, that *all* of Polybius' statistics were necessarily in stadia, nor does it mean that Strabo is only paraphrasing Polybius' number, nor does it mean that Polybius is speaking contrary to what he says about the length of the Via Egnatia to Thessalonike. "Above 2000 stadia" obviously represents a rough *calculation*. But why a rough calculation? A precise figure of 2136 stadia could have been supplied at the conversion rate of 8:1 (for direct comparison with Eratosthenes), for Polybius knew the exact distance of the Via Egnatia to Thessalonike, and Strabo reports that distance as 267 mp (7.7.4 C322). But we

---

[54] Supra n. 44.
[55] Stephanus Byzantinus, *s.v. Dyrrachion*. Tafel (supra n. 2) *Pars Occidentalis*, 16-19.
[56] Strabo 2.4.4 C106; cf. 2.1.40 C92.

must understand clearly that neither Eratosthenes nor Polybius (in presenting the numerals 900 and 2000+) is speaking of an actual distance along a winding highway; each is speaking of a distance on a map, that is, a geometrical distance.

Strabo,[57] in fact, is working out of a source (or tradition) which treats Macedonia as a parallelogram, with the Adriatic as the first side, the meridian line which passes through Cypsela and the Hebrus as its opposite and parallel side, the range of mountains in the north (Bertiscus, Scardus, Orbelus, Rhodope, and Haemus) as the third side, and the Via Egnatia "which runs from the city of Dyrrachium towards the East as fas ar Thessalonike" (plus, no doubt, the seacoast from Thessalonike to the Hebrus[58]) as the fourth. It was Eratosthenes, of course, who firmly fixed the concepts of latitude lines into the science of mapmaking, and it may have been he who invented the "Meridian of Alexandria," which passed through Rhodes, Byzantium, and the mouth of the Danube.[59] His "Parallel of Rhodes," moreover, passed through Cape Malea (which was regarded as the southernmost tip of the Peloponnesus, and thus of the Greek

---

[57] Strabo *Epitome* VII F 9 (*Epit. Vat.*), F 10 (*Epit. ed.*).

[58] Strabo 7.7.4 C323; *Epitome* VII F 33, 34, 35, 48.

[59] The inventor of the "Meridian of Alexandria," which passed through Alexandria, Rhodes, and Byzantium, is in dispute, and related to the origins of the meridian which is described as running between Lysimachia and Syene. Since Syene and Alexandria were generally believed to lie on the same line (Eratosthenes' calculation of the circumference of the earth is based on this assumption), then all the points named should be on the same meridian. Clausen, in his edition of the fragments of Hecataeus, had attributed the meridian of Alexandria to Eratosthenes himself, though Hugo Berger believed that there was reason to believe that Dicaearchus was actually responsible (*Geschichte der wissenschaftliche Erdkunde der Griechen* [Leipzig 1903] 114). There is explicit testimony that Dicaearchus had worked to improve the conception of the east-west parallel that ran from the Pillars of Hercules through Sicily, the Peloponnesus, Rhodes, Pamphylia, Cilicia, and the Taurus Mountains, to India — the "Parallel of Rhodes" (Agathemerus *Geographias Hypotyposis* 1.5 = *GGM* II 472; cf. Polybius 34.15.2 = Pliny *NH* 6.32(38).206. Berger, *Geschichte* 378. Heidel [supra n. 38] 110-13), and Eratosthenes adopted this "straight" line as a basic reference point on his map. Berger (*Die geographischen Fragmente des Eratosthenes* [Leipzig 1880] 173-76; *Geschichte*, 371 and 414-17), moreover, has indicated that the presence of Lysimachia on this line must imply a calculation made after 309 B.C., and probably made by Dicaearchus rather than Eratosthenes. The tenuous nature of the evidence and of Berger's argument is pointed out by W. A. Heidel (*Frame* [supra n. 39] 119-21), and it seems agreed that Eratosthenes was not only deeply interested in north-south meridians, but that he was responsible for the longitude drawn through Asia Minor from the Gulf of Issus to the parallel of Amisus and Sinope, which he estimated at 3,000 stadia (Strabo 2.1.3 C68; cf. 2.1.35 C87 and 14.5.22 C677. Berger, *Fragmente*, 175; *Geschichte*, 419). This parallel, and the distance assigned to it, approximates the distance from Rhodes to

Polybius, Pliny, and the Via Egnatia

peninsula),[60] at a right angle to the "Meridian of Alexandria." The Pythagorean theorem could be used (as indeed it was) to calculate various hypotenuses, once two distances on these lines were fixed or postulated. Many actual distances (variously arrived at) are recorded in the literature, and in particular it can be seen that all the geographical writers from Hecataeus, through Theopompus, Dicaearchus, Eratosthenes, Polybius and Hipparchus, down to Strabo and beyond, had at their disposal specific distances for the eastern coast of the Ionian and Adriatic Seas.[61] We can actually see Polybius at work in this field of endeavor, for he is said by Strabo to have drawn a meridian from Cape Malea to the Danube and to have calculated the distance; this calculation probably had something to do with the idea that the Danube flowed in the east-west direction (as did the Via Egnatia), that Eratosthenes had placed the mouth of the Danube on the same meridian of longitude as Alexandria, Rhodes, and Byzantium,[62] and that consequently the rectangle that resulted from these constructions could be used to calculate intermediate distances. This method of erecting geometrical figures — upon which were sited (sometimes by fairly arbitrary procedures[63]) peoples and

---

Byzantium. In any case, it was the map and the published work of Eratosthenes which became the standard guide, however much they were criticized in details by Polybius, Hipparchus, Strabo and many others. A good representation of Eratosthenes' world map can be found in C. Müller's edition of Strabo (Paris 1880) Tabula I.

[60] Strabo 2.4.8 C108. Berger, *Fragmente* (supra n. 59) 342.

[61] Hammond, *Epirus* (supra n. 1) 444-58.

[62] Strabo 7.5.1 C313; 8.8.5 C335. Berger, *Fragmente* (supra n. 59) 344-50. Polybius 34.12.12 = Strabo 8.8.5 C335 indicates that a statistic in Polybius was corrected by Artemidorus, the distance from Cape Malea (the southernmost point in the Peloponnesus) to the Danube having been given as 1000 stadia by Polybius (6500 by Artemidorus). The alleged reason for Polybius' error was that he did not reckon the distance in a straight line, but by the route some general happened to follow. The explanation of the error is manifestly absurd as it stands, and could only be relevant if Polybius had produced a figure larger than the direct geometrical distance, not smaller. The reference to some general may, however, indicate that Polybius had data at hand for a real distance. But it is impossible to believe that he actually wrote *1000 stadia*, for the distance from the "Parallel of Rhodes" to that of Byzantium was about 3000 stadia (supra n. 59), and the mouth of the Danube somewhat north of that. One might suspect that the manuscripts of Polybius had suffered some damage in the transmission of the text at a very early period, and that a word had dropped out before "thousand" ("six thousand" or "seven thousand").

[63] See e.g., D. R. Hicks, "The ΚΛIMATA in Greek Geography," *CQ* 5 (1955) 248-55; "Strabo and the ΚΛIMATA," *CQ* 6 (1956), 243-47. Polybius had apparently written a work "On the parts of the Globe under the Celestial Equator": Geminus

geographical locations — was especially useful in calculating (*not* measuring) especially long distances and distances across inaccessible, rough, or unknown territory. Apparently, Eratosthenes' calculation of the *geometrical* distance between Epidamnus and Thessalonike was based on some incorrect assumptions or statistics or calculations (or manuscript readings), and it was necessary for his successors, including Polybius, to make more accurate assessments on the basis of better information and technique. Thus, Polybius knew perfectly well that a figure in Eratosthenes of 900 stadia was wildly wrong (for, at least, he had the Via Egnatia as a control of the maximum distance)[64] though the calculation ascribed to him in the text of Strabo is only moderately successful — giving some 300 to 400 stadia more than the actual geometrical distance. This may have been a geometrical difficulty based on various technical assumptions and postulates, or Polybius may have been influenced by the fact that he had a "correct answer" at hand. In any event, it must be recognized that the Polybian distance of 2000+ stadia and the distance of 267 mp on the Via Egnatia are talking about two entirely different kind of things, geometrical distance and actual distance measured on the ground; both distances are calculated to Thessalonike, and neither distance suggests that this was the only calculation which was made. The imaginary line which connected Epidamnus and Thessalonike could have been extended eastward, through the mouth of the Strymon and the mouth of the Hebrus, and ultimately to Byzantium, producing a rectangle similar to the one erected by Polybius using the Danube and the "Parallel of Rhodes" as opposite and parallel sides. The parallelogram of which Strabo speaks, therefore, has an obvious importance for the calculation of long distances as well as intermediate ones in the neighborhood of Macedonia, Thrace and the Pontic area.

Now, after Strabo had made his way across Macedonia and Thrace, evidently proceeding in terms of natural and ethnic boundaries (east of Thessalonike this would mean the rivers Axius,

---

Elementa astronomiae 16.32-38 = Polybius 34.1.7-14; Walbank (supra n. 32) 573. Customs also played a part; in general see W. A. Heidel, *Frame* (supra n. 38) 8-55; Polybius (34.3) also identifies Homeric places by noting customs, and he attacks Theopompus (34.12) for notions which were based on the evidence of pottery.

[64] The modern distance, measured on a map and thus only approximately comparable, is 300 km, which is about 202 mp, and thus 1616 standard Greek stadia, or 1680 Greek stadia according to the Polybian reckoning. This would give an error of some 78% in the Strabonian text.

Polybius, Pliny, and the Via Egnatia

Strymon, Nestus, and Hebrus), he arrived at the Bosporus and reported various distances (We know of this only through epitomes), including the total distance "from the Ionian Gulf at Apollonia."[65] He cites Artemidorus of Ephesus, Polybius' critic, for a total distance of 7320 stadia, and remarks that "Polybius adds another 180 stadia, since he adds a third of a stadion to the eight stadia in the mile." At this point Strabo (or his epitomator) is presenting distances entirely in terms of stadia, and it has been presumed that Polybius as well was quoted *in stadia* rather than in Roman miles, relying on Strabo's remark (7.7.4 C322) that the Via Egnatia was marked with milestones as far as Cypsela and the Hebrus. This statement has been attributed directly to Polybius as though it had been a quotation, and it has been read to mean that Polybius said that the milestones existed only as far as Cypsela (which implies — a not insignificant point that the governor's authority in the third quarter of the second century extended at least that far). We have demonstrated, however, that part (if not all) of the very next sentence in Strabo is due entirely or mostly to Strabo himself, and not to Polybius; and we must wonder now what the actual status of the phrase βεβηματισμένη κατὰ μίλιον καὶ κατεστηλωμένη μέχρι Κυψέλων καὶ Ἕβρου ποταμοῦ is. For if the thought is made to begin with the word μέχρι (that is to say, if the text is taken as a Strabonian condensation rather than the actual words of Polybius), then all the text says is 1) that the Via Egnatia was measured out and marked by milestones, and 2) as far as Cypsela and the River Hebrus the distance was 535 mp, which, if converted into Greek stadia as commonly done (to take an example) would make a distance of 4280 stadia, but if converted into Greek stadia as Polybius advised would make an additional 178 mp. It is not difficult to imagine that Strabo, more intent upon the numbers than the implications of what he was saying about the milestones, attributed to Polybius in the process of condensing him much more than Polybius had actually said — or much less.

When the remark about the Polybian method of converting from miles into stadia is repeated, however, the problem is deeper. The Vatican Epitomator of Strabo first of all states that the distance from Perinthus to Byzantium was 630 stadia; he does not say whose estimate this is, and in the light of the rest of the paragraph, it seems likely that he has omitted the name of an authority in the process of

---

[65] Strabo *Epitome* VII F 57 (*Epit. Vat.*).

condensation (Strabo, I take it was the original collator of material out of Artemidorus, Polybius, Demetrius of Skepsis, and perhaps others). This distance was controversial, for Demetrius is quoted in the following sentence in Strabo as having made the distance 600 stadia instead of 630 stadia (that is, 75 or 76 mp rather than 79 mp), while the itineraries give the distance as 74 or 70 or 66 mp.[66] In any event, whether the distance is an estimate of Polybius or of Artemidorus, it is at least a plausible distance.

The Vatican Epitomator next provides a distance from Cypsela and the Hebrus River to the Cyanean Rocks of 3100 stadia, and the statement is attributed to the authority of Artemidorus. The distance in the itineraries (*Itin. Ant.* 332,1) from Cypsela to Byzantium is 168 mp, and to the Cyanean Rocks an additional 20 mp (30 km) must be included, producing a total of 188 mp from Cypsela to the Cyanean Rocks (that is, 1504 stadia in the standard Greek reckoning, or 1567 stadia according to Polybian accuracy).[67] The difference between the truth and the reported distance attributed to Artemidorus in the Vatican epitome is wrong by a factor of two, and it is hard to imagine that a careful person could have accepted such an obviously incorrect statistic. We might accuse Artemidorus of an error of such proportions (as Walbank does), and then by implication accuse Polybius and Strabo of stupidity. But if the number given by Artemidorus is to be taken seriously as a reasonably accurate distance, to what distance *might* it refer? 3100 stadia is approximately 387.5 mp (at 8:1), and if we begin a measurement with the actual total distance from the Adriatic to Byzantium of 754 mp or thereabouts, then the distance which is represented by 3100 stadia (387/8 mp) would be a point some 367 or 368 mp from Apollonia-Dyrrachium (that is, 754 − 387/8 = 367/8). Is it an accident that the 367th milestone on the Via Egnatia is at the Roman colony of Philippi? We can see that some geographers at least counted an intermediate distance using Philippi as an intermediate *caput viae*, for Pliny reports a distance from

---

[66] Demetrius of Skepsis is said by Strabo (13.1.55 C609) to have been born about the same time as Crates and Aristarchus and to have been older than his fellow townsman Metrodorus (who was killed, it seems, by Mithridates the Great in the 60's B.C.). As a boy Demetrius had visited nearby Ilium, at the time when the Romans first arrived in Asia and expelled Antiochus III. He was thus contemporary, perhaps a slightly younger contemporary, of Polybius.

Itin. Ant. 323,5-8 and 332,6-9. *Itin. Burd.* 570,2-8. See Walbank (supra n. 32) 627.

[67] Walbank (supra n. 32) 627.

Polybius, Pliny, and the Via Egnatia

Philippi to the *civitas* of Apri (which is on the Via Egnatia) of 188 mp.[68] Now, since the distance attributed to Artemidorus makes a kind of sense, it seems inappropriate to attribute the monstrosity in the text of the *Epitome Vaticana* directly to him; it is possible that at some point in the transmission of the data, or in the process of condensation (performed upon Artemidorus or upon Strabo) that a mistake was made. In the text as it survives in the *Epitome Vaticana*, the summary of distances begins with a very short distance (Perinthus-Byzantium) of 630 stadia; next appears a longer distance (Hebrus/Cypsela-Cyanean Rocks); then a number of 3100 stadia (which may be taken to be the distance from Philippi to Byzantium); and finally we are given the total distance from westernmost Macedonia to Byzantium (Ionian Sea/Apollonia-Byzantium). The appearance of the distance to the Cyanean Rocks ought to give a clue, for the rest of the distances are computed to Byzantium, thus suggesting that the distance to the Cyanean Rocks from some *caput* was a bit of raw data which was being provided for purposes of contrast, much as the variant of the first distance is provided out of Demetrius of Skepsis. Condensation or misunderstanding produced muddle. The *Epitome Vaticana* is missing the record of the number of stadia which ought to go with the distance from Cypsela to the Cyanean Rocks (which, as we have suggested, should be 1500 stadia), and immediately following that is missing the statement that "from Philippi to Byzantium it is a distance of " 3100 stadia, according to Artemidorus. If this is correct, then it may be noted that Artemidorus has calculated from city to city, whereas the mutilated entry without the numerical distance was calculated in geographical terms, from the river Hebrus to the Bosporus. It is not necessarily a correct inference that this latter calculation is Artemidorus', though it may have been found in the text of Artemidorus as a distance which he was criticizing, refining, or recalculating. It is also possible, though, that Strabo is supplying the alternative version, for the sake

---

[68] Pliny *NH* 4.11(18).47: *intus Bizye arx regum Thraciae a Terei nefasto invisa hirundinibus, regio Caenica, colonia Flaviopolis, ubi antea Caela oppidum vocabatur, et a Bizye L p Apros colonia, quae a Philippis abest* CLXXXVIIII. *Itin. Ant.* 332,2-4; *Itin. Burd.* 601,10; cf. *Itin. Ant.* 175,9. It is the Bordeaux Pilgrim who calls Apri a *civitas*; Pliny calls it a *colonia*. Apri was a colony from the time of Claudius, founded by Claudius Kalopothakes: Werner Eck, "Die claudische Kolonie Apri in Thrakien," *ZPE* 16 (1975) 295-99; *Année épigraphique* (1974) 581-83. It may have been the colonial status of Philippi and Apri, at least in part, which caused Pliny to give a distance using them as points of reference; but Apri is also the point from which the main highway went southwest into the Thracian Chersonese from the Via Egnatia.

of comparison with the statement of Artemidorus, as the reference to Demetrius of Skepsis might indicate.

The Vatican Epitomator thirdly provides a total distance, which is stated to be the distance from the Ionian Gulf at Apollonia to Byzantium, and a number, 7320 stadia, is given. This number, like the number from Cypsela to the Cyanean Rocks, is a very incorrect number, whoever the authority behind it might be (the Epitomator is not explicit). This 7320 stadia would be the equivalent of about 912 mp (at 8:1), and we know that the true distance on the Via Egnatia was only about 754 mp or 6032 stadia (at 8:1). In Walbank's discussion of this passage,[69] he suggests that the 3100 stadia (which he attributes to Artemidorus) was added by Strabo to Polybius' distance to Cypsela (which distance Walbank believes was written in stadia), and that to this sum the Polybian conversion product which is mentioned in the next phrase in the *Vatican Epitome* (180 stadia) was then added, producing a total of 7560 stadia for the entire distance (4280 + 3100 + 180 = 7560). "This [number of 7560 stades] in turn he [Strabo] rounded off to 7500 stades, but expressed this as 7,320 + 180." Thus, the 7320 stadia in the text of the *Epitome*, which appears to be attributable to Artemidorus, is actually the result of a series of computations made by Strabo, not the quotation or paraphrase of the distances indicated by one authority or another.

This theory, however, does not adequately explain the next phrase in the *Epitome*, the one about the Polybian conversion factor; neither does it attempt to account for Artemidorus' whopping mistake; neither does it attempt to account for Strabo's inattention which produced an error of 1298 stadia or 158 mp. It implies that Strabo did not notice that Artemidorus (according to Walbank) calculated to the Cyanean Rocks and not to Byzantium, and that consequently the Strabonian computation would be inaccurate by at least 160 standard Greek stadia. We have already seen, however, that Strabo is concerned to record a difference of only 30 stadia in the neighborhood of Byzantium, immediately following the remark about the Polybian conversion formula, for which difference he quotes Demetrius of Skepsis as an authority. Demetrius, indeed, is cited by name by Strabo at least thirty-eight times in what survives of Strabo's work, and as a native of the Troad, it might be thought that Demetrius had

---

[69] Walbank (supra n. 32) 627-28. His theory is committed to the idea that Polybius did not give distances in Roman miles beyond Cypsela, and that Polybius may not have given a total distance to Byzantium.

some idea of what he was talking about. He appeared to have precise information about Uranopolis and Xerxes' canal across the peninsula (Strabo *Epitome* VII F 35 [*Epit.Vat.*]); he was interested in refuting Ephorus on the subject of the Halizonii, who lived near Pallene in the Chalcidice (Strabo *Epitome* VII F 27a; Strabo 12.3.22 C550); and he claimed to have some precise knowledge of the tribes of the Molossians and Thesprotians when he talked about Dodona (Strabo 7.7.10 C328). Demetrius was quoted by Strabo at the same place (*Epitome* VII F 57) for distances to Parium, for the dimensions of the Propontus, and for the dimensions of the Hellespont, and it is not impossible that he had a distance for the width of the Greek peninsula from the Ionian Sea to Hellespont, in which the Cyanean Rocks were to be found. Whether this is relevant or not to Strabo's source material, we are still left with the need of providing an alternative explanation to Walbank's of the double problem in the *Epitome Vaticana*: first, the nature of the corruption in the number 7320 stadia, and second, the reason for the remark about the Polybian conversion formula which immediately follows the representation of the total distance as 7320 stadia.

Let us begin with the latter problem. The Epitomator says that a conversion factor of 180 mp has been applied to some number. Walbank, believing in a series of Strabonian calculations and "rounding off," makes 178 and 180 the same, and in effect merely a repetition of what was done at Apollonia by Strabo (7.7.4 C322). But, what if the number is accurate, not "rounded off." According to the formula, it implies that an original Roman mile number of 540 mp was being converted into Greek stadia of Polybian accuracy.[70] If the correction is made upon this 540 mp, the result is 4500 stadia of an accuracy required by Polybius. Now, let us assume that Polybius did know the actual distance to Byzantium, which we have been approximating as 754 mp. If this total distance is converted into stadia of Polybian accuracy, we will have 6283.3 stadia.[71] Let us

---

[70] The text of Strabo (7.7.4 C322) tells us to take the third of the number of miles and add it to eight times the number of miles to arrive at an accurate number of stadia. If the third of the number of miles is 180, then the original number of Roman miles upon which the conversion was being performed would have been 540 mp, and the complete conversion would be (540 x 8) + (540 ÷ 3) = (4320) + (180) = 4500 stadia, of a degree of accuracy required by Polybius.

[71] 27 or 28 mp: *Itin. Ant.* 320,1. 28 or 29 mp: *Itin. Ant.* 330,7-8. 30 mp: *Itin. Burd.* 605,4-606,2. The calculation backward begins with 754 mp, adds 20 mp to arrive at the Cyanean Rocks (supra n. 6), and then subtracts 540 mp, giving 234 as the *caput*. Thessalonike is at 267 mp on the Via Egnatia, from which the numbers in the

subtract the 4500 stadia of Polybian accuracy from the 6283.3 stadia of Polybian accuracy, giving a remainder of 1783.3 stadia of Polybian accuracy. If this figure is converted back into Roman mmiles, it is exactly 214 mp. Tabulated, the various calculations would look like this:

540 mp	4320 stadia	4500 Polybian
+ 214 mp	+ 1712 stadia	+ 1783.3 Polybian
754 mp	6032 stadia	6283.3 Polybian

The process by which all the numbers are filled in results, of course, in circular reasoning. But in the process of computation, the number 4320 accidentally emerged as the standard number of stadia, which represented the number of Roman miles before the Polybian correction was added. Is this similarity to our obviously incorrect total distance of 7320 just an accident? If the Greek words were written out, it is hard to see how they could be related; if represented in Greek numerals, however, we would see

and

itineraries would be subtracted; the remainders would be 240, 239, 238, and 237. We cannot be certain where a number of 540 mp reached Strabo's text from, however. If he was calculating as well as quoting (as both Walbank and I believe, however differently we conceive this calculating process), then he would have been capable of taking 4320 stadia and turning it into 540 mp by dividing by 8. Alternatively, he could have been presented with the figure 540 mp by one of his sources (which had already done the calculation from stadia into Roman miles), and then he could have performed a reconversion into both standard Greek stadia and into Greek stadia of an accuracy acceptable to Polybius. This latter procedure, to be sure, would be futile for achieving true accuracy. Finally, an accurate number of stadia could have been presented by Polybius himself according to his own reckoning (i.e., 4500 stadia), which Strabo then converted into Roman miles, using the Polybian formula (4500 ÷ 8 1/3, or, as Walbank expresses it, by dividing by 25 and multiplying the quotient [180] by 3).

The above discussion of a calculation from Pella certainly suggests a pre-Roman source. It must be confessed, however, that a post-Polybian source might have calculated from Thessalonike, using a slightly different route to Byzantium, and arrived at a distance of 540 mp; the area around the mouth of the Hebrus River can be seen in the itineraries to have been subject to such detours. A distance from Thessalonike to the Cyanean Rocks is, in any event, a reasonable possibility, and might even have been derived from Polybius — if Polybius had given the total distance to Byzantium or to the Cyanean Rocks.

which are able to be confused. But, if this is what happened, although it explains the impossible number of 7320 stadia by treating the number as an expression (corruptly transmitted) of the standard Greek stadia in the intermediate stage of calculation which was done to provide a more accurate estimate of the number of Greek stadia in a given number of Roman miles, it does not yet explain fully the meaning of 540 mp.

It must be remembered that the calculation to achieve this standard of accuracy must begin with a given number of Roman miles. When the process is first explained in Strabo, the distance of 535 mp to Cypsela was first expressed in standard Greek stadia (at 8:1), and then one-third of the number of miles was added (4280 + 178 = 4458). At Byzantium, the implied number of Roman miles is 540 mp, which would be expressed in standard Greek stadia as 4320 (at 8.1), and then one-third of the number of miles (stated to be 180) is added. Does, however, the basic datum, 540 mp, represent something real? If we begin at Byzantium and work backwards, as the other distances in the *Epitome Vaticana* are doing, we would arrive at a point some 53 mp to the west of Thessalonike, that is to say, some seven mp to the east of Edessa, or nowhere. If we begin at the Cyanean Rocks, however, and work backwards, we would arrive at a place some 33 mp to the west of Thessalonike, which is not exactly nowhere. The itineraries place the ancient capital of Macedonia and the birthplace of Alexander the Great, Pella, at a distance of 28 or 29 or 30 mp to the west of Thessalonike,[71] and it would not be an inappropriate *caput* from which to give a distance, whether in the days of its glory when it was the capital and largest city in Macedonia, or later, when it was a Roman colony. The 3 mp difference cannot bother us too much in the light of the 30 stadia difference attributed to Demetrius of Skepsis (which would be some 3.75 mp), though it need not be the case that Demetrius is responsible for this 3 mp difference. Thus, if we have correctly understood the data at our disposal, we must conclude that 1) all the data in the *Epitome Vaticana* are significant and accurate; but that 2) the Vatican Epitomator (or his predecessors) muddled the significance of the data in the process of transmission. We must further suggest that the fragment we have been discussing in no way can be said to represent anything that Polybius might have said; it must remain a question whether Polybius gave a distance from Apollonia and Dyrrachium either to

From	To	A distance of	According to
Perinthus	Byzantium	630 stadia	?
Perinthus	Byzantium	600 stadia	Demetrius of Skepsis
The Hebrus River/ Cypsela	Cyanean Rocks		?
Philippi	Byzantium	3100 stadia	?Artemidorus
?Pella	Cyanean Rocks	4320 stadia	?Demetrius ?Artemidorus ?Strabo
?Pella	Cyanean Rocks	4500 stadia	?Polybius ?Strabo
Apollonia/ Ionian Sea	Byzantium	754 mp	Romans, Itineraries
Apollonia/ Ionian Sea	Cyanean Rocks	?6200 stadia	Artemidorus (?)

Fig 3: Summary of data — stated, implied, or inferred — from the Epitome Vaticana

Byzantium or to the Cyanean Rocks.[72] A tabulation of the data in the *Epitome Vaticana*, and the deductions which have been made from it, is presented in Fig. 3.

Conclusion.

The early inscriptions inform us that roads in Macedonia were being delimited and marked with *horoi* as early as the fourth century B.C., and at least one of these early *horoi* exhibits an intermediate distance from a local *caput*. Other evidence suggests that there is a pattern of counting a distance of 1000 stadia to the west of certain major towns. In the second century B.C., probably in the third quarter of that century, the Romans built their *via militaris*, the Via Egnatia, one of whose stones has been found, establishing a certain distance of 267 Roman miles from Apollonia and Dyrrachium in the west to Thessalonike.

This distance of 267 mp agrees with a statement in Strabo that Polybius put the distance at what amounted to 267 mp as well, and that he also knew that the distance to the Hebrus River was 535 mp. These numbers are probably actual numbers provided to Strabo by the text of Polybius (now lost). Pliny also supplies a set of distances, to Thessalonike (225 mp), to Philippi (328 mp), and to Byzantium

---

[72] Polybius gives two distances to Thessalonike: a calculated one (2000+ stadia) which corrects Eratosthenes (Strabo 2.4.4. C106), and a measured one (267 mp) which is evidently dependent upon work done on the ground by Roman bematists (Strabo 7.7.4 C323). Polybius knew and discussed the "Parallel of Rhodes" (Pliny *NH* 6.23(38).206); he is on record as having erected a meridian which ran north from Cape Malea to the Danube (Strabo 8.8.5 C335); and he certainly calculated along an east-west parallel from Epidamnus to Thessalonike (Strabo 2.4.4. C106). Assuming that he knew about the "Meridian of Alexandria," which would not be unlikely if he had read Eratosthenes, which he evidently had, he would have erected a right parallelogram, with the right angles situated at Rhodes, Malea, Thessalonike and Byzantium. Since the distance from Rhodes to Byzantium was known (*ca.* 3000 standard Greek stadia), the distance from Malea to Thessalonike would be known to be the same distance. If the entire distance from Epidamnus to the Cyanean Rocks were about 6450 stadia (according to a Polybian calculation), and the distance from Epidamnus to Thessalonike were 2000+ stadia (actually 2225 stadia according to a Polybian calculation using the Via Egnatia), then a distance from Thessalonike to the Cyanean Rocks would be about 4058 stadia of an accuracy acceptable to Polybius, or a little less. That Polybius could have recorded such a distance if he chose cannot be doubted. That he did record a distance or distances (in mp and/or stadia) is not ascertainable. Polybius is on record, however, as having calculated distances in the area of the Pontus Euxinus (Pliny *NH* 4.12(24).77), and there is no reason to think that his calculations for Macedonia stopped with Thessalonike.

(711 mp); all are wrong, by 43 mp, and it is suggested that — for some unknown reason, perhaps the observed habit of geographers of treating Macedonia in sections — the first part of the Via Egnatia was treated separately, that part which ran from Dyrrachium to Clodiana. When the 43 mp is added, Pliny agrees with Polybius on Thessalonike (267), with the itineraries on Byzantium (754). He also indicates a variant on the last statistic, 720 + 43 = 763 mp, and a difference of opinion on the easternmost part of the road is apparent in Strabo and the itineraries as well. But Pliny's statistics are precise and accurate.

Strabo's relation to Polybius and his other sources presents a problem. Polybius had objected to the usual way of converting Roman miles into Greek stadia (at 8:1), and proposed a more accurate ratio of 8 1/3:1. An example in the text of Strabo shows how this was done, beginning with the number of Roman miles to Cypsela; the calculation was probably done by Strabo, using the number 535 mp found in the text of Polybius. The notion of a more accurate, Polybian conversion factor is repeated in a portion of Strabo which now survives only in the form of a condensation called the *Epitome Vaticana*. Unfortunately there is some confusion in that text — a distance which does not agree even remotely with the number of stadia assigned to it, a wildly wrong statement of the total distance from the Ionian Sea at Apollonia to the Bosporus. The Polybian correction factor expressed at that point is *not* a rounded off duplication of the one calculated for Cypsela, but a genuine separate calculation implying a distance of 540 mp; counted backward from the Cyanean Rocks, it leads to Pella. It is difficult to say whether this distance of 540 mp was also in Polybius, but the realization that it exists permits a tentative restoration of the data in the *Epitome Vaticana* and leads to a better understanding of the nature of the surviving texts and the observations found in them.

University of Virginia
The Pennsylvania State University